"Just the Facts, Ma'am"

Sergeant Joe Friday
Dragnet Television Series, 1951-1959
Creator: Jack Webb

FOREWORD

In 1997, I was visiting Venice, Italy. A festival of Taiwan artists was happening. The glossy magazine on street corners everywhere highlighted their art. A major theme was "So Long America." One painting showed the Statue of Liberty with an apple in her mouth. I was surprised because I thought Taiwan was a friend of the United States.

Now, the theme of "So Long America" feels very real, at least the America I knew. I worry about nothing less than the loss of Western Civilization during my lifetime. Pinpointing dots on a graph is a lonely business, but the dots do connect. As my friend Peter Schmidt from Leipzig used to say, "Look at it from the perspective of the moon."

--- Lynn Stewart

September 5, 2016

TABLE OF CONTENTS

I	THE CONGRESS SHALL HAVE POWER TO PAY THE DEBTS	1
	The Federal Deficit	2
	Outlays	4
	Receipts	28
2	POWER TO COIN MONEY; REGULATE VALUE; OF FOREIGN COIN	35
	Gold	36
	The Federal Reserve System	45
	Gifts and Giving	58
3	CONGRESS SHALL HAVE POWER TO REGULATE COMMERCE	72
	U.S. Most Powerful Corporations	75
	Foreign Most Powerful Corporations	77
	Employee Concerns	79
4	CONGRESS SHALL HAVE POWER TO REGULATE COMMERCE WITH FOREIGN NATIONS; COLLECT DUTIES AND IMPOSTS	92
	The Trade Deficit	93
	Winning and Losing Countries in Global Trade	94
	Trade with Japan	97
	Trade with China	105
	Majority-Owned Foreign Affiliates in U.S.	111
	Summary	112
5	IMMIGRATION: UNIFORM RULE; STATES SHALL THINK PROPER TO ADMIT; BORN UNDER JURISDICTION	114
	Laws	116
	Diversity	131
	Education	147
	Income	151
6	JUDICIAL POWER IN ONE SUPREME COURT; TRIBUNALS	158
7	A Closer Look at China	161
	Vladimir Putin's Russia	168
8	MILITIA; PEOPLE KEEP ARMS; ARMY MONEY TWO YEARS ONLY	172
9	Global Environmental Concerns	219
10	Hope	224

"THE CONGRESS SHALL HAVE POWER TO ... PAY THE DEBTS"
Article I, Section 8
Constitution of the United States

President Obama released a 2016 budget with spending of $399 trillion and a built-in deficit of $474 billion.   --nationalpriorities.org

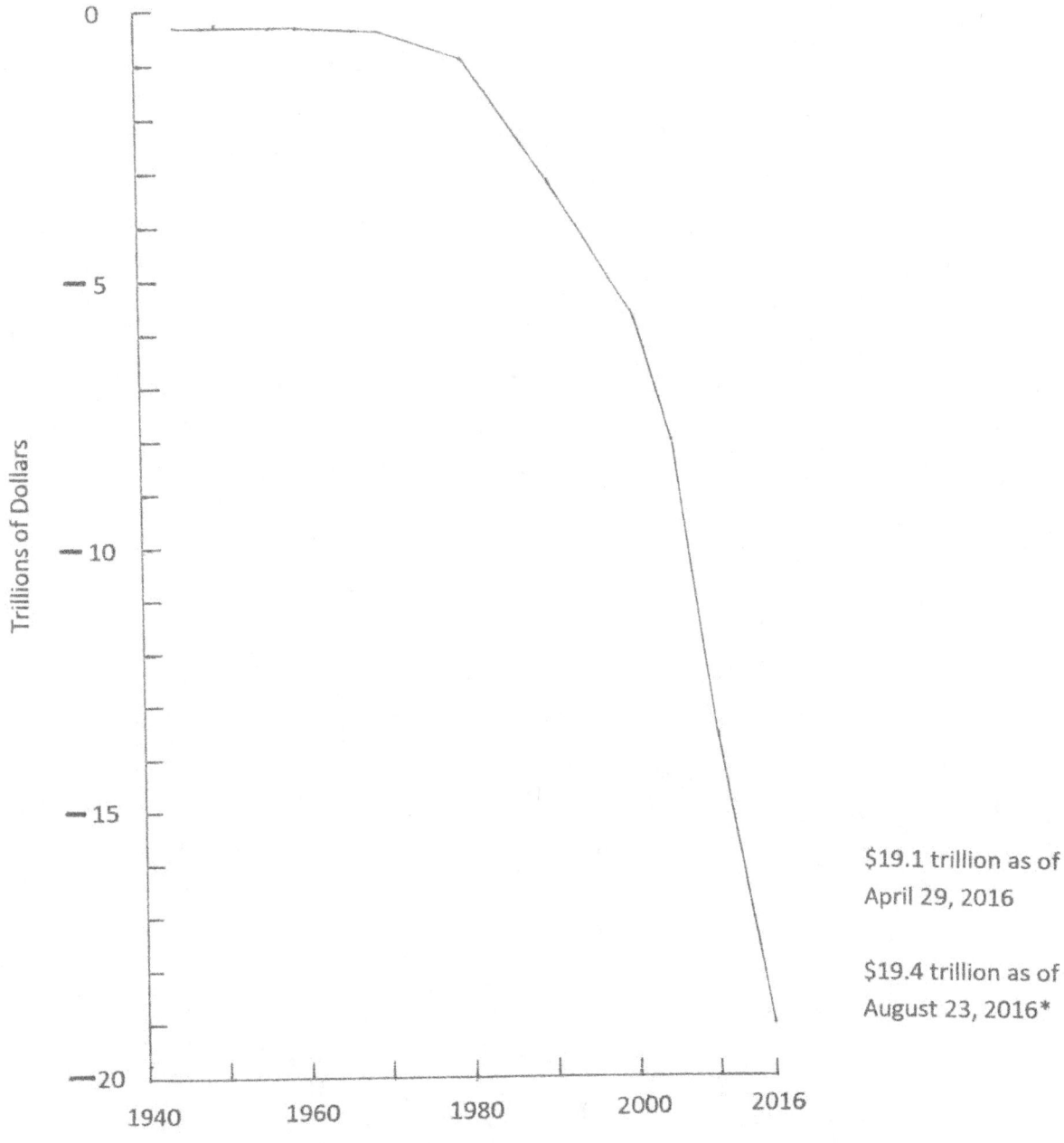

U.S. FEDERAL DEFICIT, 1945 - 2016

$19.1 trillion as of
April 29, 2016

$19.4 trillion as of
August 23, 2016*

Note: Deficit as of April 29, 2016 is 106% of the previous 12 months
of Gross Domestic Product (GDP).

Source: Statistical Abstract of the United States 1995, p 330
ProQuest Statistical Abstract of the United States 2016
Wikipedia, June 13, 2016

*Source: usdebtclock.org

INVESTORS IN UNITED STATES' FEDERAL DEBT
April 29, 2016

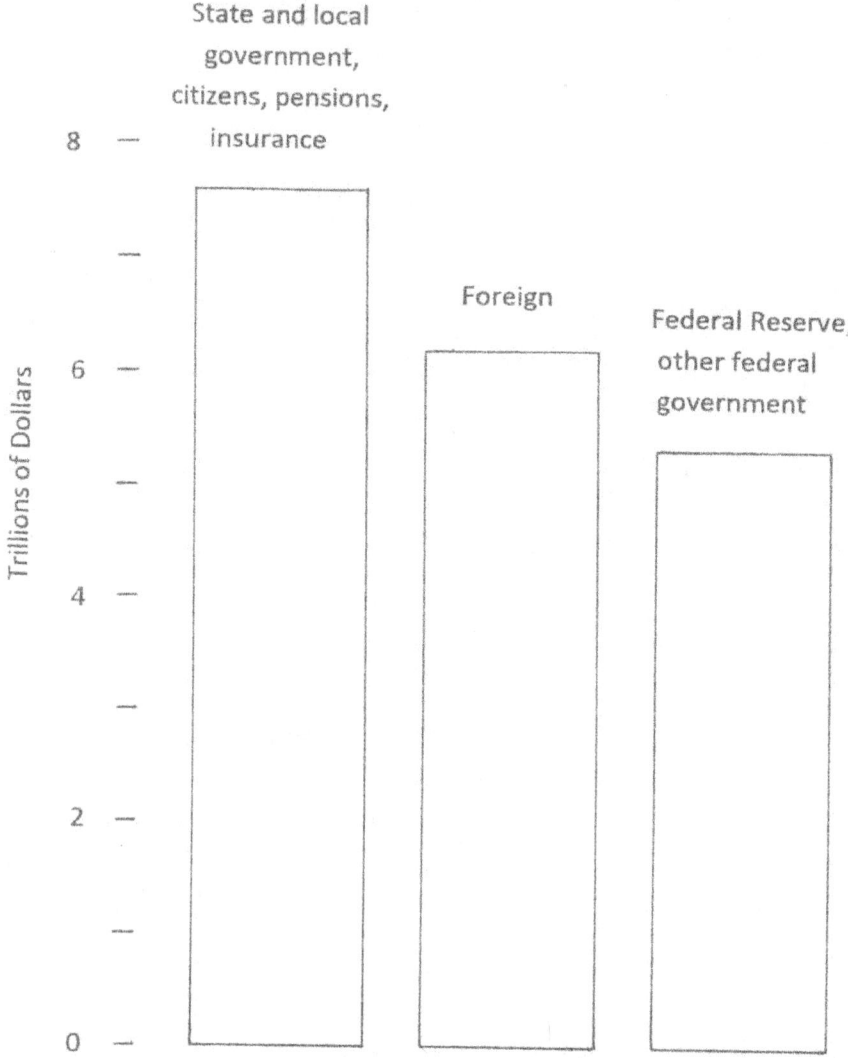

Note: China's portion of Holdings: $1.25 trillion
           Japan's portion of Holdings: $1.15 trillion
           Other foreign Holdings: $3.80 trillion (Countries not shown)

Source: wikipedia.org

Foreign investors have advantageous bargaining power over the United States because if they cashed in their loans to the Treasury in large amounts, the U.S. would not be able to meet her debt obligations.

U.S. FEDERAL TRUST FUND INCOME AND OUTLAYS, 2014 TO 2016

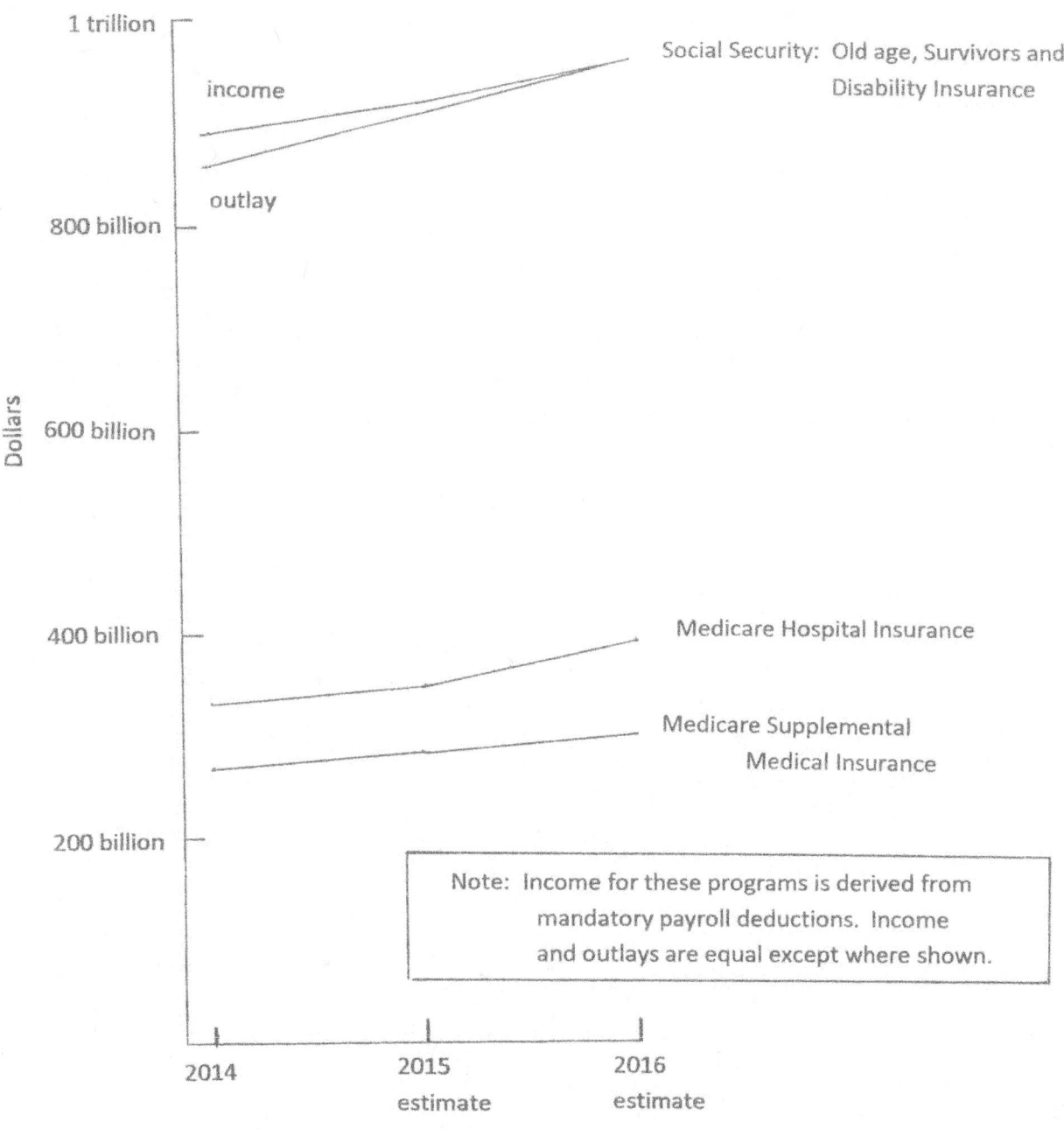

Source: ProQuest Statistical Abstract of the United States 2016, p 331

Controversy surrounds the above programs, as non-citizens can get benefits by: being "lawfully" present in the U.S, for five years; marriage to a citizen and living in the U.S. for five years; marriage to a citizen but living abroad in certain countries; working even if unlawfully in the U.S. a minimum of ten years. Treasury checks will be sent abroad to certain countries or if recipient returns to U.S. for one month every six months.

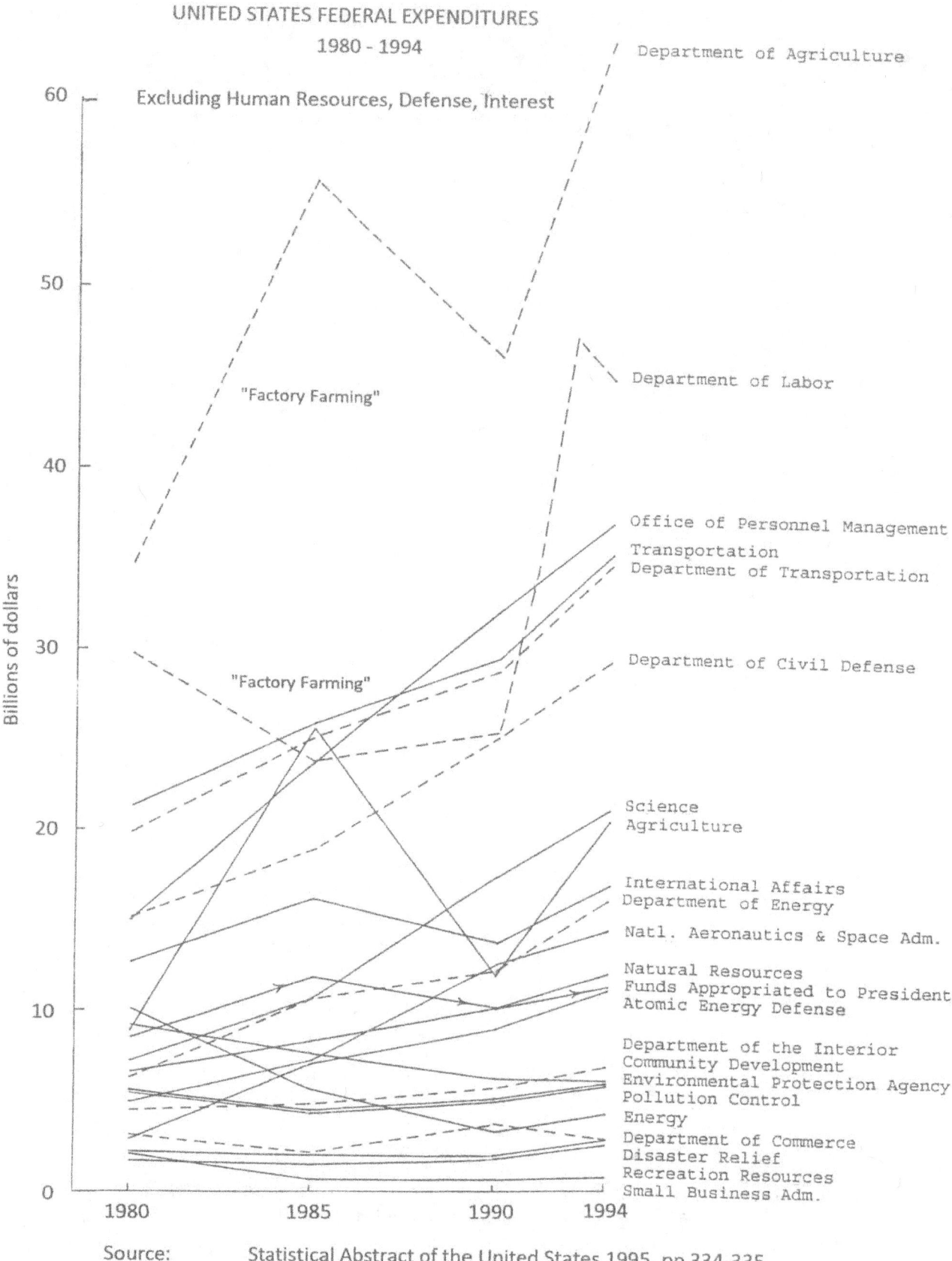

UNITED STATES FEDERAL EXPENDITURES
1980 - 1994

Excluding Human Resources, Defense, Interest

Department of Agriculture

"Factory Farming"

Department of Labor

Office of Personnel Management
Transportation
Department of Transportation

Department of Civil Defense

"Factory Farming"

Science
Agriculture

International Affairs
Department of Energy

Natl. Aeronautics & Space Adm.

Natural Resources
Funds Appropriated to President
Atomic Energy Defense

Department of the Interior
Community Development
Environmental Protection Agency
Pollution Control
Energy
Department of Commerce
Disaster Relief
Recreation Resources
Small Business Adm.

Billions of dollars

60

50

40

30

20

10

0

1980   1985   1990   1994

Source: Statistical Abstract of the United States 1995, pp 334-335

FACT   Funding for immigration is hidden in Department of Agriculture, Agriculture (farm
subsidies, H2A workers), Department of Labor, and Office of Personnel Management

5

UNITED STATES FEDERAL DEPARTMENTS SPENDING LESS THAN $100 BILLION
2015

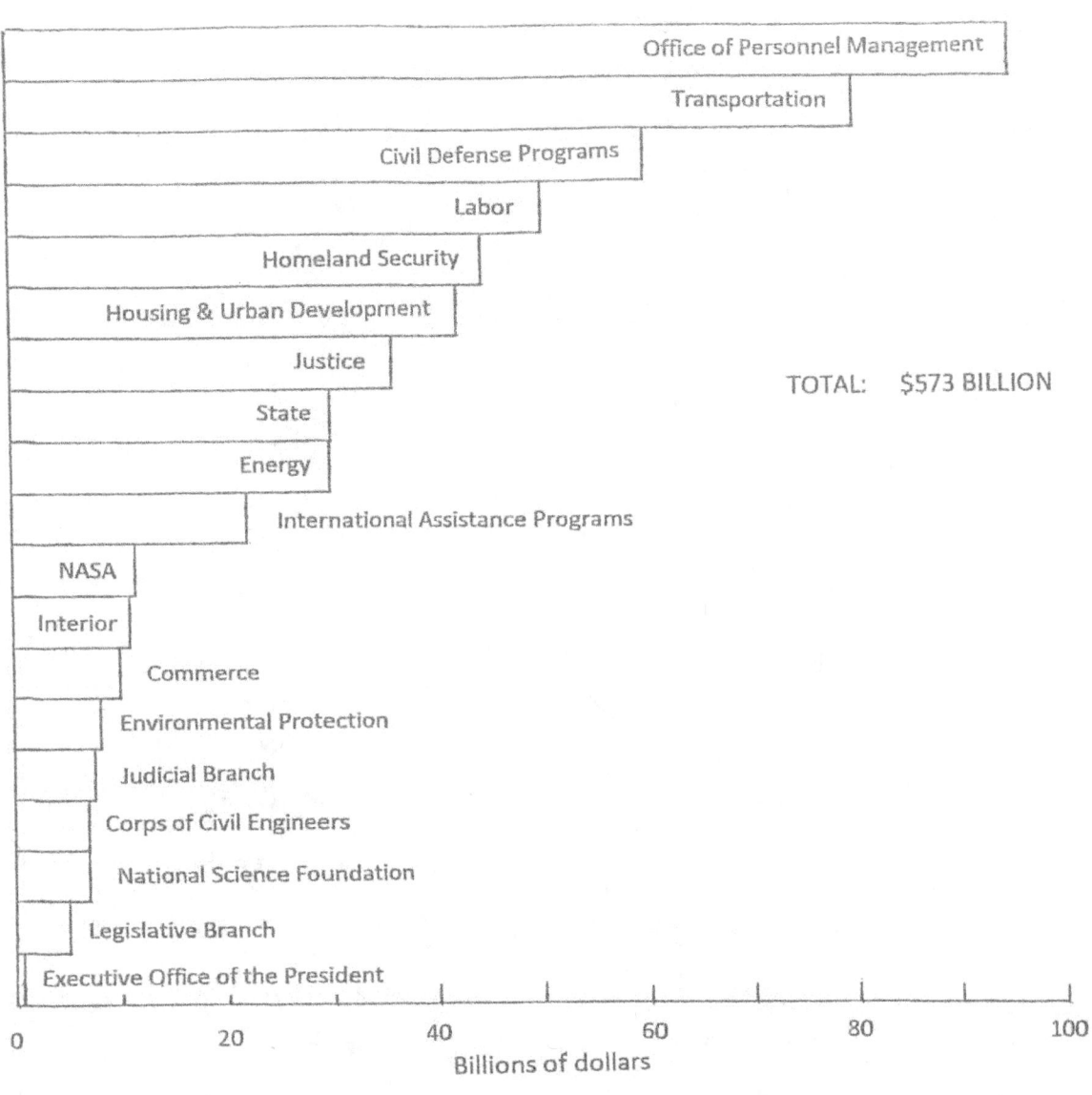

Office of Personnel Management

Transportation

Civil Defense Programs

Labor

Homeland Security

Housing & Urban Development

Justice

State

Energy

International Assistance Programs

NASA

Interior

Commerce

Environmental Protection

Judicial Branch

Corps of Civil Engineers

National Science Foundation

Legislative Branch

Executive Office of the President

TOTAL: $573 BILLION

0   20   40   60   80   100

Billions of dollars

Source: ProQuest Statistical Abstract of the United States 2016, p 328

The U.S. Federal Budget does not have a Department of Immigration. All legal and illegal immigration outlays are allocated to various other departments.

Outlays for legal and illegal immigration may reasonably be expected to occur in the Office of Personnel Management and Departments of Transportation, Labor, Homeland Security, Housing and Urban Development, Justice and State.

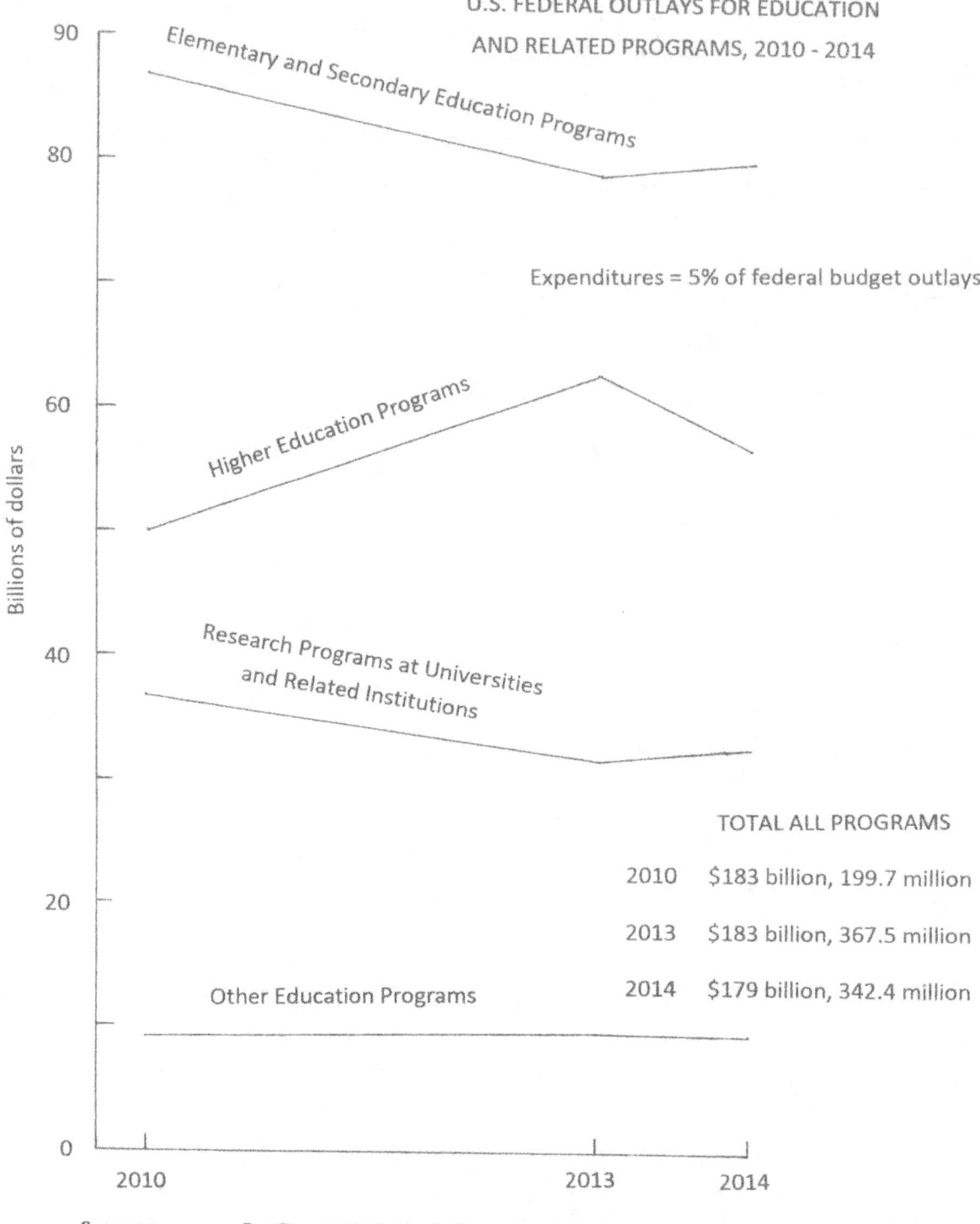

U.S. FEDERAL OUTLAYS FOR EDUCATION

AND RELATED PROGRAMS, 2010 - 2014

Elementary and Secondary Education Programs

Expenditures = 5% of federal budget outlays

Billions of dollars

Higher Education Programs

Research Programs at Universities
and Related Institutions

TOTAL ALL PROGRAMS

2010 $183 billion, 199.7 million

2013 $183 billion, 367.5 million

2014 $179 billion, 342.4 million

Other Education Programs

90

80

60

40

20

0

2010   2013   2014

Source: ProQuest Statistical Abstract of the United States 2016, p 163
                Statistical Abstract of the United States 2004-2005, p 137; 2008, p 141

In 1995 there was no federal Department of Education.
Education was and is administered by the states.
Federal Department of Education = $ 85.9 billion in 2000; $166 billion in 2006

Funding for Immigration is hidden in the Department of Education.

U.S. FEDERAL BUDGET OUTLAYS BY AGENCY, 1990 - 2015

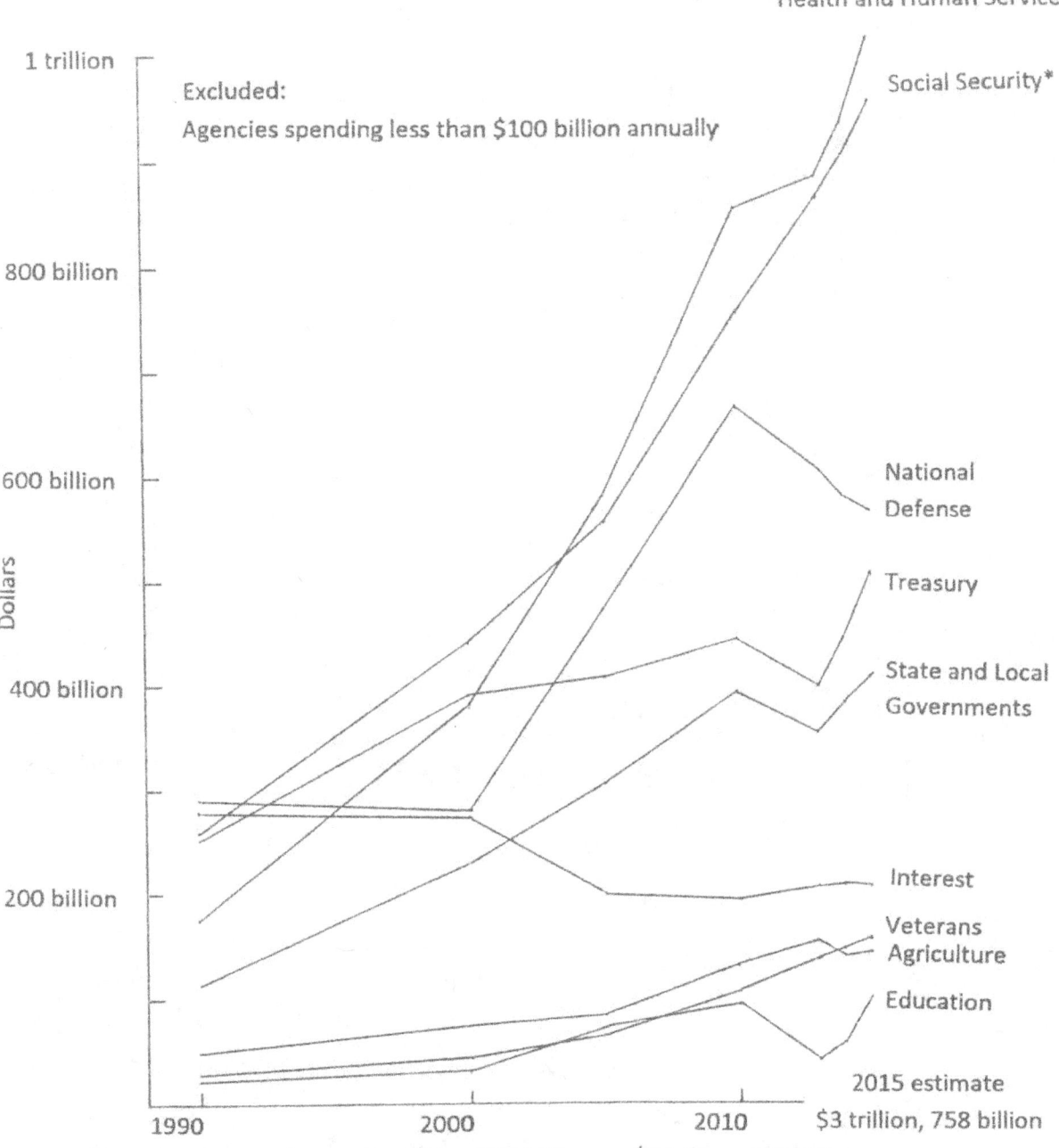

Health and Human Services

Social Security*

1 trillion

Excluded:
Agencies spending less than $100 billion annually

800 billion

National
Defense

600 billion

Treasury

State and Local
Governments

400 billion

Dollars

Interest

200 billion

Veterans
Agriculture

Education

2015 estimate

1990   2000   2010 $3 trillion, 758 billion

$1 trillion, 253 billion $1 trillion, 789 billion $3 trillion, 457 billion

*includes on and off budget

Source ProQuest Statistical Abstract of the United States 2016, p 328

Funding for Immigration is hidden in the funds for
State and Local Governments

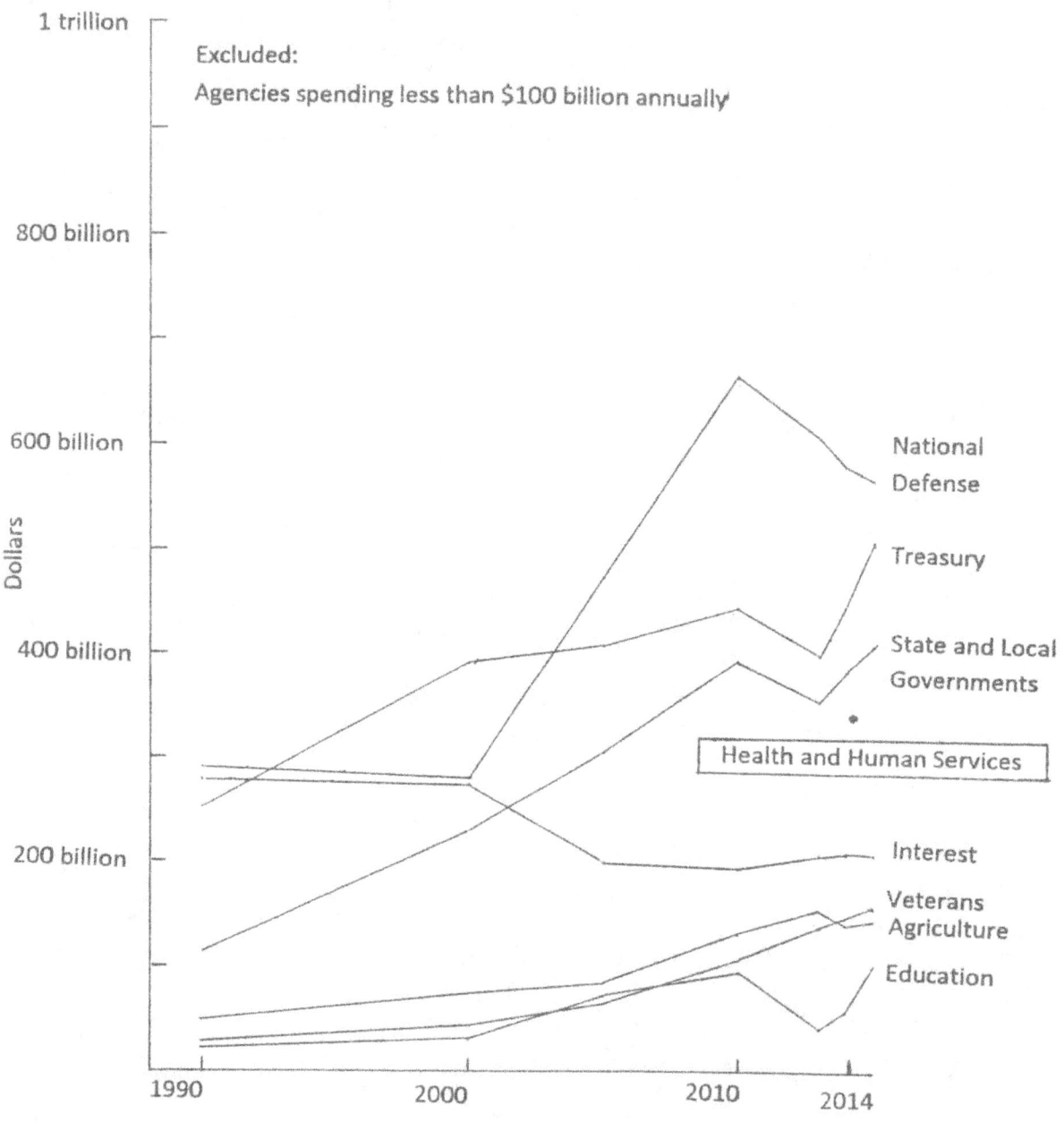

U.S. FEDERAL BUDGET OUTLAYS BY AGENCY
WITH MEDICARE AND SOCIAL SECURITY TRUST FUNDS OMITTED
1990 - 2015

Excluded:
Agencies spending less than $100 billion annually

Dollars

1 trillion

800 billion

600 billion — National Defense

Treasury

State and Local Governments

400 billion

Health and Human Services

200 billion — Interest

Veterans
Agriculture

Education

1990   2000   2010   2014

Note: When Medicare and Social Security Outlays are excluded from Health and Human
Services Outlays, the Outlay remaining is $332.3 billion in 2014 (only year available).

Source: ProQuest Statistical Abstract of the United States 2016, pp 328, 331

Funding for Immigration is hidden in the Department of Health and Human Services.

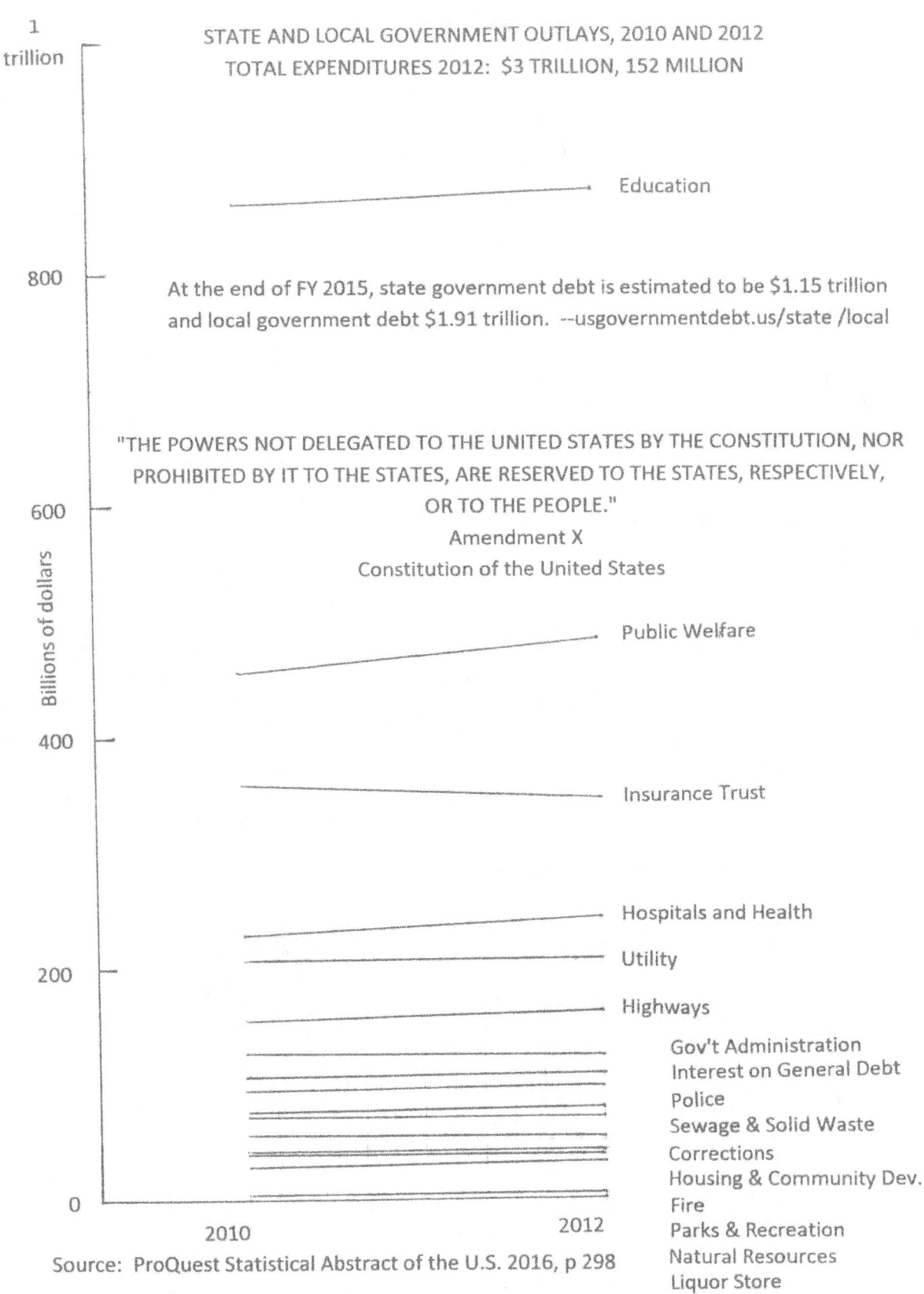

STATE AND LOCAL GOVERNMENT OUTLAYS, 2010 AND 2012
TOTAL EXPENDITURES 2012: $3 TRILLION, 152 MILLION

1 trillion

Education

800

At the end of FY 2015, state government debt is estimated to be $1.15 trillion and local government debt $1.91 trillion. --usgovernmentdebt.us/state /local

"THE POWERS NOT DELEGATED TO THE UNITED STATES BY THE CONSTITUTION, NOR PROHIBITED BY IT TO THE STATES, ARE RESERVED TO THE STATES, RESPECTIVELY, OR TO THE PEOPLE."
Amendment X
Constitution of the United States

600

Public Welfare

Billions of dollars

400

Insurance Trust

Hospitals and Health

Utility

200

Highways

Gov't Administration
Interest on General Debt
Police
Sewage & Solid Waste
Corrections
Housing & Community Dev.
Fire
Parks & Recreation
Natural Resources
Liquor Store

0

2010   2012

Source: ProQuest Statistical Abstract of the U.S. 2016, p 298

Education, Welfare, Housing, Hospitals and Health are traditionally state and local concerns.   Immigration costs are hidden in these outlays.

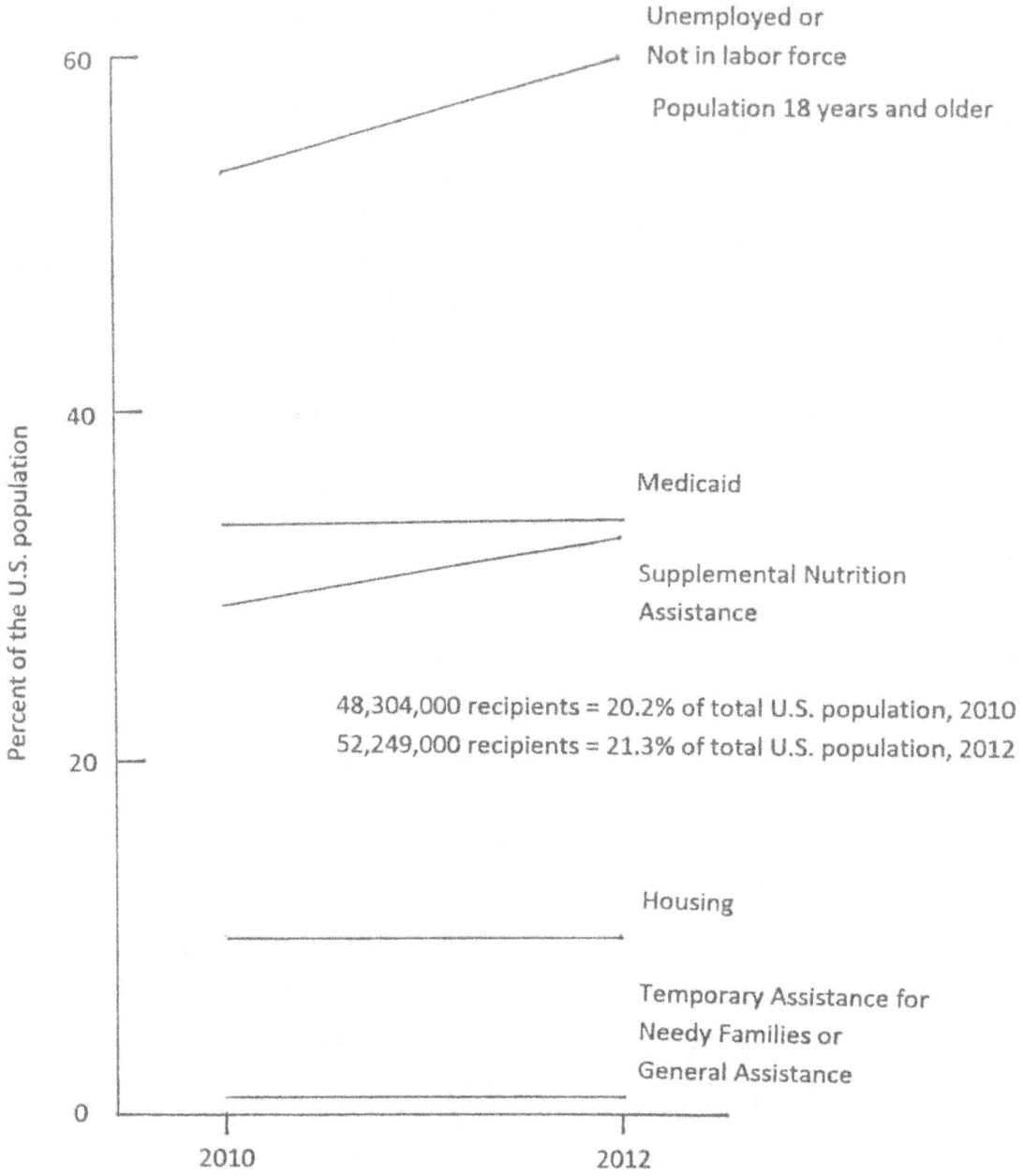

PARTICIPATION IN MEANS-TESTED U.S. FEDERAL GOVERNMENT ASSISTANCE PROGRAMS
2010 AND 2012

Unemployed or
Not in labor force

Population 18 years and older

Medicaid

Supplemental Nutrition
Assistance

48,304,000 recipients = 20.2% of total U.S. population, 2010
52,249,000 recipients = 21.3% of total U.S. population, 2012

Housing

Temporary Assistance for
Needy Families or
General Assistance

Percent of the U.S. population

60

40

20

0

2010   2012

Source U.S. Census Bureau

ProQuest Statistical Abstract of the United States 2016, p 366

"General Welfare" in the Preamble to the United States Constitution is not
a "power" given to Congress.

Funding for immigration is hidden in all of the above categories.

Financial Costs of Immigration

Ted Kennedy's Cuban Refugee Act in 1966 forced Congress to look at how to budget for immigrant expenses, especially regarding refugees from war-torn countries. Refugees rarely speak English, are traumatized, often needing medical and psychological services, as well as food and housing and other expenses of daily life, including education for their children, whom they are allowed to bring into the U.S. as well as other relatives and their concomitant expenses.

Congress made the momentous decision at that time to provide no budget for the foreseeable costs of incoming immigrants and refugees. Rather, they decided to tack expenses to other federal departments, such as the massive Health and Human Services Department, at that time called Health, Education and Welfare since Education didn't have its own department.

It was a momentous decision since it directly opposed the U.S. Constitution, in spirit if not the actual letter of the law in Article I, Section 9:

> No money shall be drawn from the Treasury, but in Consequence of Appropriations made by Law; and a Regular Statement and Account of the Receipts and Expenditures of all public Money shall be published from time to time.

The Congress does publish financial statements, including the Department of Commerce's annual Statistical Abstract of the United States, but nowhere in it are listed expenses of immigrants, legal or otherwise. Further, the federal departments where immigration expenses are hidden are questionable activities of the federal government, such as health, education and welfare, of which the Constitution is silent and which are regular departments of the various states.

Public Law 99-603 on "diversity" passed in 1986 offers proof that future expenses for immigration would be enormous. It provides for an "Immigration Emergency Fund," "status of aliens applying for benefits," "Assistance Grants," "incarceration of illegal aliens," "expeditious deportations," and a myriad of governmental reports, including one on the "sense of the Congress."

The dramatic rise in legal immigration into the United States, the rise in federal entitlements, and the rise in federal deficits beginning in 1970 show an enormously high correlation. All three categories have continued their upward trajectories to the present day. The "sense of the Congress" has not seen fit even in later years to provide a budget category for immigration.

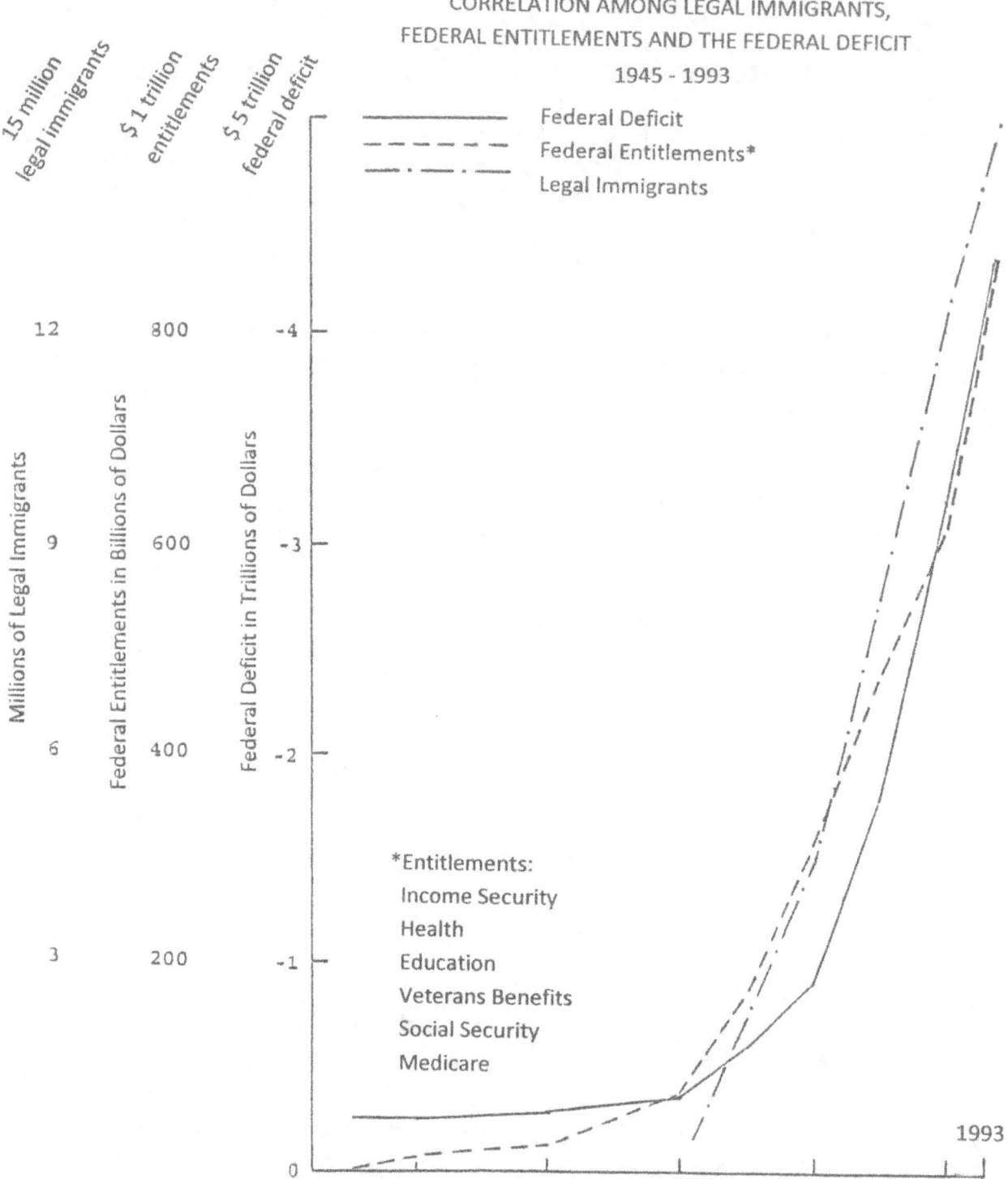

CORRELATION AMONG LEGAL IMMIGRANTS,
FEDERAL ENTITLEMENTS AND THE FEDERAL DEFICIT
1945 - 1993

——— Federal Deficit
– – – Federal Entitlements*
–·–·– Legal Immigrants

15 million legal immigrants

$ 1 trillion entitlements

$ 5 trillion federal deficit

*Entitlements:
Income Security
Health
Education
Veterans Benefits
Social Security
Medicare

Millions of Legal Immigrants

Federal Entitlements in Billions of Dollars

Federal Deficit in Trillions of Dollars

Source: Statistical Abstract of the United States 1995, pp 11, 330 332

ObamaCare, the Affordable Care Act

obamacarefacts.com

Health care insurance premiums have been rising at alarming rates over the past decade due to the rising cost of health care in the U.S. In fact, premium rates are rising faster than income, which is part of the cause of Americans lacking access to Affordable Health Insurance. Insurers have to cover high risk consumers, are no longer able to deny pre-existing conditions, and cannot charge higher rates based on health or gender. Enrollees can get reduced premium rates and lower out of pocket costs through their state health insurance marketplace, if they qualify, under a system called "exchanges."

High-end plans, covering exclusive groups due to being healthy, will see the biggest premium increases. Also, starting in 2018, high-end insurance premiums will be subject to a 40% excise tax, "greatly increasing their cost." Obamacare is a tax. Therefore, high earners will see premiums go up due to inherent "cost sharing."

In 2015, some premium increases were as low as 4%. The cost of insurance premiums varies widely by region. Employer-sponsored insurance premiums rose for a family of four from $2,949 in 2003 to $15,022 in 2011, a 62% increase. The employee premium contribution for a family of four rose from $2,283 in 2003 to $3,962 in 2011 a 74% increase. Deductible payments per person rose from $518 in 2003 to $1,123 in 2011, a 117% increase.

Small employers can get 50% off the cost of their employees' premiums, since small employers and their workers can't afford regular coverage. Since 2003, premiums have increased 80%, three times as fast as wages (31%) and inflation (27%).

Since health care costs are rising faster than the rate of inflation, making insurance more and more unaffordable for the average American, there will be an expansion of Medicaid. 50 million Americans without insurance could be covered in the next decade. Presently, over 15 million people get free insurance through Medicaid.

Insurance companies must spend 80% of their premium income on actual care and "quality improvement activities." They can spend only 20% on administration, overhead and marketing.

Health insurance under ObamaCare (aside from government programs like Medicare and Medicaid) and health care providers are not socialized, and are for profit companies. In socialized healthcare, all health care workers work for the federal government, and all the hospitals and clinics are owned by the government.

--obamacarefacts.com

Kaiser-Permanente

Henry J. Kaiser, founder of Kaiser Aluminum, wanted to provide health care to his employees, so he founded what became Kaiser Foundation Health Plan, Kaiser Foundation Hospitals, and regional Permanente Medical Groups. In December 2015, the entities reported net income of $1.9 billion. Each medical group operates as a separate for-profit partnership or corporation in its individual territory, and while none publicly report financial results, each is primarily funded by reimbursements from its respective regional Kaiser Foundation Health Plan. Kaiser Foundation Health Plan is one of the largest not-for-profit entities in the U.S. Quality of care has been highly rated, with an emphasis on preventive care. Doctors are salaried rather than paid per service, and time spent by patients in hospitals is monitored. Kaiser operates in 8 states and Washington, D.C.   --en.wikipedia.org

As with ObamaCare, each enrollee has a primary care physician, who refers patients to specialists as the need arises. Membership includes a reasonable monthly fee as well as a co-pay for each visit or prescription, often nominal, $5 to $25. Enrollment is expanding rapidly. The best thing about Kaiser Permanente is that there are no surprises, like physicians charging "out of network" fees, or hospitals charging for "services not covered." These "out-of-pocket" expenses under ObamaCare arrive in medical bills after services are rendered. They can drain a person of their lifetime savings as if they had no insurance coverage at all.

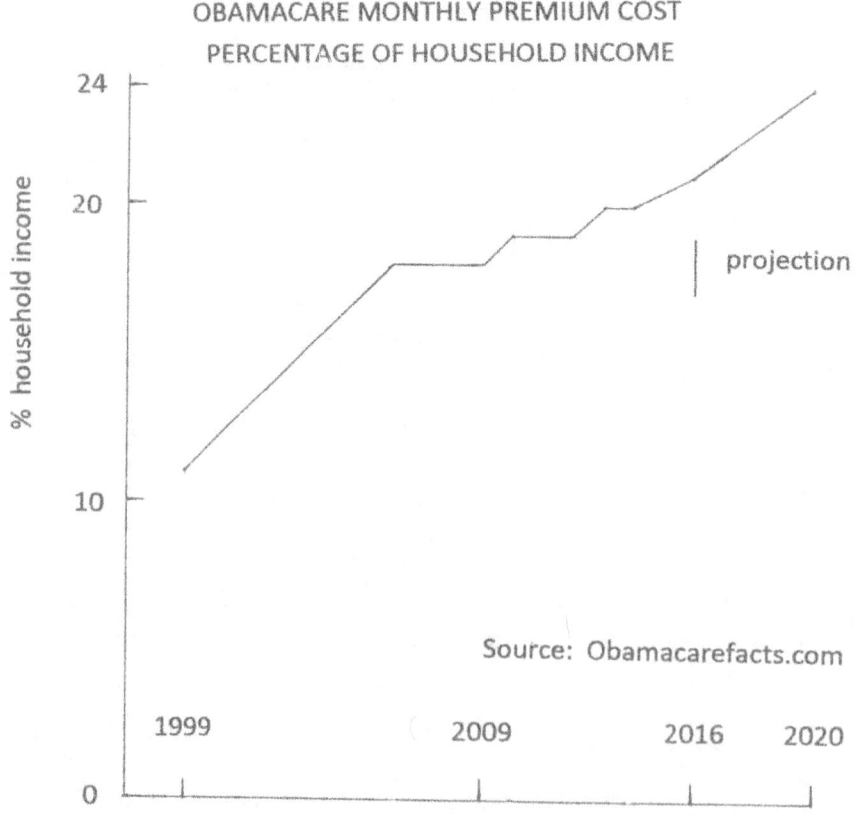

ObamaCare News

kaiserhealthnews.org

Based on 13 states only, a 40 year-old non-smoker will see his insurance premium rise from $285 in 2016 to $313 in 2017. California, Texas and Florida data is not yet available. Other facts are these:

13 million Americans bought health insurance coverage in 2016.

150 million Americans get health insurance through their employers.

100 million Americans are covered by government programs Medicare and Medicaid.

8 in 10 marketplace enrollees (through state exchanges) will get government subsidies.

--khn.org

politico.com

Large health insurance rate increases are coming November 1, 2016, the beginning date for open enrollment for 2017. Health care insurers report they are breaking even or losing money under Obamacare. Many plans have enrollees sicker than expected. The United Health Group pulled out of most ObamaCare state exchanges due to an anticipated $650 million in losses in 2016. Aetna expects to break even but is withdrawing from many ObamaCare marketplaces in 2017.   --politico.com

thehill.com

State insurance officials are feeling the pressure to accept the Affordable Care Act rate increases. For the 9 states that have approved 2017 premium increases, the average increase is 27.6%. In Tennessee, the three insurers in the state want 62%, 46% and 44% rate increases, which are actuarially justified, according to Julie McPeak, Tennessee's insurance commissioner. "Any one carrier deciding to withdraw from our marketplace could cause a disastrous effect, because the other carriers may follow suit," she said.

"North Carolina has Blue Cross/Blue Shield, which is currently the only option in much of the state," said North Carolina insurance commissioner Wayne Goodwin. Blue Cross/Blue Shield is waiting to see if its premium increase is improved by the state's Department of Insurance before deciding whether to continue to offer ObamaCare coverage statewide next year.

One county in Arizona now has no insurance companies slated to offer ObamaCare coverage in 2017, after Aetna pulled out of many markets. Senator John McCain said, after Aetna's decision, "The crumbling of ObamaCare at this alarming rate is simply unsustainable," adding that it would leave Arizona with "more expensive and less accessible health care."

--thehill.com

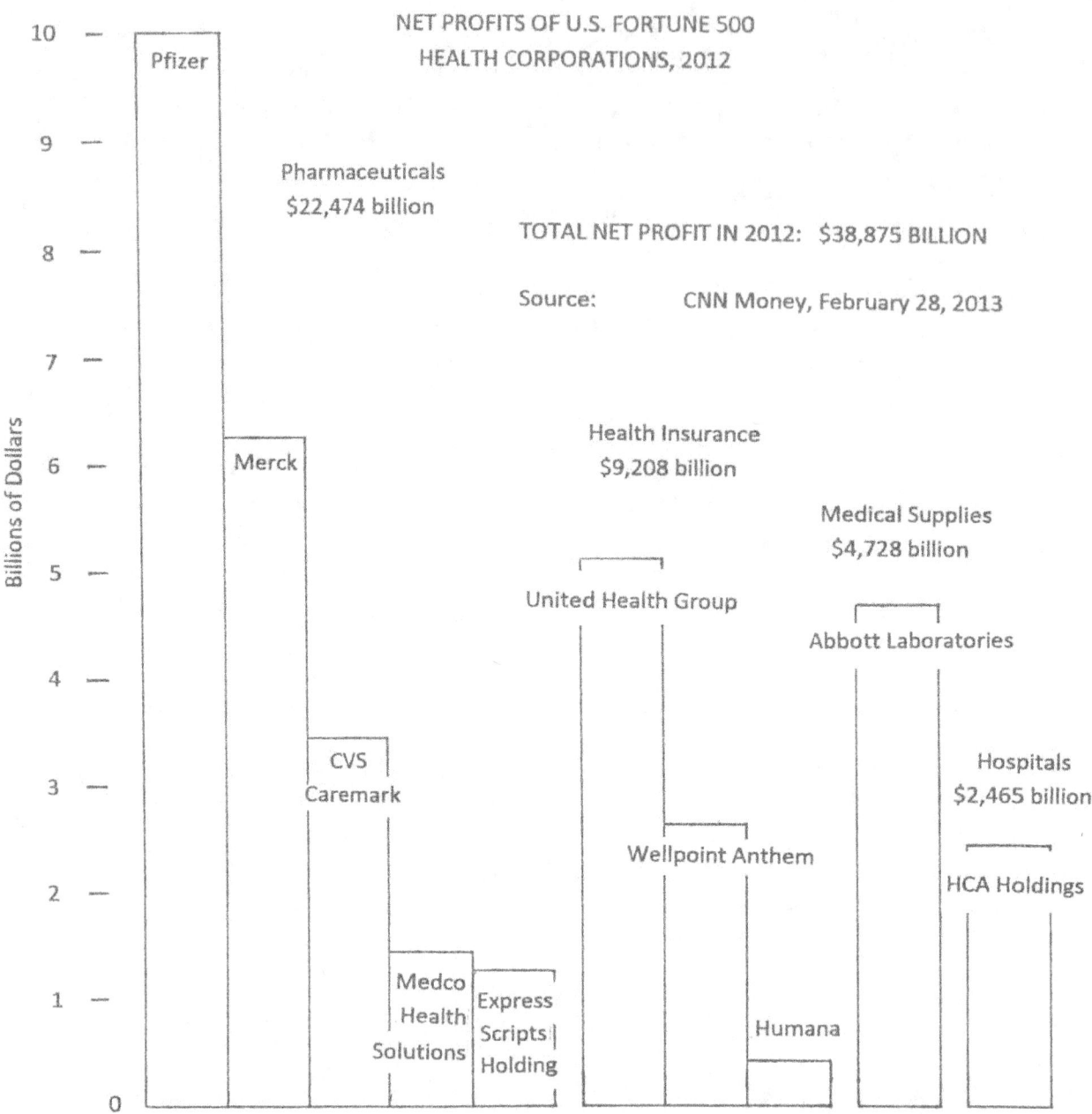

NET PROFITS OF U.S. FORTUNE 500
HEALTH CORPORATIONS, 2012

Pharmaceuticals
$22,474 billion

TOTAL NET PROFIT IN 2012: $38,875 BILLION

Source: CNN Money, February 28, 2013

Health Insurance
$9,208 billion

Medical Supplies
$4,728 billion

United Health Group

Abbott Laboratories

Hospitals
$2,465 billion

CVS
Caremark

Wellpoint Anthem

HCA Holdings

Medco Health Solutions

Express Scripts Holding

Humana

Pfizer

Merck

Billions of Dollars

10
9
8
7
6
5
4
3
2
1
0

President Obama's "Affordable Care Act," also known as "ObamaCare" mandates the purchase of health insurance by all Americans, which, with no price controls, serves to enrich the highly consolidated and global U.S. health corporations. The U.S. government subsidizes millions of Americans who cannot afford coverage, increasing U.S. deficits.

U.S. federal government spending on health care is projected to be $1.1 trillion in 2016, or 28.3% of all federal expenses.   --usgovernmentspending.com

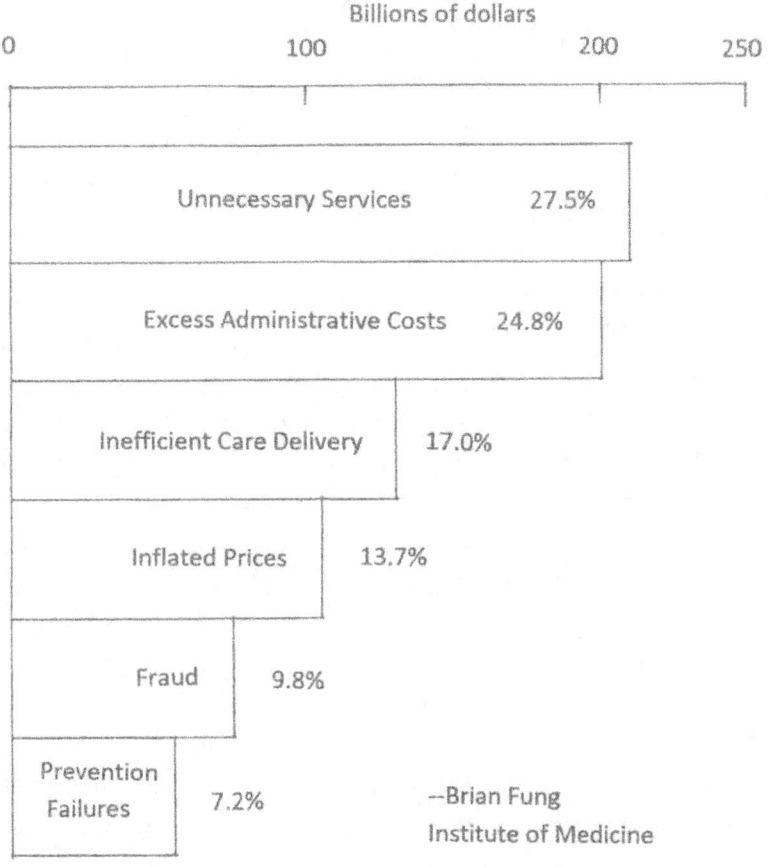

THE U.S. HEALTH CARE SYSTEM WASTES $ 750 BILLION ANNUALLY

Billions of dollars

0	100	200	250

Unnecessary Services 27.5%

Excess Administrative Costs 24.8%

Inefficient Care Delivery 17.0%

Inflated Prices 13.7%

Fraud 9.8%

Prevention Failures 7.2%

--Brian Fung
Institute of Medicine

Transformation of Health System Needed to Improve Care and Reduce Costs

Press Release - Health and Medicine Division, September 6, 2012

America's health care system has become too complex and costly to continue business as usual, says a new report from the Institute of Medicine. Inefficiencies, an overwhelming amount of data, and other economic and quality barriers hinder progress in improving health and threaten the nation's economic stability and global competitiveness, the report says. However, the knowledge and tools exist to put the health system on the right course to achieve continuous improvement and better quality at lower cost, added the committee that wrote the report.

The costs of the system's current inefficiency underscore the urgent need for a system-wide transformation. The committee calculated that about 30 percent of health spending in 2009 -roughly $750 billion - was wasted on unnecessary services, excessive administrative costs, fraud, and other problems. Moreover, inefficiencies cause needless suffering. By one estimate, roughly 75,000 deaths might have been averted in 2005 if every state had delivered care at the quality level of the best performing state.

--nationalacademies.org

18

Finding Fraud in Federal Health Programs   justice.gov

The Justice Department, combined with other federal agencies, sent a strike force on June 22, 2016 to arrest 301 individuals across the country for alleged fraud against the government's various health care programs. The arrests saved the federal government $900 million. Sixty-one doctors and nurses and other licensed health care professionals were caught up in the sweep.

In Florida, 100 individuals were targeted for $220 million on alleged false billings for home health care, mental health services and pharmacy services. In South Texas, 24 individuals were charged with $146 million in alleged fraudulent billings, one a physician with the highest number of referrals for home health services that were unnecessary or not provided. In North Texas, 11 individuals had allegedly fraudulently charged $47 million to federal health agencies; one, a physician, allowed an unlicensed person to do procedures, then billed Medicare as if he performed the services. In the Central California District, 22 individuals had billed $162 million in alleged fraud services. In East Michigan, 19 individuals charged $114 million in alleged fraud, money laundering, kickbacks and drug distribution claims unnecessary or never rendered. In North Illinois, six had billed $12 million; in East New York, 5 had billed $86 million, with money allegedly laundered through over a dozen shall companies; in South New York, a pharmacist billed $51 million in allegedly fraudulent Medicare and Medicaid services. The list goes on.   --justice.gov

Since 2009, the Justice Department Civil Division and U.S. Attorney offices around the country have saved $18.3 billion for federal health care programs under the False Claim Act cases.   --justice.gov

Prescription Drug Costs - an example

Medicine to rid an individual of Hepatitis C is extremely good news. The cost, however, can be prohibitive. A three-month supply of one tablet a day can cost $112,000. Providers of prescriptions to cure Hepatitis C and their net income, after research and development, are:

Solvadi	Gilead	San Dimas, CA	7,900 employees	$18.1 billion in 2015
Harvoni	Gilead			
Epclusa	Gilead			
Viekira	AbbVie	Chicago, IL	28,000 employees	$ 7.5 billion in 2015
Technivie	AbbVie			
Zepatier	Merck	Kenilworth NJ	70,000 employees	$ 4.4 billion in 2015
Daklinza	Bristol Myers Squibb NYC	28,000 employees		$10.6 billion in 2009
Olysio	Janssen Belgiium	parent Johnson & Johnson,	1985 in China,	no rev info
Pegasys	Roche Switz	Genentech subsid 88,509 empl	47.4 billion Swiss Francs	
Infergen	3 Rivers Pharm NY (Kadmon Corp)	250 empl,	no revenue info	

--hepatitiscnewdrugresearch.com; company web sites

Per Capita Annual Expense of Health Care by Country

$9674	Switzerland	$4612	Finland	$1455	Slovak Republic
$9522	Norway	$4239	Ireland	$1442	Uruguay
$9403	United States	$3935	United Kingdom	$1379	Czech Republic
$8149	Monaco	$3703	Japan	$1356	Kuwait
$8138	Luxembourg	$3459	San Marino	$1165	Maldives
$6808	Sweden	$3258	Italy	$1147	Saudi Arabia
$6463	Denmark	$2752	Singapore	$1136	Trinidad and Tobago
$6031	Australia	$2658	Spain	$1063	Lithuania
$5694	Netherlands	$2910	Israel	$1050	Croatia
$5580	Austria	$2471	Malta	$1037	Hungary
$5411	Germany	$2161	Slovenia	$ 947	Brazil
$5292	Canada	$2106	Qatar	$ 893	Russian Federation
$4959	France	$2097	Portugal	$ 817	Cuba
$4896	New Zealand	$2060	Republic of Korea	$ 677	Mexico
$4884	Belgium	$1743	Greece	$ 569	Colombia
$4662	Iceland	$1611	United Arab Emirates	$ 568	Turkey
				$ 420	China

North America average: $8990
European Union average: $3613
World average: $1061

data.worldbank.org

U.S. medical costs are out of proportion to other U.S. consumer costs.

U.S. medical costs are the third highest in the industrialized world.

The U.S. had a single payer system throughout its history until the 1970s,
    offering consumers voluntary catastrophic insurance coverage.

A single payer system for medical care eliminates insurance company profits.

Most European countries successfully use a single payer system for medical care.

Hopes and fears as Indonesia rolls out universal healthcare

--irinnews.org

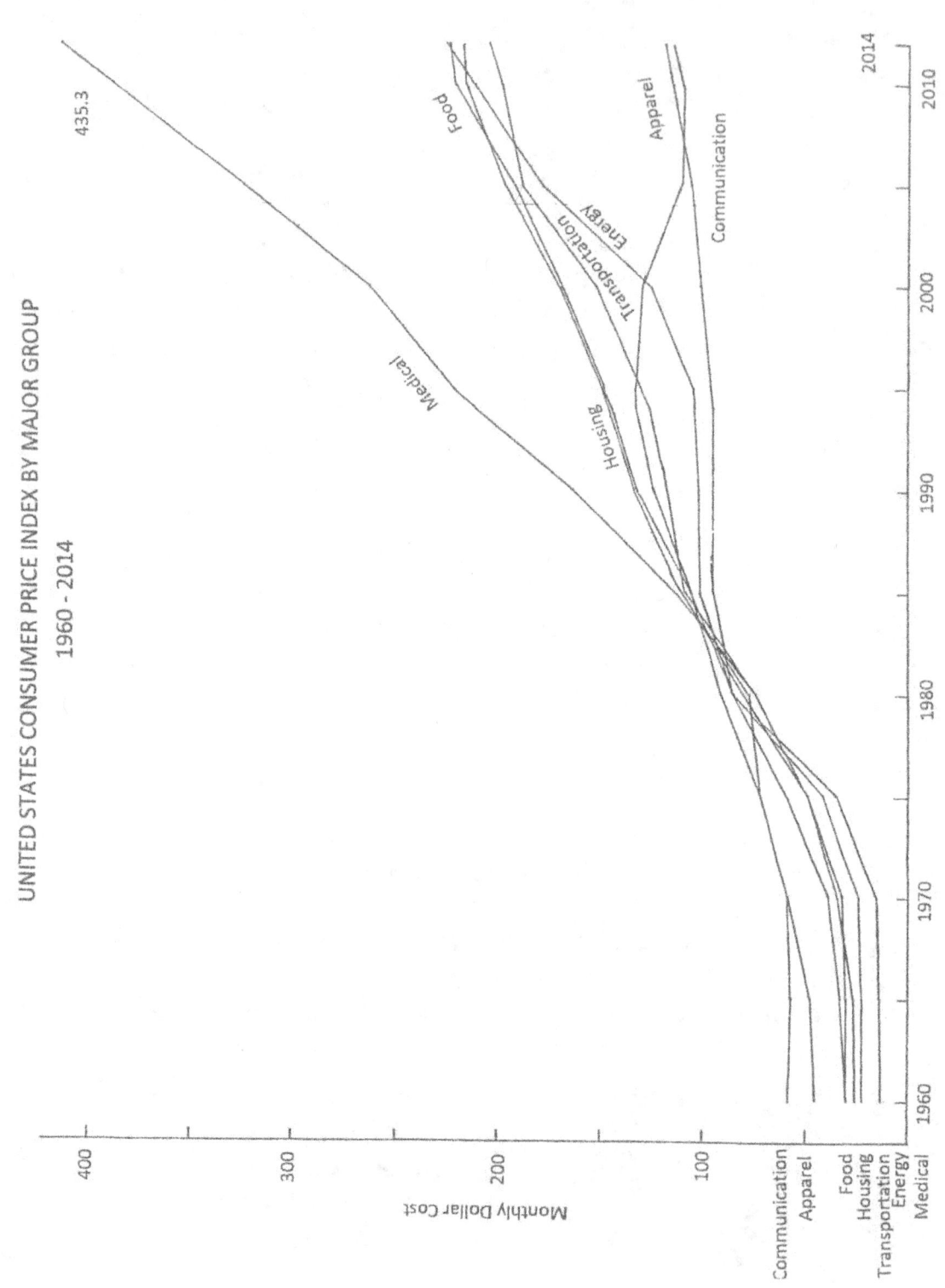

UNITED STATES CONSUMER PRICE INDEX BY MAJOR GROUP
1960 - 2014

435.3

Medical

Food

Transportation
Energy

Housing

Apparel

Communication

Monthly Dollar Cost

400

300

200

100

Communication
Apparel
Food
Housing
Transportation
Energy
Medical

1960   1970   1980   1990   2000   2010   2014

Source: ProQuest Statistical Abstract of the United States 2016, p 480
           Statistical Abstract of the United States 2012, p 474; 1995, p 492

UNITED STATES FEDERAL INVOLVEMENT IN FOREIGN AFFAIRS, 2015

Defense - Military	$567.7	billion
Veterans	$160.8	billion
Homeland Security	$ 45.7	billion
Justice*	$ 36.1	billion
State*	$ 30.5	billion
International Assistance	$ 24.0	billion

TOTAL FOREIGN INVOLVEMENT IN 2015; $ 864.8 billion

*The percentage of foreign duties in the Departments of Justice and State are unknown.

Source: U.S. Office of Management and Budget
                 ProQuest Statistical Abstract of the United States 2016, p 328

The United States does not report one dime's worth of expenditures for immigration for the simple reason that the federal budget does not include immigration as a budget category. Rather, costs for immigration are buried in the budgets of various federal agencies. The U.S. government would have the public believe that immigration is a zero sum game, or even a financial benefit to the country.

The U.S. federal deficits began their march toward the trillions under Ronald Reagan, exactly the time when immigration from non-Western European countries began to seriously kick in. Since there were no major wars during Reagan's tenure, and since the costs of the Savings and Loan fiasco weren't even announced until the beginning of Reagan's second term, and losses not fully returned to depositors until 1995, there is nowhere else to look for Reagan's massive deficits but immigration.

Clinton's relatively smaller federal deficits can be traced to the sudden rise in computer technology and the concomitant growth of Nasdaq, resulting in high income tax returns from citizens and high capital gains taxes from trades.

George Bush's and Barack Obama's federal deficits are enormous because of the "War on Terror" since 2001, but also because of growing immigration and unknown expenses thereof.

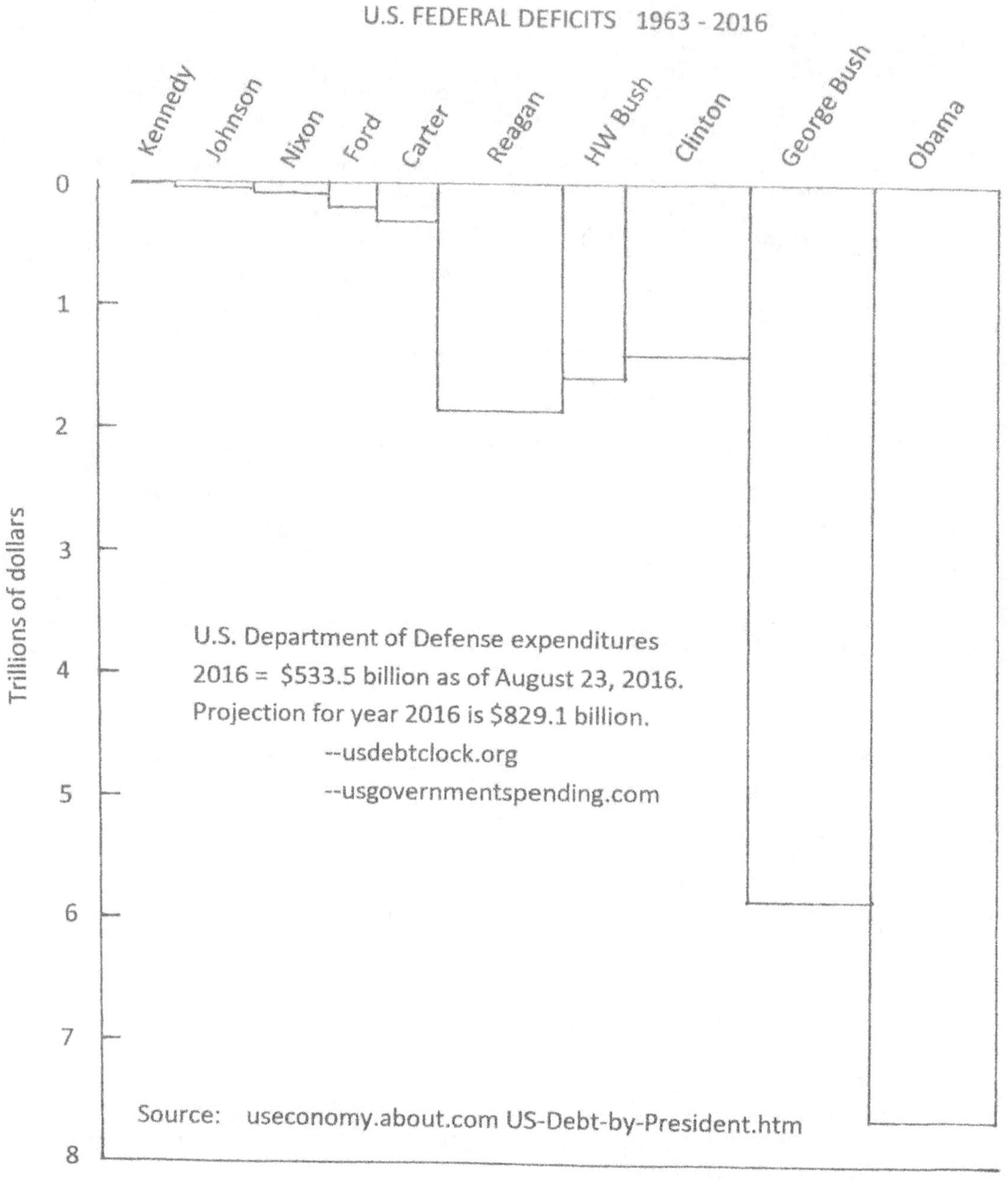

U.S. FEDERAL DEFICITS 1963 - 2016

Kennedy Johnson Nixon Ford Carter Reagan HW Bush Clinton George Bush Obama

Trillions of dollars

0

1

2

3

4

5

6

7

8

U.S. Department of Defense expenditures
2016 = $533.5 billion as of August 23, 2016.
Projection for year 2016 is $829.1 billion.
--usdebtclock.org
--usgovernmentspending.com

Source: useconomy.about.com US-Debt-by-President.htm

Harvard University researcher Linda Blimes said in a study that the U.S. has already spent "close to $2 trillion on the conflicts in Iraq and Afghanistan" but that the actual long term costs will at least double that figure.

She notes in that one out of every two veterans no longer on active duty is receiving medical care and 50% have applied for permanent disability benefits. Veterans from Vietnam and the first Gulf War are receiving benefits. Veterans often have life-long medical problems from being directly hit in combat or being close to bomb explosions.

"War's Future Cost is Vast," by Linda Blimes, Harvard Kennedy School, Harvard University, 2013   --hks.harvard.edu

UNITED STATES BUDGET FOR GLOBAL WAR ON TERROR OPERATIONS
2001 - 2014

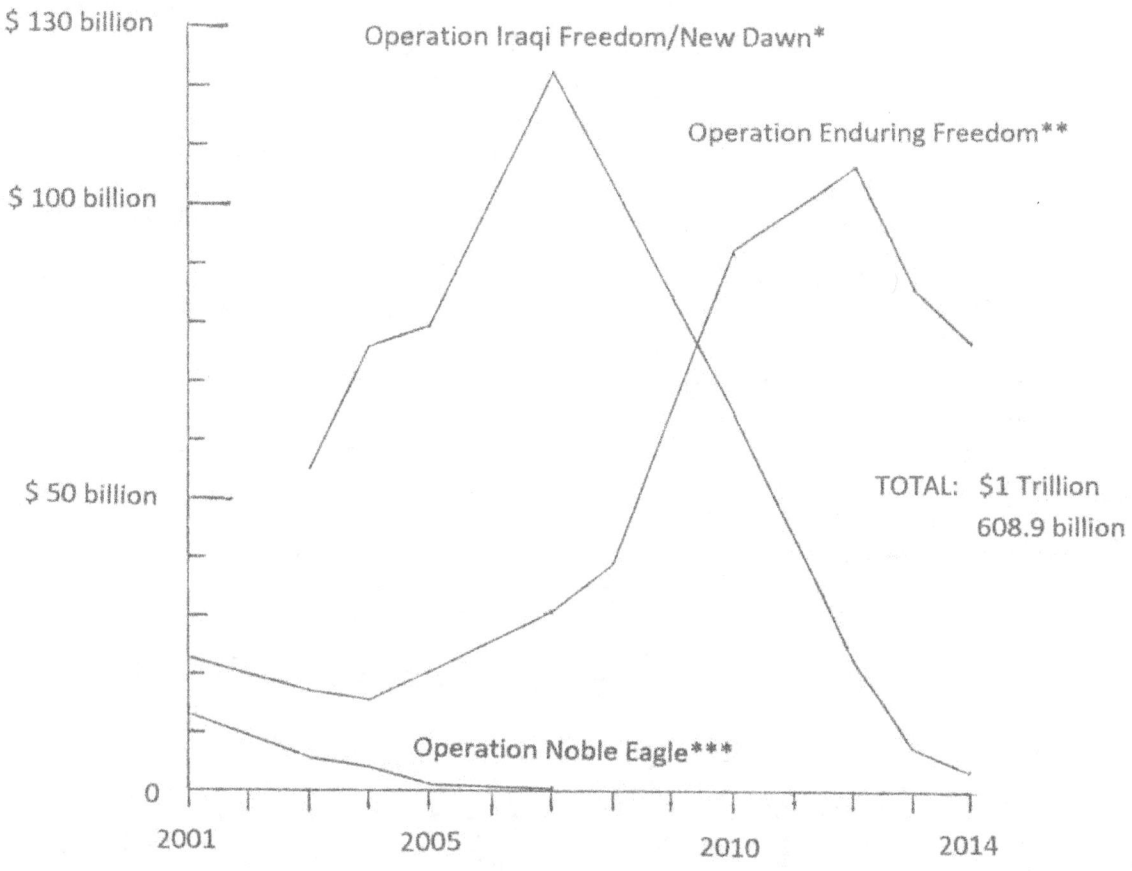

* Includes monies for reconstruction, development and humanitarian aid, embassy operations, counternarcotics, initial training of the Iraqi and Afghan armies, foreign military sales credits, and Economic Support Funds.

** Covers Afghanistan (officially ended Dec. 2014) and other Global War on Terror operations, from the Philippines to Dijbouti, that began immediately after the Sept. 11, 2001 attacks.

*** Department of Defense funds that rebuilt the Pentagon and provided higher security at U.S. military bases and other homeland security, including combat air patrol.

Source: Congressional Research Service, Library of Congress
            The World Almanac and Book of Facts 2016, p 133

"Beware the military-industrial complex."
--Dwight D. Eisenhower

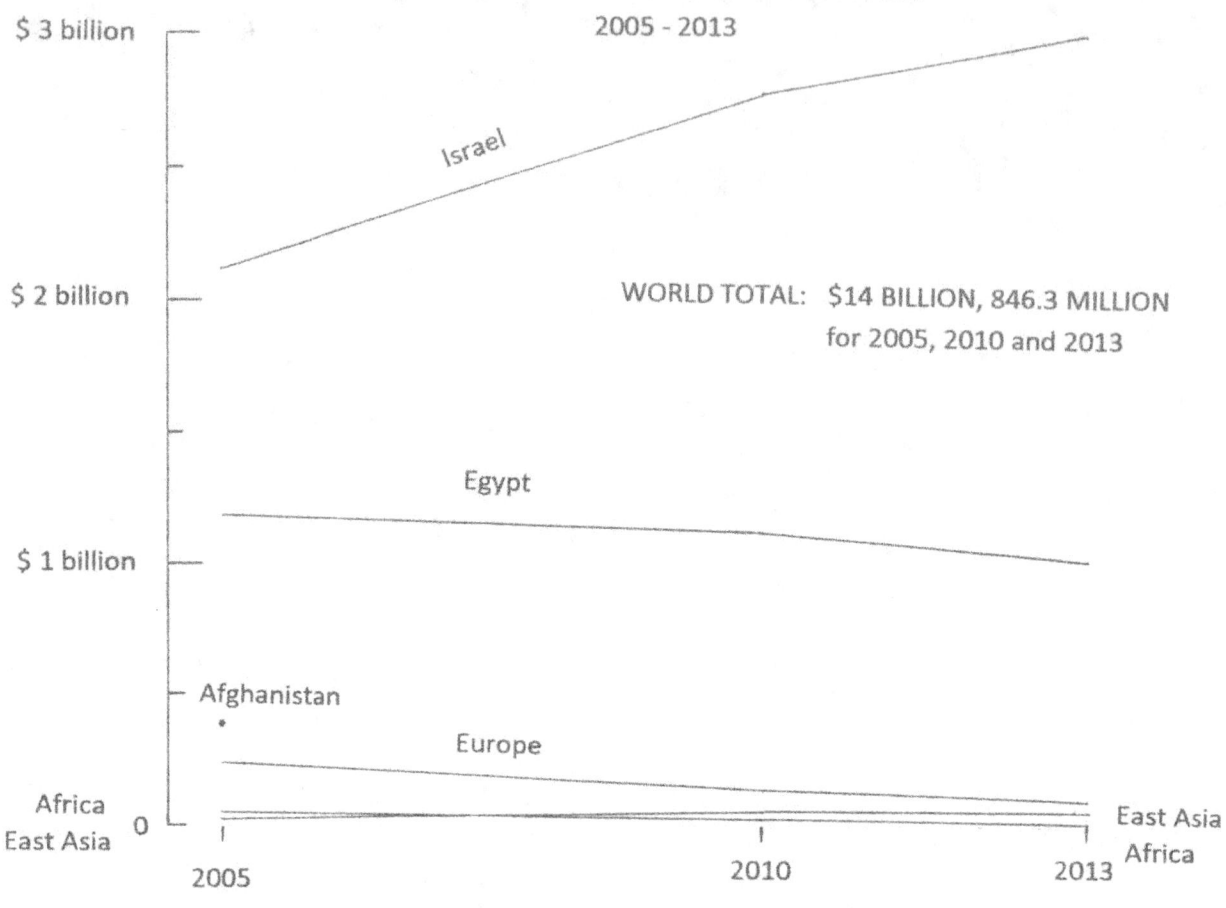

UNITED STATES FOREIGN MILITARY FINANCING
2005 - 2013

$ 3 billion

Israel

$ 2 billion

WORLD TOTAL: $14 BILLION, 846.3 MILLION
for 2005, 2010 and 2013

$ 1 billion

Egypt

Afghanistan

Europe

Africa
East Asia   0

East Asia
Africa

2005   2010   2013

Note: Grants to Bahrain, Jordan, Lebanon, Oman, Pakistan and Yemen
         totalling $ 1 billion, 635 million are not included above.

Note: Grants to Colombia, El Salvador and Mexico totalling $ 252 million, 317 thousand,
         not included above.

Note: "Listed are GRANTS EXTENDED TO FOREIGN GOVERNMENTS in a fiscal year to
         pay for military equipment and services. May be from the U.S. Department of
         Defense (DOD), or, for specific countries, negotiated directly with U.S
         military suppliers with DOD approval."

Countries in South Asia	Countries in East Asia	Countries in Europe		Countries in Africa
Afghanistan	Indonesia	Bosnia	Poland	Djibouti
Bahrain	Mongolia	Bulgaria	Romania	Liberia
Jordan	Philippines	Czech R.	Turkey	Morocco
Lebanon		Georgia	Ukraine	Tunisia
Oman		Herzegovina		
Pakistan		Macedonia		
Yemen				

Source: Defense Security Cooperation Agency, U.S. Department of Defense
          The World Almanac and Book of Facts 2016, p 134

25

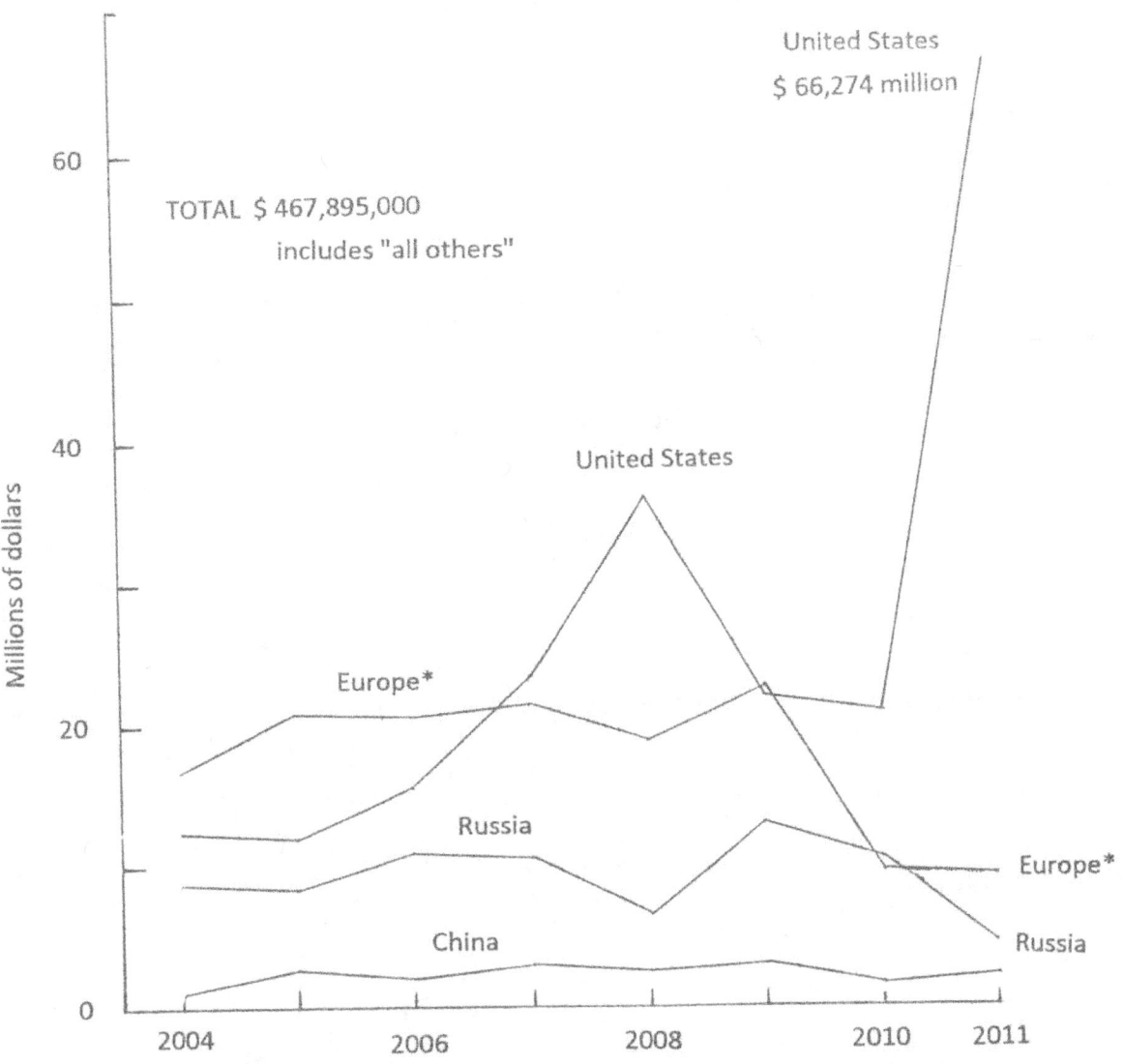

ARMS "TRANSFER AGREEMENTS WITH THE WORLD" BY SUPPLIER COUNTRY
2004 - 2011

United States
$ 66,274 million

TOTAL $ 467,895,000
includes "all others"

Millions of dollars

60

40

United States

Europe*

20

Russia

Europe*

China

Russia

0

2004   2006   2008   2010   2011

*Countries include France, United Kingdom, Germany, Italy, and "all other European"

Note: All amounts given include the values of all categories of weapons,
spare parts, construction, all associated services, military assistance,
excess defense articles, and training programs.

Source: Congressional Research Service, Library of Congress
The World Almanac and Book of Facts 2016, p 134

Everyone's bailing on this one except us.

DEFENSE CONTRACTS, 2014
COMPANIES OR ORGANIZATIONS RECEIVING LARGEST DOLLAR VOLUME
OF PRIME CONTRACT AWARDS FROM THE DEPARTMENT OF DEFENSE

Lockheed Martin Corp.

The Boeing Co.

General Dynamics Corp. PLC

Raytheon Co.

Northrop Grumman Corp.

BAE Systems

L-3 Communications Holdings, Inc.

United Technologies Corp.

Huntington Ingalls Industries, Inc.

Humana, Inc.

United Health Group, Inc.

Health Net, Inc.

TOTAL: $ 290 billion, 91.1 million
includes defense contractors
not listed

Bechtel Group, Inc.

General Electric Co.

Booz Allen Hamilton Holding Corp.

SAIC, Inc.

Exelis, Inc.

Bell Boeing Joint Project Office

McKesson Corp.

Royal Dutch Shell PLC

Textron, Inc.

General Atomic Technologies Corp.

| 0 | $10 million | $25 million |

Note: Lockheed Martin and Northrop Grumman locations combined for their totals.

Note: Amounts include contracts awarded to subsidiaries of each company.

Source: U.S. Department of Defense
              The World Almanac and Book of Facts 2016, p 134

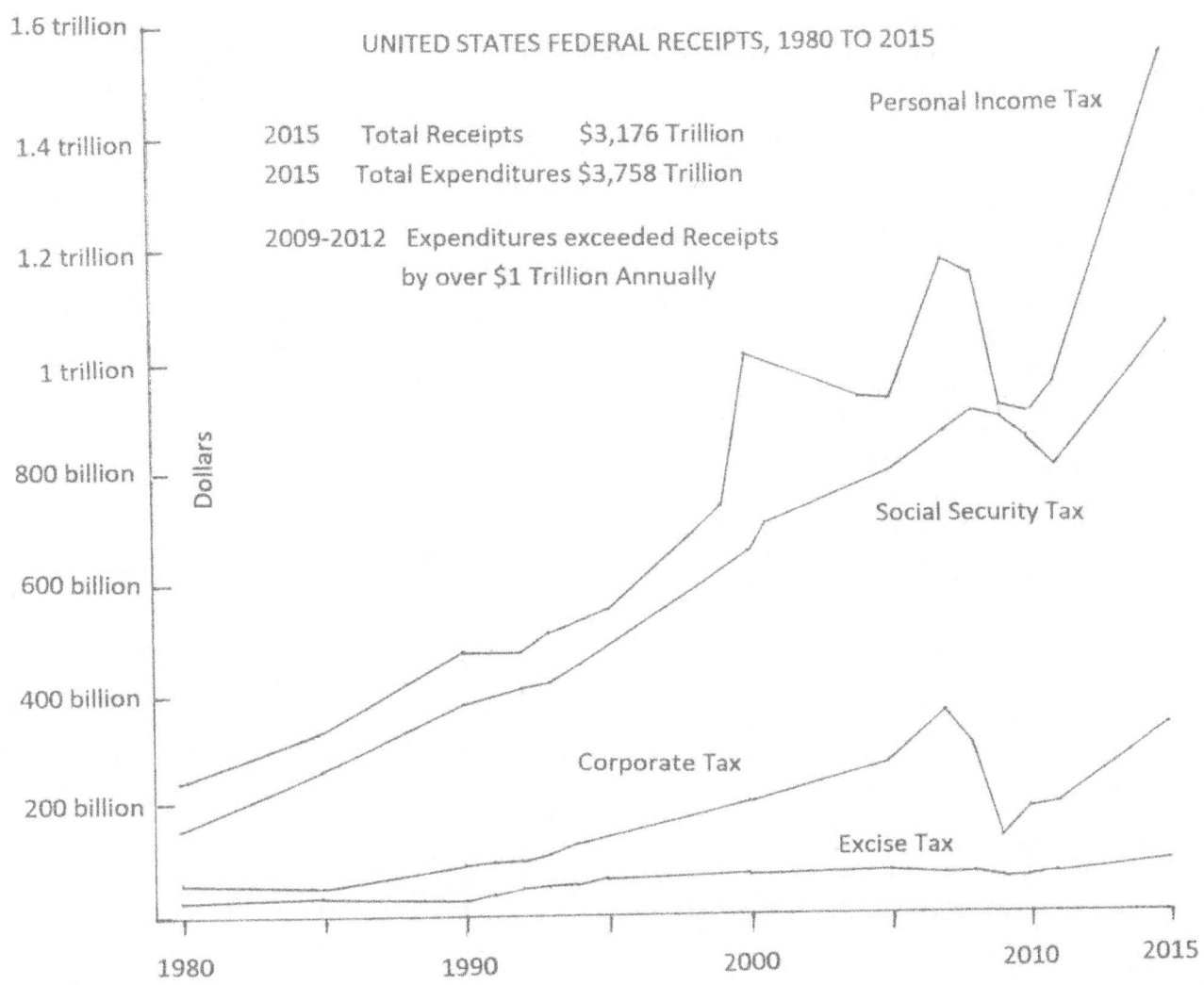

UNITED STATES FEDERAL RECEIPTS, 1980 TO 2015

2015   Total Receipts $3,176 Trillion
2015   Total Expenditures $3,758 Trillion

2009-2012 Expenditures exceeded Receipts
           by over $1 Trillion Annually

Personal Income Tax

Social Security Tax

Corporate Tax

Excise Tax

Note   Excise taxes are "inland taxes," whereas customs duties are "border" taxes.
        An excise tax is typically a per unit tax, as on gasoline, tobacco and alcohol.

Note   An "Impost" tax, also called "Customs" and "Duty" tax are taxes on imported goods.

        Source: Statistical Abstract of the United States 1994, p 332; 2012, p 314
                 ProQuest Statistical Abstract of the United States 2016, p 327

United States federal income is increasingly paid by the personal income taxes of the people
of the United States, as well as their social security, disability, and medicare payments.

The low income tax receipts from corporations contribute significantly to the annual
federal deficits of the United States.

Impost, customs or duty taxes collected are so miniscule as not to appear as a source
of federal receipts.

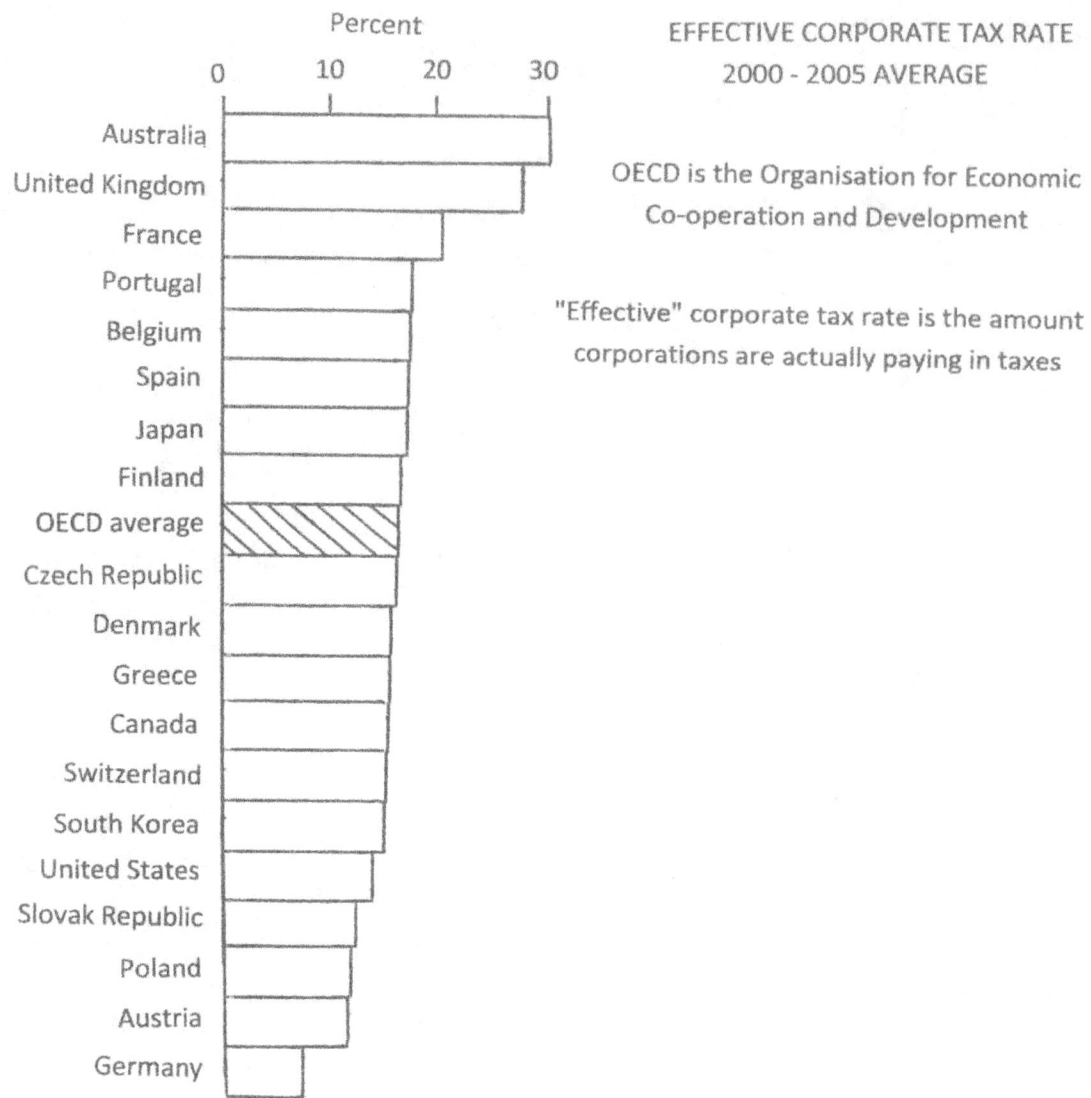

Percent

EFFECTIVE CORPORATE TAX RATE
2000 - 2005 AVERAGE

OECD is the Organisation for Economic
Co-operation and Development

"Effective" corporate tax rate is the amount
corporations are actually paying in taxes

Source: "Treasury Conference on Business Taxation and Global Competitiveness,"
23 July 2007, U.S. Treasury, p 42

The U.S. has the third highest corporate income tax in the world at 35%, the same as
Puerto Rico and exceeded by Chad and United Arab Emirates as of 2015. The worldwide
average corporate tax rate has declined from 30% in 2003 to 22.9% in 2015.

--taxfoundation.org

"In 2010, U.S. corporate tax revenue constituted about 9% of all federal revenue."

--wikipedia.org

EXECS PROFIT AT PUBLIC'S EXPENSE
Los Angeles Times   Aug 28, 2012   p B1

Twenty-five of the 100 highest paid U.S. chief executives pocketed more money in pay last year than their companies paid in federal income taxes - yet more evidence of how the 1% live in a bizarre parallel university where the normal rules don't apply.

The Institute for Policy Studies found that weak profits weren't to blame for relatively low tax bills. All had more than $1 billion in pretax income... Yet, thanks to a variety of tax breaks and loopholes, each of these companies was able to lavish an average of $20.6 million on its CEO and pay less than that amount to Uncle Sam.

Boeing enjoyed a tax refund of $605 million, according to the study, and Citigroup made the most of a $144 million refund...Sarah Anderson, an author of the study, said, "We're actually a very rich nation, but much of this money is going into the pockets of CEOs..." "They're the ones who lobbied hard for these loopholes. These loopholes aren't there by accident."

Among the loopholes cited in the report...allows companies to deduct as much "performance-based" compensation as they can cook up for their CEOs...The tax code also allows companies to kick almost unlimited sums of CEO pay down the road in the form of deferred compensation, allowing them to put off taxes on money that's already been earned...

Congress should cap the amount of CEO pay that can be deducted from a company's taxes...As it stands, CEO pay in the U.S. is 330 times what the average worker makes, according to the AFL-CIO labor union...There also should be crackdown on overseas tax havens...Senator Carl Levin (D-Mich) has introduced legislation that would...place a company's total earnings under U.S. tax laws.   by David Lazarus

U.S. oil companies enjoy between 10 and 40 million dollars every year in tax subsidies, even though they are making record profits, according to a study by the Congressional Budget Office. Senator Robert Menendez was working with President Obama on a bill in 2012 to cut about $20 billion in oil industry tax breaks, but Congress didn't pass it.

Oil industry spokesmen counter that the industry pays about $100 billion a year in taxes and provides 9.2 million jobs. The oil and gas industry also spends about $100 million a year on lobbyists.

Oil production is heavily subsidized every step of the way, beginning with exploration and ending with extraction. Oil companies can write off rent for drilling platforms, register the platforms, corporate headquarters and subsidiaries in low tax countries, and claim deductions for the lost value of tapped oil wells and platforms beyond what they actually paid for the oil rights.

Many companies besides oil companies use the same or similar tactics.

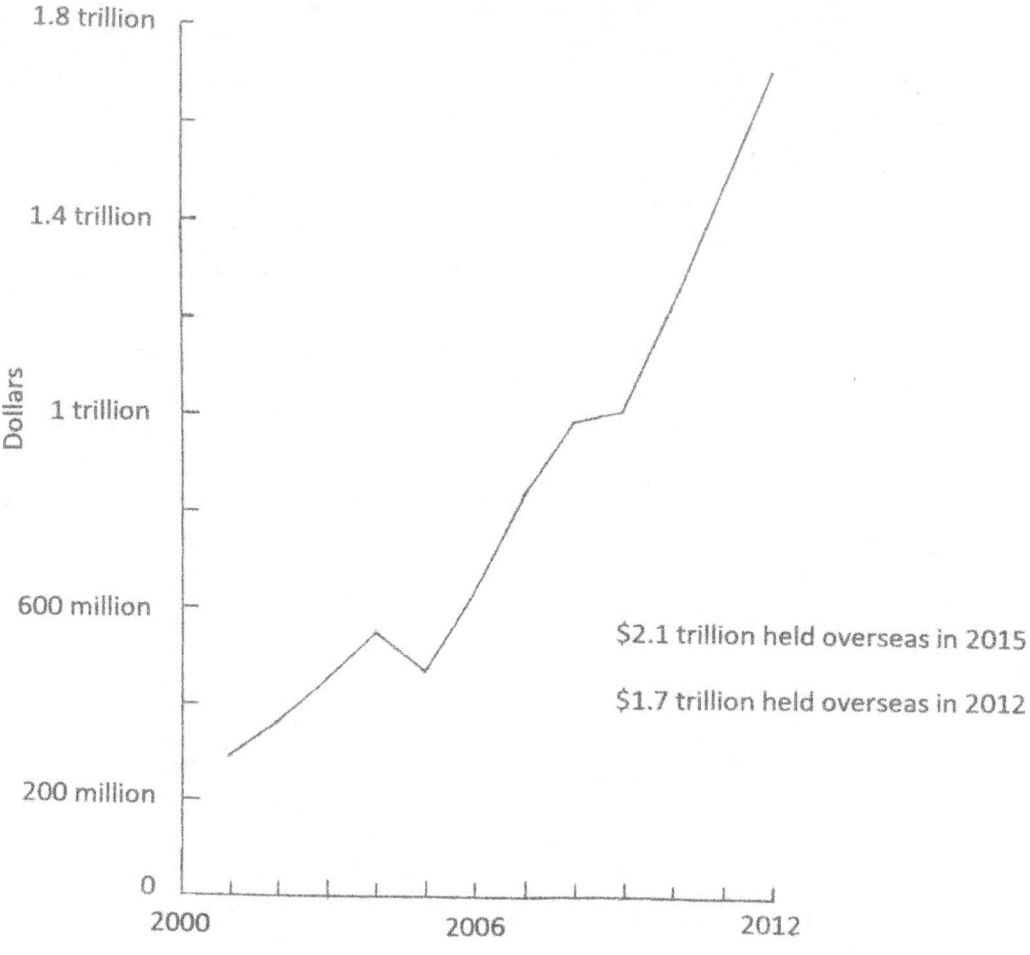

DEFERRED U.S. CORPORATE FOREIGN EARNINGS, 2001-2012

$2.1 trillion held overseas in 2015

$1.7 trillion held overseas in 2012

Source: Credit Suisse, 5 October 2012, Wikipedia Commons

A study, using company filings with the Securities and Exchange Commission, found that 72% of the 500 largest U.S. corporations hold $2.1 trillion in accumulated profits overseas to avoid U.S. taxes. The corporations pay an average of 6% overseas, rather than the 35% U.S. corporate tax rate. If the assets were brought home, the firms would collectively owe $620 billion in U.S. taxes.

The study reports that Tax haven locations include Bermuda, Ireland, Luxembourg and the Netherlands. There are 7.622 tax haven subsidiaries used by U.S. corporations. Only 30 firms hold $1.4 trillion of the $2.1 trillion profits held overseas.

FEDERAL CORPORATE TAX RATES
2015

Taxable Income

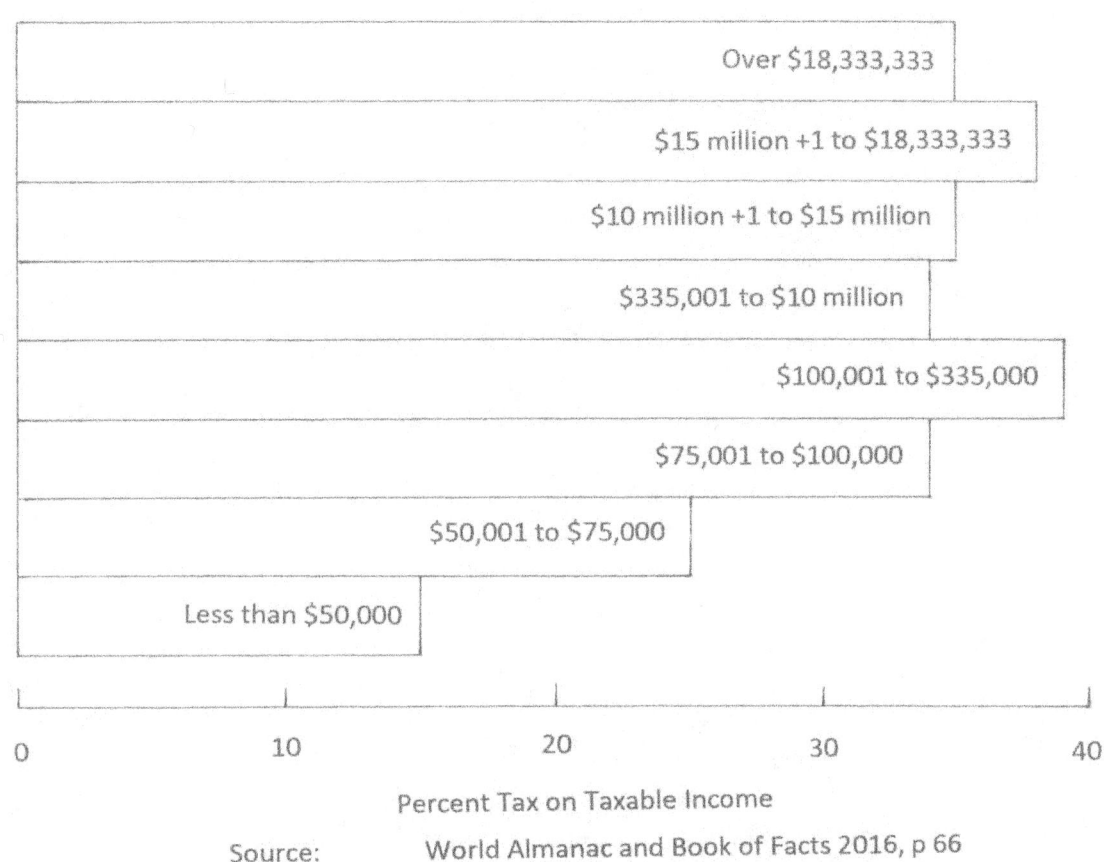

Over $18,333,333

$15 million +1 to $18,333,333

$10 million +1 to $15 million

$335,001 to $10 million

$100,001 to $335,000

$75,001 to $100,000

$50,001 to $75,000

Less than $50,000

0   10   20   30   40

Percent Tax on Taxable Income

Source: World Almanac and Book of Facts 2016, p 66

CORPORATE TAX IN THE UNITED STATES

U.S. EFFECTIVE CORPORATE TAX RATE, 1947 – 2011   U.S. CORPORATE INCOME TAX AS A SHARE OF GDP, 1945-2009

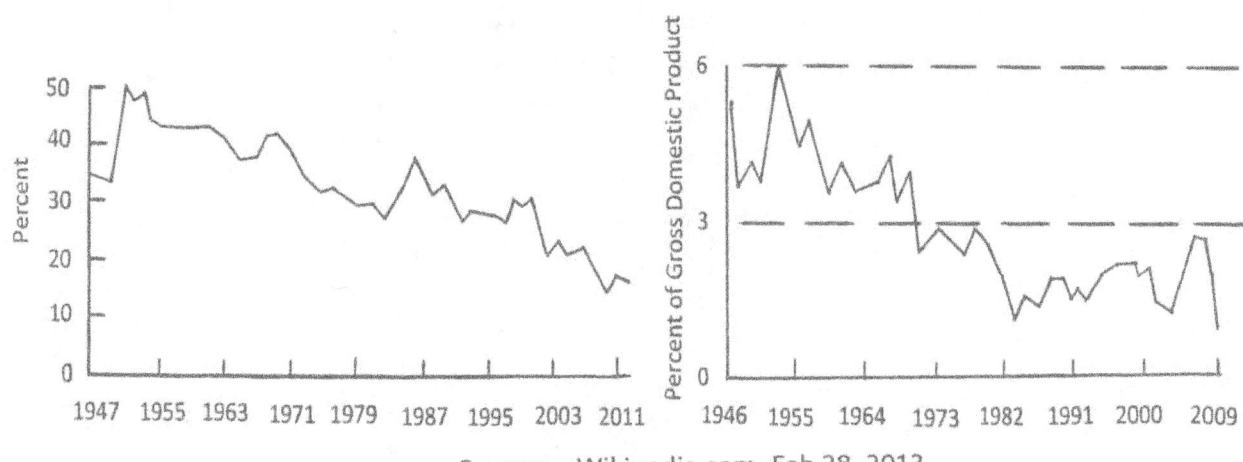

Source: Wikipedia.com, Feb 28, 2013

A GRADUATED PERSONAL INCOME TAX

It's been done before. And it levels the playing field to some degree between wealthy individuals and the middle class of the U.S. The personal income tax was as as high as 94% during the end of World War II.

THE PERSONAL INCOME TAX HELD STEADY AT 90%
FROM 1947 TO 1963

That 90% bracket for top earners in the 1950s and early 60s was what writer Ernest Hemingway griped about in his letters to his editor Max Perkins at Scribners Publishing House. Perhaps he was paying too much, for his income was modest compared to some, but certainly higher than the average Joe. The 1950s and 1960s was the heyday for the American average Joe, who could afford a nice house and two new cars every few years. There is a correlation between the ebbing of the once powerful middle class and the favorable tax bracket they enjoyed relative to the rich. High-end tax brackets also significantly increased federal government revenue. In recent decades, those earning millions annually are taxed at the same bracket as an American family earning $65,000.

A CENTURY OF THE 1040

Orange County Register   Apr 13, 2013   News 6

1862 - President Lincoln and Congress enact an income tax to
pay for the Civil War, 5% - 3%. Repealed in 1872.

1894 - Congress revives income tax. In 1895 U.S. Supreme Court
rules income tax unconstitutional on grounds it was a
direct tax and not apportioned among the states on
the basis of population.

1909 - President Taft recommends an income tax amendment
to Congress. In 1913 Wyoming is the 36th state to
ratify the 16th Amendment, giving Congress the
authority to enact an income tax.   6% - 1% and Form 1040.

1918 - During World War I, top income tax rate is 77% to help
finance the war.

1929 - Tax rates fall to 24% - 3%, but top rate rises steeply during
the Great Depression to 79% 1935 - 1940.

1941 - 1946 - During World War II, Congress introduces payroll
withholding, quarterly tax payments, and deductions for
medical and investment expenses. Tax rates rise from 1941
and peak in 1944 and 1945 at 94% - 23%.

1947 - 1963 Tax rates hold steady at 90% - 20%.

1963 - 1980 - Tax rate for top income earners holds steady at 70%,
while lowest income earners rate drops to 15% in 1963,
dropping again, to zero 1977 - 1986.

1988 - 2013 - Top and bottom tax rates hover between 40% and 10%,
reaching 39% in 2013 for top income earners and 10% for
bottom income earners.

Reporting by Sonya Quick, Graphic by Maxwell Henderson

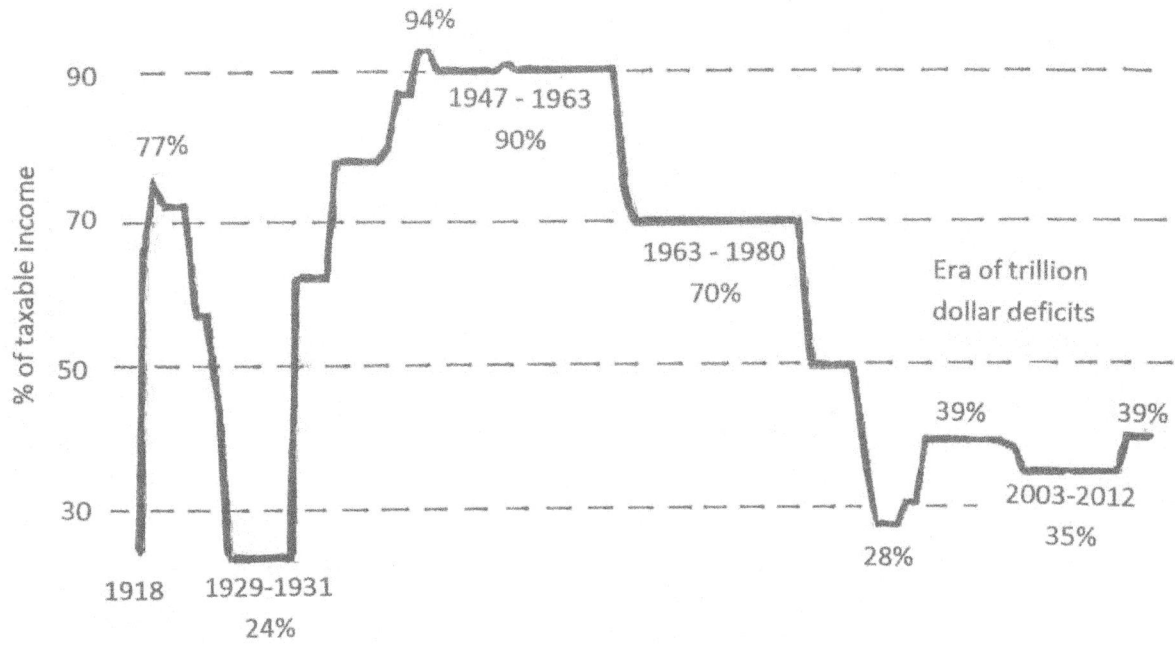

U.S. PERSONAL INCOME TAX RATES FOR HIGHEST WAGE EARNERS

Source: wikipedia.org

Personal Income Tax Rates (%) in other Countries

Sweden	56	Israel	48
Norway	56	Germany	45
Denmark	55	France	45
Netherlands	52	Australia	45
Spain	52	China	45
Finland	51	Italy	43
Great Britain	50	Luxembourg	43
Japan	50	Greece	42
Australia	50	Switzerland	40
Bulgaria	50	Croatia	40
Slovenia	50	Taiwan	40
Ireland	48	Russia	13

Federal Estate Tax

   "The Estate Tax is a tax on your right to transfer property at your death. It consists of an accounting of everything you own" (irs.gov). In 2016 any amount over $5.45 million is taxed at 40%. States are also imposing "death taxes." Complete elimination of the Estate Tax has been discussed. Such a move would significantly solidify wealth at the top, lower federal receipts, and hurt charities, since donations lower a donee's estate tax basis.

"CONGRESS SHALL HAVE POWER TO ... COIN MONEY, REGULATE THE VALUE
THEREOF, AND OF FOREIGN COIN"

Article I, Section 8

Constitution of the United States

WORLD'S LEADING GOLD PRODUCERS, 2014

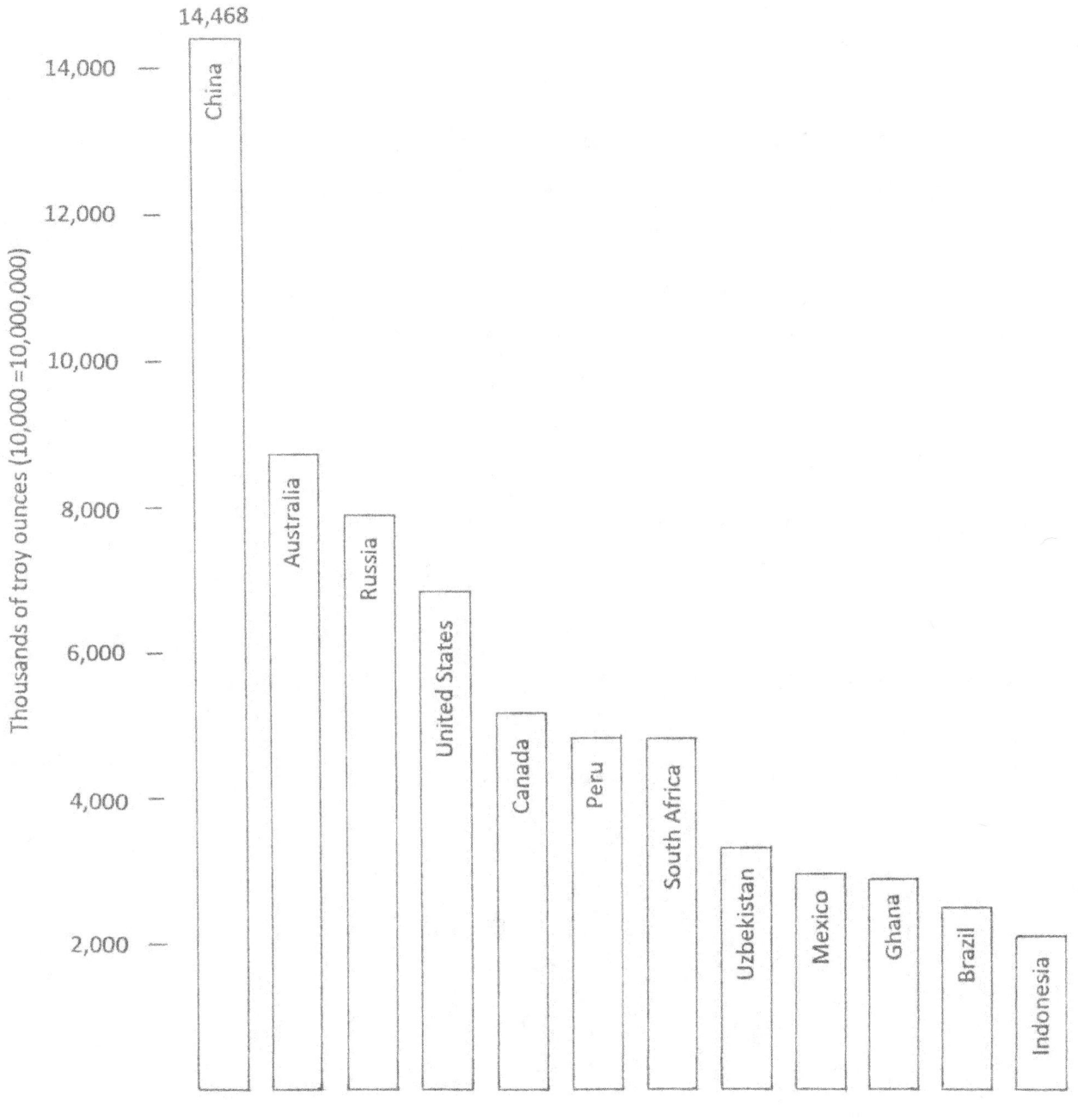

Note: 32.1507 troy oz = 1 kg

Source Mineral Commodity Summaries, 2015, U.S. Geological Survey,
U.S. Dept of the Interior; The World Almanac and Book of Facts 2016, p 68

1933
FDR takes United States off gold standard

Share this:

On June 5, 1933, the United States went off the gold standard, a monetary system in which currency is backed by gold, when Congress enacted a joint resolution nullifying the right of creditors to demand payment in gold. The United States had been on a gold standard since 1879, except for an embargo on gold exports during World War I, but bank failures during the Great Depression of the 1930s frightened the public into hoarding gold, making the policy untenable.

Soon after taking office in March 1933, Roosevelt declared a nationwide bank moratorium in order to prevent a run on the banks by consumers lacking confidence in the economy. He also forbade banks to pay out gold or to export it. According to Keynesian economic theory, one of the best ways to fight off an economic downturn is to inflate the money supply. And increasing the amount of gold held by the Federal Reserve would in turn increase its power to inflate the money supply. Facing similar pressures, Britain had dropped the gold standard in 1931, and Roosevelt had taken note.

On April 5, 1933, Roosevelt ordered all gold coins and gold certificates in denominations of more than $100 turned in for other money. It required all persons to deliver all gold coin, gold bullion and gold certificates owned by them to the Federal Reserve by May 1 for the set price of $20.67 per ounce. By May 10, the government had taken in $300 million of gold coin and $470 million of gold certificates. Two months later, a joint resolution of Congress abrogated the gold clauses in many public and private obligations that required the debtor to repay the creditor in gold dollars of the same weight and fineness as those borrowed. In 1934, the government price of gold was increased to $35 per ounce, effectively increasing the gold on the Federal Reserve's balance sheets by 69 percent. This increase in assets allowed the Federal Reserve to further inflate the money supply.

The government held the $35 per ounce price until August 15, 1971, when President Richard Nixon announced that the United States would no longer convert dollars to gold at a fixed value, thus completely abandoning the gold standard. In 1974, President Gerald Ford signed legislation that permitted Americans again to own gold bullion.

INTEL TECHNOLOGY

Source history.com/this-day-in-history/fdr-takes-united- states-off-gold-standard

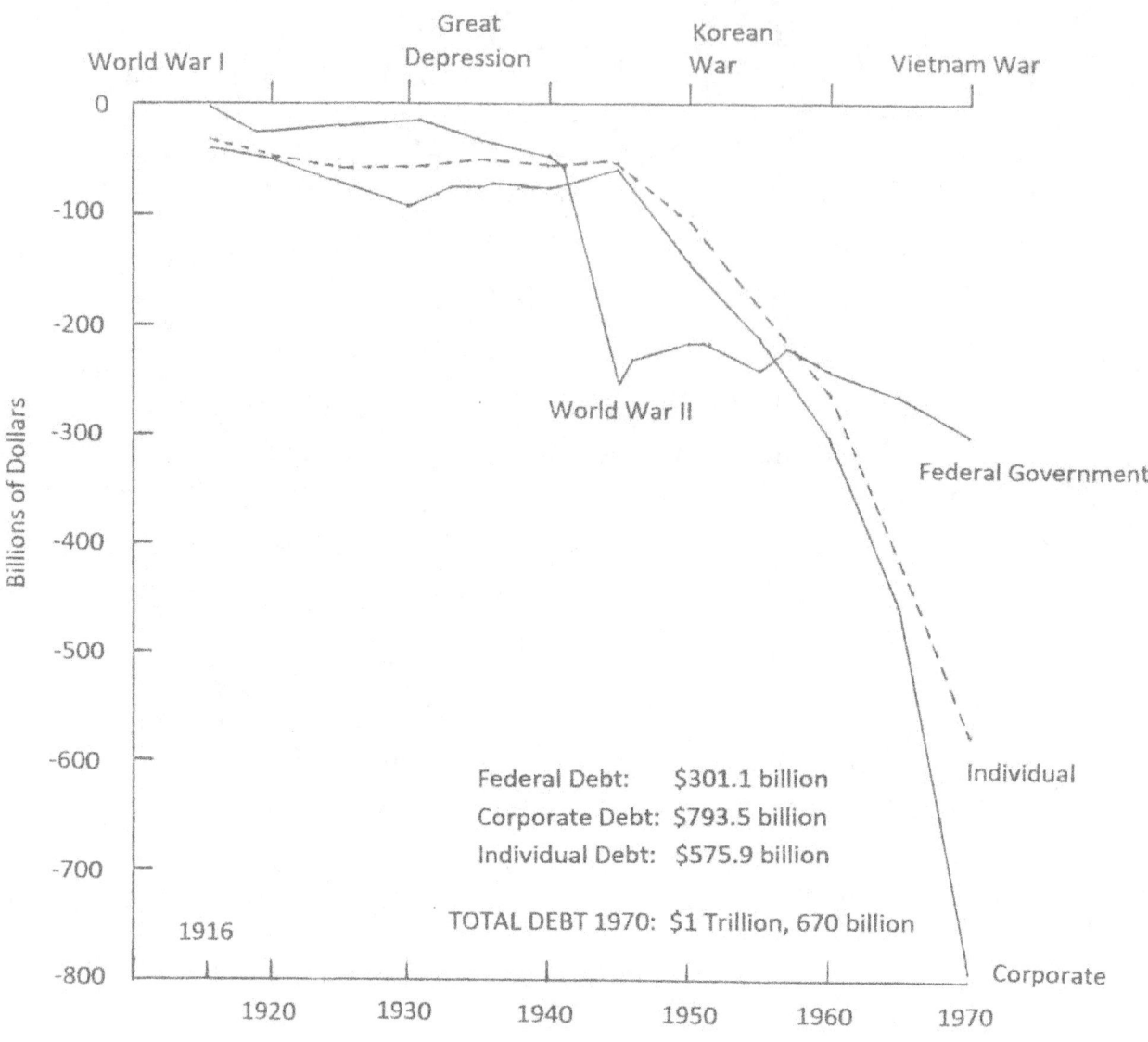

NET U.S. FEDERAL, CORPORATE AND INDIVIDUAL DEBT
1916 - 1970

Federal Debt: $301.1 billion
Corporate Debt: $793.5 billion
Individual Debt: $575.9 billion

TOTAL DEBT 1970: $1 Trillion, 670 billion

Note: Excluded: State and Local Debt $144.8 billion in 1970

Source: Historical Statistics of the United States, Colonial Times to 1970,
                 Bicentennial Edition, Part 2, p 989

The Truman and Eisenhower administrations attempted to reduce the federal
debt from World War II, but the costs of the Korean War and Vietnam War,
respectively, thwarted those attempts. By 1970, federal, corporate and individual
debt was over $1.5 trillion.

President Nixon took the nation off the Gold Standard completely on August 15, 1971.

RETHINKING GOLD

"Until recent times, gold was considered essentially a monetary metal, and most of the bullion produced each ear went into the vaults of government treasuries or central banks."
- -minerals.usgs.gov

"Most gold fabricated today goes into manufacturers of jewelry. Gold is also an essential industrial metal...in computers, communication equipment, spacecraft, jet aircraft engines. It has a unique status among all commodities as a long-term store of value."
--minerals.usgs.gov

"In 2012, the U.S. produced 230 tonnes of gold, the third largest after China and Australia. (and Russia). Most comes from large open-pit leach mines in Nevada. THE UNITED STATES IS A NET EXPORTER OF GOLD."
--wikipedia.org

China produces 90% of rare earth metals used in critical industries worldwide. When prices were high, too many producers entered mining, resulting in low metals prices. China began restricting exports of rare earths in 2010, shrinking supplies, and worrying manufacturers of high tech and clean energy products.
--mining.com

On November 5, 2015, India began manufacturing an India gold coin and an India gold bullion. The coin will join the American Eagle Coin (U.S.), Panda Coin (China), Maple Leaf Coin (Canada), Kruggerand (South Africa) and others. The India gold coin will be available in the United Kingdom, the United States, and South Africa. The MMTC, chief importer of gold and silver in India, supplies gold on loan or outright to exporters, bullion dealers and jewelry manufacturers.
--gold.org

U.S. gold is being exported largely for jewelry in India and other countries. Germany, China, Russia, Japan and India are increasing their gold reserves as of 2014.
The United States is fortunate to be a gold producing country. Given that gold is a highly sought, non-renewable commodity long used as in the U.S. as the basis of coinage and of the monetary system as recently as 1971, the U.S, would be wise to replenish and add to her gold reserves, rather than selling this precious natural resource like a bunch of bananas.

The billionaire George Soros dumped 37% of stocks to "buy up massive amounts of gold."
--investingnews.com

U.S. MONEY

*Official United States
Government-Issued
Gold Eagle Coins*

*Special Arrangements
Can Be Made for Gold
Orders Over $50,000*

U.S. Government

GOLD EAGLE

AT-COST PUBLIC RELEASE

AMERICANS OWN GOLD FOR ONLY $144!

The U.S. Money Reserve Main Vault Facility announces our latest release of U.S. government-issued gold coins previously held in the West Point Depository/U.S. Mint. U.S. citizens can buy government-issued $5 gold coins at the incredible at-cost price of only $144.00 each—an amazing price because these U.S. government-issued gold coins are completely free of dealer markup. That's correct—our cost. Take advantage of gold's low price, which is currently around $1,330 per ounce. **Please be advised: These U.S. government gold coins, currently held in our inventory, will be priced at $144.00 each while supplies last or for up to 30 days.** Call now to avoid disappointment! Orders that are not immediately received or reserved with the order center could be subject to cancellation and your checks returned uncashed.

**$5 AMERICAN EAGLE GOLD COIN
APPROVED: PUBLIC LAW 99-185**

We hope that everyone will have a chance to purchase this special U.S. government-issued gold at this price before gold could make its predicted move to higher price levels. Order immediately before our allotted inventory sells out completely! **Call toll-free 1-855-425-3297 today.** If you would have taken $150,000 of your money and bought gold in 2001, then that initial purchase would have been worth over $1 million exactly 10 years later in 2011!† This means

that specific 10-year period saw an incredible increase of 600% in the price of gold. **Even gold's recent 10-year performance has surpassed the Nasdaq, Dow and S&P 500.** When you convert money to gold, you have transferred it from a paper currency into a precious metal that can rise in both market and numismatic value. This is how the genius of owning gold may protect your money in today's volatile market.

With predictions of the gold market rising past its record high price and the potential threat of another economic meltdown, now is the time for you and your family to transfer your hard-earned money into physical gold. In our opinion, individuals are currently moving up to 30% of their assets into gold. Join the many Americans who have already converted their dollars to gold and call U.S. Money Reserve today!

U.S. MONEY

CALL NOW: 1-855-425-3297

BEGINNING TODAY, TELEPHONE ORDERS WILL BE ACCEPTED ON A FIRST-COME, FIRST-SERVED BASIS ACCORDING TO THE TIME AND DATE OF THE ORDER!

MASTERCARD • VISA • AMEX • DISCOVER • CHECK • BANK WIRE

Offer valid for
up to 30 days
Or while supplies last

**VAULT CODE:
TIM14**

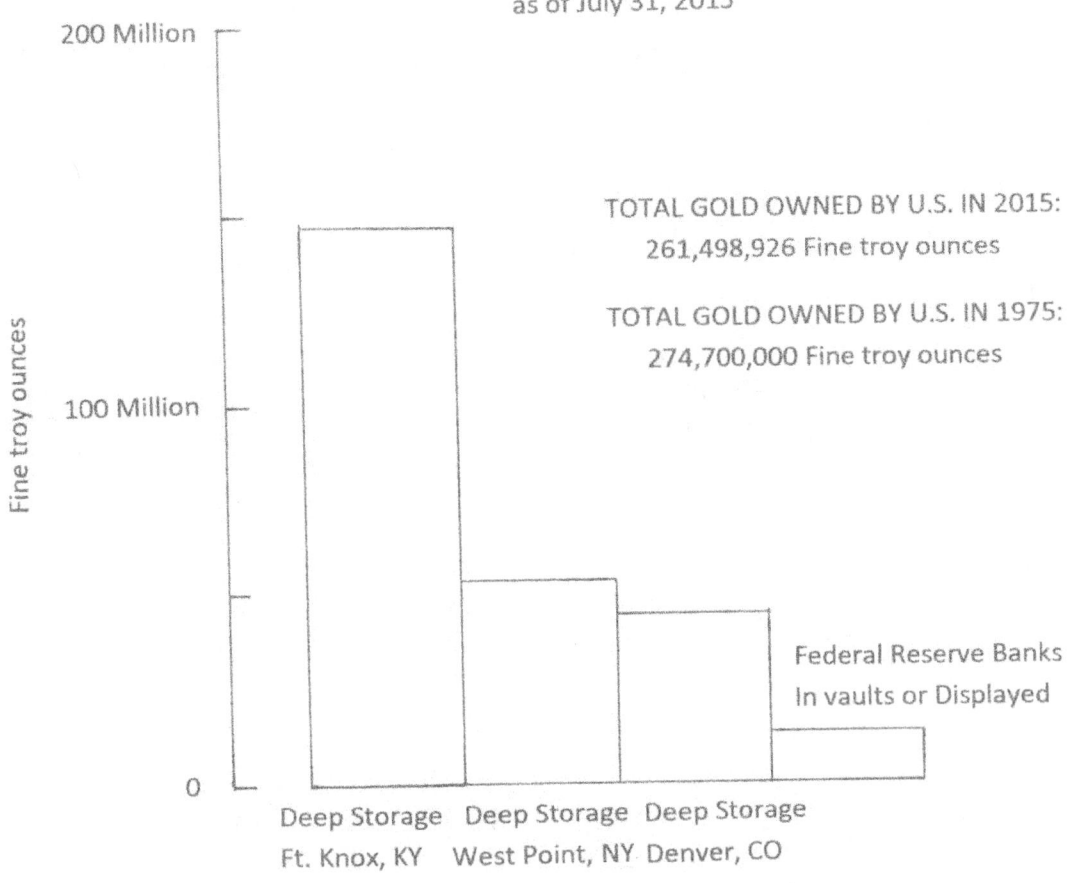

GOLD OWNED BY THE UNITED STATES
as of July 31, 2015

TOTAL GOLD OWNED BY U.S. IN 2015:
261,498,926 Fine troy ounces

TOTAL GOLD OWNED BY U.S. IN 1975:
274,700,000 Fine troy ounces

Federal Reserve Banks
In vaults or Displayed

Deep Storage   Deep Storage   Deep Storage
Ft. Knox, KY   West Point, NY Denver, CO

GOLD RESERVES OF SELECTED CENTRAL BANKS
AND GOVERNMENTS, 1975 - 2014
Fine troy ounces (millions)

Germany's reserves were 117.6 in 1975, decreased to 95.2 in 1980,
    and have increased to 108.8 in 2014

China is increasing reserves from 12.8 in 1980 to 33.9 in 2009 to 2014

Russia is increasing reserves from 9 in 1975 to 38.8 in 2014

Japan is increasing reserves from 21.1 in 1975 to 24.6 in 2014

India is increasing reserves from 7.0 in 1975 to 17.9 in 2014

France is decreasing reserves from 100.9 in 1975 to 81.9 in 1980
    up to 97.2 in 2000 and is 78.3 in 2014

Switzerland is decreasing reserves from 83.3 in 1980 to 33.4 in 2014

Netherlands is decreasing reserves from 54.3 in 1975 to 19.7 in 2014

Canada is decreasing reserves from 22 in 1975 to 3.4 in 1995, to
    .1 in 2003-2014

United Kingdom is decreasing reserves from 21 in 1975 to 10 in 2004
    to 2014

Sources: The World Almanac and Book of Facts 2016, pp 67 and 733

PURCHASING POWER OF THE DOLLAR, 1950 - 2014

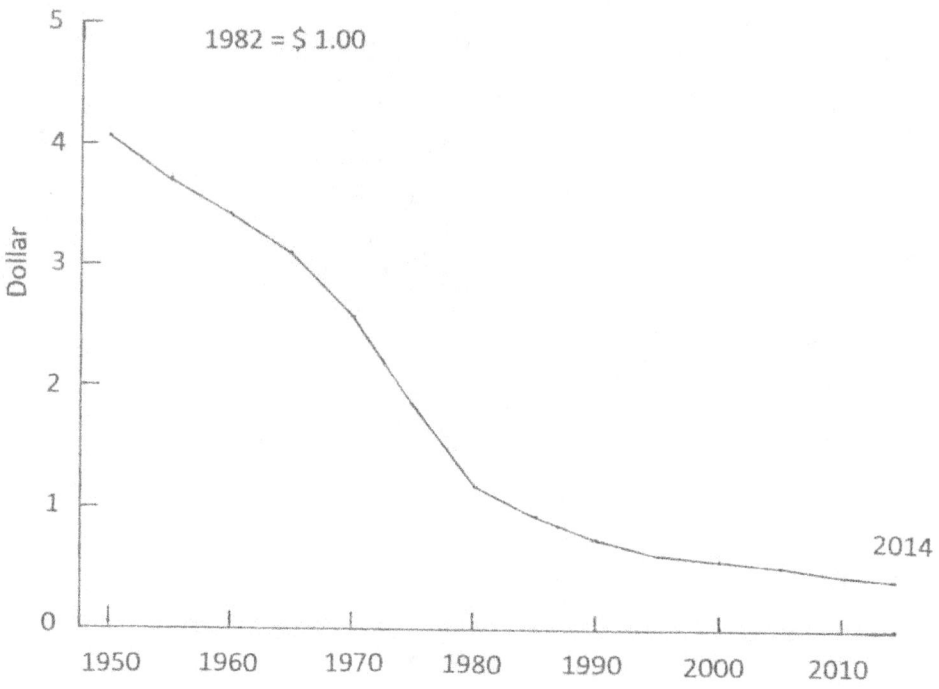

1982 = $ 1.00

2014

Source: ProQuest Statistical Abstract of the United States 2016, p 489

"Since 1913, the Federal Reserve System has managed to devalue the purchasing power of the dollar by 96%."   -- UK yahoo.com

Devaluation of the dollar is inflation in the marketplace.

In recent decades, when the U.S. dollar declines in value, other countries, notably China and Japan, devalue their yuan and yen, respectively, so as to remain competitive in the U.S. marketplace. This ongoing practice directly violates the United States Constitution, which in Article I, Section 8, states that "The Congress shall have Power To coin Money, REGULATE THE VALUE THEREOF, AND OF FOREIGN COIN ... "

If the dollar were allowed to fall without interference from foreign nations, United States goods and services would be more competitive in the worldwide marketplace because the goods and services would cost comparatively less.

REAL WEEKLY WAGES

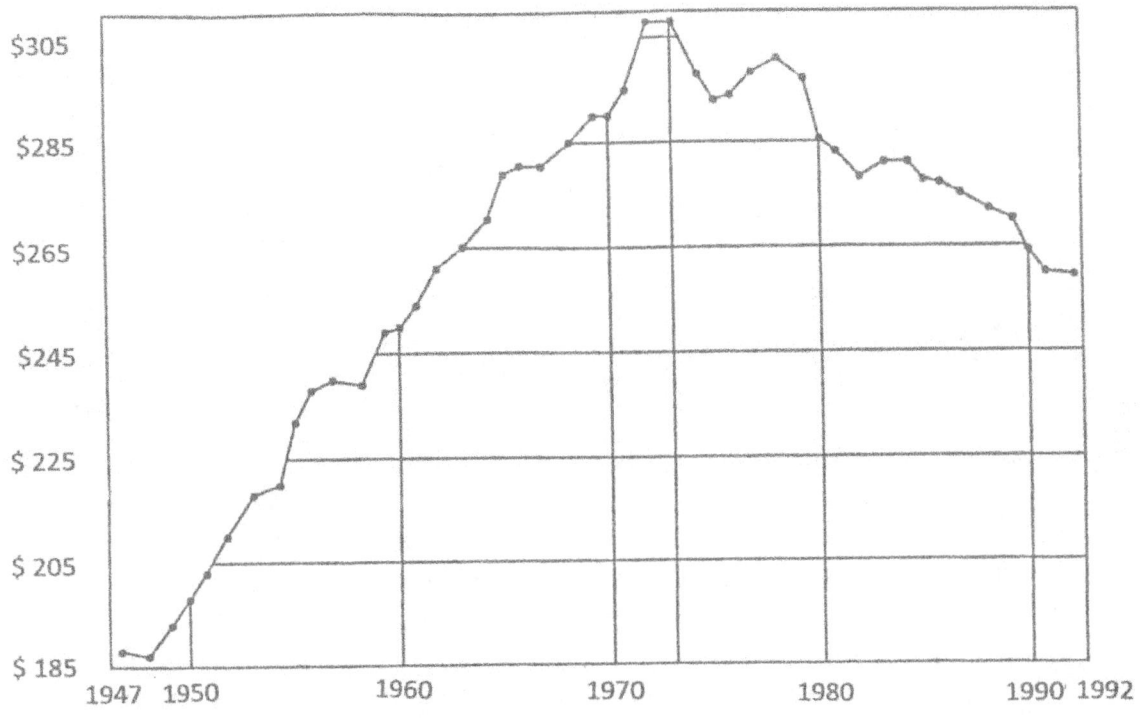

Note: In constant 1982-84 dollars

Source: Economic Report of the President, Washington, D.C.
           U.S. Government Printing Office 1991, 1993; Bureau of the Census
           Current Population Reports, ser. P-60, no. 180, 1992

STATE'S LOW-WAGE WORKERS EARN LESS THAN IN LATE '70S
Los Angeles Times   May 1, 2015   p C2

A study, released from UC Berkeley, documented the extensive growth of income inequality in California since the late 1970s. The researchers' data showed that California workers at the lowest end of the pay scale have seen a significant decline of 12% in their earnings since 1979 after adjusting for inflation, while the top 10% of California workers have seen wages grow 35%.

"We are seeing the hallowing out of middle-wage jobs over time," said Annette Bernhardt, a visiting researcher at UC. Berkeley's Institute for Research on Labor and Employment, who worked on the report. The report defines "low wage" as those in California who made less than $13.63 an hour in 2014. More than 4.7 million workers in California fit that description - a third of the state's work force.

The top five occupations expected to add the most jobs through 2022 are personal care aides, food preparation workers, retail sales workers, warehouse workers and restaurant servers, low wage positions making less than $12 an hour. Low wage workers are also contending with an erosion of their benefits.

by Chris Kirkham

THE FEDERAL RESERVE SYSTEM

The Constitution of the United States does not authorize a private banking system, such as the Federal Reserve, to have power over the monetary system of the United States.

The Constitution of the United States is silent on any banking system whatsoever.

"One of the myths about the Federal Reserve is that it is needed to stabilize the economy. Yet, it has achieved just the opposite. Destabilization is dramatically clear in the years prior to the Crash, but the same cause-and-effect continues to this day. As long as men are given the power to tinker with the money supply, they will strive to circumvent the natural laws of supply and demand."

--G. Edward Griffin
The Creature from Jekyll Island:
A Second Look at the Federal Reserve, 5th Edition
American Media, 2010, p 490
Mr. Griffin's book can be found at www.realtyzone.com/creature.html

Reprinted by permission

U.S. CORPORATE NET PROFITS BY INDUSTRY, 2015

Other Nonfinancial	$ 399.9 billion
Other Financial	339.9
Retail Trade	181.1
Wholesale Trade	170.1
Information	148.3
Federal Reserve Banks	102.9
Transportation and Warehousing	92.0
Chemical Products	88.4
Other Durable Goods	79.5
Computer and Electronic Products	74.6
Food, Beverage and Tobacco	73.3
Motor Vehicles, Bodies, Trailers and Parts	45.8
Other Nondurable Goods	45.3
Machinery	31.0
Fabricated Metal Products	28.8
Electrical Equipment, Appliances & Components	20.0
Utilities	19.0
Petroleum and Coal Products	12.9

TOTAL $1 trillion, 953 billion

Source: Statistica.com

The Federal Reserve, neither part of the federal government nor a corporation, nor a repository for emergency funds, is a private banking firm loaning the federal government money with interest, which netted them $102.9 billion in 2015.

Alexander Hamilton, appointed by George Washington as the first Secretary of the Treasury, felt it was the role of the FEDERAL GOVERNMENT to collect and disburse money. He founded the First National Bank for that purpose, and remained Secretary of the Treasury until 1795 when the debts of the American Revolution were paid.

Perhaps the United States should follow the lead of Alexander Hamilton and establish a national bank.

THE FEDERAL RESERVE SYSTEM

The Federal Reserve System is the central bank for the U.S. The system was established on December 23, 1913, originally to give the country an elastic currency, provide facilities for discounting commercial paper, and improve the supervision of banking. Since then, the system's responsibilities have been broadened. Over the years, stability and growth of the economy, a high level of employment, stability in the purchasing power of the dollar, and reasonable balance in transactions with other countries have come to be recognized as primary objectives of governmental economic policy.

The Federal Reserve System consists of the Board of Governors, the 12 District Reserve Banks and their branch offices, and the Federal Open Market Committee. Several advisory councils help the board meet its varied responsibilities. The hub of the system is the seven-member Board of Governors in Washington, D.C. The members of the board are appointed by the president and confirmed by the Senate to 14-year terms. The president also appoints the chairman and vice-chairman of the board from among the board members for four year terms...

The system's principal function is monetary policy, which it controls using three tools: reserve requirements, the discount rate, and open market operations. Uniform reserve requirements, set by the board, are applied to the transaction accounts and "nonpersonal time deposits" of all depository institutions. Responsibility for setting the discount rate (the interest rate at which depository institutions can borrow money from the Reserve Banks) is shared by the Board of Governors.

Source: The World Almanac and Book of Facts 2016, p 63

THE WALL STREET CRASH OF 1929 AND THE GREAT DEPRESSION

On October 29, 1929, Black Tuesday hit Wall Street as investors traded some 16 million shares on the New York Stock Exchange in a single day. Billions of dollars were lost, wiping out thousands of investors. In the aftermath of Black Tuesday, America and the rest of the industrialized world spiraled downward into the Great Depression (1929-39), the deepest and longest-lasting economic downturn in the history of the Western industrialized world up to that time.

Source: history.com/topics/1929-stock-market-crash

U.S. PRIME INTEREST RATE BY MONTH, 1949 TO 2016

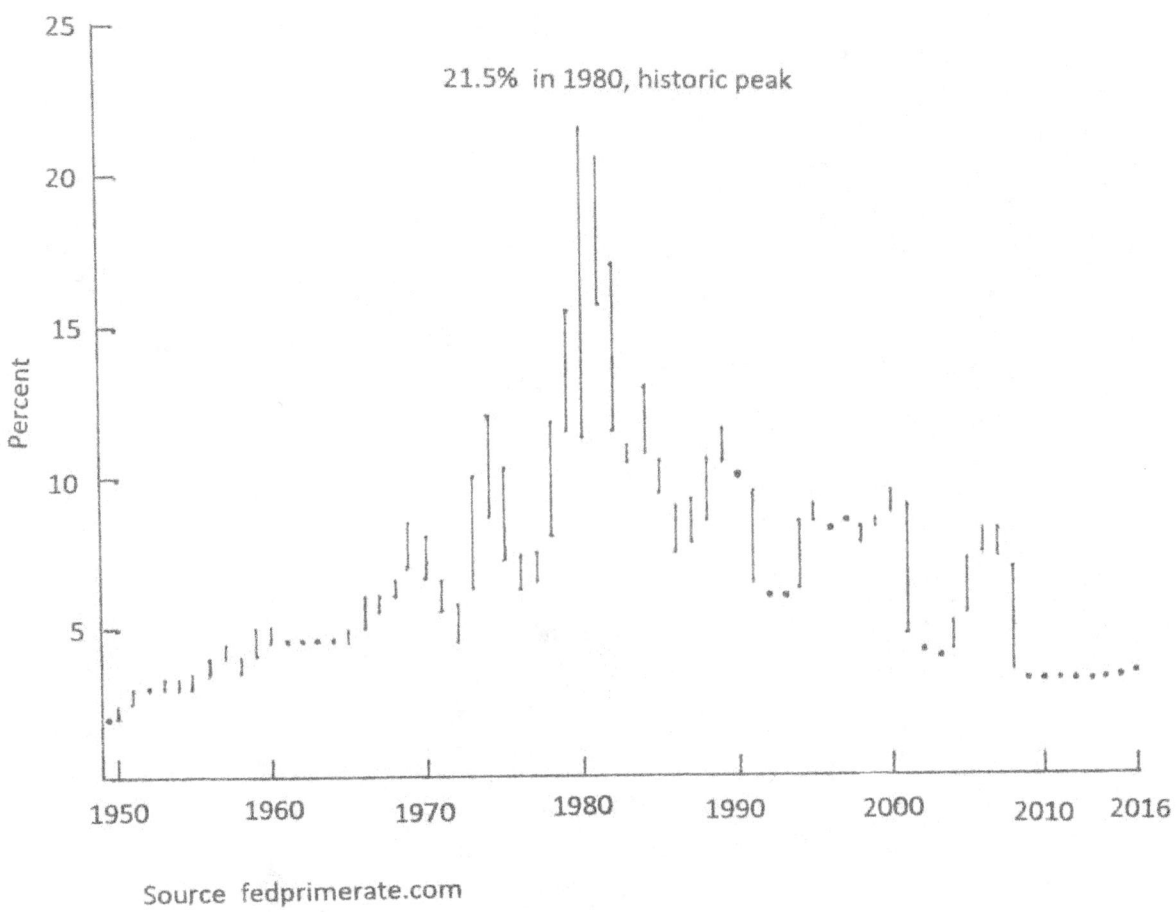

21.5% in 1980, historic peak

Source fedprimerate.com

The Federal Reserve sets the prime interest rate, the rate at which it loans dollars to the nation 's banks.

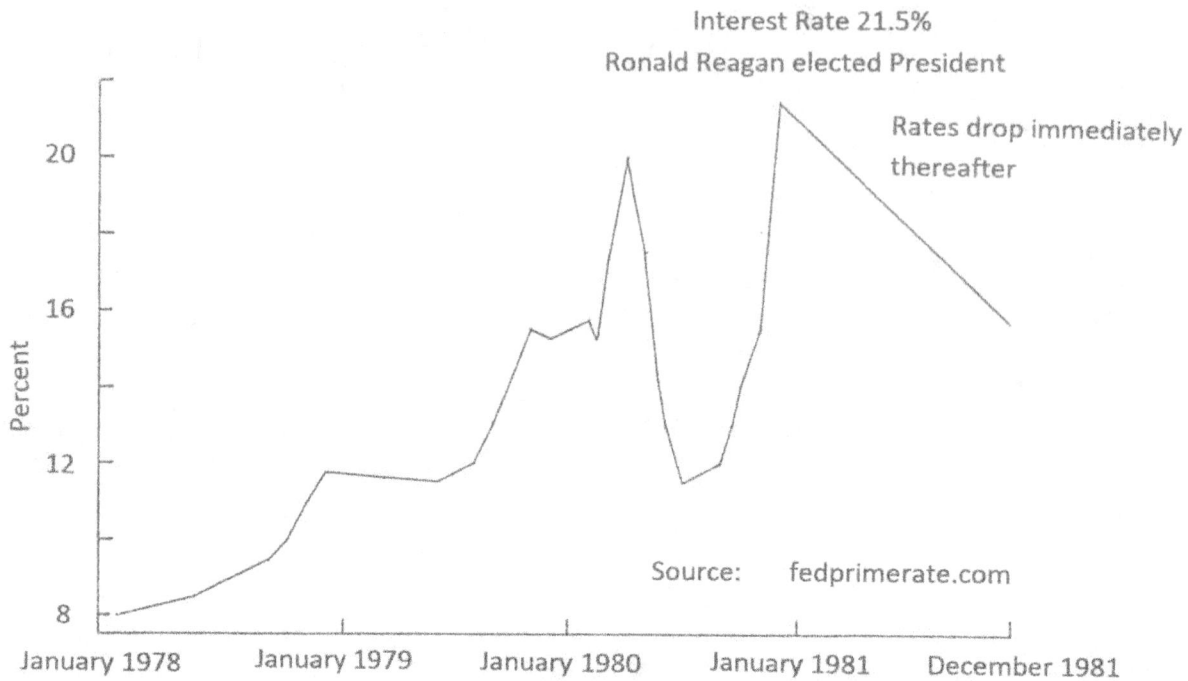

U.S. PRIME INTEREST RATE BY MONTH
1978 – 1981   DETAIL

Interest Rate 21.5%
Ronald Reagan elected President

Rates drop immediately
thereafter

Source: fedprimerate.com

Wikipedia.com:

In 1979, the Federal Reserve System of the United States raised the interest rate that it charged its member banks by 20% in an effort to reduce inflation. The Savings and Loan associations had issued long-term mortgage loans at fixed interest rates that were lower than the interest rate at which they could borrow. In addition, the S&Ls had the liability of deposits which paid higher interest rates than the rate at which they could borrow. The S&Ls were in crisis. President Jimmy Carter began the process of deregulation of the S&L industry.

Interest rates came down slightly, to 11.5%, but the feds raised the prime rate to an all-time high of 21.5% just before the Presidential election of November 1980. Carter lost to Ronald Reagan, who had run on a platform of deregulation.

In 1980, there were 400 S&Ls with assets of $600 billion. $480 billion of those were locked into long-term fixed rate home mortgage loans. Congress passed the "Depository Institutions Deregulation and Monetary Control Act of 1980," plus a second act in 1982, allowing S&Ls to offer adjustable rate mortgages and to offer a wider range of loan packages similar to what banks could do. At the same time, Congress cut funding for regulatory oversight, including lenient accounting rules, and less capital requirements. Even so, the S&Ls were backed by the FSLIC, so that the federal government would bail out bad loans.

It was a perfect storm for speculation in land deals, even though interest rates remained relatively high, and word got around. At the same time, the Iran hostage crisis was covered incessantly in the media for over a year, ending abruptly the moment Ronald Reagan was sworn in as President:

On November 4, 1979, a group of Iranian students stormed the U.S. Embassy in Tehran, taking more than 60 American hostages. The immediate cause of this action was President Jimmy Carter's decision to allow Iran's deposed Shah, a pro-Western autocrat who had been expelled from his country some months before, to come to the United States for cancer treatment. However, the hostage-taking was about more than the Shah's medical care: it was a dramatic way for the student revolutionaries to declare a break with Iran's past and an end to American interference in its affairs. It was also a way to raise the intra- and international profile of the revolution's leader, the anti-American cleric Ayatollah Ruhollah Khomeini. The students set their hostages free on January 21, 1981, 444 days after the crisis began and just hours after President Ronald Reagan delivered his inaugural address. Many historians believe that hostage crisis cost Jimmy Carter a second term as president.   history.com

The timing of the Fed's usurious prime rate of 21.5% and the release of the 60 American hostages from Iran, both events well known to weary Americans, converged to cause the defeat of Jimmy Carter for a second term. OPEC countries, oil producing countries, had a stake in American politics. Reagan's chosen vice president, H.W. Bush, was an oil man whose family had been friendly for years with the House of Saud, as revealed in the 2006 documentary, "Who Killed the Electric Car?" and Kitty Kelley's 2004 biography, "The Family: the Real Story of the Bush Dynasty." Reagan's policies proved to be unfriendly to the new, emerging field of clean energy.

The Bush family and the S&L Scandal

The Savings and Loan industry had been experiencing major problems through the late 60s and 70s due to rising inflation and rising interest rates. Because of this there was a move in the 1970s to replace the role of S&L institutions with banks.

In the early 1980s, under Reagan, regulatory changes took place that gave the S&L industry new powers and for the first time in history measures were taken to increase the profitability of S&Ls at the expense of promoting home ownership.

The problems occurred in the Savings and Loan industry as they relate to theft because the industry was deregulated under the Reagan/Bush administration and restrictions were eased on the industry so much that abuse and misuse of funds became easy, rampant, and went unchecked.

There are several ways in which the Bush family plays into the Savings and Loan scandal, which involves not only many members of the Bush family but also many other politicians that are still in office and still part of the Bush Jr. administration today. Jeb Bush, George Bush Sr., and his son Neil Bush have all been implicated in the Savings and Loan Scandal, which cost American tax payers over $1.4 *TRILLION* dollars.

Between 1981 and 1989, when George Bush finally announced that there was a Savings and Loan Crisis to the world, the Reagan/Bush administration worked to cover up Savings and Loan problems by reducing the number and depth of examinations required of S&Ls as well as attacking political opponents who were sounding early alarms about the S&L industry. Industry insiders were aware of significant S&L problems as early 1986 that they felt would require a bailout. This information was kept from the media until after Bush had won the 1988 elections.

Jeb Bush defaulted on a $4.56 million loan from Broward Federal Savings in Sunrise, Florida. After federal regulators closed the S&L, the office building that Jeb used the $4.56 million to finance was reappraised by the regulators at $500,000, which Bush and his partners paid. The taxpayers had to pay back the remaining 4 million plus dollars.

Neil Bush was the most widely targeted member of the Bush family by the press in the S&L scandal. Neil became director of Silverado Savings and Loan at the age of 30 in 1985. Three years later the institution was belly up at a cost of $1.6 billion to tax payers to bail out.

Neil Bush was charged with criminal wrongdoing in the case and ended up paying $50,000 to settle out of court. The chief of Silverado S&L was sentenced to 3.5 years in jail for pleading guilty to $8.7 million in theft.

-- rationalrevolution.net

The S&L crisis lasted until 1995, when the last of the bad loans were paid back by taxpayers through the Resolution Trust Corporation. The outlay was estimated at half a trillion dollars. After Ronald Reagan's re-election, the S&L Crisis was revealed to the public, but a similar problem with the nation's banks was unfolding, again due to speculative lending. The result was another half trillion dollars in bad loans that were paid back to depositors, this time by the FDIC. As high as 882 banks may have gone out of business between 1988 and 1992. The banks were more directly under the supervision of the Federal Reserve than were the S&Ls, but in both cases, borrowers did not have to repay their loans and there were no reports of borrowers declaring bankruptcy. The country survived the payback of the estimated trillion dollars.

Whitewater controversy

From Wikipedia, the free encyclopedia

Bill Clinton had known Arkansas businessman and political figure Jim McDougal since 1968, and had made a previous small real estate investment with him in 1977.[9]

In spring of 1978, McDougal proposed that the Clintons join him and his wife, Susan, in buying 230 acres (0.93 km^2) of undeveloped land along the south bank of the White River near Flippin, Arkansas, in the Ozark Mountains. The goal was to subdivide the site into lots for vacation homes, intended for the many people coming south from Chicago and Detroit who were interested in low property taxes, fishing, rafting, and mountain scenery. The plan was to hold the property for a few years and then sell the lots at a profit.[9]

The four borrowed $203,000 to buy land, and subsequently transferred ownership of the land to the newly-created Whitewater Development Corporation, in which all four participants had equal shares.[9]

By the time the Whitewater lots were surveyed and available for sale at the end of 1979, interest rates had climbed to near 20 percent. Prospective buyers could no longer afford to buy vacation homes. Rather than take a loss on the venture, the four decided to build a model home and wait for better economic conditions.[9]

Following the land purchase, Jim McDougal asked the Clintons for additional funds for interest payments on the loan and other expenses; the Clintons later claimed to have no knowledge of how these contributions were used.[9][14] When Bill Clinton failed to win re-election in 1980, Jim McDougal lost his job as the governor's economic aide and decided to go into banking.[11] He acquired the Bank of Kingston in 1980 and the Woodruff Savings & Loan in 1982,[15] renaming them the Madison Bank & Trust and the Madison Guaranty Savings & Loan, respectively.[12]

In 1985, Jim McDougal invested in a local construction project called Castle Grande. The 1,000 acres (4 km²), located south of Little Rock,[12] were priced at about $1.75 million, more than McDougal could afford on his own. According to current law, McDougal could borrow only $600,000 from his own savings and loan, Madison Guaranty. Therefore, McDougal involved others to raise the additional funds. Among these was Seth Ward, an employee of the bank, who helped funnel the additional $1.15 million required. To avoid potential investigations, the money was moved back and forth among several other investors and intermediaries. Hillary Clinton, then an attorney at Rose Law Firm (which is based in Little Rock) provided legal services to Castle Grande.

In 1986, federal regulators realized that all of the necessary funds for this real estate venture had come from Madison Guaranty; regulators called Castle Grande a sham. In July of that year, McDougal resigned from Madison Guaranty. Seth Ward fell under investigation, along with the lawyer who helped him draft the agreement. Castle Grande earned $2 million in commissions and fees for McDougal's business associates, as well as an unknown amount in legal fees for Rose Law Firm, but in 1989, it collapsed, at a cost to the government of $4 million.[18] This in turn helped trigger the 1989 collapse of Madison Guaranty, which federal regulators then had to take over.[18] Taking place in the midst of the nationwide savings and loan crisis, the failure of Madison Guaranty cost the United States $73 million.[19]

--wikipedia.org

The Clintons lost between $37,000 and $69,000 on their Whitewater investment; this was less than the McDougals lost.[20] The reasons for the unequal capital contributions by the Clintons and McDougals are unknown but the President's critics cited the discrepancy as evidence that then-Governor Clinton was to contribute to the project in other ways.[14]

The White House and the President's supporters claimed that they were exonerated by the Pillsbury Report. This was a $3 million study done for the Resolution Trust Corporation by the Pillsbury, Madison & Sutro law firm at the time that Madison Guaranty Savings & Loan was dissolved. The report concluded that James McDougal, who had set up the deal, was the managing partner, and Bill Clinton was a passive investor in the venture.

David Hale, the source of criminal allegations against the Clintons, claimed in November 1993, that Bill Clinton had pressured him into providing an illegal $300,000 loan to Susan McDougal, the Clintons' partner in the Whitewater land deal.[3] Clinton supporters regarded Hale's allegations as questionable, as Hale had not mentioned Clinton in reference to this loan during the original FBI investigation of Madison Guaranty in 1989; only after coming under indictment in 1993, did Hale make allegations against the Clintons.[4] A U.S. Securities and Exchange Commission investigation did result in convictions against the McDougals for their role in the Whitewater project. Jim Guy Tucker, Bill Clinton's successor as governor, was convicted of fraud and sentenced to four years of probation for his role in the matter.[5] Susan McDougal served 18 months in prison for contempt of court for refusing to answer questions relating to Whitewater. The Clintons themselves were never prosecuted, after three separate inquiries found insufficient evidence linking them with the criminal conduct of others related to the land deal,[6] and Susan McDougal was granted a pardon by President Clinton before he left office.

The term **Whitewater** is also sometimes used to include other controversies from the Bill Clinton administration, especially Travelgate, Filegate, and the circumstances surrounding Vince Foster's death, that were investigated by the Whitewater independent counsel.[7]

More information on Whitewater and other controversies is available in the book, "The Secret Life of Bill Clinton," by Ambrose Evans-Pritchard, Regnery Publishing, Inc., Washington, D.C., 1997

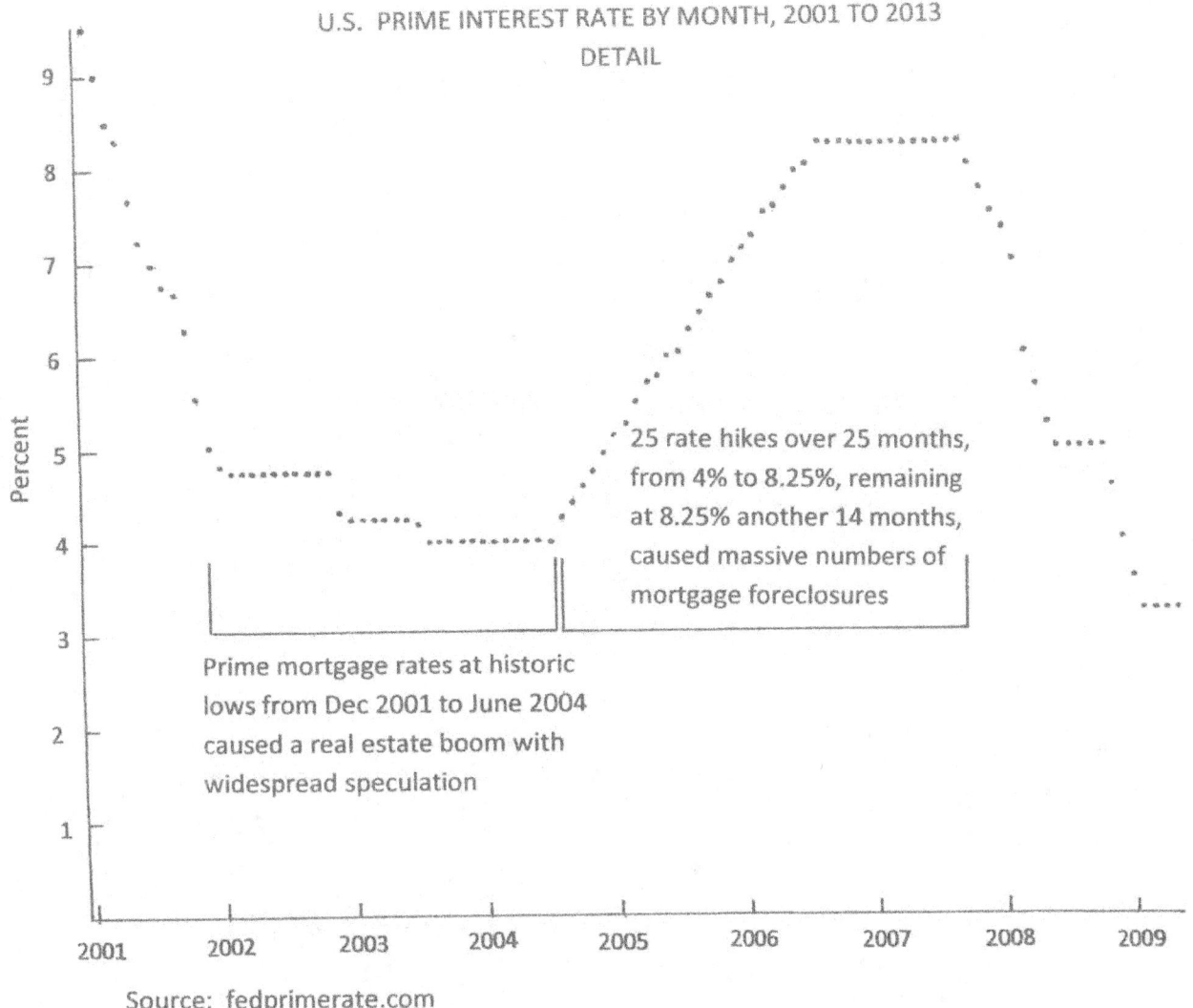

U.S. PRIME INTEREST RATE BY MONTH, 2001 TO 2013
DETAIL

25 rate hikes over 25 months,
from 4% to 8.25%, remaining
at 8.25% another 14 months,
caused massive numbers of
mortgage foreclosures

Prime mortgage rates at historic
lows from Dec 2001 to June 2004
caused a real estate boom with
widespread speculation

Source: fedprimerate.com

The Federal Reserve rate hikes coupled with deregulated loans and foreign
sales of subprime loan packages led to the worldwide financial collapse of 2008.

It was foreseeable that borrowers would not be able to keep up with
their ever-increasing mortgage payments.

Alan Greenspan served as Chairman of the Federal Reserve from 1987 to 2006.

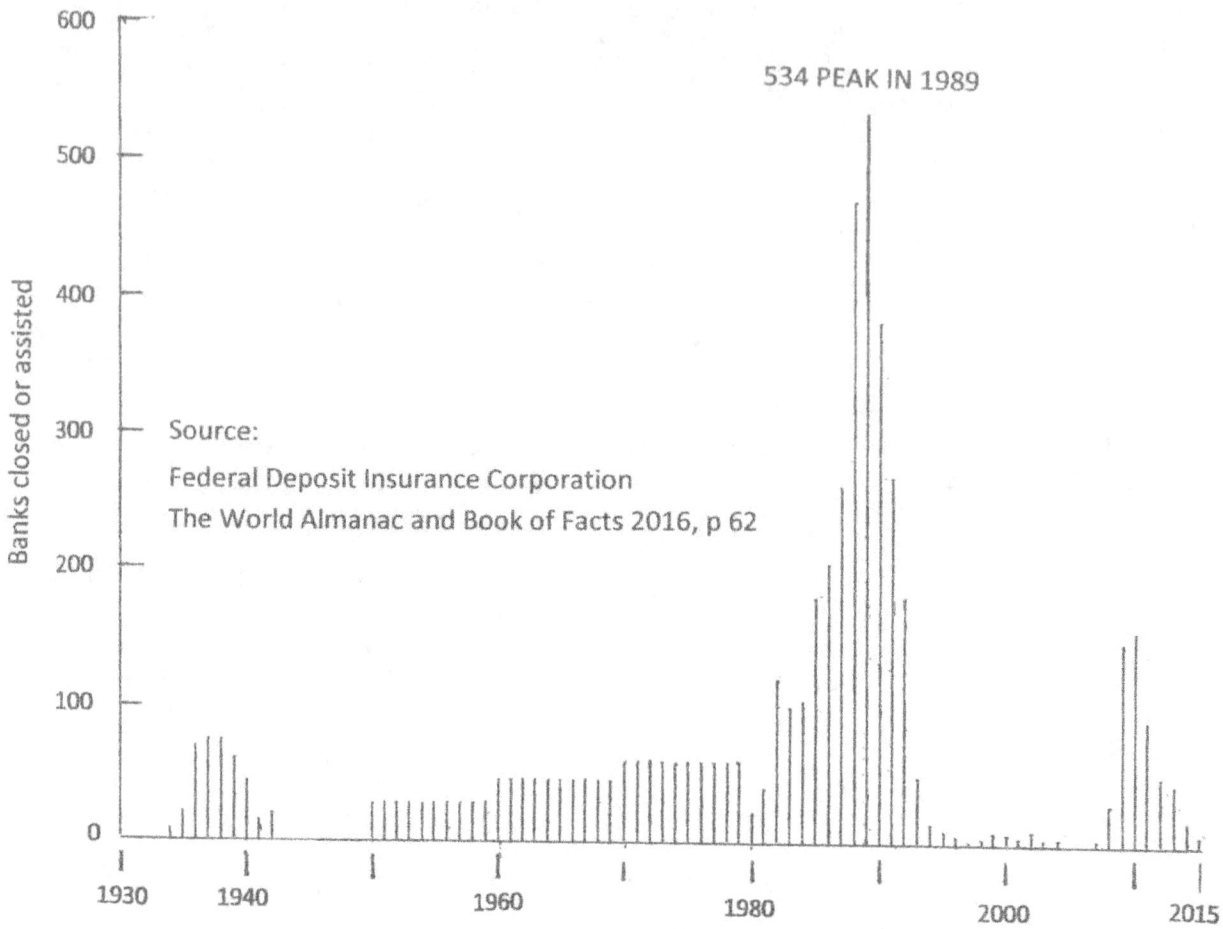

U.S. BANK FAILURES, 1932 – 2015

534 PEAK IN 1989

Source:

Federal Deposit Insurance Corporation

The World Almanac and Book of Facts 2016, p 62

Note: Includes all FDIC-insured commercial and savings banks
(including savings and loan institutions FSLIC-insured of 1980 and after)

Wikipedia, the free encyclopedia:

The Glass-Steagall Act, part of the Banking Act of 1933, was intended to control speculation. It gave the Federal Reserve the power to regulate interest rates in savings accounts, but this provision was repealed by "Depository Institutions Deregulation and Monetary Control Act of 1980."

In 1999 the Graham-Leach-Bliley Act further eviscerated Glass-Steagall. The Graham Act allowed banks to make investments in securities, a function far beyond their traditional role of making loans for business purposes. The deregulation also allowed officers of investment houses to serve as officers of commercial banks, thus allowing Wall Street to use depositors' money for investments. The distinction between secure deposits and speculative, risky investment packages was now blurred. The banking industry had been lobbying for deregulation since the 1980s, especially since securities investments are more loosely regulated than banks.

The repeal enabled commercial lenders such as Citigroup, which was in 1999 the largest U.S. bank by assets, to underwrite and trade instruments such as mortgage-backed securities and collateralized debt obligations and establish "structured investment vehicles" that could buy those securities. Buyers for the SIVs included some of the biggest banks in Europe.

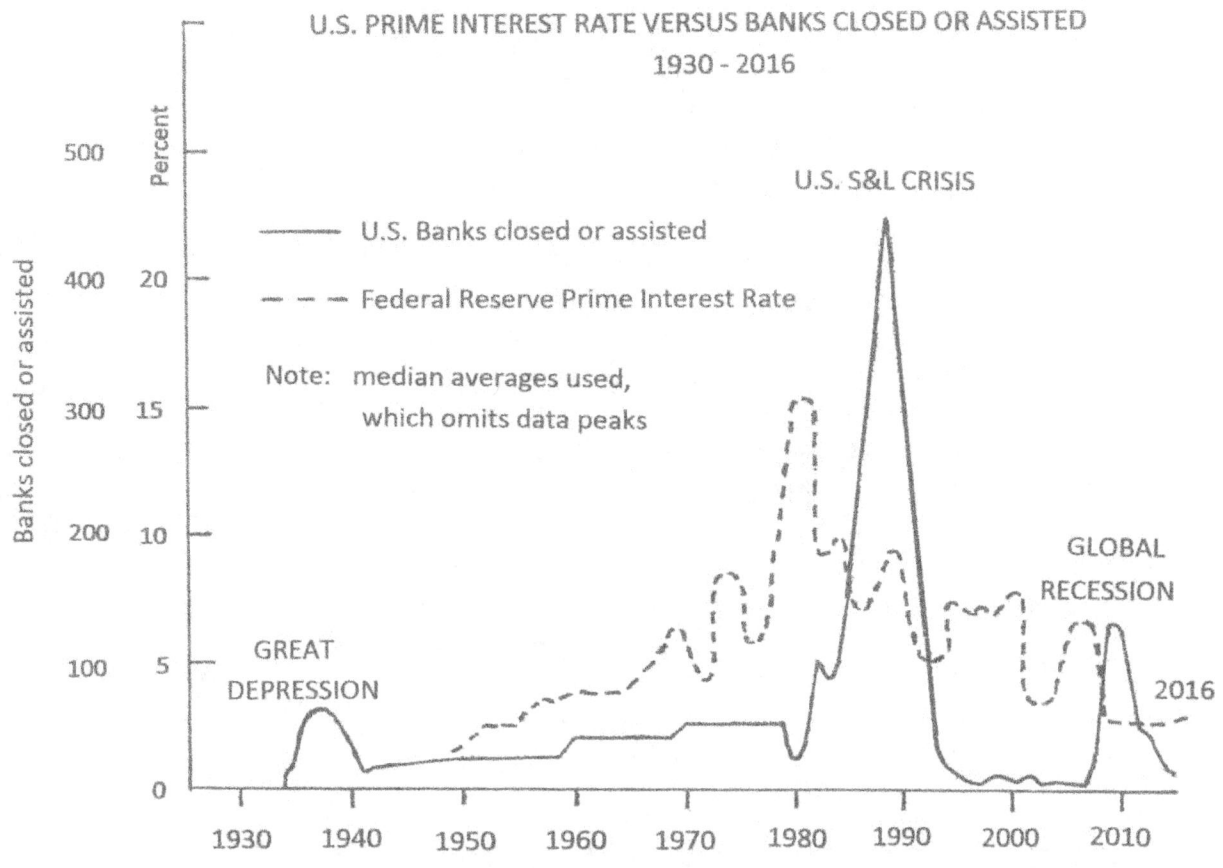

U.S. PRIME INTEREST RATE VERSUS BANKS CLOSED OR ASSISTED
1930 - 2016

Source: fedprimerate.com; The World Almanac and Book of Facts 2016, p 62

There is an extremely high correlation between the Federal Reserve Prime Interest Rate and economic chaos, evident in the U.S. Savings and Loan Crisis and the 2008 global recession. In both cases, the Fed hiked interest rates to the point borrowers could not repay their loans. In both cases, the results were foreseeable.

Dodd–Frank Wall Street Reform and Consumer Protection Act

Nicknames   Dodd–Frank

Enacted by   the 111th United States Congress

Effective   July 21, 2010

Wikipedia, the free encyclopedia

Long title   an Act to promote the financial stability of the United States by improving accountability and transparency in the financial system, to end "too big to fail", to protect the American taxpayer by ending bailouts, to protect consumers from abusive financial services practices, and for other purposes.

Why not reinstitute Glass-Steagall?

RIGHT WING ASSAILS DODD-FRANK
Los Angeles Times   Jul 27, 2014   p B1

Dodd-Frank was signed into law four years ago last Monday...
Dodd-Frank cast a wide net to put a collar on irresponsible banking
practices.. the rollout of regulations has been painfully slow.
But the blame should be directed at the financial industry, which has
sedulously fought every proposal, and Congress, which has hobbled
rule making...

The most popular target of Dodd-Frank critics may be the
Consumer Financial Protection Bureau, which is thoroughly detested
by the financial services industry, with good reason. The bureau has
extracted billions of dollars in fines and consumer refunds from
financial services companies, including a massive $772-million
settlement from Bank of America in April for deceitful credit card
practices.

The nation's biggest banks have grown only bigger since the
2008 crisis - by as much as a third, according to some estimates...
Bank of America, Citigroup, JP Morgan Chase and Goldman Sachs,
among other big firms, have all cut back on their trading or shed
"non-core" assets in recognition that in the post-Dodd-Frank world,
simpler is better.

by Michael Hiltzik

SUMMARY OF DEREGULATION OF U.S. BANKING RULES

President Bill Clinton, on November 12, 1999 just weeks before leaving the Presidency,
signed the complete repeal of the Glass-Steagall Act of 1933, which had been partially eroded
in 1980 by H.W. Bush. The 1999 repeal had been prepared in Congress and was known as
the cumbersome Graham-Leach-Bliley Act.

By 2005, housing speculation and deal-making were at their peak. Risky and murky
investment packages were selling briskly and globally. Depositors' money in banks was now
legally being used by Wall Street "investment banking" firms. The biggest investment houses
such as Lehman Brothers, the biggest banks, such as Bank of America and Citigroup, the biggest
insurance companies, such as AIG, and federal housing lenders Fannie Mae and Freddie Mac
were involved. In 2006 the house of cards began to unravel. The writer Michael Lewis
described it in "The Big Short," a book made into a movie of the same name.

Reaction to the Dodd-Frank Reform Act was mixed. Some critics say, according to
Wikipedia.com, that it will be "insufficient to avoid another financial crisis." A think tank
called the "World Pensions Council" argues that "the dismantlement of the Glass-Steagall
Act was only the symptom of a much deeper problem: the emergence of a new economic
paradigm associating the worst interpretations of Keynesian monetary stimulus with
unbridled deregulation that came to define the Clinton and Bush eras."

"NO TITLE OF NOBILITY SHALL BE GRANTED BY THE UNITED STATES:
AND NO PERSON HOLDING ANY OFFICE OF PROFIT OR TRUST
UNDER THEM, SHALL, WITHOUT CONSENT OF CONGRESS,
ACCEPT ANY PRESENT, EMOLUMENT, OFFICE, OR TITLE,
OF ANY KIND WHATEVER, FROM ANY KING, PRINCE,
OR FOREIGN STATE"
Article I, Section 10
Constitution of the United States

'THE PRESIDENT, VICE PRESIDENT AND ALL CIVIL OFFICERS OF THE UNITED STATES,
SHALL BE REMOVED FROM OFFICE ON IMPEACHMENT FOR, AND CONVICTION OF
TREASON, BRIBERY, OR OTHER HIGH CRIMES AND MISDEMEANORS"
Article II, Section 4
Constitution of the United States

U.S. FEDERAL POLITICAL ACTION COMMITTEES, QUANTITY, 1980 TO 2014

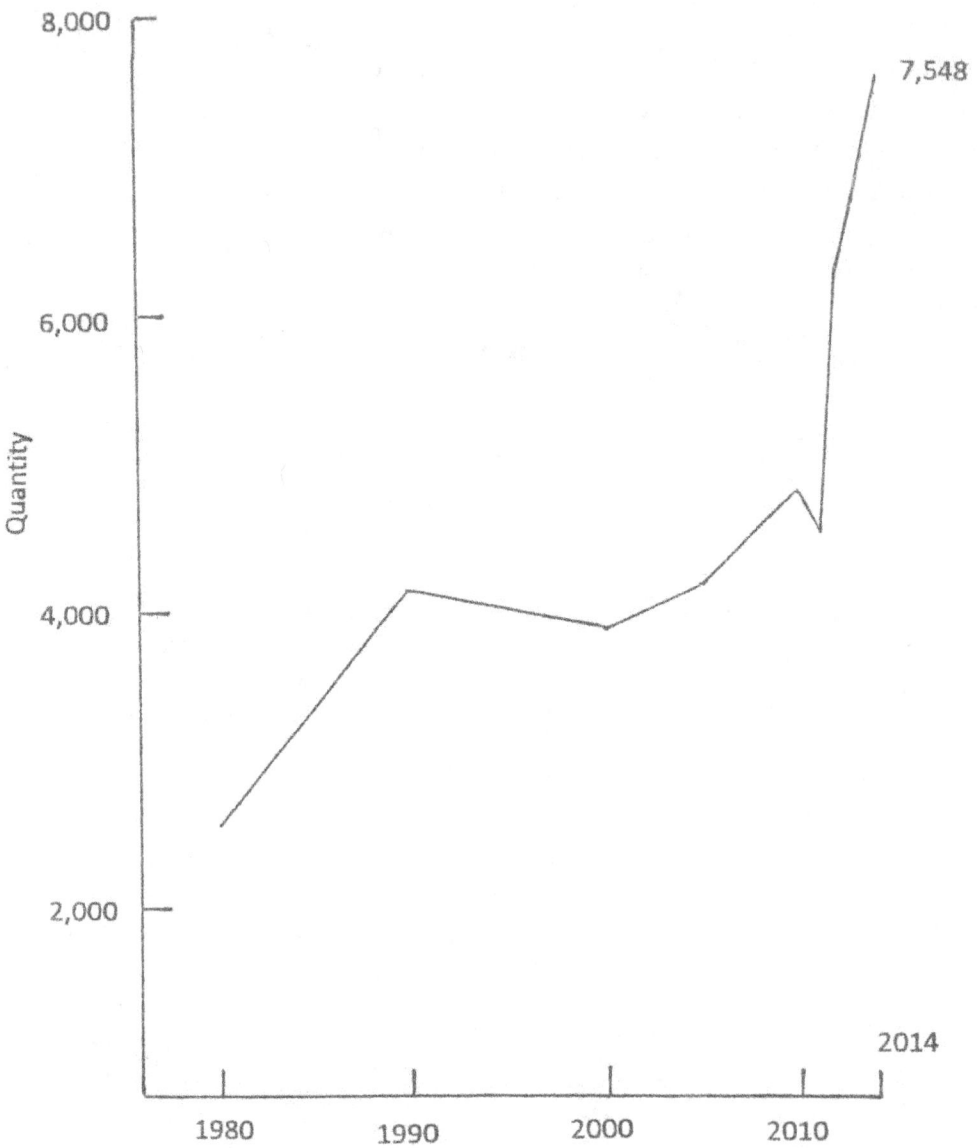

Source "U.S. Federal Election Commission, "Campaign Finance Statistics"
ProQuest Statistical Abstract of the United States 2016, p 291

An unknown percentage of lobbyists are foreign.

U.S. FEDERAL POLITICAL ACTION COMMITTEES BY TYPE
CONTRIBUTIONS TO ELECTED OFFICIALS, 2009 - 2014

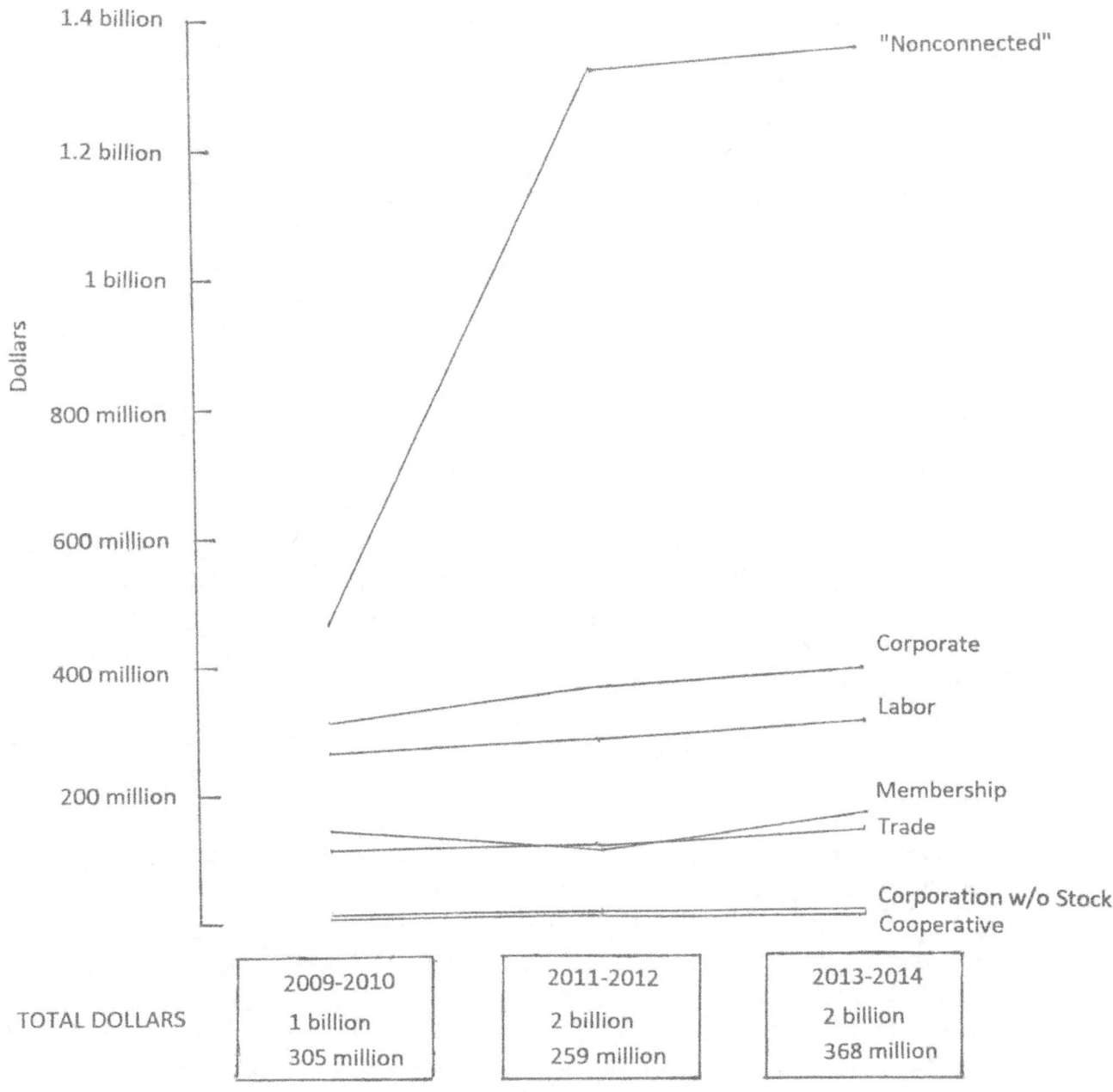

	2009-2010	2011-2012	2013-2014
TOTAL DOLLARS	1 billion	2 billion	2 billion
	305 million	259 million	368 million

Note: Health organizations are no longer an organization type but are included
in either the trade or membership categories.

Source: U.S. Federal Election Commission, "Campaign Finance Statistics"
ProQuest Statistical Abstract of the United States 2016, p 291

Citizens United vs. Federal Election Commission

In 1907, Congress passed the Tillman Act, banning corporations from funding federal election campaigns. In 1947, Congress' Taft-Hartley act extended that ban to include unions. In 1971, Congress passed the Federal Election Campaign Act, requiring full reporting of campaign contributions and expenditures. It also limited spending on media advertisements. In 2002 Congress passed the Bipartisan Campaign Reform Act, prohibiting advertising for or against political candidates within 60 days of a general election and 30 days of a primary election. All were designed to keep money and influence out of political elections.

In 2008, a small nonprofit called Citizens United wanted to run advertisements on television for a film called "Hillary: the Movie," before the 2008 elections when Hillary Clinton was running for president. They wanted to run the ads within 60 days of the general election, but ran afoul of the 60 day rule, so they sued the Federal Election Commission, lost in a lower court and appealed to the U.S. Supreme Court and won in January, 2010.

The U.S. Supreme Court reasoned that the nonprofit had the same right of free speech as people have, and could therefore run political ads within 60 days of a federal election. The Court said they still had to disclose donors of the ads. Another lawsuit was filed, this time by a corporation, on the grounds it should have the same right to free speech as the nonprofit, and won. Citizens United was a 5-4 decision. The two women justices joined the dissent, which argued that the decision "threatened to undermine the integrity of elected institutions across the nation" and would likely "diminish the voice of the individual against vast corporate political investment." Polls have reported that 80% of the people oppose the ruling as a corporate method to gain unfair legislative access.

Speechnow.org v. Federal Election Commission

SpeechNow is a nonprofit that wanted to pool individual contributions to pay for campaign advertisements, and sued in March, 2010, to be able to exceed federal limits, arguing that limiting contributions to the nonprofit violates the individual contributors' rights to free speech, based on the Citizens United precedent. The D.C. Court of Appeals agreed, ruling that the government has no anti-corruption interest in limiting independent expenditures within a group setting. The ruling extended to individual contributions to corporations. In effect, the Court allows corporations to spend what they want on ads calling for the election or defeat of individual candidates, establishing super PACs (political action committees) that can accept unlimited donations from billionaires through corporations to buy advertising in political campaigns. Direct contributions to candidates still have financial limits.

Foreign corporations can now make unlimited donations to PACs through their U.S. subsidiaries, so long as U.S. employees run the PAC and contribute the money, saying the individuals should have the same donation rights as individuals in U.S. corporations. Political advertising is uncontrolled in electronic media anyway. The solution is to ignore the ads.

UNITED STATES PRESIDENTIAL CAMPAIGN FINANCES
2016

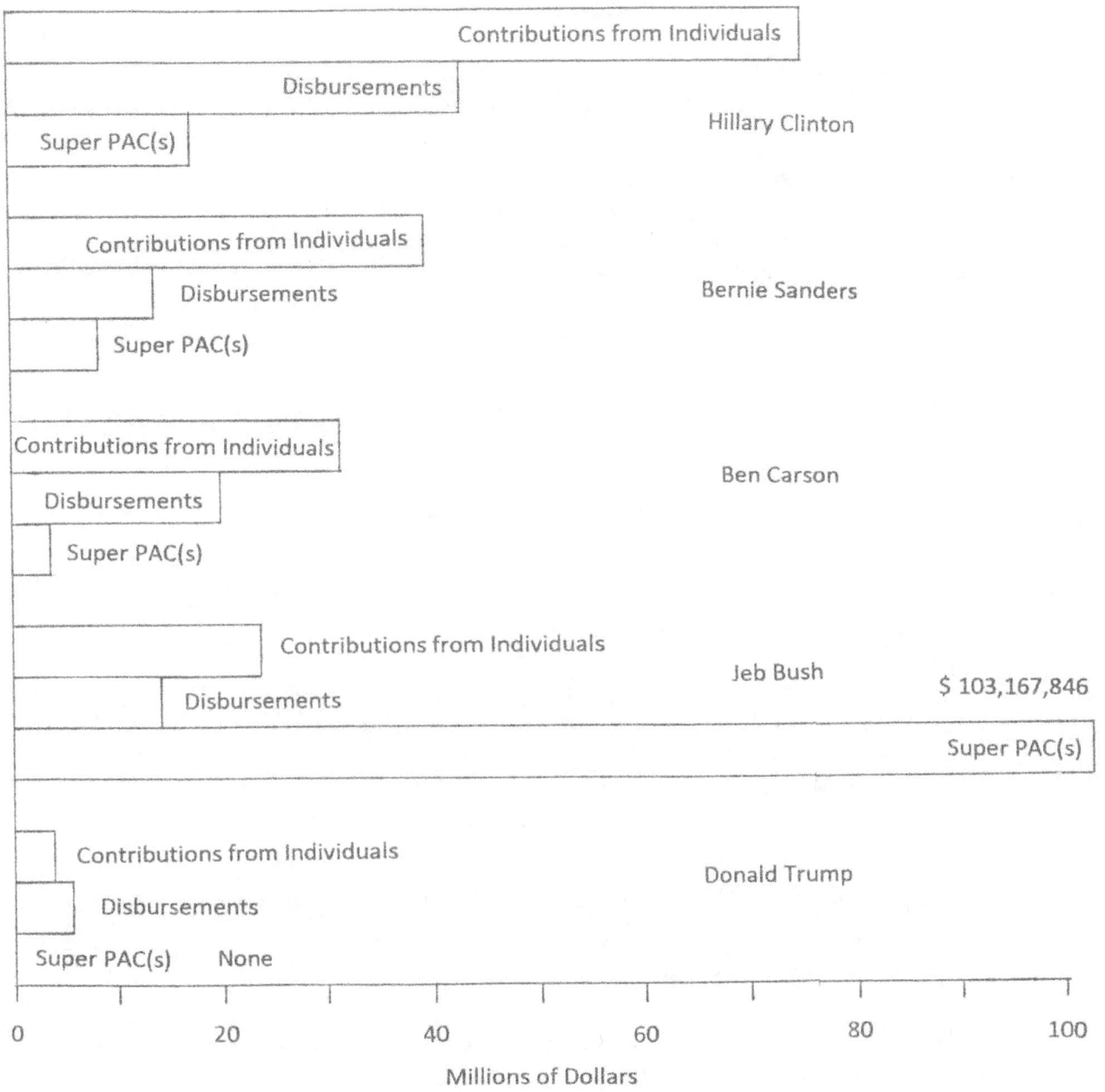

Contributions from Individuals

Disbursements

Hillary Clinton

Super PAC(s)

Contributions from Individuals

Disbursements

Bernie Sanders

Super PAC(s)

Contributions from Individuals

Ben Carson

Disbursements

Super PAC(s)

Contributions from Individuals

Jeb Bush

$ 103,167,846

Disbursements

Super PAC(s)

Contributions from Individuals

Donald Trump

Disbursements

Super PAC(s)   None

0   20   40   60   80   100

Millions of Dollars

Note: Super PAC funds are "Affiliated"

Source: Federal Election Commission as of Sept. 30, 2015
               The World Almanac and Book of Facts 2016, p 6

FOREIGN GIFTS TO CLINTON FOUNDATION CLIMB
The Wall Street Journal   Feb 18, 2015   p A4

The Clinton Foundation has dropped its self-imposed ban on collecting funds from foreign governments and is winning contributions as at accelerating rate, raising ethical questions as Hillary Clinton ramps up her expected bid for the presidency.

Recent donors include the United Arab Emirates, Saudi Arabia, Oman, Australia, Germany and a Canadian government agency promoting the Keystone XL pipeline.

Since leaving the State Department in early 2013, Mrs. Clinton officially joined the foundation, which changed its name to the Bill, Hillary and Chelsea Clinton Foundation, and has become a prodigious fundraiser as the foundation launched a $250 million endowment campaign, officials said...

"Now that she is gearing up to run for president, the same potential exists for foreign governments to curry favor with her as a potential president of the United States," said Kirk Hanson, director of the Markkula Center for Applied Ethics at Santa Clara University in California.

A previous donor, the Kingdom of Saudi Arabia, has given between $10 million and $25 million since the foundation was created in 1999.

by James V. Grimaldi and Rebecca Ballhaus

Wikipedia, the free encyclopedia:

The Lobbying Disclosure Act of 1995 was aimed at bringing a "level of accountability to federal lobbying practices in the United States... Under provisions that took effect on January 1, 2006, lobbyists are required to register with the Clerk of the House of Representatives and the Secretary of the Senate. Anyone failing to do so is punishable by a civil fine of up to $50,000. The clerk and secretary must refer any acts of non-compliance to the U.S. Attorney for the District of Columbia," (of the Department of Justice).

Also included are definitions of what actions must be disclosed, which "includes lobbying to certain members of the Executive Branch who are included on specific payrolls. Also included are members of Congress."

"Any organization that contributes more than $10,000 towards lobbying activities must be registered, (but) amounts even slightly below this threshold are exempt from reporting. DUE TO SEVERE UNDERSTAFFING, the (two offices named above) ARE UNABLE TO CHECK FOR ILLEGAL ACTIVITIES OR CORRUPT PRACTICES. THIS IS THE SIGNIFICANT FAILURE OF THIS BILL."

"During a hearing before the Senate Committee on Rules and Administration, Senator Christopher Dodd stated that, 'since 2003, the Office of Public Records has referred over 2,000 cases to the Department of Justice, and nothing's been heard from them again.'"

--wikipedia.org

CNN Interviews Bill Clinton

Bill Clinton was interviewed by CNN on August 18, 2016, as follows:

He said Hillary has a "Clinton Global Initiative" meeting scheduled in New York for September, 2016, and that it will be the "final meeting."

He said that he will not do any more paid speeches if Hillary wins in November, or during the time up to the election. He added that the Clinton Foundation "will not accept foreign or corporate donations if Hillary is elected president in November," and that he would "resign from the Clinton Foundation Board" should she win.

CNN commented that Bill's statements were an admission that the Foundation needs to be "retooled" if his wife wins in November. CNN cited the Foundation's "pay to play" schemes, which connect her actions as Secretary of State under Obama to contributions to the Foundation. The example used was that the State Department was approached by Lebanese-Nigerian businessmen brothers Ronald and Gilbert Chagoury. They suggested the State Department purchase their Chagoury Group's land in Lagos, Nigeria, and build an embassy there. In exchange, the Chagoury Group pledged to commit $1 billion to fight coastal erosion.

Gilbert Chagoury donated more than $1 million to the Clinton Foundation.

A Boston Globe editorial stated that the Clinton Foundation should "remove a political - and actual - distraction and stop accepting funding." Both the FBI and Department of Justice met several months ago to discuss opening a public corruption case against the Clinton Foundation after the FBI received, from a bank, notification of "suspicious activity from a foreigner who had donated to the foundation."

Hillary Clinton told Anderson Cooper at a CNN town hall meeting in June regarding the Clinton Foundation's future if she were elected president: "We'll cross that bridge if and when we come to it."   --cnn.com

Clinton Global Initiative   --wikipedia.org

The Clinton Global Initiative was founded in 2005 by former President Bill Clinton. The CGI is a nonpartisan organization that convenes global leaders to devise and implement innovative solutions to the world's most pressing problems. CGI hosts an Annual Meeting every September scheduled to convene with the U.N. General Assembly.

Each CGI member develops a Commitment to Action. Commitments must be "new, specific and measurable," but beyond those three criteria, members have wide latitude to determine which actions to take. CGI then monitors the progress and success of these commitments throughout the year. Funding pledged through commitments does not come through CGI, and is not donated to CGI. Rather, organizations commit to raise and distribute money on their own.

Clinton Global Initiative International

Bill Clinton launched CGI International to supplement the Annual Meeting in New York with additional meetings in various regions of the globe. In December 2008 Clinton convened the first CGI International meeting in Hong Kong (China) to address local, regional and global challenges.

Clinton Global Citizenship Awards

Clinton Global Initiative has been giving Clinton Global Citizen Awards every year since 2007. Awards are given to, in the opinion of the Clinton Foundation, "outstanding individuals who exemplify global citizenship through their vision and leadership."

Other Sub-Organizations of the Clinton Foundation

Other organizations spearheaded by the Clinton Foundation include the Clinton Climate Initiative, the Clinton Development Initiative, the Alliance for a Healthier Generation, the Clinton Economic Opportunity Initiative, the Clinton Giustra Sustainable Growth Initiative, the Clinton Health Matters Initiative, Disaster Relief (which included Hurricane Katrina and the Haiti earthquake), and the "No Ceilings Project." The list might not be exhaustive.

In the fall of 2015, the Department of State issued a Subpoena to the Clinton Foundation ordering "documents about the charity's projects that might have required approval from the federal government during Hillary Clinton's term as Secretary of State."

--wikipedia.org

The Clinton Foundation

Share this post!

MAY 12, 2015   CRC STAFF

By Barbara Joanna Lucas, *Foundation Watch*, May 2015

Before Obama even took office, the Clinton Foundation's chairman of the board, Bruce Lindsey, signed a Memorandum of Understanding on Dec. 12, 2008 with Valerie Jarrett, then co-chair of President-elect Obama's transition team. The document provided that "During any service by Senator Clinton as Secretary of State, the Foundation will publish annually the names of all new contributors." We now know that the foundation cast aside its promise to make timely disclosure of donations it took in from foreign sources.

The memorandum further asserted that the State Department would review any paid speeches by the secretary's husband. The Obama transition team at the time said in a statement, "We believe the agreement with the Clinton Foundation meets our goals of transparency and goes above and beyond in preventing conflicts."

Foreign Donors

While Hillary Clinton served as Secretary of State, the governments of Kuwait, Qatar, Oman, Australia, Norway, Algeria, and the Dominican Republic all lavished millions of dollars on the Clinton Foundation. While acting coy when questioned about most of these, the Clinton Foundation has admitted it should have sought approval from the State Department before accepting $500,000 from the government of Algeria.

The foundation received between $1 million and $5 million from Friends of Saudi Arabia, a pro-Saudi advocacy group in the United States. The foundation also received between $1 million and $5 million from Sheikh Zayed bin Sultan Al Nahyan, who served as president of the United Arab Emirates from 1971-2004. In 1999, his family set up the Zayed Center for Coordination and Follow-Up, which became a haven for anti-Israel sentiment, terrorist sympathizers, and Holocaust deniers (DiscoverTheNetworks.org).

Bill's Big Speaking Gigs

Under the same Memorandum of Understanding with the Obama transition team, a designated ethics official from the State Department's legal office was to review any "potential or actual conflict of interest" for Secretary Clinton regarding her family's interests.

Bill Clinton delivered 215 paid speeches across the world while his wife served as Secretary of State, earning $48 million for the foundation and other Clinton family interests. For each of these speeches, he received an "ethical waiver" from the State Department, whether the speech was in the United States or overseas, or sponsored by a U.S. or foreign corporation.

As Hillary was in charge of running America's foreign policy, Bill was giving high-dollar speeches in China, Russia, Saudi Arabia, Egypt, United Arab Emirates, Central America, Turkey, Thailand, Taiwan, India, and the Cayman Islands, according to Judicial Watch. Certainly some of these should have raised eyebrows by reviewers at the State Department, considering tenuous U.S. relations with Russia and China. And the fact that the list of donors includes Muslim nations that are known for mistreating women, ought to set off the hypocrisy alarm bells because Mrs. Clinton has long positioned herself as a champion of women's rights.

Then there are the massive financial institutions sponsoring the speeches that would certainly have an interest in currying favor with the Department of State. These sponsors included Goldman Sachs, Bank of America, Deutsche Bank, and American Express.

Spanning the Globe

The Clinton Foundation has $277.8 million in assets. It took in $144.3 million and doled out $8.8 million in fiscal year 2013. FoundationSearch ranks it 472nd in the Top 10,000 U.S. Foundations by Assets and 4th in Top Foundations by Assets for Arkansas.

The organization was established in 2001 shortly after the Clintons moved out of the White House. The stated goal was to "alleviate poverty, improve global health, strengthen economies, and protect the environment." It has multiple sub-organizations, most notably the Clinton Global Initiative. The Foundation has 350 employees in 180 countries.

U S CODE, TITLE 18, SECTION 2071

(a) Whoever willfully and unlawfully conceals, removes, mutilates, obliterates, or destroys, or attempts to do so, or, with intent to do so takes and carries away any record, proceeding, map, book, paper, document, or other thing, filed or deposited with any clerk or officer of any court of the United States, or in any public office, or with any judicial or public officer of the United States, shall be fined under this title or imprisoned not more than three years, or both.

(b) Whoever, having the custody of any such record, proceeding, map, book, document, paper, or other thing, willfully and unlawfully conceals, removes, mutilates, obliterates, falsifies, or destroys the same, shall be fined under this title or imprisoned not more than three years, or both; and shall forfeit his office and be disqualified from holding any office under the United States. As used in this subsection, the term "office" does not include the office held by any person as a retired officer of the Armed Forces of the United States."

Former United States Attorney General Michael Mukasey tells MSNBC that not only is Hillary Clinton's private email server illegal, it "disqualifies" her from holding any federal office.   August 26, 2016

On MSNBC's Morning Joe, Mukasey said, "I think the more dangerous part of this, from her standpoint, is not so much the placement of the material here as wiping the server. Number one, that's a felony, but that statute disqualifies you from holding any further office in the U.S., and she's running for a further office under the United States."

Seth Barrett Tillman, a former teacher at Rutger's Law School, now at Maynooth University in Ireland, immediately wrote that "applying the statute to candidates for president would be unconstitutional. The only limits on qualifications to be president are in the Constitution - having U.S. citizenship, being at least 35, and having lived in the U.S. at least 14 years." Tillman quoted from a recent court opinion that said, "The democratic presumption is that any adult member of the polity...is eligible to run for office," and Congress cannot "supplement these requirements."

Tillman's objection was picked up by a legal blog maintained by UCLA law professor Eugene Volokh. On Thursday, August 29, Volokh said he received an email from Mukasey that said, "On reflection...Professor Tillman's (analysis) is spot on, and mine was mistaken." Mukasey added in the email, "The disqualification statute may be a measure of how seriously Congress took the violation in question, and how seriously we should take it, but that's all it is."   --Pete Williams, nbcnews.com

Friends of Bill and Hillary

Mr. and Mrs. Kahn

Mr. and Mrs. Khizr Muazzam Khan stood on the podium at the Democratic National Convention where Hillary Clinton easily won her party's nomination to run for the office of president of the United States. Mr. Kahn chided Republican nominee Donald Trump for suggesting immigrants from terrorist countries be vetted thoroughly before entering the U.S. as legal residents. The couple's son, a Purple Heart and Bronze Star hero, was killed in 2004 in the Iraq War. The Kahns are Pakistani immigrants.

What the media did not mention was that Mr. Kahn is a lawyer with the law firm of Hogan, Hartson and Lovells, renamed Hogan Lovells. Clients of the law firm include the Royal Court of Saudi Arabia, Bill and Hillary Clinton, and the Clinton Foundation.

Loretta Lynch also worked at the Hogan Lovells law firm before she became the Attorney General of the United States on April 27, 2015. Appointed by President Barack Obama, Attorney General Lynch spearheaded the federal investigation of Hillary Clinton's use of a private email server in her Chappaqua, New York home while serving as Secretary of State. During the investigation, Lynch met privately with Bill Clinton for a few minutes on the tarmac of the Phoenix Sky Harbor International Airport, creating a media controversy over the meeting as a conflict of interest. Bill Clinton and Loretta Lynch have said that the conversation was personal, and that the investigation was not discussed.

Hogan Lovells Law Firm

wikipedia.org

Hogan Lovells is a multinational law firm headquartered in London and Washington, D.C. It was formed May 1, 2010 by the merger of United States-based Hogan and Hartson and London-based Lovells. Hogan Lovells has around 2500 lawyers working out of more than 40 offices in the United States, Europe, Latin America, the Middle East and Asia. In 2013 Hogan Lovells was the eleventh largest law firm in the world by revenues, earning around $1.8 billion that year.

Lovells in early 2000 opened offices in Beijing and Shanghai, becoming the second largest foreign firm in China. In 2007, Lovells opened an office in Dubai, offering legal services to corporations, financial institutions and individuals in the middle east, and at the beginning of 2009 opened an office in Hanoi. Also in 2009, Lovells opened an associated office in Riyadh, the capital of Saudi Arabia and home to the royal family.

At the time of the merger with Hogan Hartson in 2010, Lovells was a global law firm with over 300 partners and around 3,150 employees operating from 26 offices in Europe, Asia and the United States.

Hogan Lovells Law Firm (continued)

In December 2013, Hogan Lovells merged with South African firm Routledge Modise. The addition of about 120 lawyers in the Johannesburg office made up the first physical location for Hogan Lovells in Africa.

> Hogan Lovells is among the largest lobbying firms in the United States, servicing $12.3 million in lobbying in 2013.   --wikipedia.org

Hogan Lovells' Los Angeles office opened in 1996 and includes 30 lawyers, located in Century City, along the Avenue of the Stars.

Lynn Forester de Rothschild

Lady Rothschild met Sir Evelyn Robert de Rothschild at a 1998 Bilderberg Group meeting in Scotland. Introduced by Henry Kissinger, the couple married in 2000. She heads an independent wealth management firm in the U.S. and heads the political movement, "Inclusive Capitalism," the goal of which is to adjust the capitalist system to include more people. She is a member of the Council on Foreign Relations (U.S.), The Institute for Strategic Studies (UK), the International Advisory Council of Asia House (UK) and the Foreign Policy Association (U.S.). Sir and Lady Rothschild have homes in New York, London, the Rothschild historic country estate in England, and a summer home on Martha's Vineyard.

Lady Rothschild hosted a fundraiser for Hillary Clinton on August 25, 2016 at her Martha's Vineyard home, which raised $1 million for Hillary's presidential campaign. Before the dinner, a cocktail party at another Martha's Vineyard home raised $2 million.

--wikipedia.org

Edward Mezvinsky

Mr. Mezvinsky served in the U.S. House of Representatives as a Congressman from Iowa from 1973 to 1977. A democrat, he served on the House Judiciary Committee along with new law school graduate and fellow democrat Hillary Clinton. Both voted to impeach President Richard Nixon. He and the Clintons remained in touch. Mr. Mezvinsky's second marriage was to Marjorie Margoles, who became a member of the U.S. House of Representatives. In 1993, she cast the deciding vote to get President Bill Clinton's tax package through the House of Representatives. Eight years later, in 2001, Mr. Mezvinsky pleaded guilty to 31 of 69 counts of bank, mail and wire fraud for embezzling $10 million in a Ponzi scheme. After serving less than five years in federal prison, he was released in April, 2008. He still owes $9.4 million to his victims. Meanwhile, Mr. Mezvinsky's son Marc married Chelsea Clinton in George Soros' mansion.

George Soros

A Hungarian-American with dual citizenship, George Soros is chairman of the Soros Fund Management, LLC. He is also chairman of the Open Society Foundations, which supports democracy and human rights in more than 100 countries. --georgesoros.com

George Soros had recognized the unfavorable position of the United Kingdom in the European Exchange Rate Mechanism. The UK rate was too high, their inflation was also much too high (triple the German rate). On September 16, 1992, Black Wednesday, Soros fund sold short more than $10 billion in English pounds, profiting from the UK's reluctance either to raise its interest rate to a level comparable to those of other European Exchange Rate Mechanism countries, or to float its currency. The UK finally withdrew from the European Exchange Rate Mechanism, devaluing the pound. Soros' profit on the bet was estimated at over $1 billion. He was dubbed "the man who broke the Bank of England." The estimated cost of Black Wednesday to the UK treasury was 3.4 billion pounds.

In 1999, Paul Krugman wrote of Soros' effect on financial markets:

"Nobody who has read a business magazine in the last few years can be unaware that these days there really are investors who not only move money in anticipation of a currency crisis, but actually do their best to trigger that crisis for fun and profit."

Regarding the 2008 recession, Soros referred to it as the most serious crisis since the 1930s. In reaction, he founded the "Institute for New Economic Thinking" in October 2009. This is a think tank composed of international economic, business and financial experts, mandated to investigate radical new approaches to organize the international economic and financial system. --wikipedia.org

"CONGRESS SHALL HAVE POWER TO REGULATE COMMERCE
WITH FOREIGN NATIONS, AND AMONG THE SEVERAL STATES ..."

Article I, Section 8

Constitution of the United States

DOW JONES AND NASDAQ MILESTONES

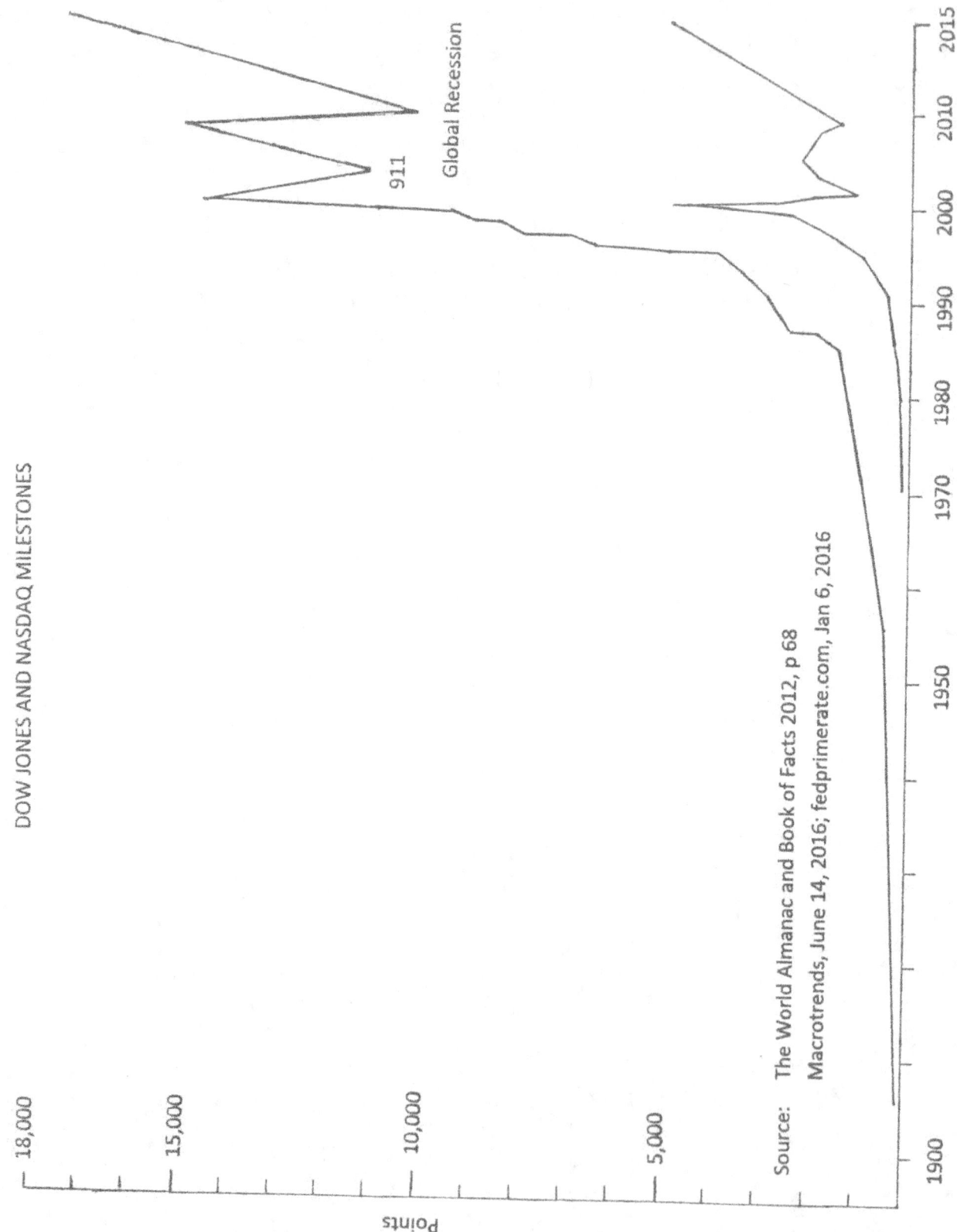

Source: The World Almanac and Book of Facts 2012, p 68
           Macrotrends, June 14, 2016; fedprimerate.com, Jan 6, 2016

73

U.S. NET CORPORATE PROFITS, 1947 - 2015

$1 trillion, 844 billion

Billions of Dollars

Global Recession

2015

Source: Federal Reserve Board, St. Louis, May 27, 2016
U.S. Corporate Profits after Tax

United States corporate profits benefit the top 1% of the U.S. population,
who own the vast majority of corporate stocks, and foreign owners.

GAP WIDENS AS THE RICH GET RICHER
Los Angeles Times Jan 21, 2014   p B1

As business and political leaders gather in Davos, Switzerland to discuss the
world economy, new evidence emerged about how much the rich have become
richer - and how much further the poor are falling behind.

The 85 richest people on earth now have the same amount of wealth as
the bottom half of the global population.

The bottom half of the population - about 3.5 billion people - account for
about $1.7 trillion, or about 0.7% of the world's wealth, according to Oxfam
International, a British humanitarian group. Those wealthy 85 are a small part of
the richest 1%, who hold 46% of the world's wealth, or $110 trillion.

A Gallup poll released Monday found two-thirds of Americans were
dissatisfied with the way income and wealth are distributed in the nation. Oxfam
said the United States has led a worldwide growth in wealth concentration. Since
2009, the bottom 90% of Americans have become poorer, Oxfam said.

Falling taxes for the rich and increased use of tax havens have helped widen
income inequality, Oxfam said. Oxfam called on corporate executives at Davos to
take steps to reverse the trend: support progressive taxation, pledge not to dodge
taxes, pay a living wage to workers at their companies, and push governments
"to provide universal healthcare, education and social protection" for their citizens.

by Jim Puzzanghera.

WORLD'S LARGEST COMPANIES, 2015
UNITED STATES COMPANIES

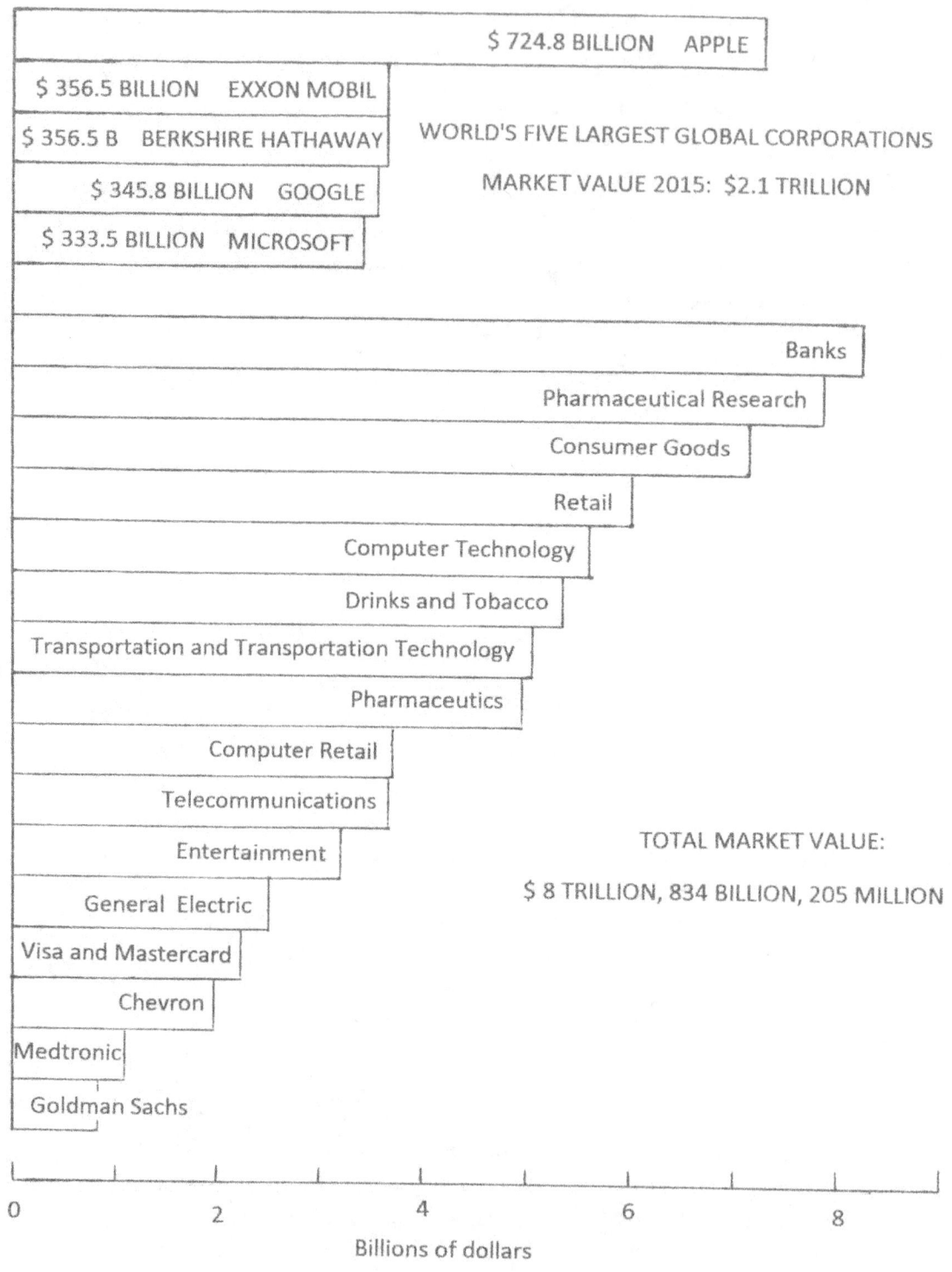

$ 724.8 BILLION   APPLE

$ 356.5 BILLION   EXXON MOBIL

$ 356.5 B   BERKSHIRE HATHAWAY

WORLD'S FIVE LARGEST GLOBAL CORPORATIONS

$ 345.8 BILLION   GOOGLE

MARKET VALUE 2015: $2.1 TRILLION

$ 333.5 BILLION   MICROSOFT

Banks

Pharmaceutical Research

Consumer Goods

Retail

Computer Technology

Drinks and Tobacco

Transportation and Transportation Technology

Pharmaceutics

Computer Retail

Telecommunications

Entertainment

TOTAL MARKET VALUE:

General Electric

$ 8 TRILLION, 834 BILLION, 205 MILLION

Visa and Mastercard

Chevron

Medtronic

Goldman Sachs

0   2   4   6   8

Billions of dollars

Source: World Almanac and Book of Facts 2016, p 54

Rank	Type of Business	Name
1	Computer Retail	Apple
2	Fuel	Exxon Mobil
3	Financial	Berkshire Hathaway
4	Computer Retail	Google
5	Computer Retail	Microsoft
7	Bank	Wells Fargo
17	Bank	JP Morgan Chase
37	Bank	Bank of America
40	Bank	Citigroup
43	Pharm Research	Gilead Sciences
52	Pharm Research	Amgen
54	Pharm Research	Actavis
65	Pharm Research	United Health Group
77	Pharm Research	Biogen Idec
84	Pharm Research	AbbVie
86	Pharm Research	Celgene
8	Consumer Goods	Johnson & Johnson
18	Consumer Goods	Proctor & Gamble
68	Consumer Goods	Bristol Myers Squibb
73	Consumer Goods	3-M
12	Retail	Wal-mart
41	Retail	Home Depot
83	Retail	McDonald's
85	Retail	Walgreens
38	Computer Tech	IBM
42	Computer Tech	Intel
46	Computer Tech	Cisco Systems
62	Computer Tech	Qualcomm
32	Drinks & Tobacco	Coca-Cola
45	Drinks & Tobacco	Pepsi Co
60	Drinks & Tobacco	Philip Morris Intl
78	Drinks & Tobacco	Altria Group
69	Transport Tech	Schlumberger
70	Transport Tech	United Technologies
72	Transport Tech	Boeing
81	Transport Tech	Union Pacific
89	Transport Tech	Kinder Morgan
20	Pharmaceutics	Pfizer
36	Pharmaceutics	Merck
59	Pharmaceutics	CVS Caremark
28	Computer Retail	Oracle
29	Computer Retail	Facebook
33	Computer Retail	Amazon.com
22	Telecom	Verizon Comm
34	Telecom	AT&T
13	Elec Appliance	General Electric
30	Entertainment	Walt Disney
44	Entertainment	Comcast
48	Credit	Visa
80	Credit	Mastercard
23	Fuel	Chevron
67	Medical Devices	Medtronic

UNITED STATES' LARGEST COMPANIES 2015

Source: World Almanac and Book of Facts 2016, p 54

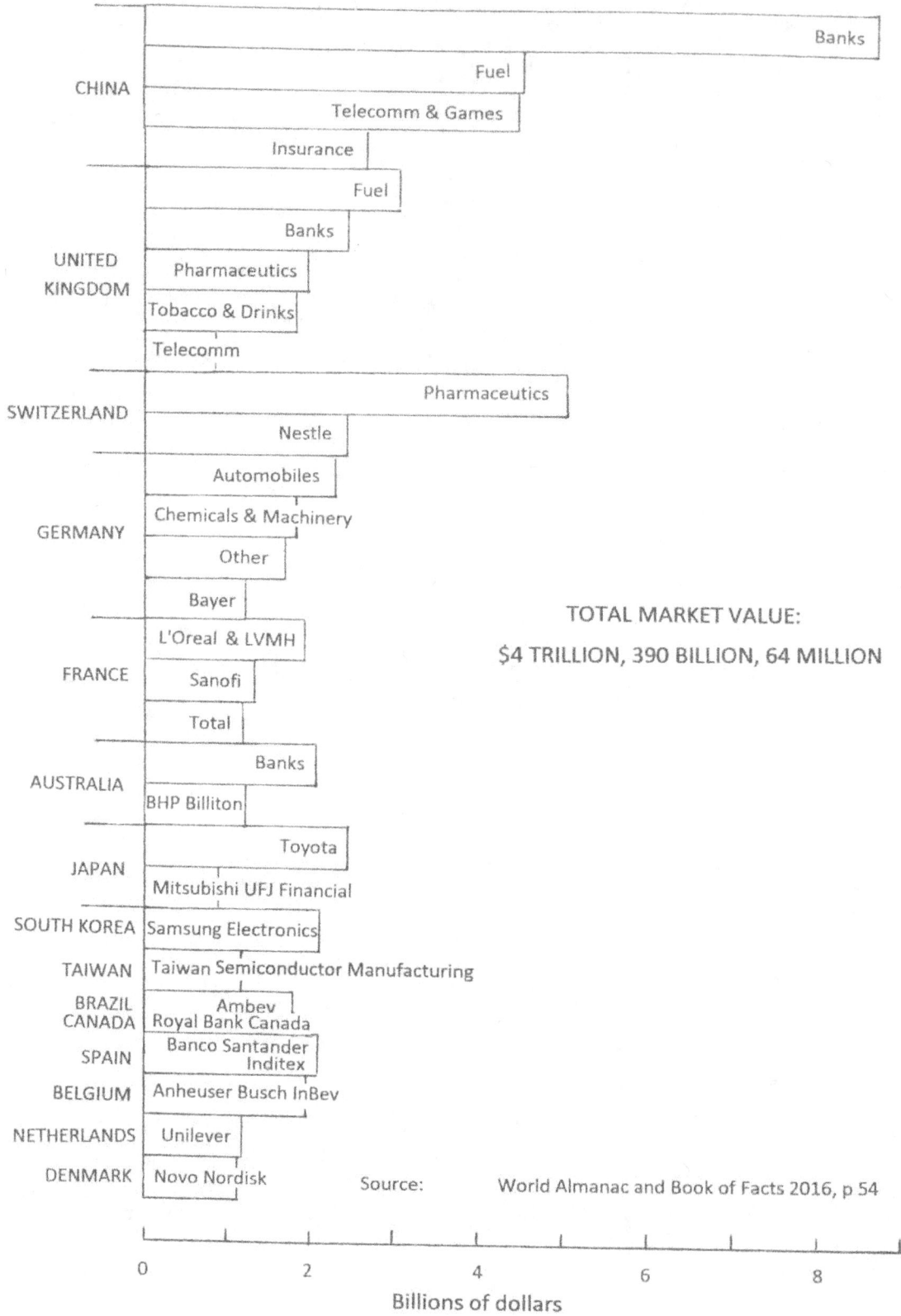

WORLD'S LARGEST COMPANIES, 2015

COMPANIES OTHER THAN UNITED STATES COMPANIES

CHINA
- Banks
- Fuel
- Telecomm & Games
- Insurance

UNITED KINGDOM
- Fuel
- Banks
- Pharmaceutics
- Tobacco & Drinks
- Telecomm

SWITZERLAND
- Pharmaceutics
- Nestle

GERMANY
- Automobiles
- Chemicals & Machinery
- Other
- Bayer

FRANCE
- L'Oreal & LVMH
- Sanofi
- Total

AUSTRALIA
- Banks
- BHP Billiton

JAPAN
- Toyota
- Mitsubishi UFJ Financial

SOUTH KOREA — Samsung Electronics

TAIWAN — Taiwan Semiconductor Manufacturing

BRAZIL — Ambev

CANADA — Royal Bank Canada

SPAIN — Banco Santander, Inditex

BELGIUM — Anheuser Busch InBev

NETHERLANDS — Unilever

DENMARK — Novo Nordisk

TOTAL MARKET VALUE:
$4 TRILLION, 390 BILLION, 64 MILLION

Source: World Almanac and Book of Facts 2016, p 54

0   2   4   6   8

Billions of dollars

77

WORLD'S LARGEST COMPANIES OTHER THAN UNITED STATES COMPANIES, 2015

Rank	Country	Type of Business	Name
6	China	Fuel	Petro China
9	China	Bank	Industrial & Commercial Bank of China
11	China	Telecom	China Mobile (Hong Kong)
21	China	Bank	China Construction Bank
24	China	Bank	Bank of China
27	China	Bank	Agricultural Bank of China
31	China	Entertainment	Tencent (Hong Kong)
39	China	Insurance	China Life Insurance
55	China	Fuel	Sinopec
63	China	Insurance	Ping An Insurance
26	United Kingdom	Fuel	Royal Dutch Shell
35	United Kingdom	Bank	HSBC
58	United Kingdom	Fuel	British Petroleum
66	United Kingdom	Pharmaceutics	Glaxo Smith Kline
79	United Kingdom	Tobacco & Drinks	British American Tobacco
95	United Kingdom	Pharmaceutics	AstraZeneca
96	United Kingdom	Telecom	Vodafone Group
97	United Kingdom	Tobacco & Drinks	SABMiller
99	United Kingdom	Bank	Lloyds Banking Group
10	Switzerland	Pharmaceutics	Novartis
14	Switzerland	Food	Nestle
16	Switzerland	Pharmaceutics	Roche
49	Germany	Automobile	Volkswagen
50	Germany	Pharmaceutics	Bayer
74	Germany	Automobile	Daimler
87	Germany	Chemical	BASF
90	Germany	Machinery	Siemens
92	Germany	Computer Software	SAP
98	Germany	Telecom	Deutsch Telekom
47	France	Pharmaceutics	Sanofi
57	France	Fuels	Total
75	France	Luxury	L'Oreal
91	France	Luxury	LVMH
51	Australia	Mining	BHP Billiton
61	Australia	Bank	Commonwealth Bank of Australia
82	Australia	Bank	Westpac Banking
15	Japan	Automobile	Toyota
93	Japan	Bank	Mitsubishi UFJ Financial
19	South Korea	Electronics	Samsung Electronics
53	Taiwan	Electronics	Taiwan Semiconductor Mfg
71	Spain	Bank	Banco Santander
76	Spain	Apparel	Inditex
25	Belgium	Drink	Anheuser Busch InBev
56	Netherlands	Food	Unilever
64	Denmark	Pharmaceutics	Novo Nordisk
94	Canada	Bank	Royal Bank Canada
88	Brazil	Drink	Ambev

Source: The World Almanac and Book of Facts 2016, p 54

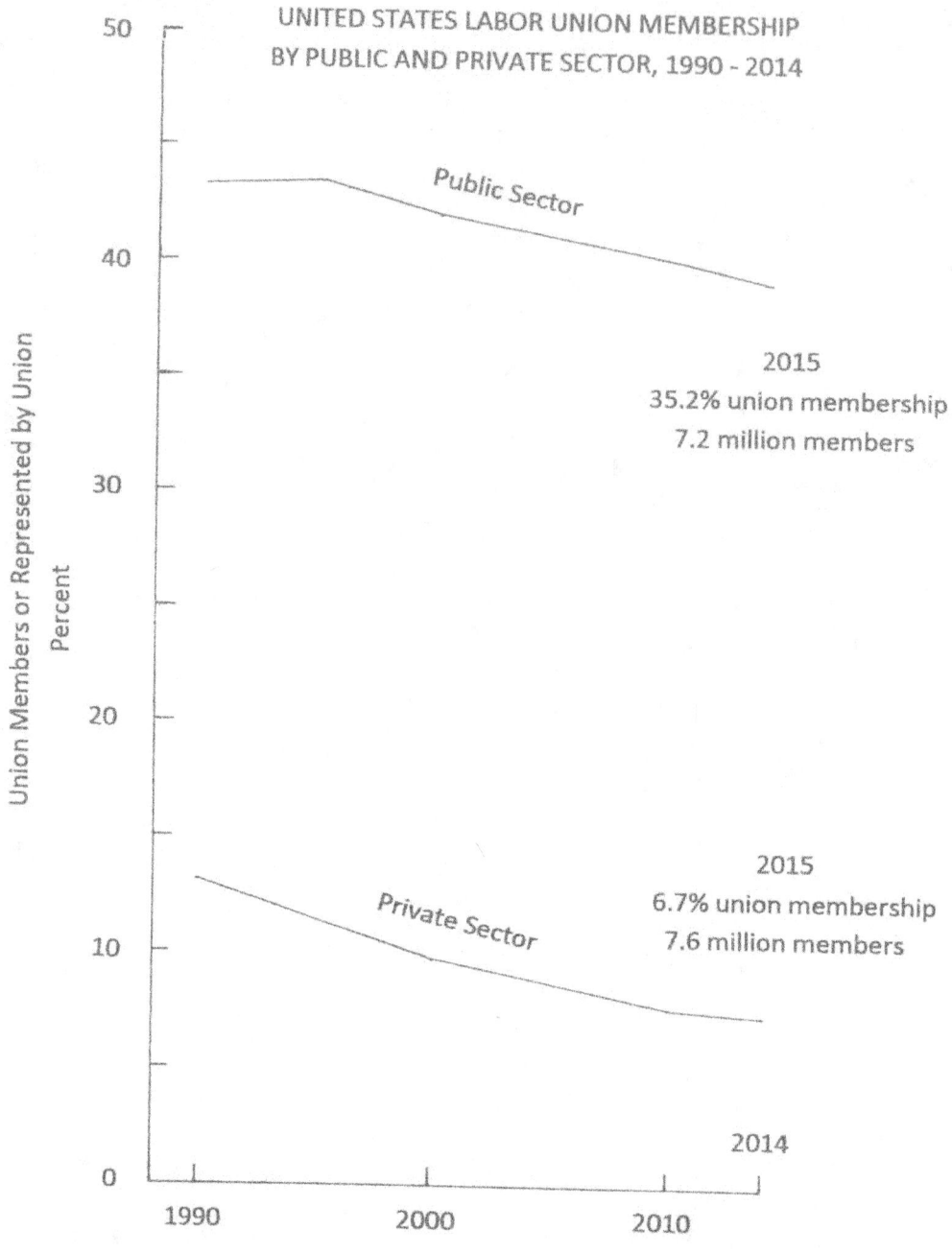

UNITED STATES LABOR UNION MEMBERSHIP
BY PUBLIC AND PRIVATE SECTOR, 1990 - 2014

Public Sector

2015
35.2% union membership
7.2 million members

Union Members or Represented by Union
Percent

2015
6.7% union membership
7.6 million members

Private Sector

2014

50

40

30

20

10

0

1990   2000   2010

Source: ProQuest Statistical Abstract of the United States 2016, p 445; bls.gov

Labor Unions are legally recognized as representatives of workers in many industries
in the United States. Their activity today centers on collective bargaining over wages,
benefits, working conditions for their membership, and on representing their members
in disputes with management over violations of contract provisions.   --wikipedia.org

A federal government review showed that employees in a labor union earn up to 33%
more income than their nonunion counterparts, as well as having more job security,
and safer and higher-quality work conditions. The median weekly income for union
workers was $973 in 2014 compared with $763 for nonunion workers. --wikipedia.org

U.S. Private Sector Unions

"The American Federation of Labor," founded in 1886 and led by Samuel Gompers until his death in 1924 proved durable. It arose as a loose coalition of various local unions. It helped coordinate and support strikes and eventually became a major player in national politics. American labor unions benefited greatly from the New Deal policies of Franklin Roosevelt in the 1930s. The Wagner Act, in particular, legally protected the right of unions to organize, but pro-business conservatives gained control of Congress in 1946, and in 1947 they passed the Taft-Hartley Act. President Truman vetoed it, but the conservatives in Congress overrode the veto."   --wikipedia.org

The Taft-Hartley was designed to change much of the Wagner Act, greatly restricting the power of labor unions. The Taft-Hartley permits union shops only after a majority of employees vote for them. It allows the president to appoint a board of inquiry to investigate union disputes if he believes a strike would endanger public health or safety. It ended the check-off system whereby the employer collects union dues. It declared all 'closed shops' illegal."   --ushistory.com

Labor union membership peaked in 1954 at almost 35%. Jimmy Hoffa, President of the powerful International Brotherhood of Teamsters, was reported by the media as corrupt, misusing union dues paid by the membership, and having ties with the powerful mafia underworld. The federal government charged him with jury tampering, bribery and fraud. He was convicted and sentenced to jail in 1967 for 13 years but kept his Teamsters presidency. President Nixon released Hoffa from jail in 1971 with the stipulation that he give up control of the Teamsters and refrain from union activities until 1980. Jimmy Hoffa disappeared in 1975. It is widely believed he ended up in a 55-gallon barrel of cement

Private sector union membership was viewed by the public after the Jimmy Hoffa matter as corrupt, criminal and dangerous. The Landrum-Griffin Act, passed in 1959, was intended to prevent labor union leaders from colluding with dishonest employers. It regulated control of union bosses as well as union funds. With the new restrictions on their activities, union leaders pushed less for their members, and the labor union movement in the private sector continued its decline.

Other factors contributed to the decline. In the 1970s, a rapid increase in imports undermined the jobs of U.S. workers at the same time as workers themselves were increasing due to immigration. By 1980 with Reagan's deregulation policies, manufacturers were seeking cheaper labor outside the country. Some relocated to southern states where unions were weak, where companies could threaten to close or move a plant if workers demanded higher wages or benefits.

U.S. Public Sector Unions

It is ironic that public sector workers are thriving in settings that offer far greater security than private sector workers enjoy. Federal, state, county and city governments won't disappear, move offshore, be taken over, or have foreign or domestic competition.

Wisconsin in 1959 was the first state in the U.S. to grant collective bargaining rights to public employees. In 1962, John F. Kennedy signed Executive Order 10988, upgrading the status of federal employee unions. In the 1960s and 1970s, public employee unions expanded rapidly. Now, 3/4ths of the states have public employee unions.

Public sector unions can contribute directly to the people who have the ultimate responsibility for their livelihood.

The public union giving pattern is "overwhelmingly democratic."

TOP CONTRIBUTORS, 2015-2016

National Education Association*	$ 15.8 million
American Federal/State/County/Municipal Employees*	$ 3.9 million
American Federation of Teachers*	$ 3.2 million
International Association of Fire Fighters	$ 1.6 million
American Federal Government Employees	$ 1.2 million
National Association of Letter Carriers	$ 949,921
American Postal Workers Union*	$ 533,760
National Afge Headquarters	$ 500,000
Rural Letter Carriers Association	$ 395,000
National Active & Retired Federal Employees Assn	$ 373,000
National Treasury Employees Union	$ 316,999
Aft Solidarity 527	$ 268,946
National Association of Postal Supervisors	$ 257,500
Federal Aviation Administration Managers Assn	$ 238,500
National Postal Mail Handlers Union	$ 153,000
National Association of Postmasters	$ 94,430
National Weather Service Employees Organization	$ 61,000
California School Employees Association	$ 60,821
Professional Engineers in California Government	$ 54,061
American Foreign Service Association	$ 31,580

*Top lobbying clients

Source: opensecrets.org   TOP RECIPIENT: HILLARY CLINTON $121,510

Public sector unions didn't suffer a setback when President Reagan fired 11,000 air traffic controllers during their strike around the nation in 1981. They had refused Reagan's order to return to work. Their jobs were covered by 3000 supervisors, 2000 non-striking controllers and 900 military controllers, who soon resumed 80% of air travel. That same year, the Professional Air Traffic Controllers Organization was decertified. Reagan ordered that none of the strikers could ever work in their chosen profession again.

Today, 31% of federal workers, 35% of state workers and 46% of local employees are members of unions. An analyst in 2011 stated that "in today's public sector, good pay, generous benefits, and job security make possible a stable middle-class existence for nearly everyone from janitors to jailers." He added that "generous pension systems are too heavy a drain on state budgets."

The $18 billion Chapter 9 bankruptcy in 2013 by Detroit left the city teetering but still standing. The city survived by cutting pensions 10% and reducing health care benefits by 90%. Orange County, California, filed a $1.7 billion bankruptcy in 1994, and Jefferson County, Alabama, got through a $4 billion bankruptcy in 2011. The cities of Stockton and San Bernardino, California, also filed for bankruptcy protection.

The cities of San Jose and Vallejo, California, filed for bankruptcy protection largely because of their public pension obligations. San Jose's pension and health costs for retirees approached $400 million. The city had to cut city services to the bone to make ends meet. The city of Vallejo was facing creditor claims from public safety employees, which in 2008 was taking up 80% of the city budget. Vallejo's acerbic city manager remarked to his interviewer, Michael Lewis, that the city "failed to persuade its public safety workers that it could not afford to make them rich." (Michael Lewis, "Boomerang," 2011, p 202, W.W. Norton & Co., NY).

The U.S. Bureau of Labor Statistics surveyed the histories of union membership rates in industrialized countries from 1970 to 2003, and found that of 20 advanced economies which had union statistics going back to 1970, 16 of them had experienced drops in union density over the period. The Bureau reported, "All the English-speaking countries studied saw union membership drop to some degree, with some countries having even steeper drops than the United States." Four countries which had gained in union membership were Finland, Sweden, Denmark and Belgium.   --wikipedia.org

Outsourcing

Handing out company processes to subcontractors began in 1981. The practice shifts responsibility for in-house benefits packages and legal issues, including terminations, to outside vendors. Staffing agencies advertise their workers, who willingly work without benefits, wage increases, or steady hours and on an hourly basis subject to termination at any time. 30% of the U.S. labor force now works for such agencies, and subcontracting is on the rise.

In January, 2010, Walmart outsourced 11,200 jobs over the month, ridding itself of 10,000 food sampling demonstrators and 1,200 recruiting jobs, hiring instead a marketing firm, Shopper Events, LLC. It was an attempt to lure shoppers from Costco by having better food samples and displays. One of the contract employees reported that Shopper Events, LLC, paid her less than minimum wage. She had to put in long hours with no overtime pay, endure illegal and falsified pay records, work in hazardous conditions, including dangerously high temperatures and unstable warehouse storage stacking. When she complained, she was threatened with termination.   --eoionline.org

One of the most egregious examples of outsourcing are workers who repair or maintain the engines on top of wind farm projectiles. An extremely dangerous job, workers sometimes are hired several layers of subcontractors away from wind farm owners so as to avoid responsibiility for any deaths that occur. When a death or injury occurs, the subcontractor at the end of the line who has responsibility often doesn't have the insurance or resources to cover the claim.

The safety net from employers has disappeared for U.S. low wage workers and some middle income earners. It's not only outsourcing that threatens workers. There's also inshoring, where companies bring in third party firms to replace whole departments, such as payroll, accounting, claims processing, and inventory, again avoiding employee responsibility or expense. Offshoring is another way of replacing in-house employees, in fields such as customer service, with widespread use of English-speaking workers from India.

Technology

Workers around the world increasingly will be losing jobs to automation.
A consultant at Yale reports that technology is now destroying more jobs than it is creating.
Fields most at risk are cashiers and checkers, phone operators, teachers, travel agents and interpreters. The consultant adds that machines may replace half of human jobs worldwide. Robots already staff a hotel in Japan.   --techinsider.io

Technology has replaced real estate agents locally and worldwide. Realtor.com provides properties globally in an assortment of languages, with photos and digital tours, and availability for purchasing on-line. Operational since 2010, foreign buyers have been investing upwards of $100 billion in the U.S. annually, causing prices to skyrocket.

Book sellers are finding book buyers through Amazon.com, but struggle to survive because Amazon offers books on-line inexpensively. Competitor Barnes and Noble offers Kindle for reading books on-line as well as new books for purchase. Brick and mortar retailers of all description sell merchandise on-line around the world, giving up stores, overhead and employees.

Mergers and Acquisitions

The Sherman Antitrust Act of 1890, intended to combat anti-competitive practices, is still on the books, as well as the Clayton Antitrust Act of 1914, which prohibits mergers and acquisitions that "substantially reduce market competition," according to Wikipedia.

Standard Oil of New Jersey vs. United States was the first major antitrust case in the U.S. The Court in 1911 found against Standard Oil, saying it was guilty of a series of "abusive and anticompetitive actions." Standard Oil was divided into several separate firms that soon were competing against each other, but has emerged today intact.

In the early 1980s, Reagan went after AT&T, arguing that it was monopolistic. Again, the company was broken into smaller parts. Today, AT&T is one of the largest corporations in the world, albeit with competitors. The government went after Microsoft on the same grounds but stopped short of splitting it up. The latest is Apple, but at this point, Ayn Rand's statement kicks in, "Antitrust law is penalizing of ability for being ability."

Antitrust law is receding into the background as the biggest U.S. corporations in their fields merge or buy each other. In 1990 the magazine Time, Inc., merged with Warner Communications to become the largest media company. In 1995, Lockheed Corporation merged with Martin Marietta as the second and third largest defense contractors became the largest. The Boeing Company in 1997 spent $13.3 billion in stock to purchase McDonnell Douglas to become the world's largest aerospace company. Two of the most powerful banks in the U.S. became one when Chase Manhattan purchased J.P. Morgan in 2000 for $28.6 billion. In 2013, US Air bailed out American Airlines from bankruptcy for $11 billion as the two became the world's largest airline.

As corporations merge, they not only gain in size and financial strength, they eliminate competition, giving them superior bargaining position relative to workers, who experience less job availability in the marketplace. Corporations after merging increase efficiency and avoid duplication by "downsizing," terminating excess employees, which further increases competition among workers seeking employment.

Global competition among corporations is now the norm. While U.S. companies move offshore, companies outside the U.S. are moving in. The numbers are huge. One of the most aggressive buyers of U.S. corporations is Wang Jianlin, who founded the Wanda-Group in 1988 and has turned it into a multinational conglomerate. As the world's biggest private property developer, Wanda generated net income of $2.06 billion in 2013 with a chain of luxury hotels worldwide. He expanded into entertainment in 2012 when his subsidiary Wanda Cinema purchased AMC theatres for $2.6 billion. In 2015 he bought Hoyts, Australia's leading cinema chain. Also in 2015 his Dalian Wanda subsidiary purchased the World Triathlon Corporation, a U.S.-based corporation, for $650 million. In January 2016, he acquired Legendary Entertainment for $3.5 billion. He also purchased IMAX. Wanda has quickly become the highest revenue-generating film company in the world. In 2016, he began to show interest in buying Hollywood's iconic Paramount Studios.

Foreign involvement in U.S. business transactions is not new, and they compete with U.S. companies for government projects. One would hope that governmental entities would hire U.S. companies to keep profits in the U.S. and provide jobs for American workers, but such is not the case. In 2016, a real estate developer from China wants to build on sixteen acres in North Hollywood that surround the Red Line commuter train station. The Los Angeles County Metropolitan Transportation Authority wants to have housing near their train station, so they are negotiating building an immense project in a joint venture with a U.S. firm and the Chinese businessman, who is already building a complex in downtown Los Angeles.

The LACMTA in the 1980s began building the Red Line and Green Line commuter tracks. They purchased the train cars from a Japanese firm at a cost of $1 million per car.

Hiring Practices based on Race

National Center for Biotechnology Information

Although there have been some remarkable gains in the labor force status of racial minorities, significant disparities remain. African Americans are twice as likely to be unemployed as whites (Hispanics are only marginally so), and the wages of both blacks and Hispanics continue to lag well behind those of whites. A long line of research has examined the degree to which discrimination plays a role in shaping contemporary labor market disparities.

Experimental audit studies focusing on hiring decisions have consistently found strong evidence of racial discrimination, with estimates of white preference ranging from 50% to 240%. In a study, researchers mailed equivalent resumes to employers in Boston and Chicago using racially identifiable names to signal race (for example names like Jamal and Lakisha signaled African Americans, while Brad and Emily were associated with whites). White names triggered a callback rate that was 50% higher than that of equally qualified black applicants. Further, their study indicated that improving the qualifications of applicants benefited white applicants but not blacks, thus leading to a wider racial gap in response rates for those with higher skill.

Statistical studies of employment outcomes likewise reveal large racial disparities unaccounted for by observed human capital characteristics. Evidence from a fixed-effects model indicate that black men spend significantly more time searching for work, acquire less work experience, and experience less stable employment than do whites with otherwise equivalent characteristics... Controlling for age, education, urban location, and occupation, black male high school graduates are 70% more likely to experience involuntary unemployment than whites with similar characteristics, and that this disparity increases among those with higher levels of education. At more aggregate levels, research points to the persistence of occupational segregation, with racial minorities concentrated in jobs with lower levels of stability and authority and with fewer opportunities for advancement. Of course, these residual estimates cannot control for all relevant factors, such as motivation, effort, access to useful social networks, and other factors that may produce disparities in the absence of direct discrimination. Nevertheless, these estimates suggest that blacks and whites with observably similar human capital characteristics experience markedly different employment outcomes.

--NCBI.nlm.nih.gov

White women earn 78% of what white men earn. Asian women earn 79% of what Asian men earn. Hispanic and African-American women each earn 89% of what Hispanic and African-American men earn, respectively.   --pay-equity.org

Asian men are paid the highest, $56,817, followed by white men, $52,148, then African-American men, $37,526, followed by Hispanic men, $31,427. Asian women are paid on average $45,164, followed by white women, $40,558, African-American women, $33,251 and Hispanic women, $27,892.   --pay-equity.org

UNITED STATES FULL TIME WAGE AND SALARY WORKERS' EARNINGS
BY RACE, 2010 - 2014

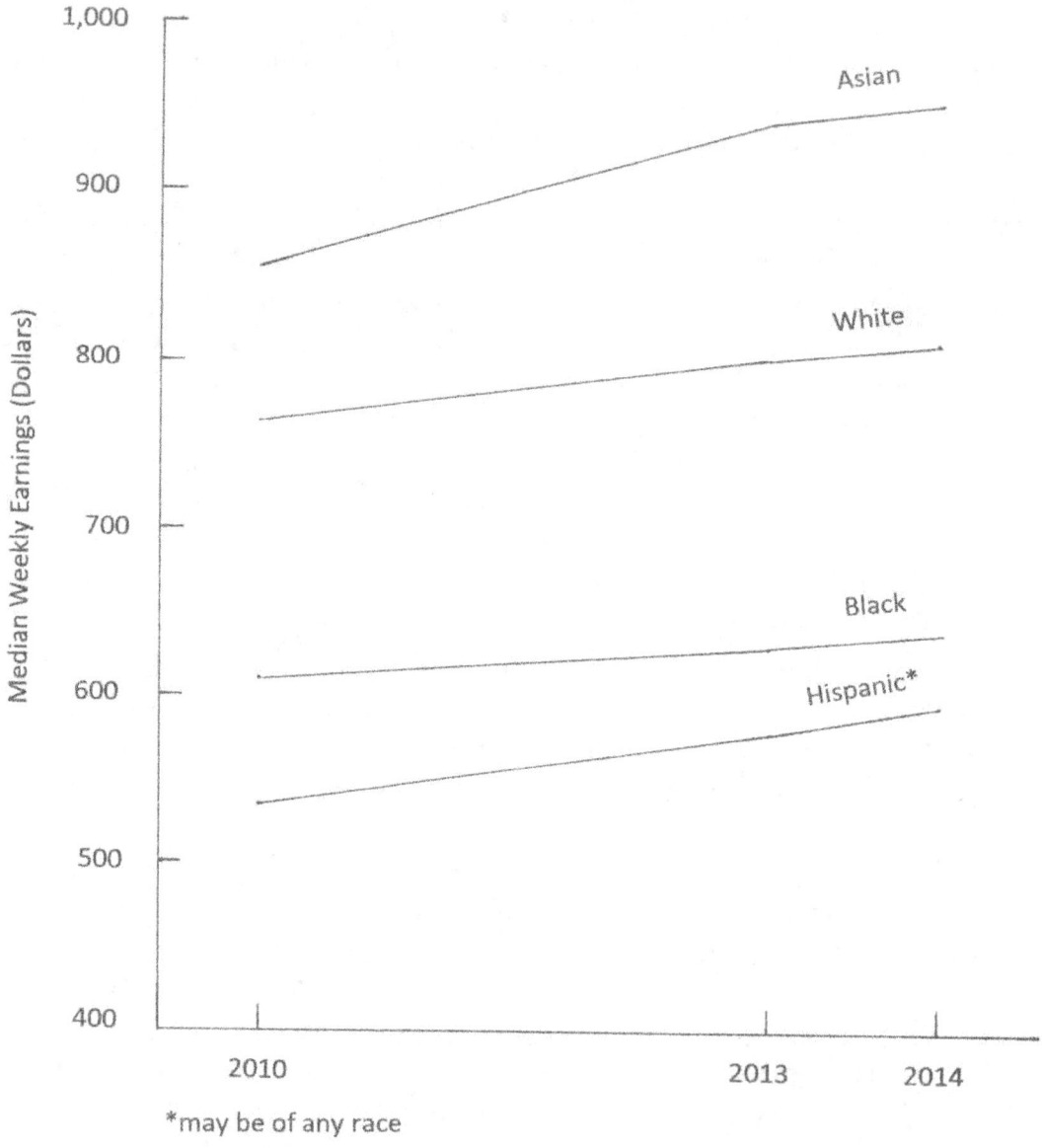

*may be of any race

Source: ProQuest Statistical Abstract of the United States 2016, p 435

U.S. WOMEN'S EARNINGS AS A PERCENTAGE OF MEN'S BY OCCUPATION
2014

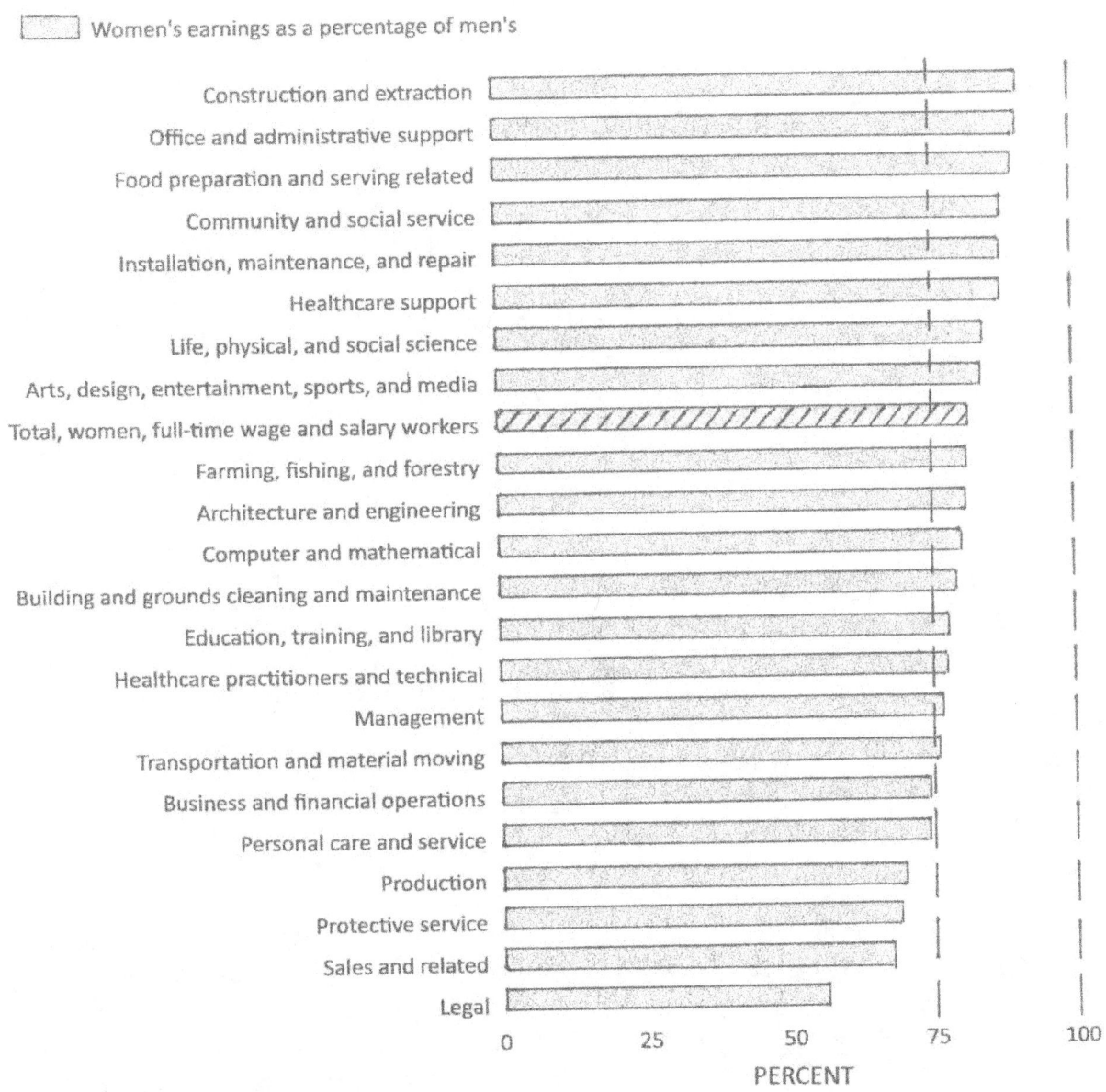

Women's earnings as a percentage of men's

"In 2014, women who worked full time in wage and salary jobs had median usual weekly earnings of $719, which was 83% of men's earnings of $871."

Source: United States Bureau of Labor Statistics

http://www.bls.gov/opub/ted/2016/womens-earnings-83-percent-of-mens-but-vary-by-occupation.htm

UNITED STATES FULL-TIME WAGE AND SALARY WORKERS,
WOMEN'S EARNINGS AS PERCENT OF MEN'S BY EDUCATION
1980 - 2014

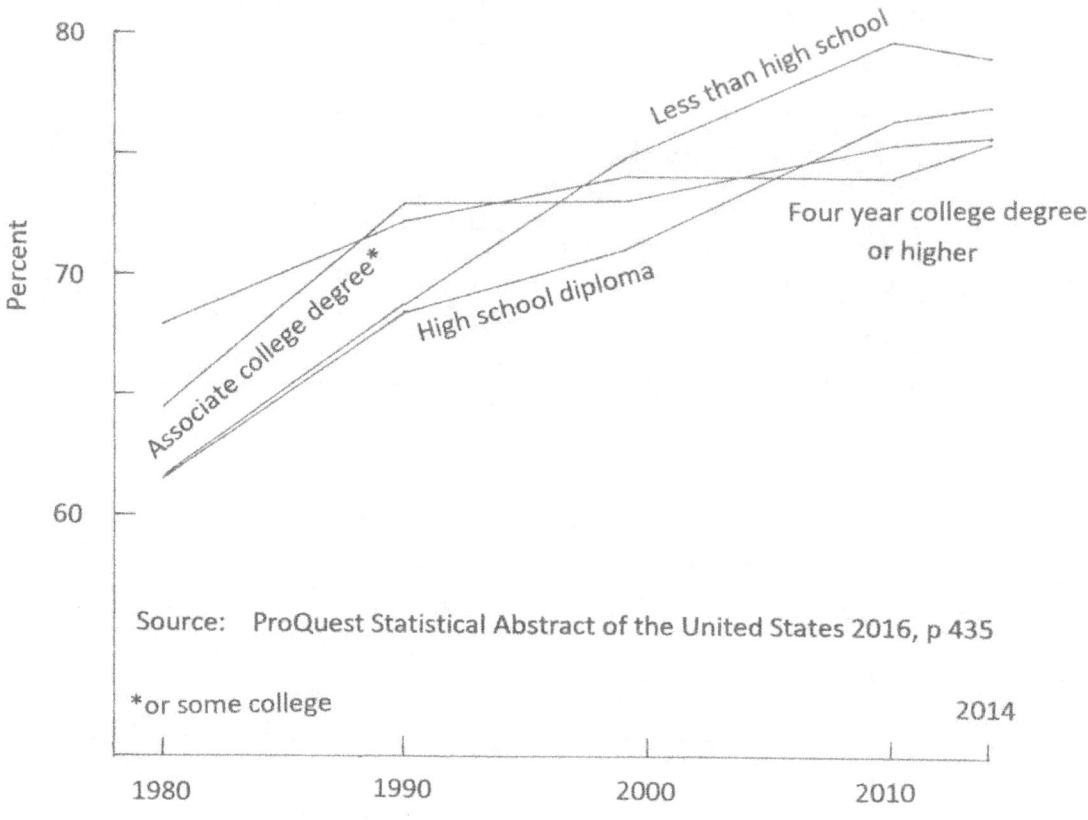

Source: ProQuest Statistical Abstract of the United States 2016, p 435

*or some college

"Only Asian-American women showed gains, with their median salary increasing from $42,335 to $46,334 or 91.9% of the earnings of all men."   --pay-equity.org

"The Gender Pay Gap is Alive and Well In All 50 States," shows a study by the AAUW, American Association of University Women, in 2014. The study covers full-time, year-round workers 16 and up.

> "In 2014, women earnings on average were 79% less than that of men's."

--huffingtonpost.com

In all 50 states, women on average earn 23% less than men. Washington, D.C. had the smallest gap, where women's pay of $60,116 equaled 90% of men's of $66,754. Wyoming came in last, where women's pay of $33,152 was 64% to men's $51,932.   --pay-equity.org

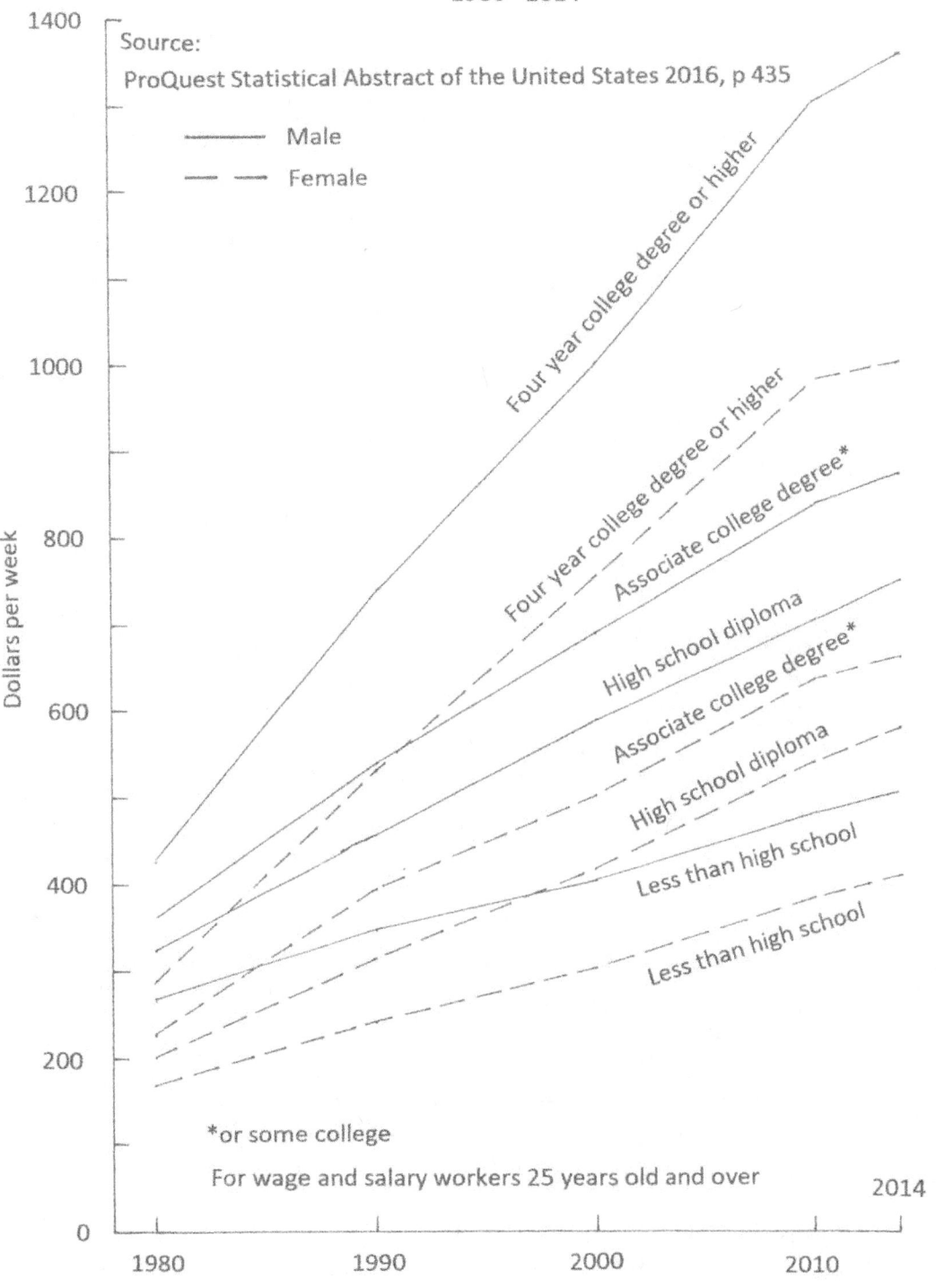

UNITED STATES MEDIAN USUAL WEEKLY EARNINGS OF FULL-TIME
WAGE AND SALARY WORKERS BY SEX AND EDUCATION
1980 - 2014

Source:
ProQuest Statistical Abstract of the United States 2016, p 435

Male
Female

Dollars per week

Four year college degree or higher

Four year college degree or higher

Associate college degree*

High school diploma

Associate college degree*

High school diploma

Less than high school

Less than high school

*or some college

For wage and salary workers 25 years old and over

1400
1200
1000
800
600
400
200
0

1980   1990   2000   2010   2014

"While greater education does increase women's overall earnings, it does not
significantly close the gender wage gap. At every academic achievement level,
women's median salaries are less then men's by AT LEAST 21%." --pay-equity.org

UNITED STATES CORPORATE PROFITS VERSUS LEGAL IMMIGRATION
1970 - 1993

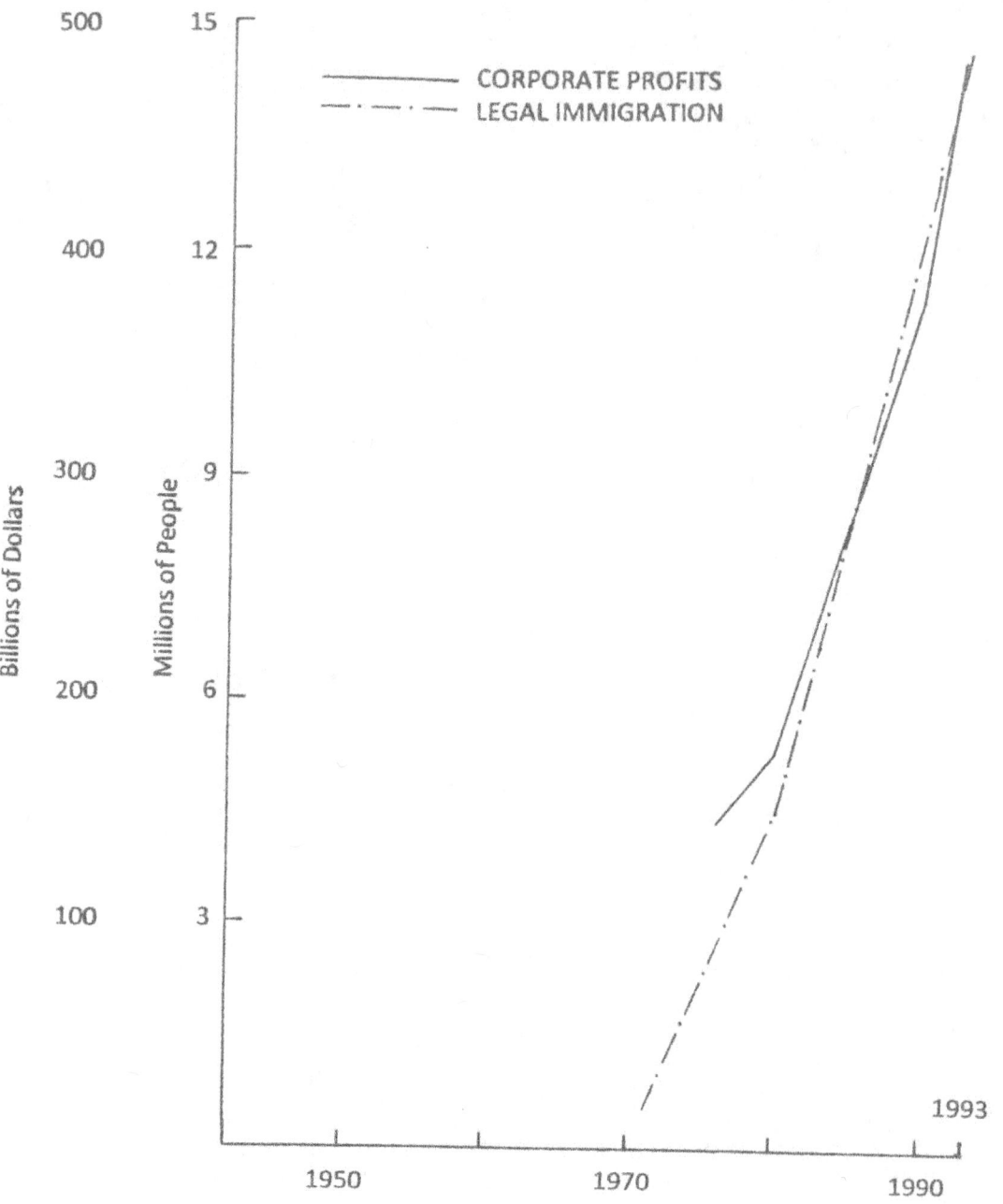

Source: Statistical Abstract of the United States 1995, p 11

Standard & Poor's Statistical Service 1995, pp 98-100

The greater the number of customers, the larger the profit potential.

Going global is the greatest profit potential of all.

"CONGRESS SHALL HAVE POWER TO ... REGULATE COMMERCE
WITH FOREIGN NATIONS"

Article I, Section 8
Constitution of the United States

"CONGRESS SHALL HAVE POWER TO LAY AND COLLECT TAXES, DUTIES
IMPOSTS AND EXCISES"

Article I, Section 8
Constitution of the United States

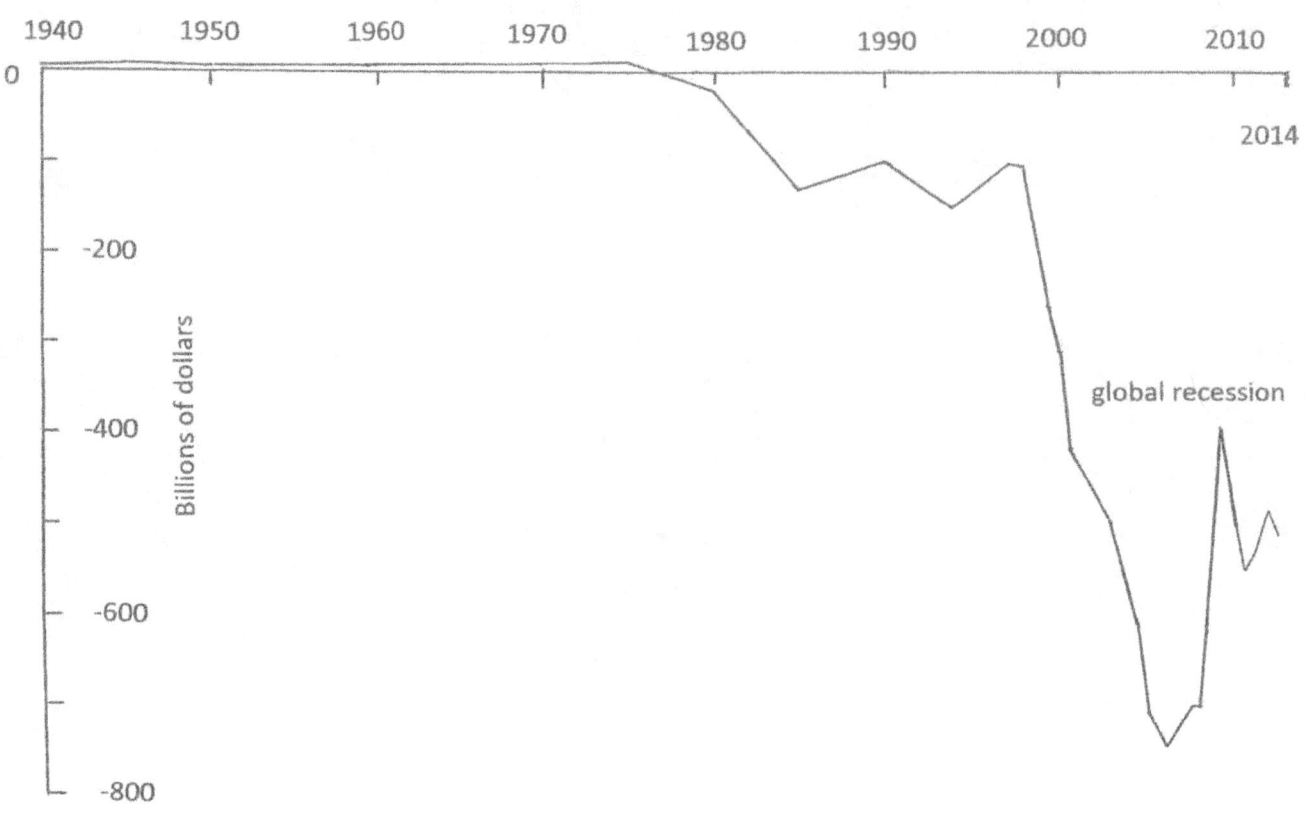

U.S INTERNATIONAL TRADE BALANCE IN GOODS AND SERVICES
1940 - 2014

Billions of dollars

global recession

2014

Sources: ProQuest Statistical Abstract of the United States 2016, p 824
Statistical Abstract of the United States 2012, p 804; 2004-2005, p 811

Since 2000 U.S. trade in goods and services has a deficit
average of over half a trillion dollars.

U.S. trade in services is consistently profitable.

U.S. trade in exported goods is high, reaching $784 billion in 2000,
$1.29 trillion in 2010 and consistently growing to $1.63 trillion in 2014.

U.S. trade losses are due to imported goods, reaching $1.23 trillion
in 2000 and growing to $2.37 trillion in 2014.

Controlling imported goods would keep a half trillion dollars in the
U.S. annually, provide manufacturing jobs, higher tax receipts for
government at all levels, and reduce poverty and its costs.

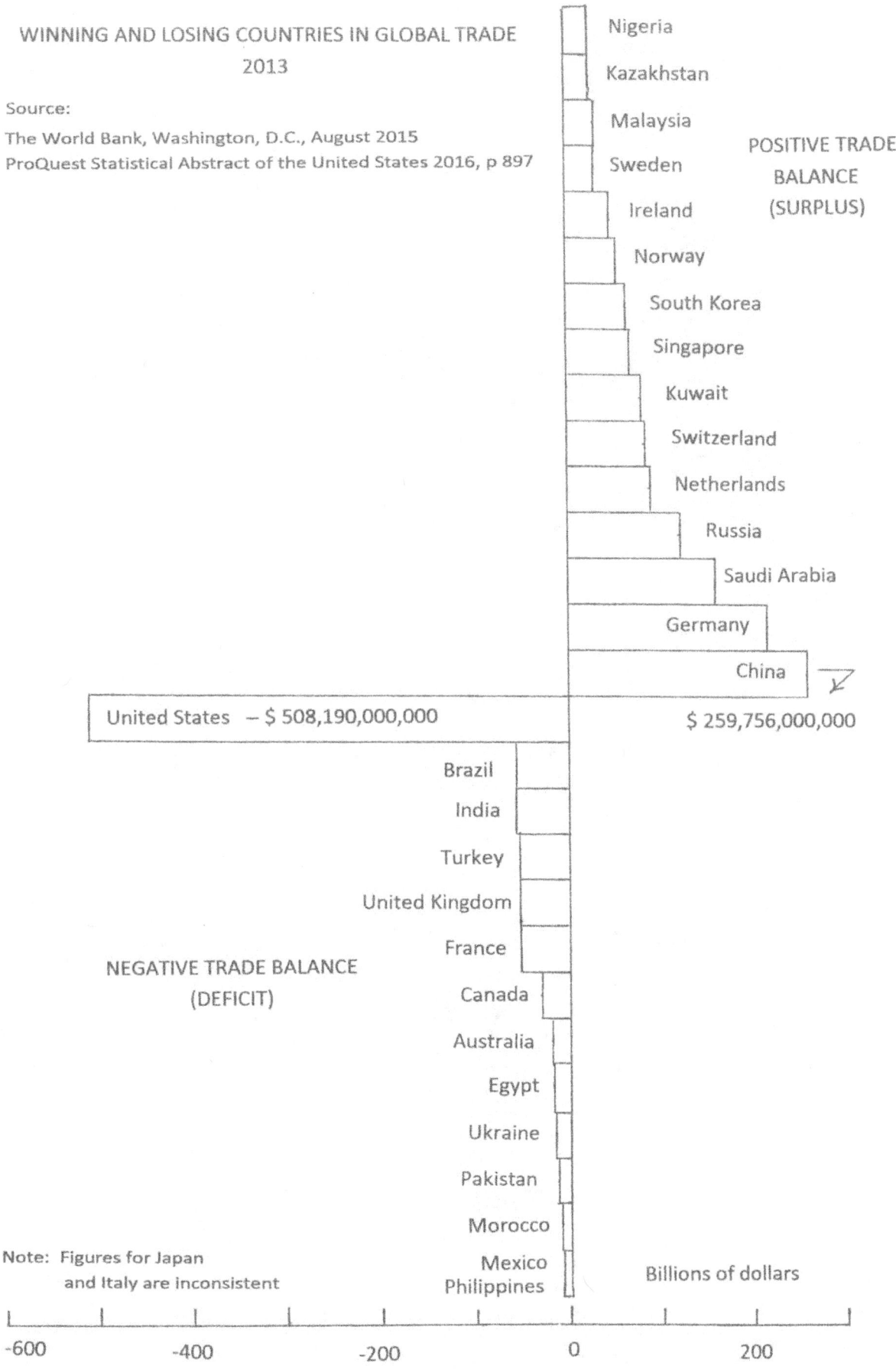

WINNING AND LOSING COUNTRIES IN GLOBAL TRADE
2013

Source:

The World Bank, Washington, D.C., August 2015
ProQuest Statistical Abstract of the United States 2016, p 897

POSITIVE TRADE
BALANCE
(SURPLUS)

Nigeria
Kazakhstan
Malaysia
Sweden
Ireland
Norway
South Korea
Singapore
Kuwait
Switzerland
Netherlands
Russia
Saudi Arabia
Germany
China

United States   − $ 508,190,000,000

$ 259,756,000,000

Brazil
India
Turkey
United Kingdom
France
Canada
Australia
Egypt
Ukraine
Pakistan
Morocco
Mexico
Philippines

NEGATIVE TRADE BALANCE
(DEFICIT)

Note: Figures for Japan
        and Italy are inconsistent

Billions of dollars

-600   -400   -200   0   200

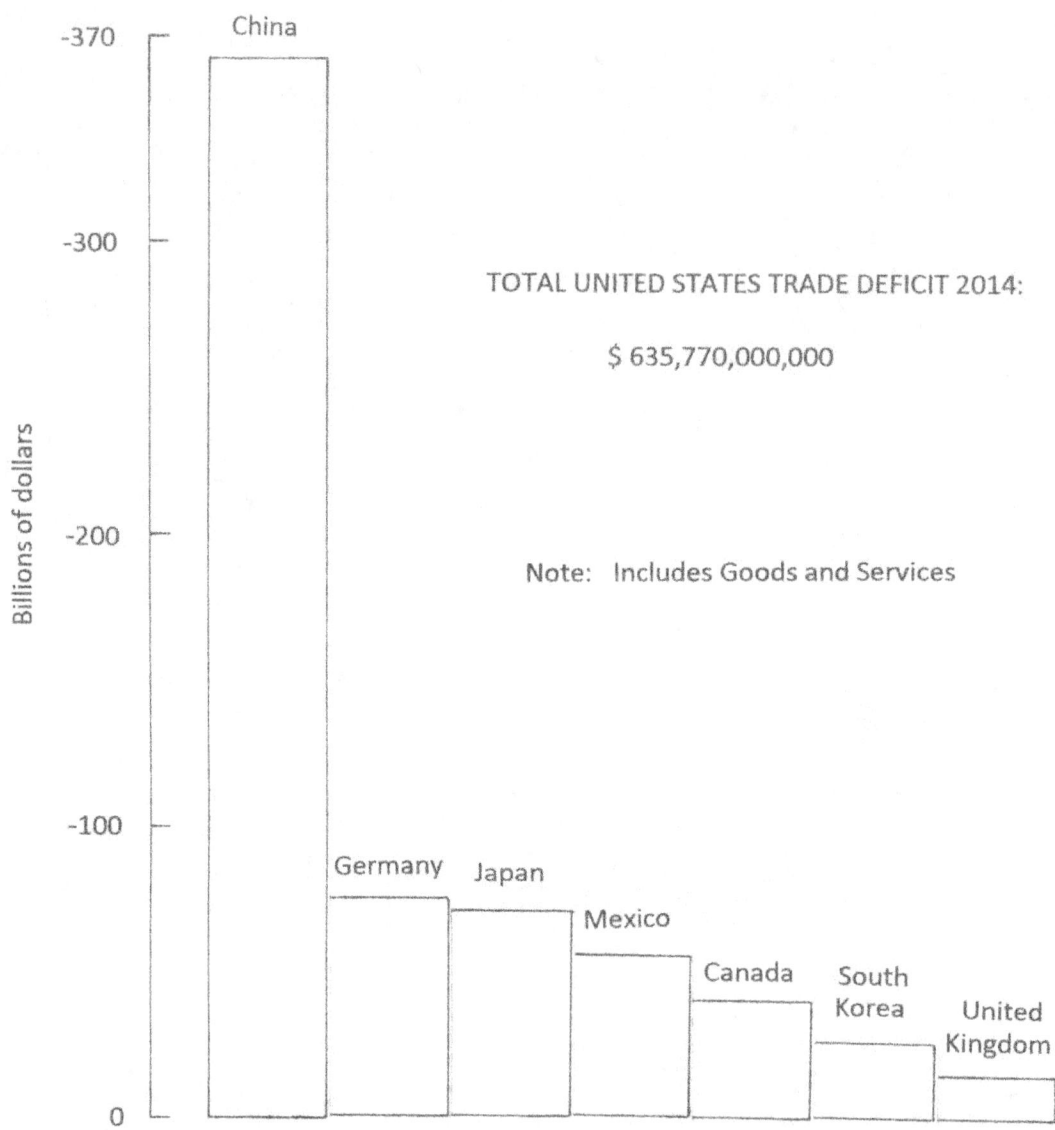

UNITED STATES TRADE DEFICIT BY COUNTRY, 2014

TOTAL UNITED STATES TRADE DEFICIT 2014:

$ 635,770,000,000

Note: Includes Goods and Services

Billions of dollars

-370   China

-300

-200

-100

Germany   Japan

Mexico

Canada   South
Korea   United
Kingdom

0

Source: The World Almanac and Book of Facts 2016, p 75

TRADE RESULTING IN UNITED STATES DEFICITS, BY COUNTRY
2010

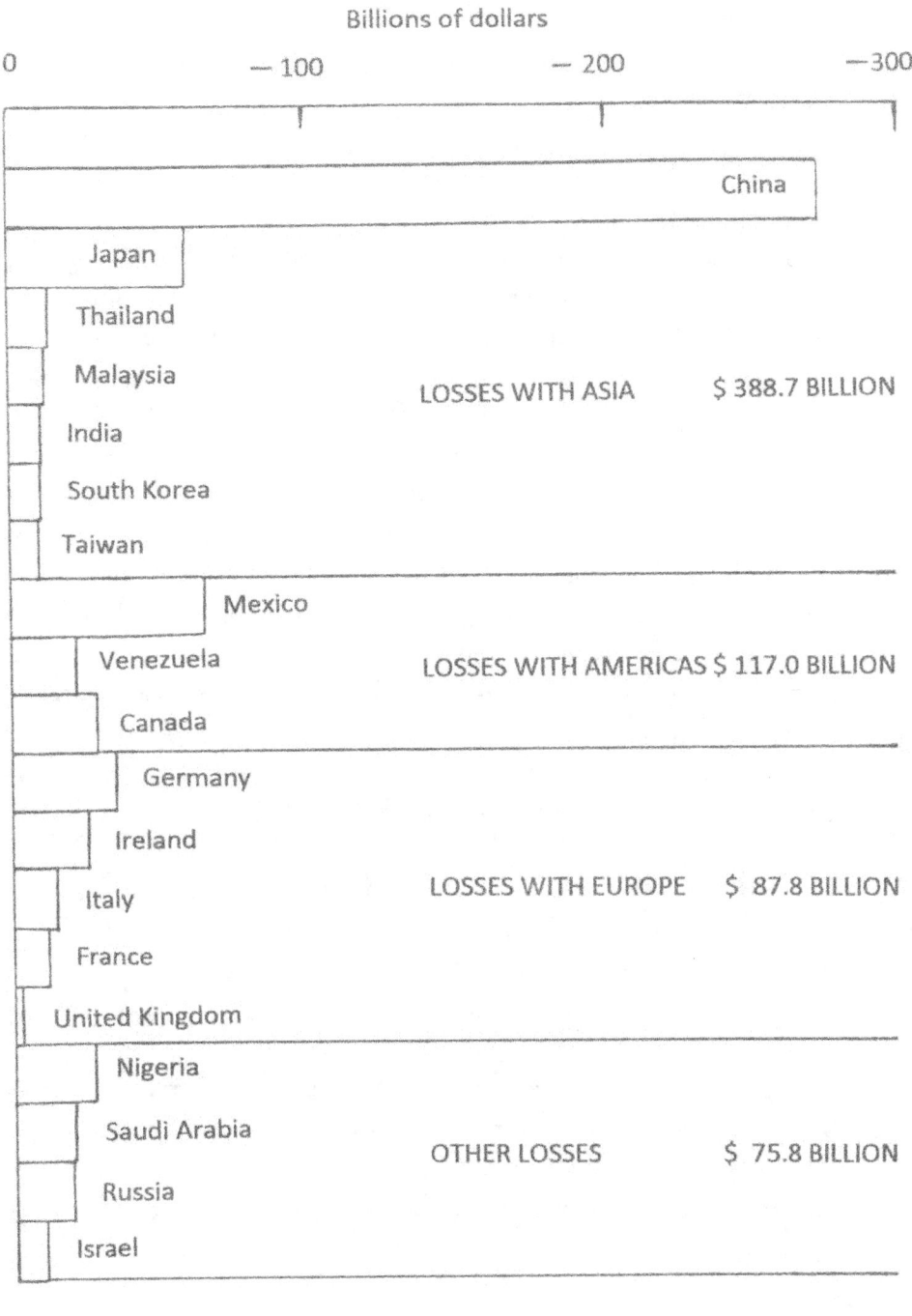

Billions of dollars

| 0 | — 100 | — 200 | — 300 |

China

Japan

Thailand

Malaysia

LOSSES WITH ASIA $ 388.7 BILLION

India

South Korea

Taiwan

Mexico

Venezuela   LOSSES WITH AMERICAS $ 117.0 BILLION

Canada

Germany

Ireland

Italy   LOSSES WITH EUROPE $ 87.8 BILLION

France

United Kingdom

Nigeria

Saudi Arabia   OTHER LOSSES $ 75.8 BILLION

Russia

Israel

TOTAL U.S. LOSS: $ 669.3 BILLION

Source: The World Almanac and Book of Facts 2012, p 55

96

Trade with Japan

After World War II, when most of the world was devastated, Japan looked ahead. The country decided that exports would pave their way to growth and prosperity. They sent colorful paper umbrellas that restaurants used in kids' Shirley Temple drinks. They sent hibachis, monkey pod bowls, beach mats and paper lanterns to places like Trident Imports on the Seattle waterfront.

They were selling plywood to Weyerhauser in Longview, Washington, because the Japanese could make it cheaper, especially since Weyerhauser sent over the wood. By the 1950s, they were selling Sony and Mitsubishi TV sets in Whitefront discount stores cheaper than the Admirals and RCAs. In 1974, the Hondas and the Datsuns started flooding in.

1974 was a pivotal year. For one thing, it was the year Americans first became aware of limited resources. In the early 1970s, the OPEC oil producing countries instituted a trade embargo, and by January 1974, for the first and only time, Americans were waiting in long lines to pump gas at the few stations that had gasoline. A gallon went from 25 cents to 75 cents in the next few months. Americans began thinking about the fuel mileage of their cars. Suddenly these new smaller, lighter cars from Japan appeared with great mileage and easily passed new government smog regulations. It was almost like a setup.

"Look, this metal's so thin you can dent it with your thumb," said one UCLA professor in a parking lot by the Molecular Biology Institute.

American car companies didn't think the cheap little Japanese cars would hit the mainstream. They kept building big gas guzzlers. The cheap little cars and light trucks were exported around the world. Along with consumer electronics, the auto industry was quickly making Japan the second largest economy in the world, after the United States.

The government of Japan had organized MITI, the Ministry of International Trade and Industry, in 1952 in Osaka for the purpose of export promotion. In 1958 they renamed it METI, the Ministry of Economy, Trade and Industry, half funded by the government. In 2003 they established JETRO, the Japan External Trade Organization, with offices in fifty-five countries as of 2011. These agencies were the global promoters of Japanese exports.

When Ronald Reagan became president of the United States in January 1981, he pursued his platform of deregulation. One of his first moves was to allow Japanese car companies to set up "Foreign Trade Zones" so they could manufacture cars in the United States that would not be classified as imports. Ten plants were established in the 1980s, mostly in Midwest states but also Ontario, Canada, plus hundreds of auto parts companies nearby.

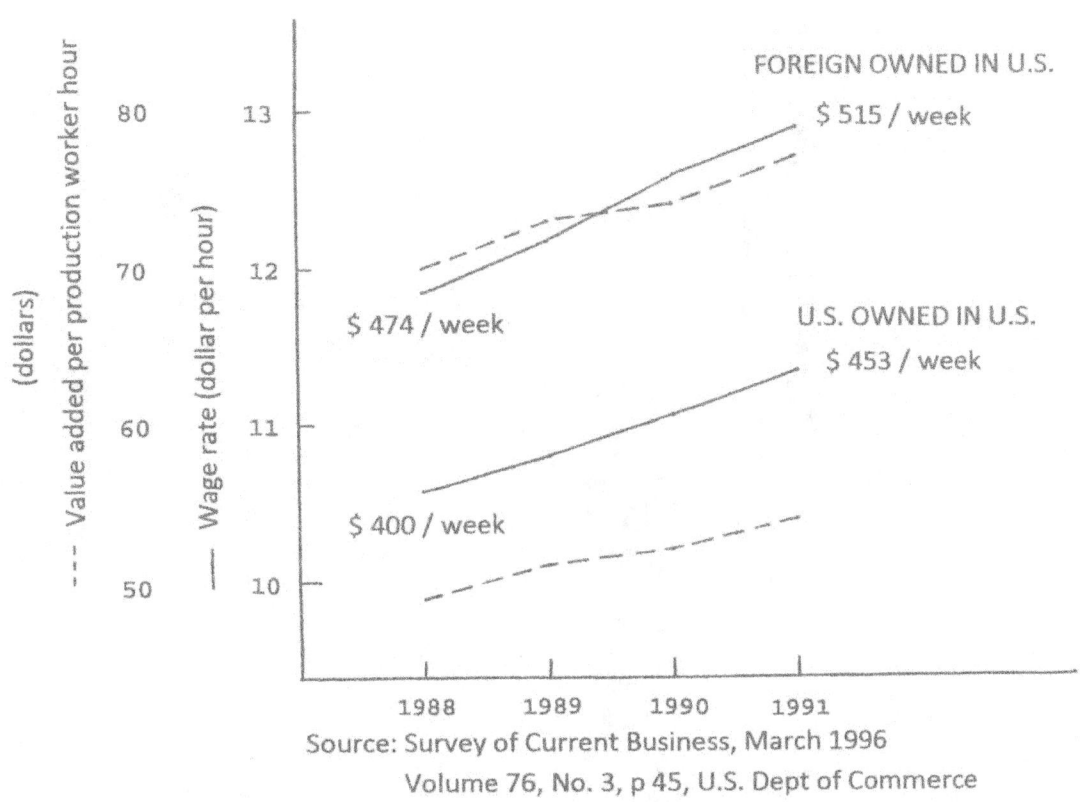

FOREIGN AND DOMESTIC WAGE DIFFERENTIAL IN U.S.

FOREIGN OWNED IN U.S.
$ 515 / week

U.S. OWNED IN U.S.
$ 453 / week

$ 474 / week

$ 400 / week

Value added per production worker hour (dollars)

Wage rate (dollar per hour)

1988   1989   1990   1991

Source: Survey of Current Business, March 1996
Volume 76, No. 3, p 45, U.S. Dept of Commerce

State and local governments offered incentives such as delayed taxes or reduced leases to woo the Japanese companies and the jobs they would provide. The Japanese paid higher wages than the prevailing rates so that U.S. workers would not seek union membership. As the cars flooded the marketplace, the profits went across the Pacific, as did corporate income taxes. The IRS has murky income tax rules country by country.

It wasn't just foreign car companies that came to the U.S. to set up shop. Financial institutions such as Union Bank, oil companies such as Royal Dutch Shell, consumer products such as Nestle, pharmaceuticals such as Bayer, and retailers such as Ikea, came, too. At the same time, U.S. companies could relocate overseas, expanding their customer base while finding tax advantages in being offshore.

When Reagan left office, the Japanese invited him and Nancy to Japan. There the couple was feted for a week, which purportedly cost $6 million, plus another $2 million that was an outright gift to the Reagans, newspapers reported.

H.W. Bush became president in January 1989. In 1990, the U.S. suddenly awarded China "most-favored-nation" status, sharply reducing tariffs and quotas on Chinese imports. Bush also signed a new bill called NAFTA, the North American Free Trade Agreement between the United States, Canada and Mexico on December 17, 1992, weeks before leaving office. While media attention in 1992 concentrated on NAFTA and the incredible emergence of the internet, the other new phenomenon had quietly begun: the importation of consumer goods from China.

UNITED STATES - JAPAN WORLD TRADE
1995

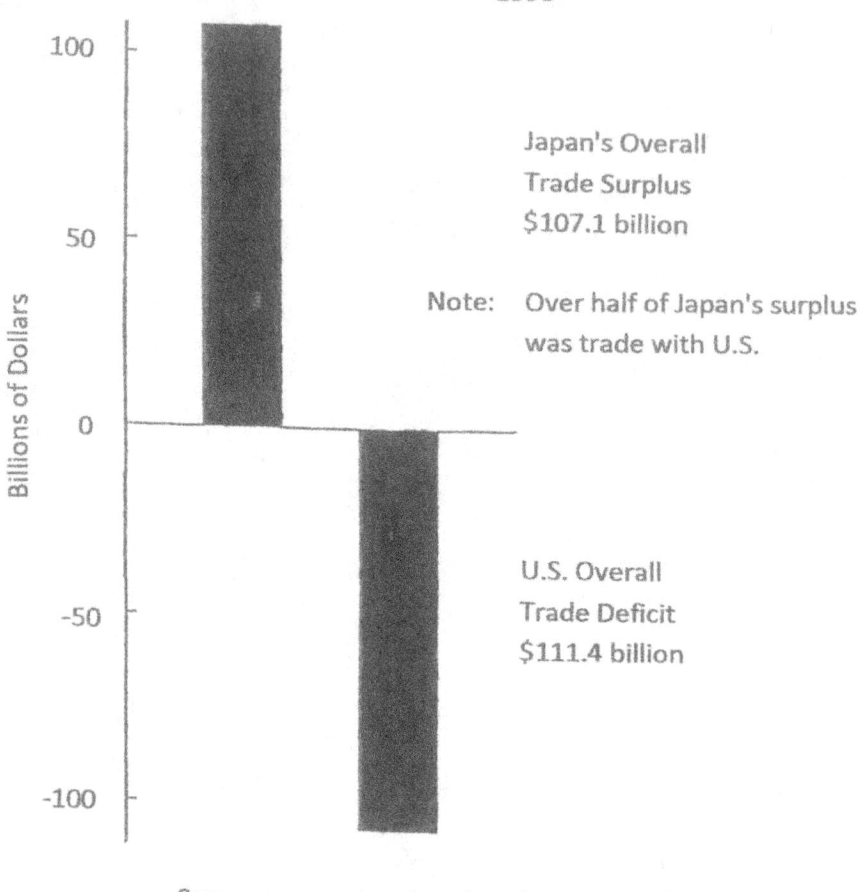

Japan's Overall
Trade Surplus
$107.1 billion

Note: Over half of Japan's surplus
was trade with U.S.

U.S. Overall
Trade Deficit
$111.4 billion

Sources: Los Angeles Times, Jan. 24, 1996, p D2;
Feb 29, 1996, p D2

There was no media coverage. Americans just started seeing merchandise, inexpensive merchandise, on the shelves labeled, "Made in China." The immediate impact was the demise of the U.S. apparel industry, which had been producing 94% of clothing for Americans. Soon shelves were flooded with Chinese goods, crowding out goods "Made in the U.S.A."

Bill Clinton confirmed NAFTA by signing off on it December 8, 1993, for implementation on January 1, 1994. In a speech, he said:

"This is a defining moment for our nation, and it's important to the rest of the world. We decided we would compete and not retreat. 200,000 jobs in the U.S. alone will be created. We will have social progress plus economic growth, leading toward world trade. For two decades Americans have been losing jobs. The way to growth is exports. We have the opportunity to re-create the world. Once again, we are leading. We will build security and prosperity for our people."

WORLD'S 100 MOST POWERFUL CORPORATIONS, 1992

Gross Revenues in Billions of Dollars

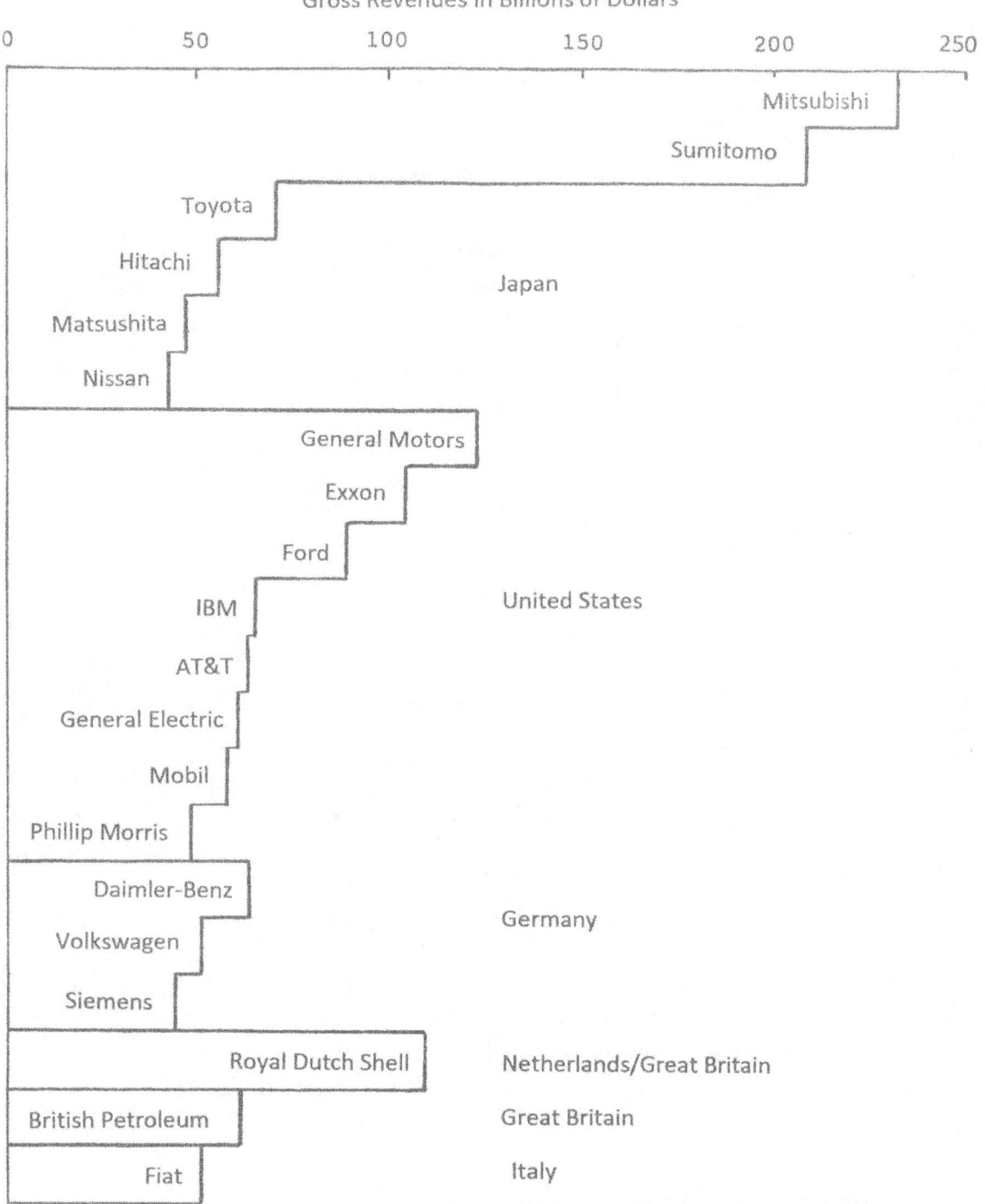

"The globalization of business has given a new prominence to the leading multinational companies. They, rather than governments, increasingly are the primary players in the world economy."

—Philip Mattera, p xi

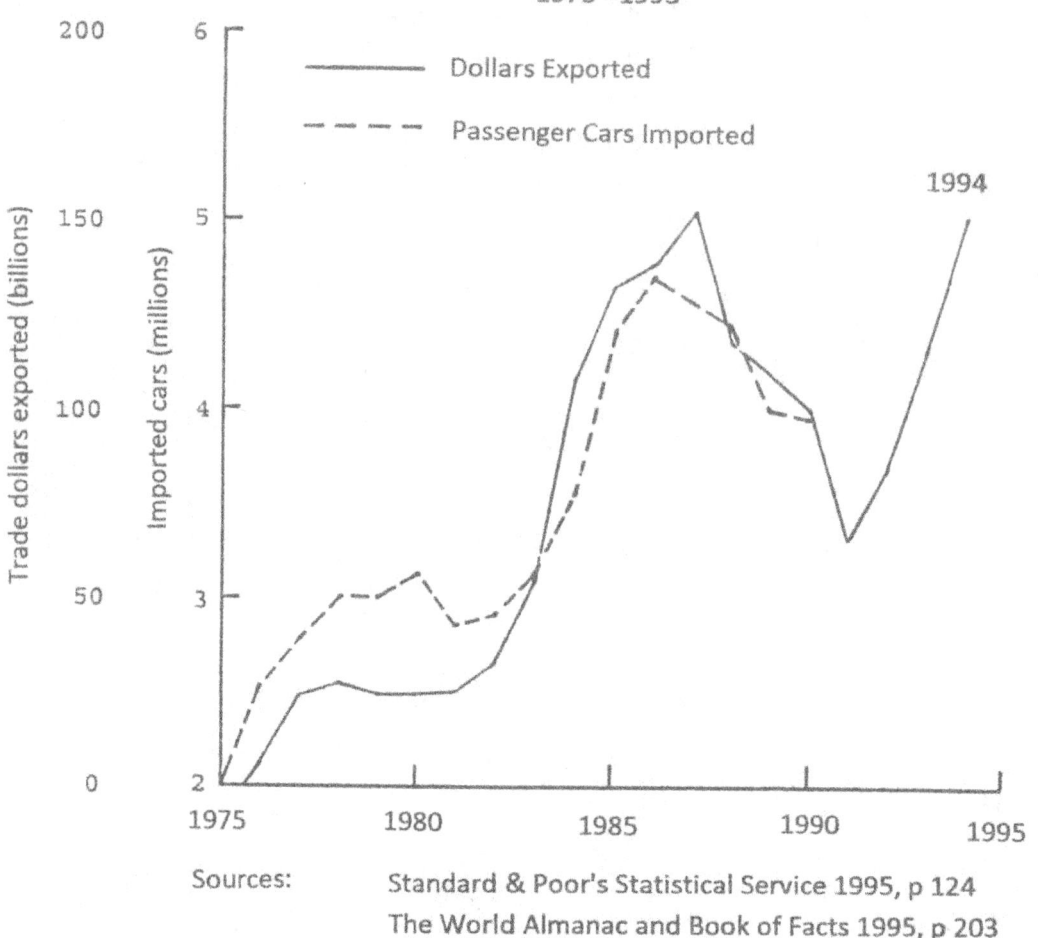

AUTOS IMPORTED TO THE UNITED STATES, DOLLARS EXPORTED
1975 - 1995

Dollars Exported

Passenger Cars Imported

1994

Trade dollars exported (billions)

Imported cars (millions)

Sources: Standard & Poor's Statistical Service 1995, p 124
             The World Almanac and Book of Facts 1995, p 203

Every person in the United States who purchases a new foreign car or light truck
is sending corporate profits thereof out of the United States, enriching a
foreign country and depleting the United States.

The United States was most prosperous when nearly all new cars and light trucks
were produced by U.S. companies on U.S. soil for U.S. consumption.

Importing new cars and light trucks for consumption is a drain on any country.

When Bill Clinton became president in January 1993, a steady stream of Asian
businessmen with Chinese ties visited the White House, including Charlie Trie and Johnny
Chung. The media didn't report the comings and goings of the foreign White House visitors
until Clinton was re-elected, but by 1997 the media was saturated with reports of lavish
White House dinners at taxpayer expense with Chinese dignitaries who could stay as guests
in the Lincoln bedroom. The press reported a myriad of campaign contributions, often to the
Democratic National Committee. Many donations were returned when it was discovered
they had come from foreign sources, which were illegal.

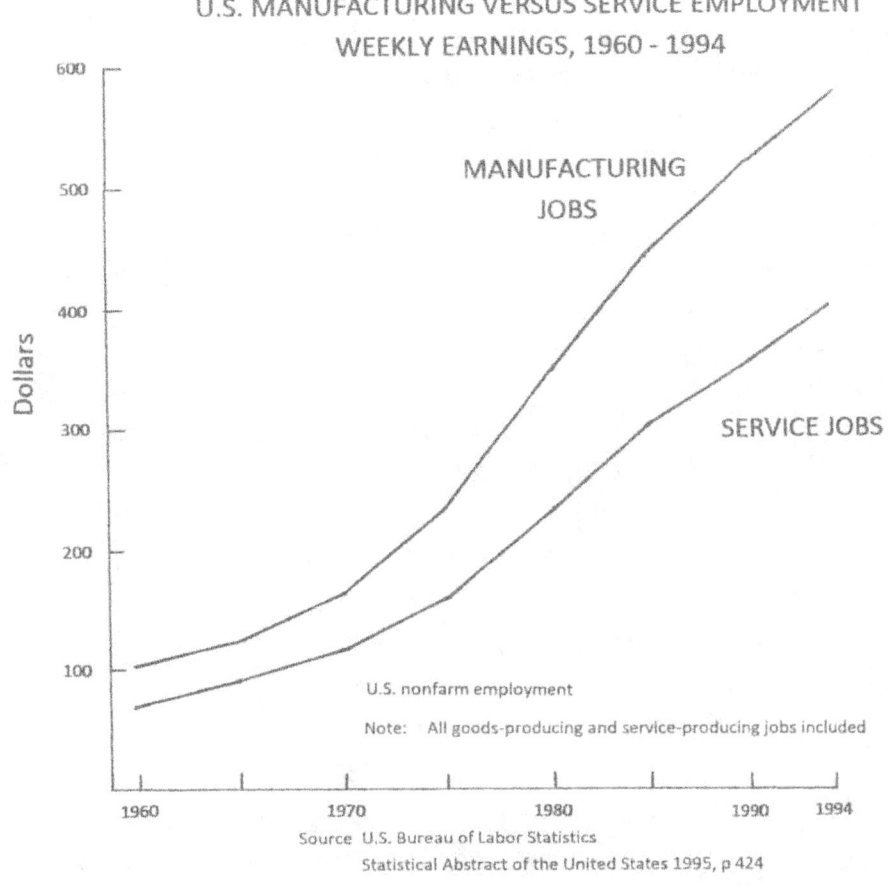

U.S. MANUFACTURING VERSUS SERVICE EMPLOYMENT
WEEKLY EARNINGS, 1960 - 1994

MANUFACTURING JOBS

SERVICE JOBS

U.S. nonfarm employment

Note: All goods-producing and service-producing jobs included

Source U.S. Bureau of Labor Statistics
Statistical Abstract of the United States 1995, p 424

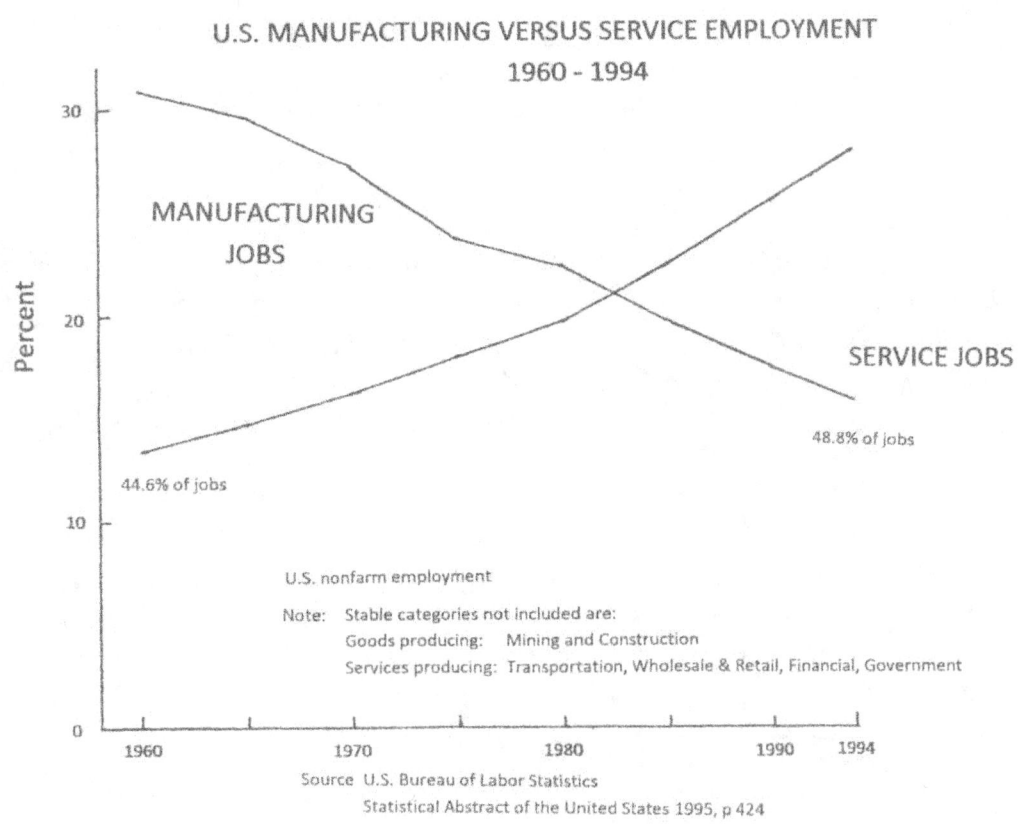

U.S. MANUFACTURING VERSUS SERVICE EMPLOYMENT
1960 - 1994

MANUFACTURING JOBS

SERVICE JOBS

44.6% of jobs

48.8% of jobs

U.S. nonfarm employment

Note: Stable categories not included are:
Goods producing: Mining and Construction
Services producing: Transportation, Wholesale & Retail, Financial, Government

Source U.S. Bureau of Labor Statistics
Statistical Abstract of the United States 1995, p 424

In 1992, democrat Dianne Feinstein was elected Senator from California. Her husband, Richard Blum, had business dealings in China that expanded dramatically in the mid 1990s. While the Feinsteins deny that her Senate seat had any effect on her husband's businesses, she made several trips to Beijing in the mid 1990s to visit Chinese President Jiang Zemin with her husband by her side.

Federal investigations began. Chinese visitors to the Clinton White House were not registering their affiliations. They were making illegal campaign contributions. They were currying favor, evident when Clinton asked for a "fast track" authority on trade agreements, which Congress denied. A Canadian intelligence official wrote in 1996 that the Chinese had agents of influence in government, academia, the media, and the private business sector in both Canada and the U.S.

> A think tank writer, John Bolton, said,
> "These accusations go beyond old fashioned bribery.
> Now you are talking about subversion."

Meanwhile, the consequences of NAFTA began to appear. Companies immediately realized they could build factories in Mexico and Canada for importation of goods to the U.S. without having to deal with U.S. environmental concerns or high wages and benefits for workers, at least in Mexico. Plus they would have access to cheap land and close proximity to middle class consumers in both Canada and the U.S. It was a win-win for foreign companies and our two neighboring countries, plus a big win for their workers. The price predictably was a substantial loss of jobs for U.S. workers, the loss of federal income tax revenue both individual and corporate, and a draining economy resulting in a U.S. recession in the early nineties.

Cosco, the Chinese Ocean Shipping Company, has been operating in the Port of Long Beach, California, since 1981, but when the Pentagon closed the Long Beach Naval Station at the port in 1991, Cosco's operations took off. Cosco, China's state-run shipping line, agreed to lease a wharf if the Port of Long Beach would build a huge terminal on the site. The Ports of Long Beach and Los Angeles now comprise the largest port in the U.S.

By 1992, another event that barely made the news was the fallout from the takeover of Hong Kong from Britain to China, due to be take place July 1, 1997. The largest group of emigres left in 1992 to Vancouver and Toronto, Canada, and Sydney, Australia. Prime Minister Margaret Thatcher attempted to keep control of Hong Kong, but immediately encountered fierce aggression from the Communist party leaders and backed off. The timing of the Chinese takeover of Hong Kong, the signing of NAFTA, and the expansion of the Port of Long Beach converged to feel like another plan was brewing.

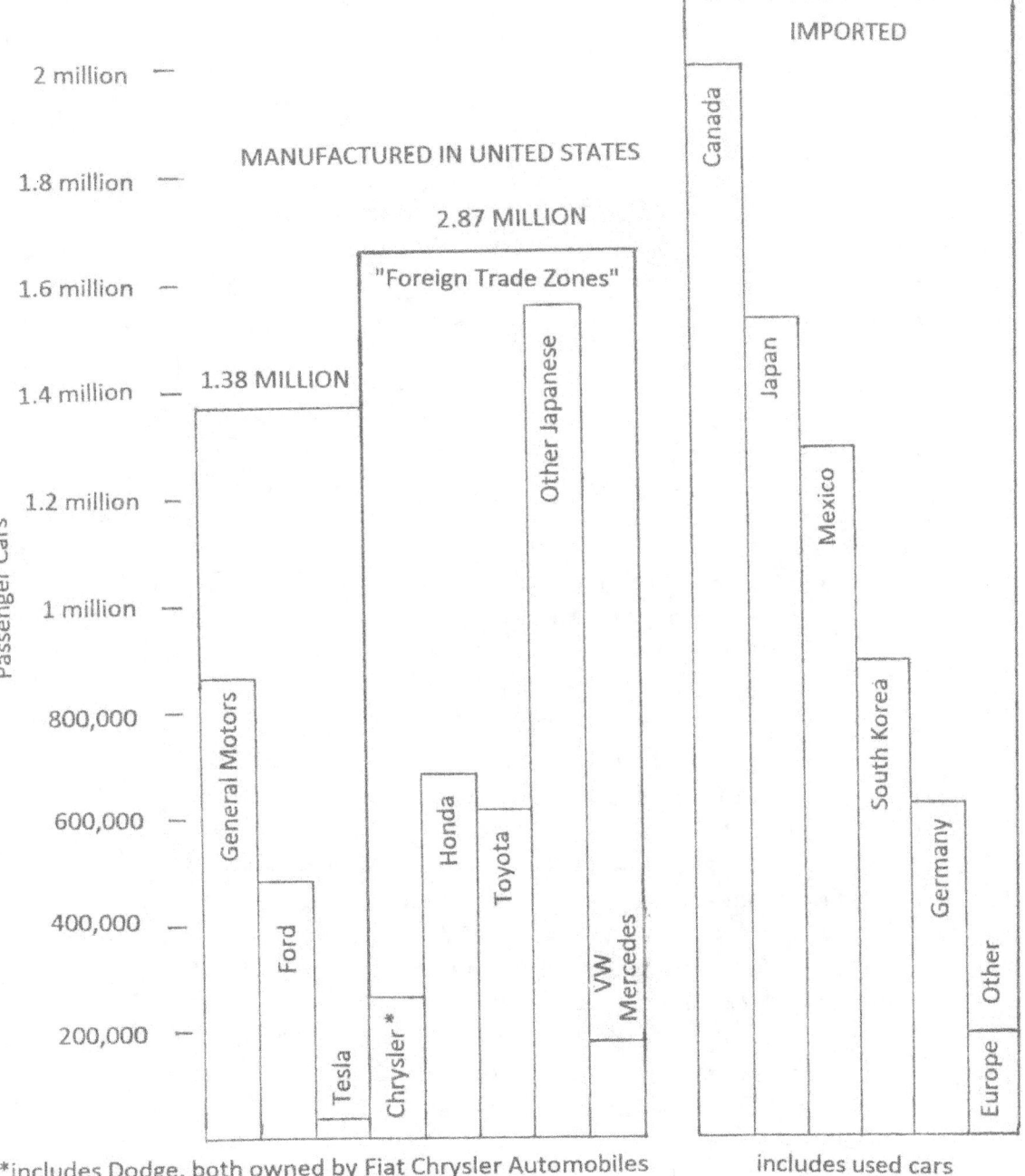

PASSENGER CARS
MANUFACTURED FOR U.S. MARKET, 2014

TOTAL AUTOS: 10.79 MILLION

MANUFACTURED OUTSIDE
UNITED STATES
6.54 MILLION

IMPORTED

Canada

MANUFACTURED IN UNITED STATES

2.87 MILLION

Japan

"Foreign Trade Zones"

Mexico

1.38 MILLION

Other Japanese

2 million

1.8 million

1.6 million

1.4 million

1.2 million

1 million

800,000

600,000

400,000

200,000

Passenger Cars

General Motors

Ford

Tesla

Chrysler *

Honda

Toyota

VW

Mercedes

South Korea

Germany

Other

Europe

*includes Dodge, both owned by Fiat Chrysler Automobiles

includes used cars

Source: The World Almanac and Book of Facts 2016, pp 79-80

Trade with China

The country was barely absorbing the profound effects of NAFTA when suddenly a new trade agreement was on the table. The WTO, the World Trade Organization, was started on January 1, 1995. U.S. government officials signed on that very day. Based in Geneva, Switzerland, the WTO has a staff of 640. The founders are:

Hong Kong
Japan
Dominica
France
Austria
Denmark

Lest we forget, Hong Kong at that very moment was being absorbed into China.

> The WTO touts itself as "the only international organization dealing with trade between nations." It "ensures that trade flows as smoothly, predictably and freely as possible."   WTO.org

For the benefit of whom? China, obviously, but certainly not for the benefit of the United States, nor such places as Kano, Nigeria:

THE ROAD FROM BEGGAR TO MILITANT
Los Angeles Times   Aug 17, 2014   p A3

KANO, Nigeria - They scurry between vehicles in the traffic-choked cities of northern Nigeria, small boys in tattered clothing armed with begging tins.

Known as the almajiri, the youngsters, some no older than 5, have flooded the streets for the nearly 15 years since a tsunami of cheap Chinese imports and a dysfunctional electrical system began destroying the region's once-thriving textile manufacturing industry. Many more children have streamed in from rural areas since similar collapses of the fishing and agriculture sectors left their parents unable to feed them...

After Nigeria joined the World Trade Organization in 1995, removing tariffs and quotas that had protected the textile and food industries, cheap Chinese goods became available in quantity. Kano's factories started closing around 2000.

Meanwhile, Lake Chad and its fishing catch began to shrink, caused by overuse and climate change. The joint collapses have left a generation with limited ways to scrape by: washing cars; hawking candies, beads, water and fruit; panhandling; or stealing. The entire Muslim-dominated northern region has suffered, including Maiduguri, the birthplace of Boko Haram and a trade center dependent on Kano.

"In my factory, it costs $1 to make a shirt," said Nasir Adhama, the oldest son of the Adhama business. "But the Chinese make a dozen for a dollar, so how can I compete with them?"

Panhandling was recently banned in Kano in an attempt to reduce the sea of almajiri on the streets. Yet they remain visible, hollow-cheeked, anxious, their hands extended.   by Robyn Dixon

Enormous U.S. trade deficits with China are enriching China, a Communist country not particularly friendly to its neighbors or even to its own people. As of July 2016, 164 countries are members of the WTO, according to Wikipedia, so now goods from all over the world are being imported to the United States, with the concomitant loss of U.S. jobs.

DO JOBS DATA REFLECT HEALTH OF ECONOMY?
Los Angeles Times   July 22, 2016   p C1

On Friday, California will release its monthly jobs report...One month's results will not reveal much, unless they're stacked against several past reports covering a longer period of economic activity.

The 440,300 jobs that employers officially added in the last 12 months include anyone who worked at least one hour per week.

California's manufacturing jobs shrunk from 1.84 million in 2000 to 1.28 million in 2016. California's manufacturing workforce makes up 10% of the nation's total, but it is expected to continue to shrink.   by Natalie Kitroeff

In 2014, Ford, General Motors and Tesla had less than 7% of U.S. market share in passenger cars, whereas in the booming 1950s U.S. companies had close to 100%. Japanese car advertisements flood the marketplace, and consumers generally feel that Japanese cars are better made than American cars, but most of the recalls for defective parts are in Japanese cars. Toyota had the most recalls in 2013. Their cars had defective gas pedals causing "forced acceleration," a condition that caused fatalities and launched a U.S. criminal investigation. Honda recalled vehicles for stability system problems.

There is a growing consensus that automobiles are becoming less reliable. The problem may be quality control at the factories where they are produced. 3.3 million cars were imported from Canada and Mexico in 2014, but neither country has its own brands being sold in the U.S., so the brands coming in are brands U.S. customers know, but without U.S. regulation. The latest scare is potential explosions from faulty air bags in millions of cars.

28.8 million cars in the U.S. were recalled in 2013, followed by 35 to 40 million more recalls in 2014 due to possibly faulty Takata air bags It was the biggest automotive recall in U.S. history. The airbags were exploding, blowing pieces of metal shrapnel in the faces of drivers. Takata Corporation, based in Tokyo since 1933, has 48,775 employees. Ammonium nitrate in the airbags is supposed to explode in a crash to cause the airbags to inflate. In June 2014, the company said a Mexican subsidiary mishandled the manufacturing of the airbag explosive elements and improperly stored the chemicals. It also said moisture might be the cause.

In July 2014, a pregnant Malaysian driver was going thirty miles per hour when she was involved in a crash, which caused a metal fragment from a ruptured airbag to slice into her neck. Both she and her baby daughter, born later, were killed. In November 2014, BMW announced they were moving their orders from a Mexican plant to a Takata plant in Germany. In August 2016, a truck in Texas hauling Takata parts crashed, causing the cargo to explode. The explosion destroyed a house and killed the woman inside.

China and Japan have a tacit agreement not to compete with each other in the United States and elsewhere. It is now clear that since 1992 Japan was to keep its tight rein on automobiles and consumer electronics, while China could manufacture everything else. China has just completed the widening of the Panama Canal, which it leases from Panama, so that its newer, larger ships can get through, which may deplete harbor jobs and income up and down the west coast of the U.S. At the same time, a railroad line from Mexico to San Diego is being repaired, to avoid long wait times for trucks at U.S. southern borders.

NEW FIRM WILL TAKE OVER REPAIRS OF RAIL LINE
Los Angeles Times   Jun 12, 2016   p B4

SAN DIEGO - A new company will take over repairs and eventual operations of the beleaguered Desert Line railroad, clearing the way for work to begin this summer and for trains to move goods made in Mexico into the United States in 2018.

The Baja California Railroad will sublease the old and dilapidated line from Pacific Imperial Railroad, a company that has leased the tracks from its landlord, the San Diego Metropolitan Transit District, since 2012.

Officials said the sublease is a crucial step in getting the Desert Line running again so that products made in Mexico's maquiladoras can be efficiently shipped into the United States by rail rather than sitting for hours in trucks at the region's border crossings.

"The rehabilitation of the cross-border railroad provides a much needed alternative for moving goods through one of the most vibrant centers of commerce in the world," said Jerry Sanders, the president and chief executive of the San Diego Regional Chamber of Commerce.   by Joshua Stewart

China is the world's top export economy at $2 trillion, 275 billion in 2016, according to statistica.com. China has surpassed Japan as the world's second largest economy, with the U.S. the world's largest. If the U.S. deficit of $19 trillion is factored in, China and Japan would be the world's largest economies.

MILKING NEW ZEALAND'S IDYLLIC COUNTRYSIDE

The Wall Street Journal   Feb 18, 2015   p A11

POKENO, New Zealand - Ken and Patricia Graham have an unwelcome new neighbor on the farm where they retired to raise sheep and cattle and tend a vineyard - a gigantic Chinese-owned infant-formula factory.

The $165 million plant emblazoned with the company's name - Yashili - in Chinese characters fills the view from their wooden deck. Its size is out of proportion to the surrounding village of Pokeno, which has a population of around 400 in the heart of New Zealand's dairy country...

How do they feel? "Actually - yuck," says Mrs. Graham. "We like living in a nice rural place." Mr. Graham is more damning about the broader industrial development in the area spearheaded by Yashili. "It's an absolute abomination," he says...

China now relies heavily on New Zealand's pristine farms. They provide 70% of Chinese dairy imports...China is no longer content merely to buy New Zealand's dairy exports: it wants a stake in the entire production chain...

The company that built the infant-formula plant in Pokeno is majority-owned by Chinese state-backed giant China Mengniu Dairy Co...All of China's top three dairy producers now manufacture in the country..."They've got wealth that we don't understand in New Zealand," says Helen Clotworthy, who with her husband is bailing out now to a quieter spot nearby.   China's World, by Andrew Browne

Europe is China's biggest trading partner. In 2013 Europe spent 1 billion euros a day on Chinese goods and services. Europe imports industrial and consumer goods, machinery and equipment, shoes and clothes, lamps, furniture and toys. China imports industrial and consumer goods, machinery and equipment, automobiles , aircraft and chemicals.

Europe was running a "significant trade deficit with China, partly due to access barriers." Europe sought redress through the WTO, charging that China wasn't trading fairly and was taking intellectual property without compensation. They also protested China's increasing act of withholding "raw earths," essential components in many manufacturing processes and products. The WTO confirmed Europe's claim, saying China must conform to its WTO obligation regarding exportation of raw earths. Europe's other grievances were that China discriminates against foreign companies, lacks transparency, and has a strong degree of "government intervention in the economy, resulting in a dominant position of state-owned companies."

Another dispute was over solar panels. Europe accused China of "dumping" panels to wrench the business from European competitors. From 2011 to 2013 China had to pay 47.7% duty to export solar panels to Europe, and that was the duty charged on the companies "that cooperated" with WTO rules. Companies that didn't cooperate had to pay anti-dumping fees, which were higher.   --ec.europe

UNITED STATES INTERNATIONAL TRADE IN GOODS, 2010

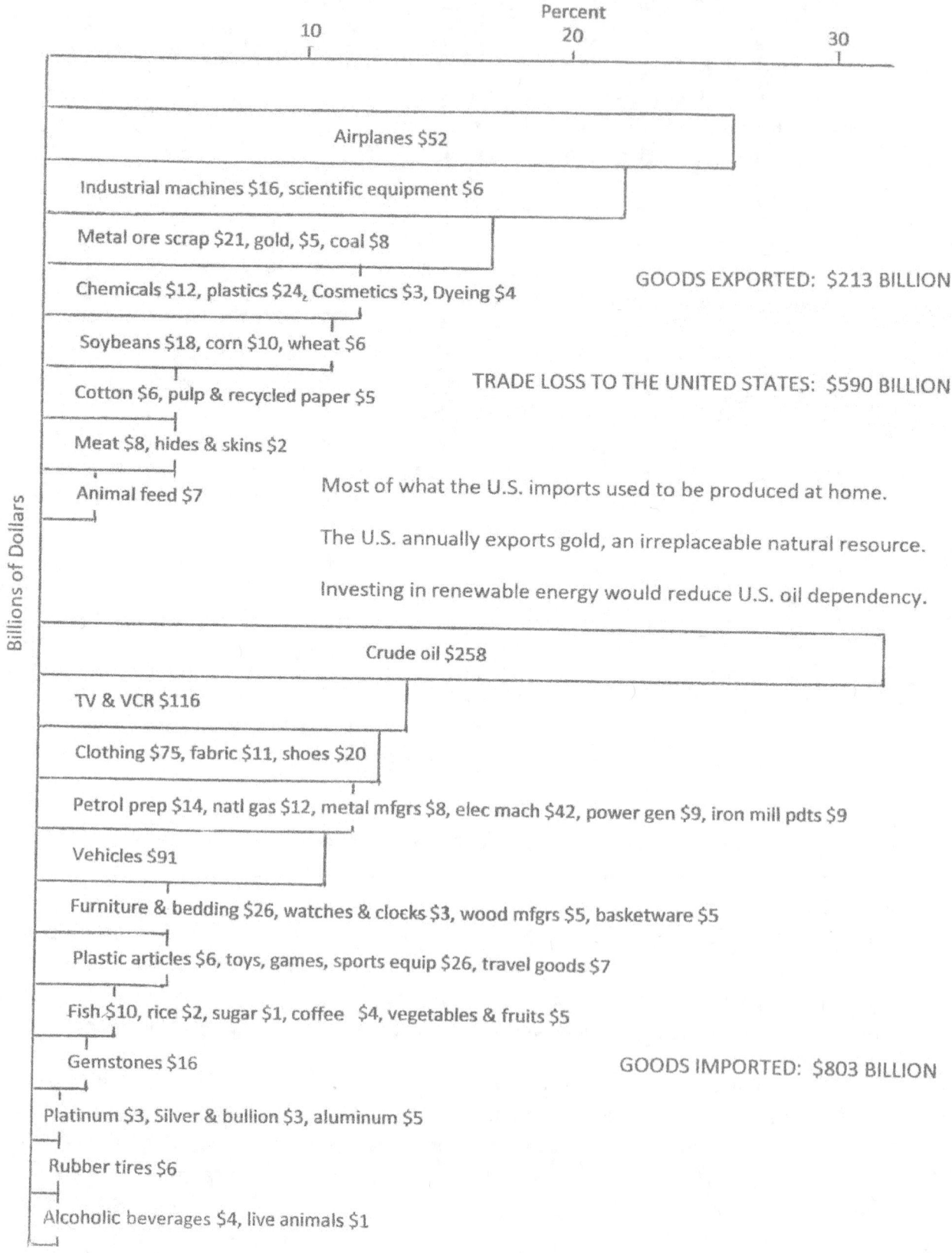

Percent

| | 10 | 20 | 30 |

Airplanes $52

Industrial machines $16, scientific equipment $6

Metal ore scrap $21, gold, $5, coal $8

Chemicals $12, plastics $24, Cosmetics $3, Dyeing $4

Soybeans $18, corn $10, wheat $6

Cotton $6, pulp & recycled paper $5

Meat $8, hides & skins $2

Animal feed $7

GOODS EXPORTED: $213 BILLION

TRADE LOSS TO THE UNITED STATES: $590 BILLION

Most of what the U.S. imports used to be produced at home.

The U.S. annually exports gold, an irreplaceable natural resource.

Investing in renewable energy would reduce U.S. oil dependency.

Crude oil $258

TV & VCR $116

Clothing $75, fabric $11, shoes $20

Petrol prep $14, natl gas $12, metal mfgrs $8, elec mach $42, power gen $9, iron mill pdts $9

Vehicles $91

Furniture & bedding $26, watches & clocks $3, wood mfgrs $5, basketware $5

Plastic articles $6, toys, games, sports equip $26, travel goods $7

Fish $10, rice $2, sugar $1, coffee $4, vegetables & fruits $5

Gemstones $16

GOODS IMPORTED: $803 BILLION

Platinum $3, Silver & bullion $3, aluminum $5

Rubber tires $6

Alcoholic beverages $4, live animals $1

Billions of Dollars

Source: The World Almanac and Book of Facts 2011, p 85

Misc. Manufact   EXPORTS

Scientific equip, photo equip, apparel, footwear, furniture, misc mfg IMPORTS

Petroleum   EXPORTS

Petroleum   IMPORTS

Automobiles   EXPORTS

Automobiles   IMPORTS

by Material   EXPORTS

Manufactured Goods by Material   IMPORTS

Chemicals and Pharmaceutics   EXPORTS

Chemicals and Pharmaceutics   IMPORTS

Machinery   EXPORTS

Machinery   IMPORTS

Elec mach EXPORTS

Electrical machinery   IMPORTS

Tele   EXPORTS

Telecommunications IMPORTS

Food   Animals EXPORTS

Food Live Animals IMPORTS

EXPORTS $ 1 TRILLION, 620 BILLION, 532 MILLION

Offic   EXPORTS

IMPORTS $ 2 TRILLION, 347 BILLION, 026 MILLION

Office Machinery   IMPORTS

Gold EXPORTS

"special transactions"

$727 BILLION, 153 MILLION

Gold IMPORTS

Transportation Equipment   EXPORTS

TRADE LOSS TO UNITED STATES 2014

Transp   IMPORTS

Crude (Raw) Matl   EXPORTS

Crude   IMPORTS

Re-Exports

350

0   100   Billions of dollars 200   300

Source: The World Almanac and Book of Facts 2016, p 74

MAJORITY-OWNED FOREIGN AFFILIATES IN THE UNITED STATES
VALUE ADDED BY INDUSTRY OF AFFILIATE AND COUNTRY
2012

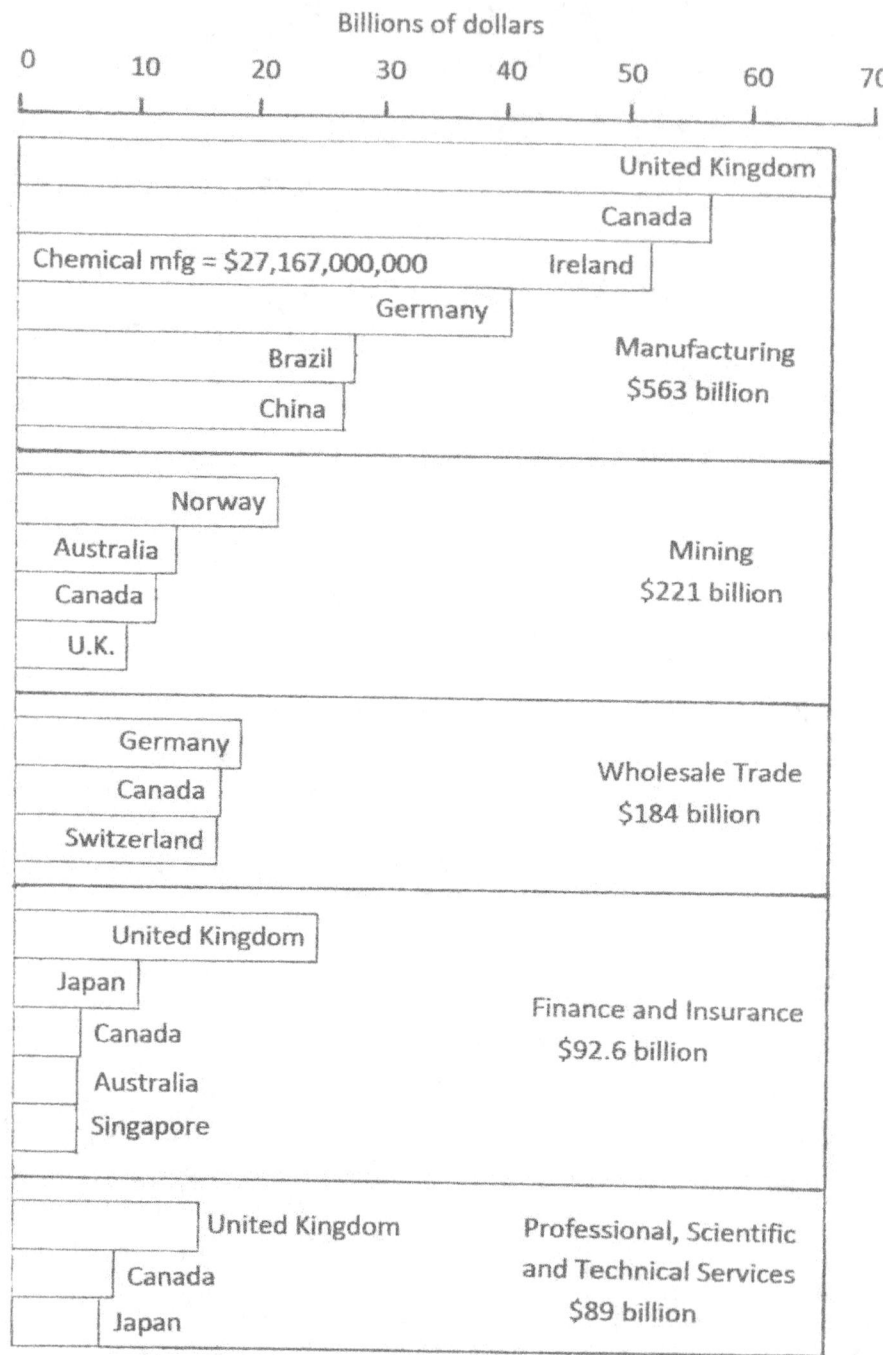

Billions of dollars

United Kingdom

Canada

Chemical mfg = $27,167,000,000   Ireland

Germany

Brazil

China

Manufacturing
$563 billion

Norway

Australia

Canada

U.K.

Mining
$221 billion

Germany

Canada

Switzerland

Wholesale Trade
$184 billion

United Kingdom

Japan

Canada

Australia

Singapore

Finance and Insurance
$92.6 billion

United Kingdom

Canada

Japan

Professional, Scientific
and Technical Services
$89 billion

"VALUE ADDED" = $ 1 TRILLION, 420 BILLION, 679 MILLION

Other country affiliates: France, Mexico, Netherlands, Italy.
"Includes other countries, not shown separately."

Source: ProQuest Statistical Abstract of the United States 2016, p 538

111

SUMMARY

Modest trade surpluses in the United States began to fall in 1975, reaching $-25 billion in 1980, $-130 billion in 1985 and a record $-748 billion in 2006. HALF A TRILLION DOLLARS in annual trade deficits for the United States is now the norm.

The Congress of the United States HAS YIELDED SOVEREIGNTY OF THE UNITED STATES CONSTITUTION to various trade agreements, including The General Agreement on Tariffs and Trade (GATT) in 1967, The North Atlantic Free Trade Agreement (NAFTA) in 1992, and The World Trade Organization (WTO) in 1995. The WTO "administers trade agreements and treaties between nations, attempts to settle disputes, and keeps track of trade measures and statistics."* The WTO "seeks to promote free trade by eliminating barriers to trade."** NONE OF THESE OR OTHER TRADE AGREEMENTS SEEK TO DIMINISH THE DEFICITS OF UNITED STATES TRADE.

Foreign countries shipping goods and services to the United States pay little or no customs fees or duties to the United States, IN DIRECT VIOLATION OF THE CONSTITUTION OF THE UNITED STATES WHICH MANDATES CONGRESS TO LAY AND COLLECT DUTIES AND TO REGULATE COMMERCE WITH FOREIGN NATIONS.

Massive importation of foreign goods at lower prices has WIPED OUT ENTIRE INDUSTRIES such as apparel, consumer electronics and household goods, leaving citizens of the United States to compete for fewer jobs with less pay and benefits, a phenomenon which began in the 1980s and continues to this day.

FOREIGN INDUSTRIES ARRIVED in the United States to provide jobs as early as the 1980s, beginning with Japanese passenger cars. Cities and states welcomed foreign businesses, enticed by potential sales taxes, and competed with each other by offering foreign businesses discounts on land, property taxes and other inducements.

By 2012 foreign businesses in the United States produced ONE TRILLION, 420 BILLION DOLLARS WORTH OF GOODS AND SERVICES. The businesses are statistically recorded as "Majority-owned Foreign Affiliates," and their profits are "Value Added." If these value added dollars are shipped home as profits, and these annual profits are added to the United States half trillion dollar yearly trade deficits, TRADE IS ACTUALLY COSTING THE UNITED STATES TWO TRILLION DOLLARS A YEAR.

*The World Almanac and Book of Facts 2016, p 742
**The World Almanac and Book of Facts 2016, p 74

U.S Population Profile before 1974

U.S. Population Profile after 1974

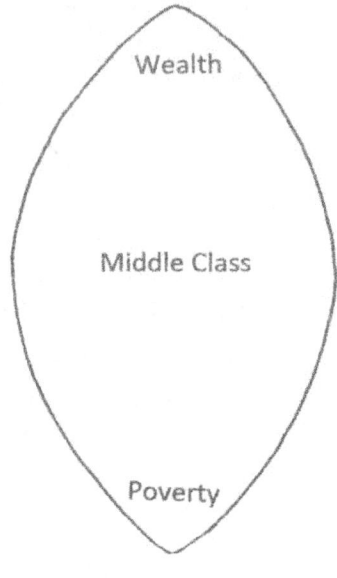

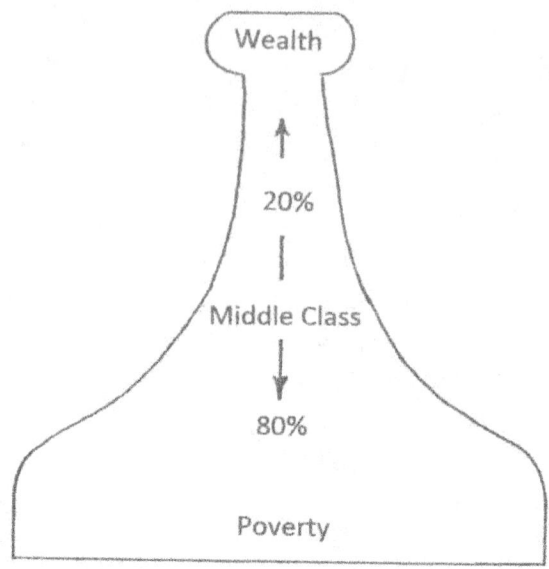

The middle class of the United States, that Great Silent Majority, shaped like the football of their favorite sport, has morphed into the profile of a pawn in the great global chess game.

WHERE THE JOBS ARE

Los Angeles Times Jan 2, 2014 p A17

The city of New York decreed a few years ago that each bedroom in the city must have a carbon monoxide detector. There are roughly 11 million bedrooms in New York City, so the law created a huge market. Further, the devices have a life of five years, after which they must be replaced, so the continuing market was also guaranteed.

Was there a rush of companies here in the United States gearing up to manufacture 11 million devices for this guaranteed sale? No. Almost all the detectors were made in China or Taiwan.

At the same time, India and other Asian nations have rapidly moved into global trade. This has meant millions more workers around the world competing with American workers to make stuff and offer services. And since the international workers are willing to accept extremely low wages, they have the advantage.

And during this entire period, what did the United States government do to meet this challenge? Nothing. Our clueless, bellowing national leaders took no action to meet the effect of this new competition. Many American companies embraced the changes, happy to make profits off underpaid Asian workers while allowing huge swaths of American industry to die.

It's hard to explain all this to younger Americans, who are generally a hopeful and cheerful lot. The information is no fun to deliver.

by Jeff Danziger

"THE CONGRESS SHALL HAVE POWER ... TO ESTABLISH AN UNIFORM RULE
OF NATURALIZATION"
Article I, Section 8
Constitution of the United States

"THE MIGRATION OR IMPORTATION OF SUCH PERSONS AS ANY OF THE
STATES NOW EXISTING SHALL THINK PROPER TO ADMIT
SHALL NOT BE PROHIBITED BY THE CONGRESS ... "
Article I, Section 9
Constitution of the United States

"ALL PERSONS BORN OR NATURALIZED IN THE UNITED STATES,
AND SUBJECT TO THE JURISDICTION THEREOF,
ARE CITIZENS OF THE UNITED STATES
AND OF THE STATE WHEREIN THEY RESIDE."
Amendment XIV, Section 1
Constitution of the United States

POPULATION OF THE WORLD BY CONTINENT
1990 - 2014

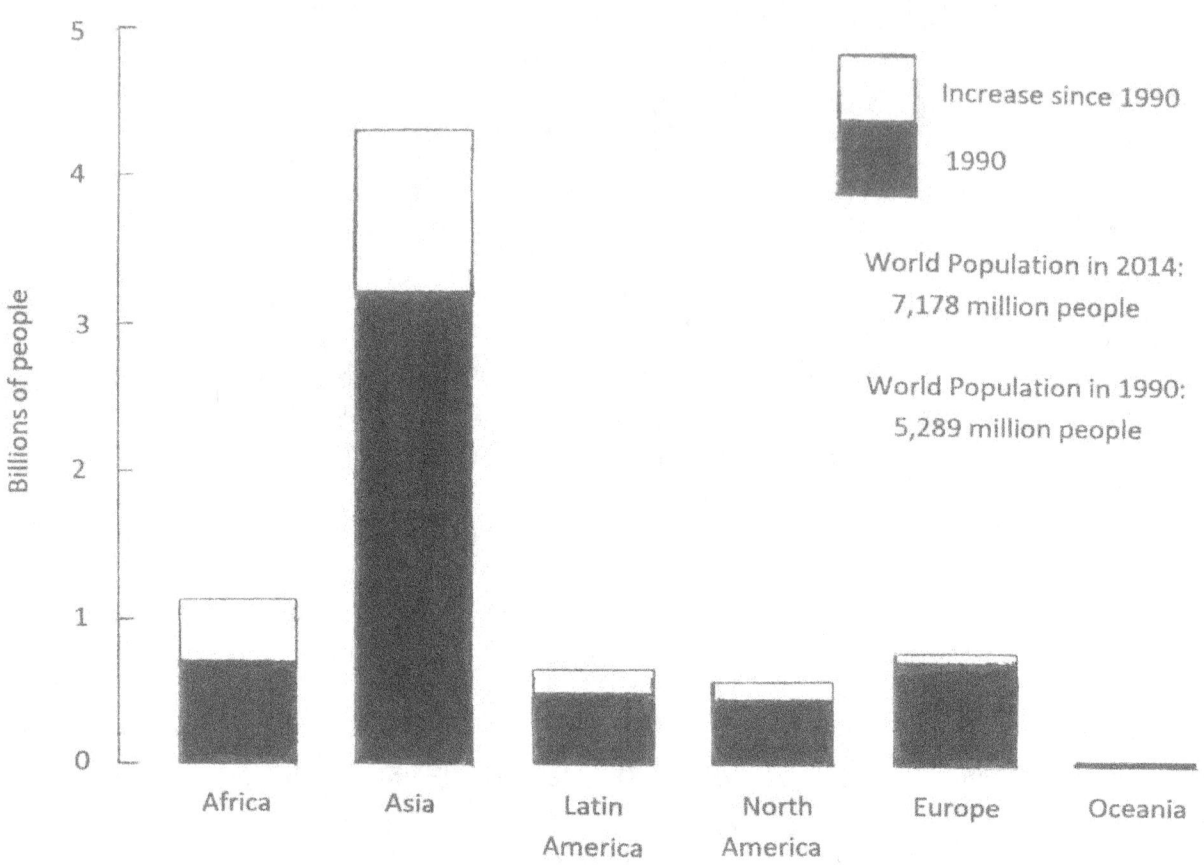

Source: ProQuest Statistical Abstract of the United States 2016, p 860

World's Population as of August 30, 2016:

7,447,109,688

--worldometers.info

FEDERAL LAWS ON IMMIGRATION
VERSUS
THE U.S. CONSTITUTION

JURISDICTION

There is a problem with the term, "Nativity." The federal government definition is, "The native population consists of all persons born in the United States..." whereas the U.S. Constitution states, "All persons born or naturalized in the United States, and subject to the jurisdiction thereof, are citizens."

> **Nativity.**—The native population consists of all persons born in the United States, Puerto Rico, or an outlying area of the United States. It also includes persons born at sea or in a foreign country who have at least one American parent. All others are classified as "foreign born."

Source: Statistical Abstract of the United States 1995, p 5

The founders put in the jurisdiction phrase for a reason. Webster's defines jurisdiction as "1. the right of making and enforcing laws" and "2. the domain over which a given authority extends," neither of which help to clarify the founders' intent, since the Constitution is the law, and the "domain" is the United States in both cases.

A reasonable person might interpret "jurisdiction" to mean the government is aware of the person in question. Some sort of documentation, such as a birth certificate or a visa, or other form of government-issued identification, would meet the test of jurisdiction.

Such an interpretation would prevent millions of foreign women from entering the United States illegally for the purpose of giving birth. Foreign women who are issued visas but only for the purpose of giving U.S. citizenship to their offspring might face fraud charges. People born to a U.S. citizen outside of the U.S., or on the high seas or in the military, without the U.S. citizen parent's knowledge or consent might not receive U.S. citizenship. As it is, they all get citizenship, and can apply for citizenship for their extended families.

RAIDS TARGET 'BIRTH TOURISM'
Los Angeles Times Mar 4, 2015 p A1

It is not necessarily illegal for foreign nationals to give birth in the U.S. Many agencies openly advertise services offering assistance in getting newborns a U.S. passport and extolling the benefits that come with American citizenship, including public education and immigration benefits for parents.

The practice has become particularly popular in recent years with the newly wealthy Chinese middle class, but Taiwanese, Korean and Turkish mothers are also known to engage in birth tourism. About 40,000 of the 300,000 children born to foreign citizens in the U.S. each year are the product of birth tourism. Star Baby Care boasted on its site that it had served 4,000 women from China since it was founded in 1999.

Even though the mothers paid birth tourism operators thousands of dollars in fees, they paid local hospitals nothing or a reduced sum for uninsured, low-income patients. One of the women paid $4,080 out of $28,845 in hospital bills when her bank account showed charges at Wynn Las Vegas and purchases at Rolex and Louis Vuitton stores. The reported top fee for guiding pregnant women through the birth process in the U.S. is $50,000.   by Victoria Kim and Frank Shyong

The vast majority of U.S. citizens are unaware of these liberal laws, but foreigners are not. Few Americans know that as far back as the Vietnam War, a child born to an American soldier is an American citizen has been extended to a child born of any American anywhere in the world is an American citizen.

The biggest problem with jurisdiction regarding immigration is that the federal government arguably doesn't have it: the states expressly do, as stated in the U.S. Constitution, Article I, Section 9. True, the Constitution limits the states' authority to 1808 and discusses a ten dollar per capita tax. But beyond 1808, the Constitution is silent, except that immigration shall be "uniform" and "subject to jurisdiction" for citizenship. At this point, the Tenth Amendment kicks in:

> "The powers not delegated to the United States by the Constitution, nor prohibited by it to the States, are reserved to the States, respectively, or to the people."

The issue then becomes: Can one federal judge, or even the United States Supreme Court, overrule a state or the people? The U.S. Constitution is, after all, "Of the people, by the people, and for the people." The biggest question of all is: Why would the judiciary want to overrule the will of a state or the people in the first place? It is the states and the people in them who have to live with the consequences of immigration.

LANGUAGE

> "Every applicant for naturalization must demonstrate an understanding of the English language, including an ability to read and write, and speak words in ordinary usage in the English language."

A "lawyer or social service agency representing the applicant may be present." Since the 1970s this statement has opened the door to a booming business helping immigrants past the barriers to U.S. citizenship.

LANGUAGE SPOKEN IN U.S. HOMES AND ENGLISH SPEAKING ABILITY
2013

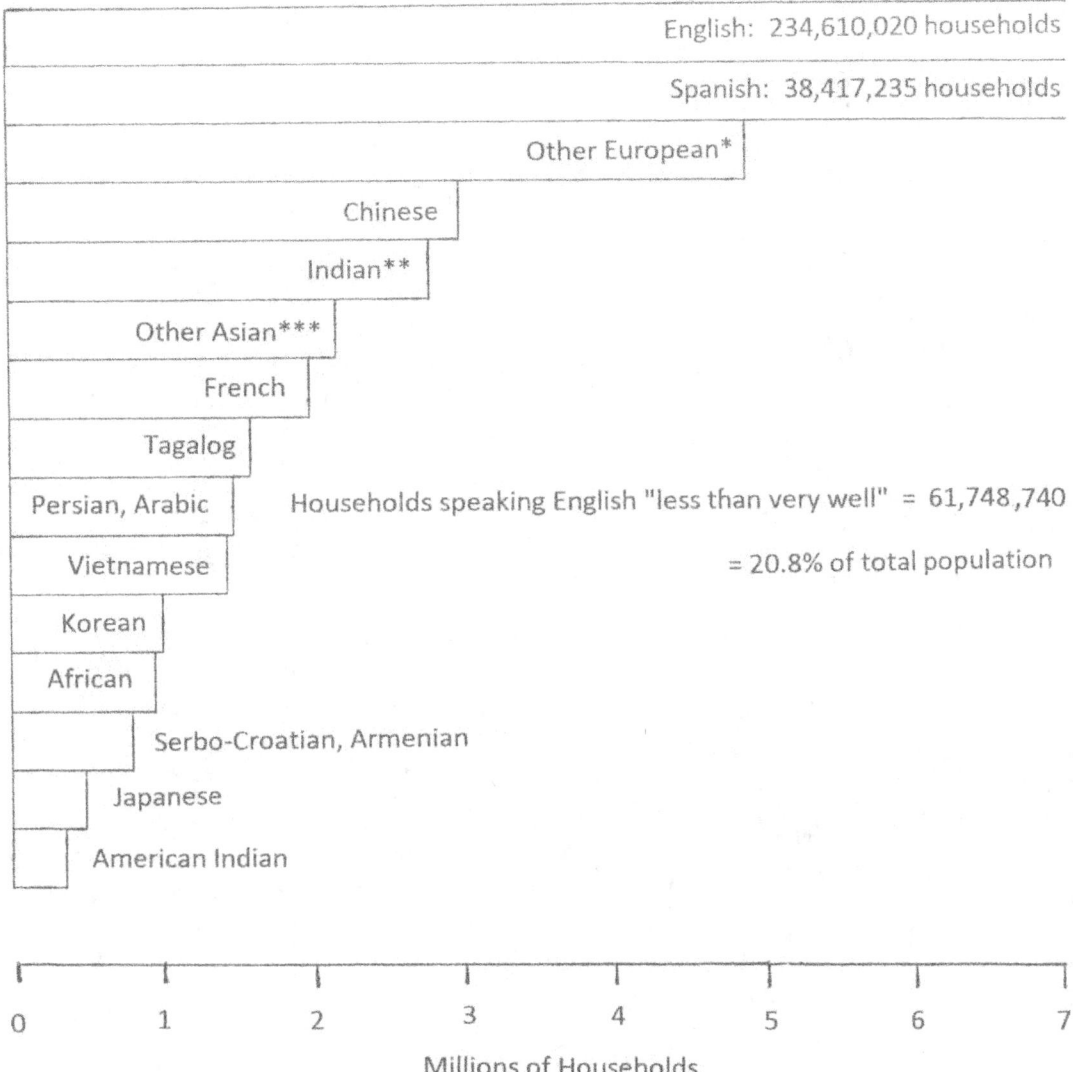

English: 234,610,020 households

Spanish: 38,417,235 households

Other European*

Chinese

Indian**

Other Asian***

French

Tagalog

Persian, Arabic

Households speaking English "less than very well" = 61,748,740

Vietnamese

= 20.8% of total population

Korean

African

Serbo-Croatian, Armenian

Japanese

American Indian

0   1   2   3   4   5   6   7

Millions of Households

* Italian, Portuguese, Germanic, Yiddish, Hebrew, Scandinavian, Greek, Russian
Polish, Hungarian, Other West Germanic languages

**Gujarathi, Hindi, Urdu, Other Indic, Other Indo-European languages

***Mon-Khmer, Cambodian, Hmong, Thai, Laotian, Other Asian,
Other Pacific Island languages

Source: ProQuest Statistical Abstract of the United States 2016, p 46

The Los Angeles Unified School District teaches entire classrooms in foreign languages,
for example, South Korean, taught by South Korean - American teachers.

★★★★★★★★★★★★★★

OFFICIAL SAMPLE BALLOT

AND VOTER INFORMATION PAMPHLET

★★★★★★★★★★★★★★

COMPILED BY JUNE LAGMAY, CITY CLERK

GENERAL MUNICIPAL AND SPECIAL ELECTIONS
TUESDAY, MAY 21, 2013

INTERNET - http://clerk.lacity.org/elections/

For Election Information,
please call 1-888-873-1000

Under federal law, voter information pamphlets are
available in English as well as in the following languages:

若您希望索取本手冊的中文譯本
請致電：1-800-994-VOTE (8683)

यदि आपको यह पैम्फलेट हिन्दी में चाहिए,
तो कृपया 1-800-994-VOTE (8683) पर फोन करें

このパンフレットの日本語版をご希望の方は、
お電話ください。1-800-994-VOTE (8683)

이 팸플릿을 한국어로 원하시면 다음 전화번호로
연락하십시오. 1-800-994-VOTE (8683)

Si usted desea obtener una copia de este folleto en español,
por favor llame al 1-800-994-VOTE (8683)

Kung kailangan ninyo ng kopya ng pamplet na ito sa Tagalog,
tumawag po lamang sa 1-800-994-VOTE (8683)

ถ้าท่านต้องการขอรับสำเนาจุลสารนี้ในภาษาไทย
กรุณาโทรศัพท์ติดต่อที่หมายเลข 1-800-994-VOTE (8683)

Nếu quý vị muốn có tập sách này bằng tiếng Việt,
xin gọi số điện thoại 1-800-994-VOTE (8683)

LOYALTY

The federal government still requires applicants for citizenship to take a loyalty oath:

> I hereby declare, on oath, that I absolutely and entirely renounce and abjure all allegiance and fidelity to any foreign prince, potentate, state or sovereignty, to whom or which I have heretofore been a subject or citizen; that I will support and defend the Constitution and laws of the United States of America against all enemies, foreign and domestic; that I will bear true faith and allegiance to the same...

Persons in direct violation of the Oath of Allegiance to the United States should include:

Any person who maintains dual citizenship

Any person who maintains dual passports

Any Islamic person, because in Islam, there is no separation between church and state. In the U.S., there is complete separation between church and state

> "ORTHODOX ISLAM IS NOT ONLY A SYSTEM OF BELIEFS BUT ALSO A LEGAL SYSTEM"
> wikipedia.org:

All of the above routinely obtain U.S. citizenship.

UNIFORM RULE

The only "uniform rule" of naturalization, as required Article I, Section 8 of the U.S. Constitution, is that the federal government has amassed its intricate body of laws into one document, the laws of which are diverse by definition.

Perhaps the "uniform rule" of naturalization the founders of this country were talking about was the immigration from western Europe that comprised the vast majority of immigration from 1607 to 1965. The founders sought a "more perfect union," which suggests a population of similar background, values and culture. All newcomers eagerly learned English, gave up old passports, and fully embraced their new lives as Americans.

Morever, the founders were wary of "foreign entanglements."

121

"In the first place, we should insist that if the immigrant who comes here in good faith becomes an American and assimilates himself to us, he shall be treated on an exact equality with everyone else, for it is an outrage to discriminate against any such man because of creed, or birthplace, or origin. But this is predicated upon the person's becoming in every facet an American, and nothing but an American... There can be no divided allegiance here. Any man who says he is an American, but something else also, isn't an American at all. We have room for but one flag, the American flag... We have room for but one language here, and that is the English language ... and we have room for but one sole loyalty and that is one loyalty to the American people."

--Theodore Roosevelt, 1907

THE IMMIGRATION AND NATIONALITY ACT OF 1965

Immigrants admitted to the U.S. by "class of admission" is the list still used by the United States for legal immigration. It incorporates all immigration laws, including the 1980 Refugee Act. It is the consolidation of U.S. immigration policy "into one body of text," which is the government's idea of the "Uniform Rule" of the U.S. Constitution.

The Immigration and Nationality Act of 1965 was introduced to Congress by Senator Ted Kennedy and his brother Bobby to bring 5,000 Cuban rebels who had attempted to overthrow Fidel Castro at Cuba's Bay of Pigs, but failed because the United States withdrew its support of the attempt at the last minute. Bobby Kennedy testified to Congress that after those 5,000 Cuban refugees came to the United States, immigration "from that source" would stop. As they threw away the quota system allowing immigrants largely from Europe, Ted Kennedy prophetically had this to say:

> First, our cities will not be flooded with a million immigrants annually. Under the proposed bill, the present level of immigration remains substantially the same.... Secondly, the ethnic mix of this country will not be upset.... Contrary to the charges in some quarters, [the bill] will not inundate America with immigrants from any one country or area, or the most populated and deprived nations of Africa and Asia.... In the final analysis, the ethnic pattern of immigration under the proposed measure is not expected to change as sharply as the critics seem to think.

> —— Ted Kennedy, chief Senate sponsor of the Immigration and Nationality Act of 1965

In 1973, after eight years of combat in Vietnam, the United States withdrew, having lost the war. Communist Viet Cong from the north were sweeping southward, and by 1975 were approaching Saigon. The United States airlifted 58,000 Vietnamese into Camp Pendleton in Southern California. They came as refugees under the Indochinese Refugee Act of 1977. Their numbers approached the number of body bags of U.S. soldiers airlifted home from that war: 57,605 dead Americans.

There were refugees from the Korean War, too, as evidenced by the Refugee Relief Act of 1953, but the numbers were fewer. When General Eisenhower became President of the United States in 1953, he abruptly ended the three year war and ordered U.S. troops to blockade the 38th parallel so that Communist North Korean troops could not move southward. The blockade is still in effect. The "forgotten" Korean War resulted in 54,246 U.S. soldiers returning home in body bags.

In all three cases, the United States entered into conflicts which she did not win but which created refugees. It was the beginning of the current trend of perpetual war and perpetual refugees, which has now reached global proportions.

When Dwight Eisenhower became President in 1953, illegal aliens were entering the United States from the south, crossing the Rio Grande and other rivers. He ordered over one million turned back in "Operation Wetback," and the influx briefly stopped. Presidents Reagan and H.W. Bush took the opposite tack: they granted Amnesty to millions of illegal aliens in 1980 and 1985, plus 1990 through 1993, rewarding their presence with legal status. Amnesties obviously encourage millions more to illegally cross into the United States or overstay visas.

By 1994, illegal immigration was so overwhelming Californians that they passed an initiative, garnered by gathering signatures. Approved by 59% of the voters, Proposition 187 allowed law enforcement agents to investigate and report the immigration status of persons under arrest, and disallowed health care and education benefits to illegal aliens. One federal judge, Mariana Pfaelzer quickly declared Proposition 187 unconstitutional on the basis it interfered with the federal government's "exclusive jurisdiction" over immigration. She wrote:

"California is powerless to enact its own legislative scheme to regulate immigration. It is likewise powerless to enact its own legislative scheme to regulate alien access to public benefits."

Bill Clinton, President during Proposition 187's passage, referred to it as "an impediment to federal policy on immigration." Clinton asked voters to allow the federal government "to keep working on what we're doing," so wrote Philip Martin in "Proposition 187 in California," published in "International Migration Review," Vol. 29, No. 1, pp 258-259.

Ten other states filed similar statutes, to no avail. In April 2010, Governor Jan Brewer of Arizona signed SB 1070, requiring illegal immigrants to have alien registration documents, requiring police to question immigration status if "there is a reason," illegality of hiring or transporting illegals, and allowing citizens to sue government agencies that hinder enforcement of immigration laws, according to Wikipedia.com.

Arizona v. United States was reviewed by the U.S. Supreme Court in 2012 on the issue whether federal law preempts state law. The justices relied on "long-standing interpretation of federal sovereignty in areas pertaining...to foreign nations," and that "federal law will prevail when state and federal laws conflict," citing Article VI, paragraph two of the U.S. Constitution, and Article 1, Section 8's "uniform rule" for immigration. The justices allowed only the "show me your papers" doctrine. Nine states and 81 Congressmen were for Arizona. Eleven countries filed amicus briefs against Arizona, according to Wikipedia.com.

One federal official said after the verdict that Arizona v. United States was consequential in that it stopped an anti-immigration movement "dead in its tracks." The justices struck down a provision that would have made it a state crime for illegal immigrants to be "unlawfully present in the United States," ironic since Governor Brewer's SB 1070 was dubbed "Support our Law Enforcement and Safe Neighborhoods Act."

Even agents of ICE, the U.S. Immigration and Customs Enforcement branch of the U.S. Department of Homeland Security, is suing its employer, the federal government, for not allowing them to do their jobs. ICE, according to Wikipedia.com, is responsible for "identifying, investigating, and dismantling vulnerabilities regarding the nation's border, economic, transportation, and infrastructure security." With an annual budget of over $5 billion and 19,330 employees as of 2014, ICE handles Enforcement and Removal Operatiions.

A group of immigration agents filed a lawsuit against the Obama administration in 2012, saying they are sick of being told not to do their jobs, a feeling intensified by a non-deportation policy and a directive not to arrest certain illegal immigrants. Ten Immigration and Customs Enforcement (ICE) agents filed the lawsuit in federal court, asking to be allowed to do their jobs.

The Obama administration has shut down numerous Border Patrol stations, ended a crucial ICE program that allowed local law enforcement agencies to enforce federal immigration law, and actually instructs Border Patrol agents not to make arrests.

The ICE agents say they are between a rock and a hard spot. They can either enforce the law and be reprimanded by their superiors, or fail to enforce the law and violate their oaths of service. A 1996 law requires the agents to demand proof of legal status from individuals they suspect are in the country illegally. "ICE agents are being told to violate federal law. They're being told that any illegal alien under the age of 31 is going to be let go," said Kris Kobach, attorney for the agents, according to theblaze.com

The agents won the case, and deportations are proceeding again.

With an estimated 12 to 20 million illegal immigrants in the United States in 2016, it would be expected that border states would enact strict voter ID verification. Along with 15 other states, neither Arizona nor California require voter identification at the polls, while 22 states have strict voter ID rules. Sizable undocumented populations in both Arizona and California could swing elections, but liberal, mostly democratic politicians don't want voter I.D. requirements. On the contrary, politicians woo undocumented immigrants for their votes.

IMMIGRANTS ADMITTED TO THE U.S. BY CLASS OF ADMISSION, 1965 - PRESENT

Preference Immigrants

Family-sponsored:

Unmarried sons/daughters of U.S. citizens and their children

Spouses, unmarried sons/daughters of alien residents, and their children

Married sons/daughters of U.S. citizens*

Brothers or sisters of U.S. citizens*

Employment-based immigrants:

Priority workers*

Professionals with advanced degrees*

Skilled workers, professionals, unskilled workers*

Special immigrants*

Employment creation*

Professional or highly skilled immigrants*

Needed skilled or unskilled workers*

Immediate relatives:

Spouses of U.S. citizens

Children of U.S. citizens

Orphans

Parents of U.S. citizens

Refugees and asylees:

Cuban Refugee Act, Nov. 1966

Indochinese Refugee Act, Oct. 1977

Refugee-Parolee Act, Oct. 1978

Asylees, Refugee Act of 1980

Refugees, Refugee Act of 1980

Other refugees

Other immigrants:

Children born abroad to resident aliens
or subsequent to issuance of visa

Diversity Programs - includes categories of immigrants
admitted under three laws intended to diversify
immigration: P.L. 99-603, P.L. 100-658 and P.L. 101-649

Amerasians: Under Public Law 100-202, Amerasians are
aliens born in Vietnam between January 1, 1962, and
January 1, 1976, who were fathered by U.S. citizens.

Legalization dependents: Spouses and children of
persons granted permanent resident status under
provisions of the Immigration Reform and Control
Act of 1986.

Other

*includes spouses and children

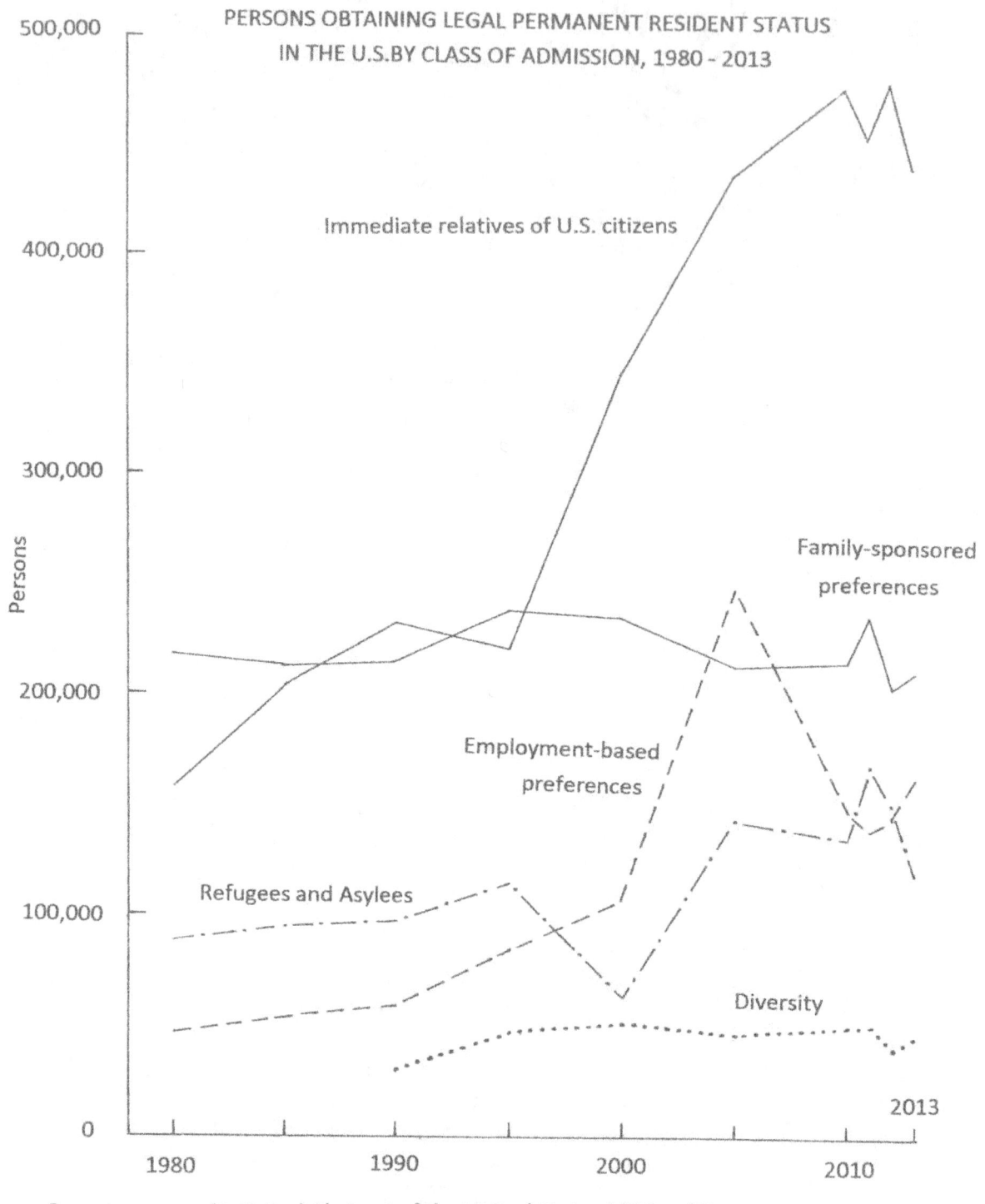

PERSONS OBTAINING LEGAL PERMANENT RESIDENT STATUS
IN THE U.S.BY CLASS OF ADMISSION, 1980 - 2013

Immediate relatives of U.S. citizens

Family-sponsored
preferences

Employment-based
preferences

Refugees and Asylees

Diversity

2013

Persons

500,000

400,000

300,000

200,000

100,000

0

1980   1990   2000   2010

Source: Statistical Abstract of the United States 1995, p 10;
2004-2005, p 9; ProQuest Statistical Abstract of the United States 2016, p 44

"We're drowning in people."
Anna Banana, Hollywood, CA

Finally, no population anywhere in the world at any time has been told, not asked, by their own government to absorb so many foreigners from every country into their midst. It is a tribute to the generosity and openness of the American people that they have accepted more than half of their own number from alien cultures with very little complaint. No one can call Americans racist.

There are stresses, financial, environmental and cultural. One of the greatest is space. Urban gridlock is everywhere, on freeways and highways, in intersections and mall parking lots. Frustration expresses itself as road rage, sometimes deadly. There are long lines in stores and at sporting events to the point that the crowds, combined with ubiquitous traffic, make venturing out hardly worth the effort.

The United States is already the third most populous country on earth, after China and India. We are taking immigrants in very large numbers precisely from those most populated countries. Somewhere, sometime, as with federal deficits and trade deficits, a line must be drawn in the sand. If not now, when?

ASIANS TO TOP LATINOS AS LARGEST IMMIGRANT GROUP
Los Angeles Times   Sep 28, 2015   p A14

Immigrants and their children are likely to make up 88% of the country's population growth over the next 50 years, according to the study by the Pew Research Center.

The foreign-born, who made up just 5% of the nation's population in 1965, when Congress completely rewrote the country's immigration laws, make up 14% today.

Increasingly, that population growth will involve Asians. The census category of Asian encompasses a vast array of ethnic and language groups, including Japanese, Chinese, Koreans, Filipinos, Indians and Pakistanis. Already, Asian Americans make up about 6% of the nation's population, up from just 1% in 1965.

Asians are expected to constitute 36% of the immigrant population by 2055, surpassing Latinos, who by then will be 34% of immigrants, the study indicates, but Latinos will remain a larger share of the total population, close to one-quarter of all Americans by mid-century.

The Pew study was designed to look at how immigration has changed the racial and ethnic makeup of the U.S. since Congress passed the 1965 Immigration and Naturalization Act. That law abolished a quota system based on national origin, which had barred most immigrants from outside Western Europe.   by Kate Linthicum

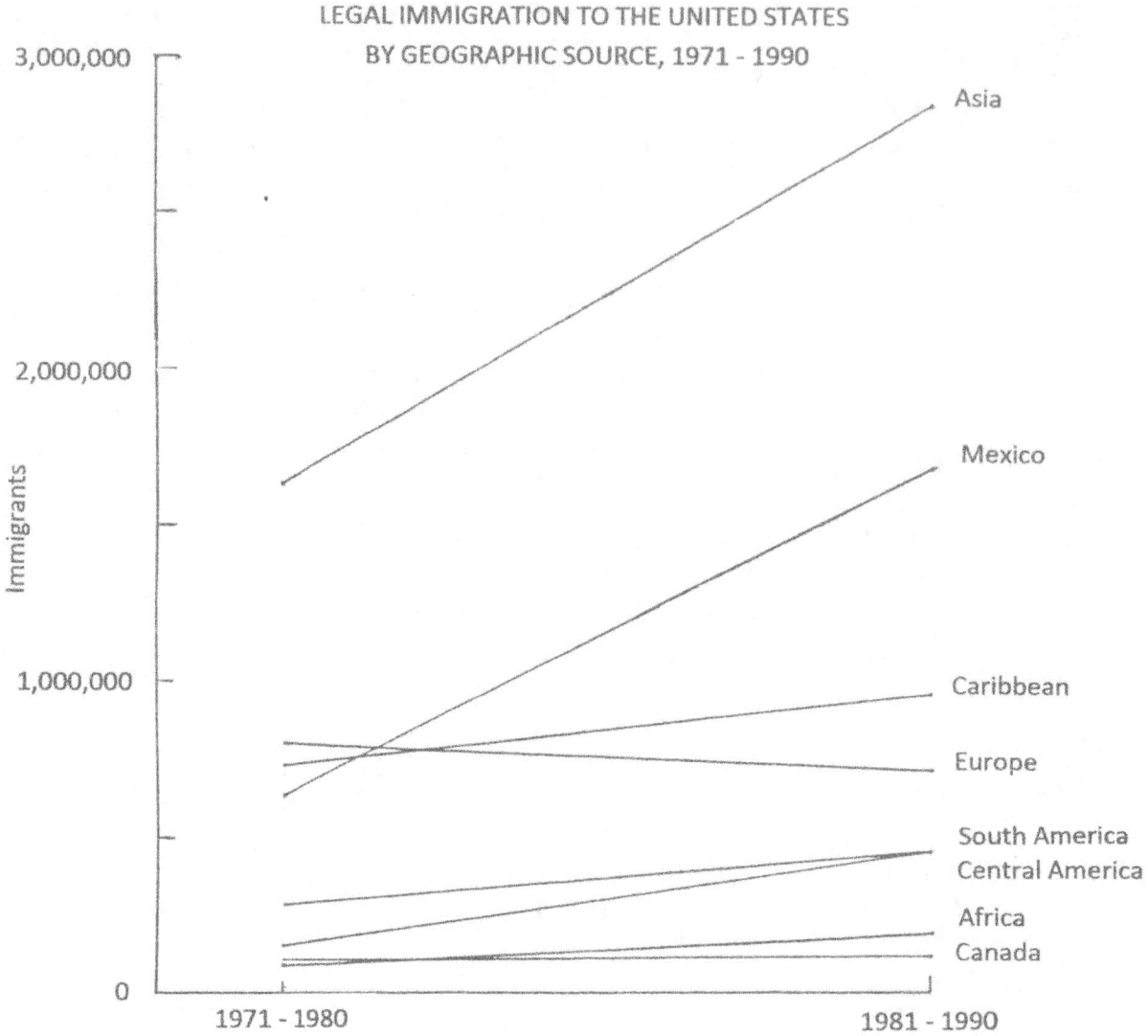

LEGAL IMMIGRATION TO THE UNITED STATES
BY GEOGRAPHIC SOURCE, 1971 - 1990

Source: Statistical Abstract of the United States 1995, p 11

NUMBER OF ASIANS IN U.S. SURGES
Los Angeles Times   Mar 23, 2012   p AA2

The nation's Asian population grew faster than any other racial or ethnic group over the last decade, surging almost 46% between 2000 and 2010, says a new Census Bureau report...The number of Americans who identify as Asian...rose to more than 17 million during the decade, the report showed. That was more than four times the rate of growth for the U.S. population as a whole, which increased about 10% over that period.

By comparison, the Latino population rose 43%...African American grew by 15%, while those identifying as white increased by 7%. The rising Asian population was propelled mainly by immigration...Those identifying as Asian or partly Asian rose by at least 30% over the decade in every state except Hawaii, where Asians already make up a majority.

by Rebecca Trounson

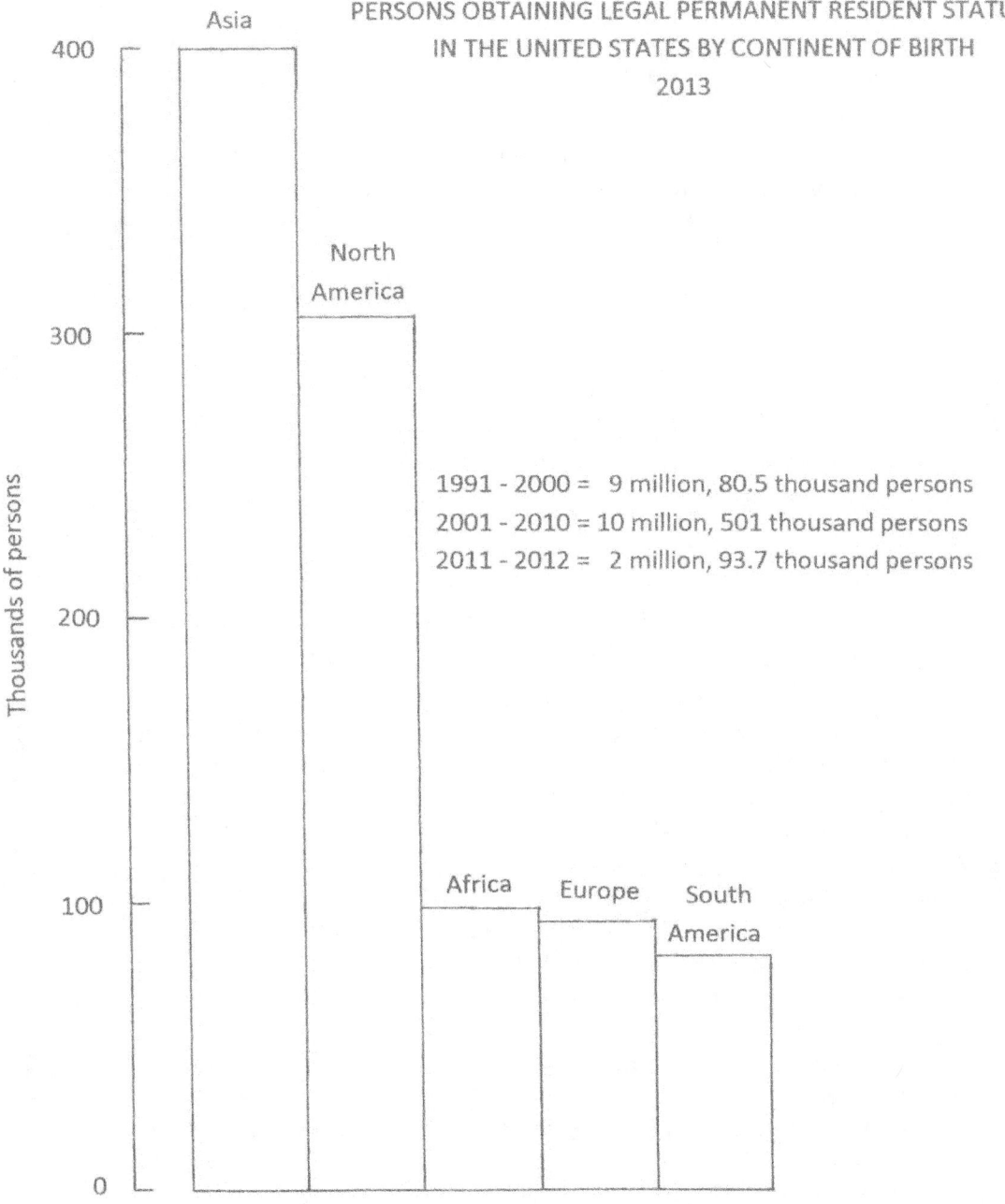

PERSONS OBTAINING LEGAL PERMANENT RESIDENT STATUS
IN THE UNITED STATES BY CONTINENT OF BIRTH
2013

1991 - 2000 = 9 million, 80.5 thousand persons
2001 - 2010 = 10 million, 501 thousand persons
2011 - 2012 = 2 million, 93.7 thousand persons

Source: ProQuest Statistical Abstract of the United States 2016, p 45

"Today, U.S. government policy is literally dissolving the people and electing
a new one... the fact is undeniable. Americans have told pollsters long and loudly
that they don't want any more immigration, but the politicians ignore them."

   --Peter Brimelow

"Alien Nation - Common Sense about America's Immigration Disaster,"
1995, p xv, xvi, Penguin Random House, New York, New York;
The Wylie Agency, LLC, New York, New York   Reprinted by permission

Diversity

There are, incredibly, four federal laws not only allowing diversity but mandating it, and they have been on the books for a long time. The first one "Public Law 99-603," is part of the 1986 Immigration Control and Reform Act. It is not known when "Public Law 100-658" or "Public Law 101-649" were passed or what they say. In 1994 the "Diversity Immigrant Visa Lottery" was passed, so that countries without enough residents In the United States can get citizens into the U.S. anyway.

Public Law 99-603

Diversity Program: Public Law 99-603 passed by Congress as "Immigration Control and Reform Act of 1986"

Forbids hiring of illegal aliens

Provides for a list of owners and operators of international bridges and toll roads to prevent unauthorized landing of aliens

Provides for an Immigration Emergency Fund
Verification of immigrant status of aliens applying for benefits under certain programs

State legalization impact – Assistance Grants

Permanent Residence for certain special agricultural workers

G-IV special immigrants

Making visas available for non-preference immigrants

Provides for Reports on unauthorized alien employment

Reports on H2A program (agricultural)

Reports on legalization program

Reports on visa waiver pilot program

Reports on Immigration and Naturalization Service

"Sense of the Congress"

Title V – State Assistance for Incarceration costs of illegal aliens and certain Cuban nationals

Expeditious deportation to nations of convicted aliens

Identification of facilities to incarcerate deportable or excludable aliens

Making Employment of Unauthorized Aliens Unlawful

In general, it is unlawful for a person or other entity to hire, or to recruit or refer for a fee, for employment in the United States

---

Diversity Program Public Law 100-658 - not available on the internet
Diversity Program Public Law 101-649 - not available on the internet

Today, the British capital probably has more mosques than any other city in the west...The whole world is in London...The city of eight million inhabitants has 50 minority groups of at least 10,000 each, including the most Bangladeshis anywhere besides Bangladesh. More than 300 languages, from Armenian to Zulu, are spoken in the schools...

With Britain mired in a double dip recession and saddled with a high unemployment rate, immigration remains a fraught political issue...

Violent clashes have occasionally erupted between Muslims and anti-immigrant demonstrators. Riots in August resulted in the deaths of five people, caused hundreds of millions of dollars in property damage...

Newcomers from the Continent eventually gave way to arrivals from former British colonies and, more recently, refugees from conflict-ridden countries such as Afghanistan, Iraq and Zimbabwe. On the other end of the scale, Russian oligarchs and Saudi sheiks have made London's toniest neighborhoods their private playgrounds.   by Henry Chu

Nations — U.S. Immigration Law:

Diversity Immigrant (DV) Category

The Immigration and Nationality Act provides 55,000 immigrant visas each fiscal year (beginning with FY 1995) to provide immigration opportunities for persons from countries other than the principal sources of current immigration to the US. DV visas are divided among six geographic regions. Not more than 3,850 visas (7% of the 55,000 visa limit) may be provided to immigrants from any one country.

The allotment of FY 1995 visa numbers for each region is as follows: Africa, 20,200; Asia, 6,837; Europe, 24,549; North America (Bahamas), 8; South America, Central America, and the Caribbean, 2,589; and Oceania, 817.

Diversity Immigrant Visa Lottery (DV) Drawing

On Aug. 12, 1994, the National Visa Center in Portsmouth, NH, began the selection of winners of the DV lottery. The first notices were sent to the winners in September.

The DV registration mail-in was held June 1-30, 1994. During this one-month period, the National Visa Center received approximately 6.5 million qualified entries. An additional 1.5 million entries received during those dates were disqualified for not providing the requested information or following published guidelines.

In order to issue all 55,000 visas in FY 1995, the National Visa Center planned to notify 110,000 principal applicants. Persons whose entries were not selected were not notified. Winners were sent instructions on how to apply for an immigrant visa. During the visa interview, applicants must provide proof of a high school education or its equivalent or must show two years of work experience within the past five years in an occupation that requires at least two years of training or experience.

Those selected needed to act on their immigrant visa applications quickly. As soon as 55,000 visas were issued, the program for FY 1995 would end.

The four diversity laws extend far beyond federal governmental preference in admitting Asians as legal residents to the U.S. The agenda to promote diversity extends to rewarding businesses and universities with financial incentives of they hire and promote diversity in their employee and student populations. Data like this is not easy to find, but there are clues, such as the "Business and Legal Resources" ad published on the internet, excerpted herein on page 134. The fact that the ad casually closes with the statement that "ALL FIFTY STATES HAVE DIVERSITY REQUIREMENTS" indicates how widespread, pervasive and insidious the federal government agenda is, especially when the immigration "body of text," including the four diversity laws, have been kept a secret, along with the costs of immigration, from the American people since 1965.

STATE AIMS TO CREATE EQUAL ACCESS
Los Angeles Times   Jul 4, 2016   p B1

The state agency in charge of handing out hundreds of millions of dollars in tax credits to companies that promise Californians jobs is moving closer to requiring those businesses to say how they plan to make their workforce more diverse.

Businesses soon will have to describe their hiring and recruiting practices to ensure women and people of color have equal access to jobs as part of their applications for tax dollars, according to a plan unveiled last month by Go-Biz, the state's economic development department. The new rules are expected to be in place by November.

Madeline Janis said, "It's essentially a taxpayer investment in the private company, so there has to be a public purpose."

The state's tax credit program, California Competes, began after Gov. Jerry Brown signed legislation in 2013 to allow businesses to forgo some of their income taxes if they agreed to create a more diverse work force.   by Liam Dillon

The four diversity laws smack the face of the "uniform rule" the Constitution requires and the Constitution's goal of forming a "more perfect UNION."

By aiding and abetting illegal immigrants, giving them Amnesty over four decades, whether republicans or democrats are in charge, thereby flaunting the immigration laws they themselves wrote; by making a sham of language, loyalty, jurisdiction and uniform rule; by ignoring border control; by ignoring the departure of visa holders; by offering all immigrants regardless of legal status far more freebies than U.S. citizens get; by refusal to let ICE officers carry out deportation duties; by refusal to let the states or the people have a voice in immigration matters; and by legal enforcement of four diversity laws to ensure every race, creed and culture on earth has access to the United States; all these combined lead to no other conclusion but that immigrants are valued far more highly by the U.S. government than her own citizens.

"Simplify Compliance"

Diversity: What you need to know:

Workforce diversity extends beyond affirmative action and protected classifications like gender, race, age, religion, national origin, and disability. It is not based solely on changing the representation of various groups in the workplace. Rather, workplace diversity focuses on recognizing uniqueness in every individual, valuing each person's contributions, and creating an inclusive environment where awareness of and respect for individual differences are promoted and encouraged. Diversity includes life experiences, language, skills, talents, education, thought processes, and personal styles - in essence, the entire package of personal attributes that each employee contributes to the workplace.

> For a Limited Time receive a FREE HR Report on the "Critical HR Recordkeeping". This exclusive special report covers hiring records employment relationships, termination records, litigation issues, electronic information issues, tips for better recordkeeping, and A LIST OF LEGAL REQUIREMENTS.

Companies with a diverse workforce are better positioned to attract the best talent and maintain a competitive edge. A company that has (and fully utilizes) employees who have varied backgrounds and personalities is better equipped to serve a wide range of customers than one where most of the employees are alike or only certain types of employees have input.

Internals. Internally, diversity drives creativity, which helps employees come up with new and better products and processes. A workplace that includes employees with diverse backgrounds and perspectives will have a broader range of ideas, experiences, and insights to draw on when tackling issues like product creation, business planning, decision making, and development. Furthermore, a diverse group is more likely to question and challenge past practices, leading to improved products and services.

Another internal benefit of a diverse workplace is an improved employee relationship from start to finish.

This movie-like version of the powerpoint presentation with audio makes it easy to deliver diversity training to supervisors.

> There are also "State Requirements" in all 50 states.

Business and Legal Resources (BLR)

During H.W. Bush's Presidency, the EB-5 visa program was added to the Immigration Act of 1990, whereby foreign nationals could buy a fast track to U.S. citizenship for a $500,000 investment in the United States. The purpose stated was to encourage jobs in rural or economically depressed areas of the United States. The number of jobs the applicants had to create? Ten.

In 2011, according to Wikipedia.com, the U.S. made a "number of changes" in the program to encourage more foreign investors.

There are "Regional Centers" in case the foreign investor does not want the hassle of actually hiring employees. The Regional Centers will create the jobs in exchange for management fees. State agencies in California, Florida and Washington provide lists of areas suitable for the investments.

The system is dubbed, "Green Card through Investment," and it is run by a federal agency called USCIS, the U.S. Citizenship and Immigration Services.

IN U.S. VISA PROGRAM, MONEY TALKS
Los Angeles Times   Sep 4, 2011   p A1

Those who invest $500,000 in a U.S. enterprise that creates at least ten jobs in a rural area or a community with a high unemployment rate are eligible for special visas that put them and their families on the fast track to becoming permanent residents...It's the fastest way to establish permanent residency apart from marrying a U.S. citizen. Investors aren't required to work in the business or participate in its management; some never even see the enterprises they buy into.

The federal program, known as EB-5 is relatively small, capped at 10,000 visas annually. But applications nave skyrocketed since 2006 as entrepreneurs and cash-strapped towns have begun aggressively wooing wealthy foreigners as a low-cost source of capital...

Congress created the program in 1990 to attract wealthy Hong Kong residents looking to flee the British colony before the 1997 transfer to Communist China. Australia, Canada and New Zealand were courting these emigres...

The rules were complicated, and the program proved vulnerable to fraud...A flurry of EB-5 related websites has popped up with pitches written in Chinese, Korean, Spanish and Arabic. Promoters regularly offer seminars in hotel ballrooms in China, as well as in the U.S., proffering deals and collecting hefty fees...

"The government is selling access to this country and what are we getting in return? Very little," said David S. North, a research fellow with the Center for Immigration Studies in Washington.

The U.S. Citrizenship and Immigration Services which administers the program, by its own admission, has failed to closely track the flow of EB-5 money, how the projects are being sold to investors or whether the projects are successful. Its focus has been on making sure jobs are created - but not that the jobs will last.   by P.J. Huffstutter

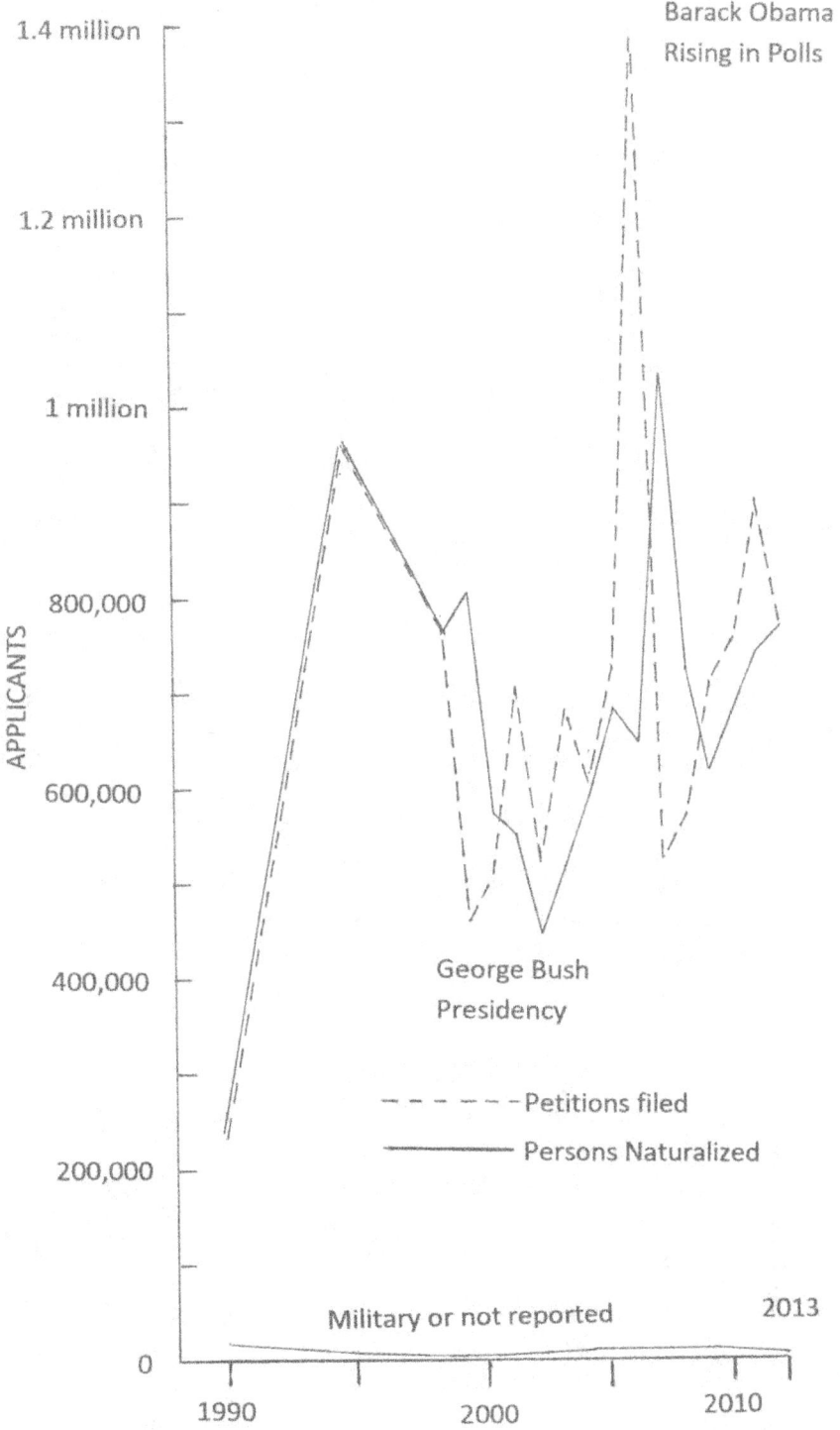

PETITIONS FOR NATURALIZATION
1990 - 2013

Barack Obama
Rising in Polls

APPLICANTS

1.4 million

1.2 million

1 million

800,000

600,000

400,000

George Bush
Presidency

– – – – – Petitions filed

——— Persons Naturalized

200,000

Military or not reported   2013

0

1990   2000   2010

Source: ProQuest Statistical Abstract of the United States 2016, p 43

Consider the annual administrative cost of admitting and managing hundreds of thousands of immigrants as reflected in the "Office of Personnel Management." The federal budget for this category ballooned from $15 billion in 1980 to $88 billion in 2014.

LEGAL IMMIGRANTS ADMITTED INTO U.S.
AND ILLEGAL IMMIGRANTS GRANTED AMNESTY, 1980 - 1993

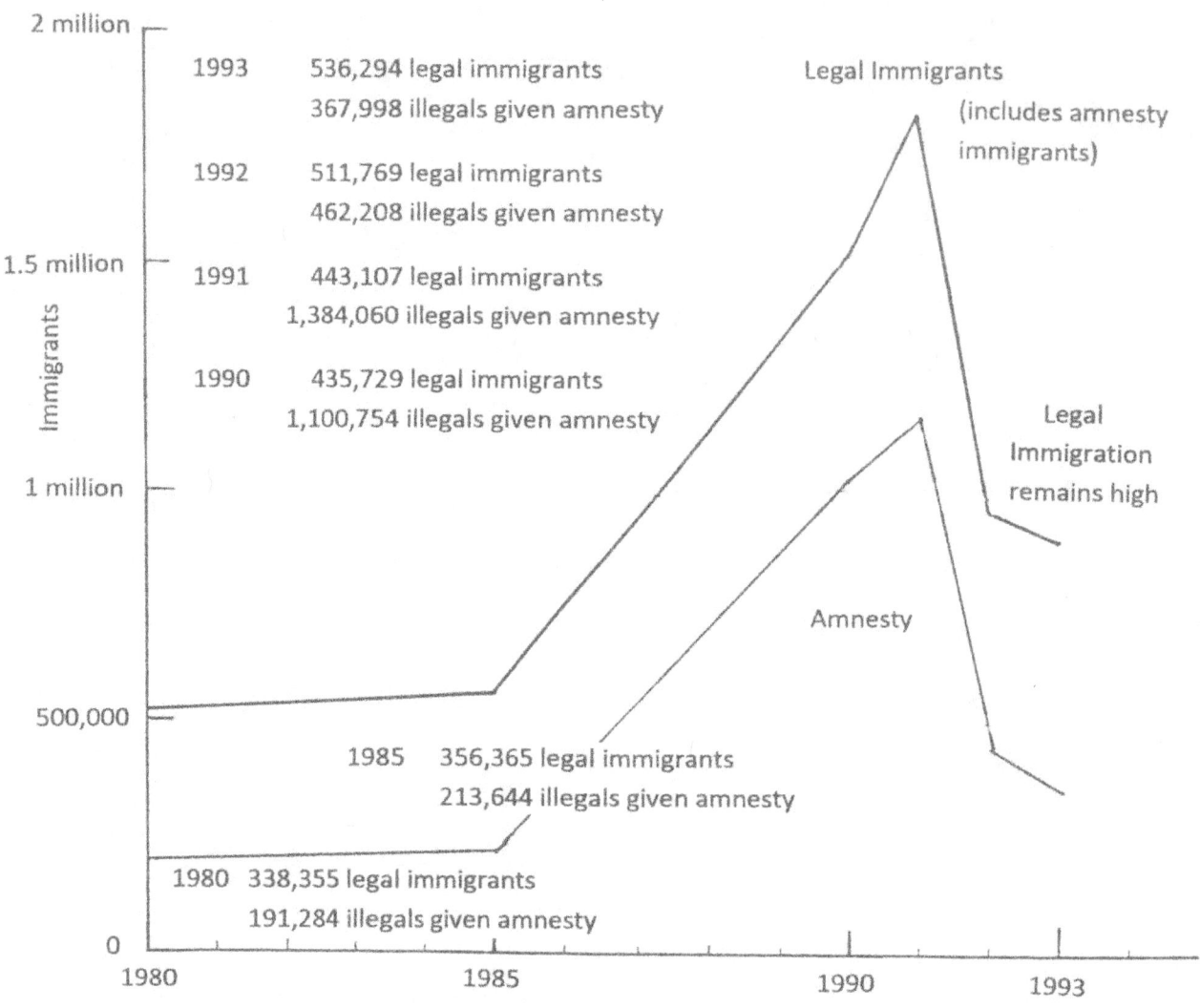

Note: Amnesty grants legal status to illegal immigrants.

Note: "Amnesty" and "illegal immigrants" are terms not used by the federal government. It uses the term, "Legalization Adjustments"

Source: Statistical Abstract of the United States 1995, p 10; 2004-2005, p 8

A reasonable person could conclude that granting legal status to illegal immigrants for four consecutive years for a total of 3 million, 315 thousand and 20 persons encourages more illegal immigration.

While media attention focused on amnesty, legal immigration increased to 804,000 by 1994.

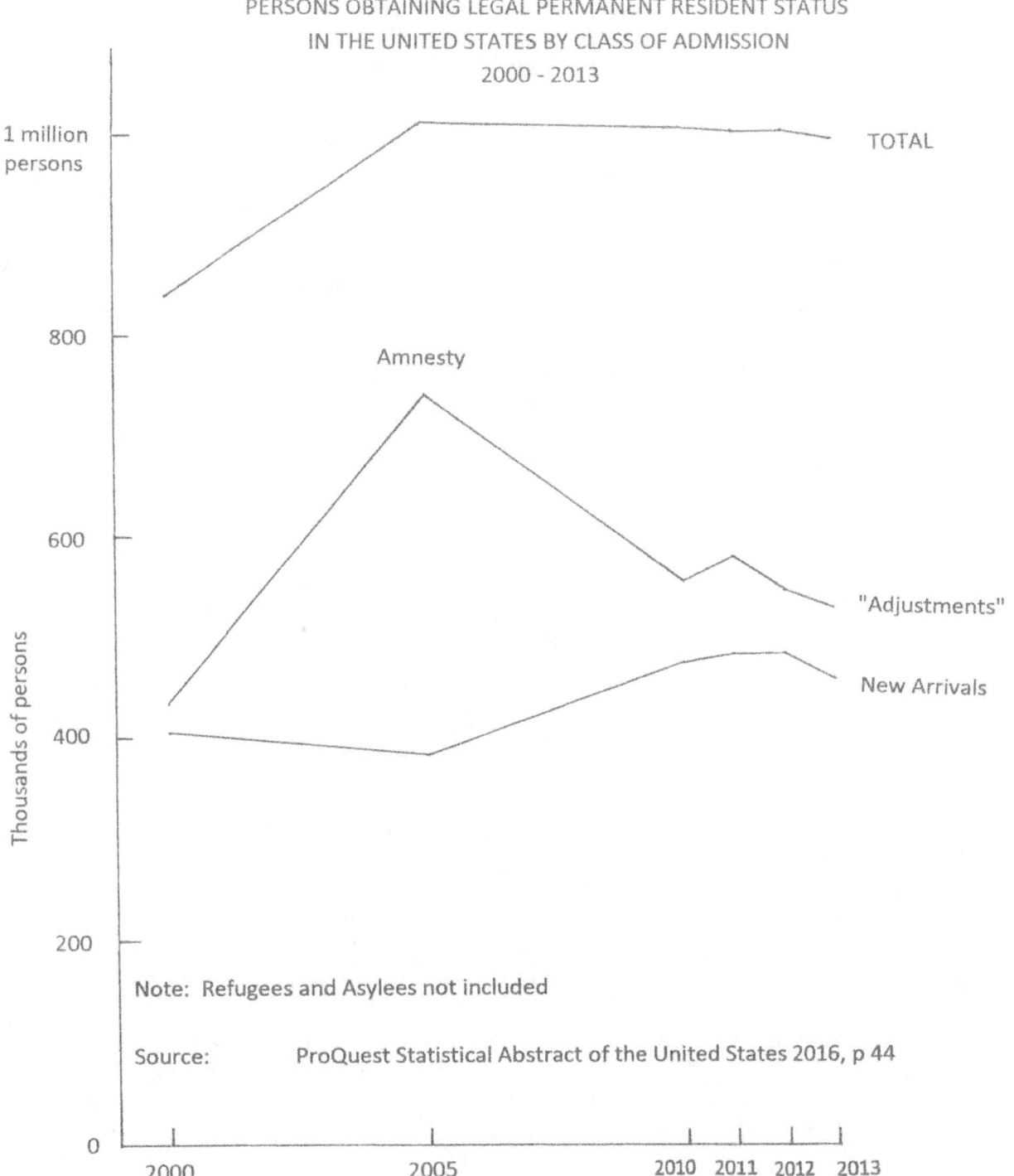

PERSONS OBTAINING LEGAL PERMANENT RESIDENT STATUS
IN THE UNITED STATES BY CLASS OF ADMISSION
2000 - 2013

TOTAL

Amnesty

"Adjustments"

New Arrivals

Thousands of persons

1 million persons

800

600

400

200

0

Note: Refugees and Asylees not included

Source: ProQuest Statistical Abstract of the United States 2016, p 44

2000   2005   2010 2011 2012 2013

"Adjustments" are non-citizens already living in the United States who are
granted legal permanent resident status. These include humanitarian migrants
(such as refugees) and persons illegally present in the United States."

Factoring out Refugees and Asylees for the listed six years (780,885 persons)
"adjustments" for the listed six years alone totals 2 million, 616.2 thousand persons.

PERSONS OBTAINING LEGAL PERMANENT RESIDENT STATUS
IN THE UNITED STATES BY SELECTED COUNTRY OF BIRTH
2013

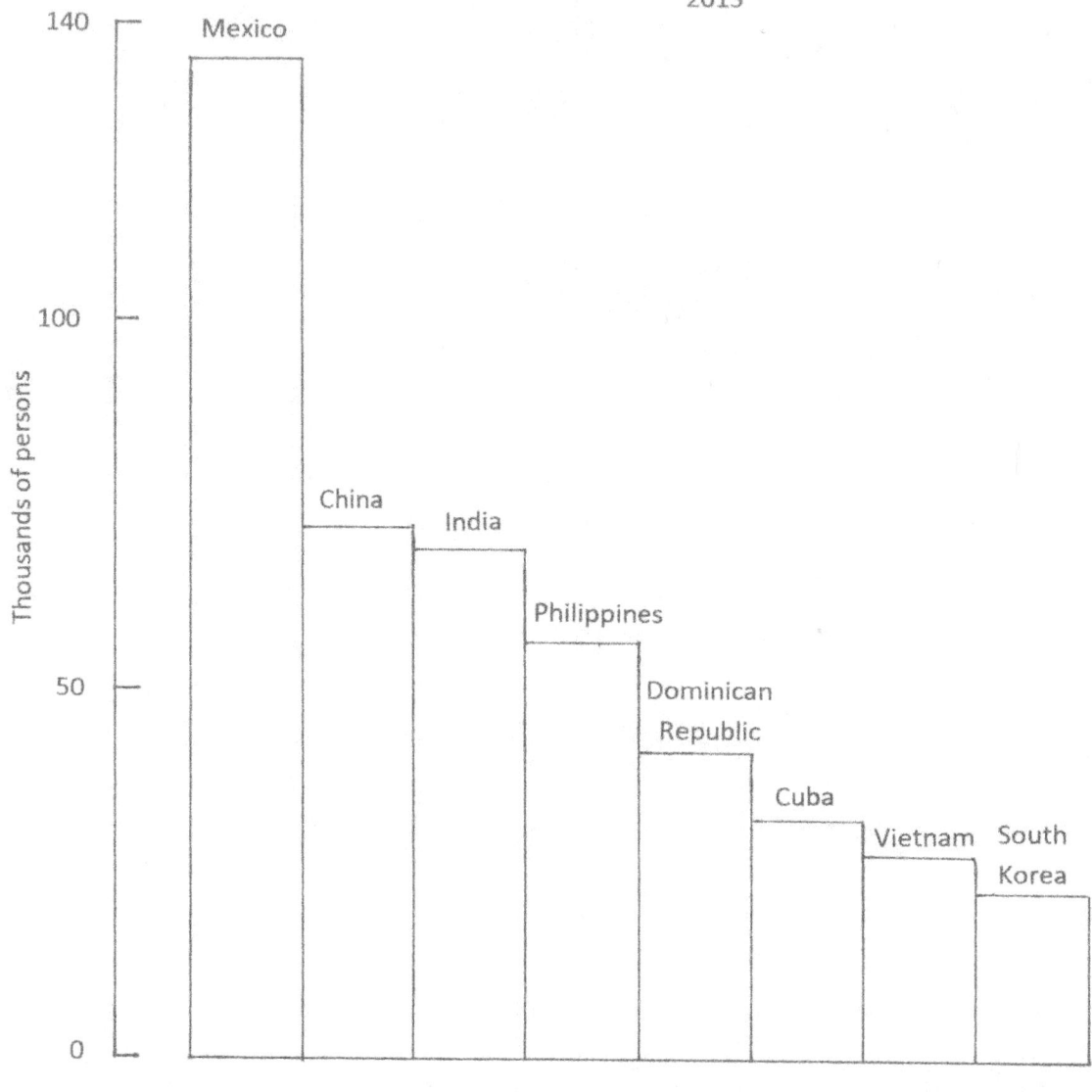

Source: ProQuest Statistical Abstract of the United States 2016, p 44

"The United States clearly cannot take all of the world's surplus population, and it would be insane for us to try. The United States is no longer an empty continent that can absorb endless streams of population. The melting pot, like any pot, is finite."

From THE IMMIGRATION TIME BOMB: THE FRAGMENTING OF AMERICA by
Richard D. Lamm and Gary Imhoff, copyright © 1985 by Richard D. Lamm and Gary Imhoff. Used by
permission of Dutton, an imprint of Penguin Publishing Group, a division of Penguin Random House LLC.

Richard Lamm was governor of Colorado 1975 - 1987.

UNDOCUMENTED (ILLEGAL) IMMIGRANTS
BY RATE OF INCREASE

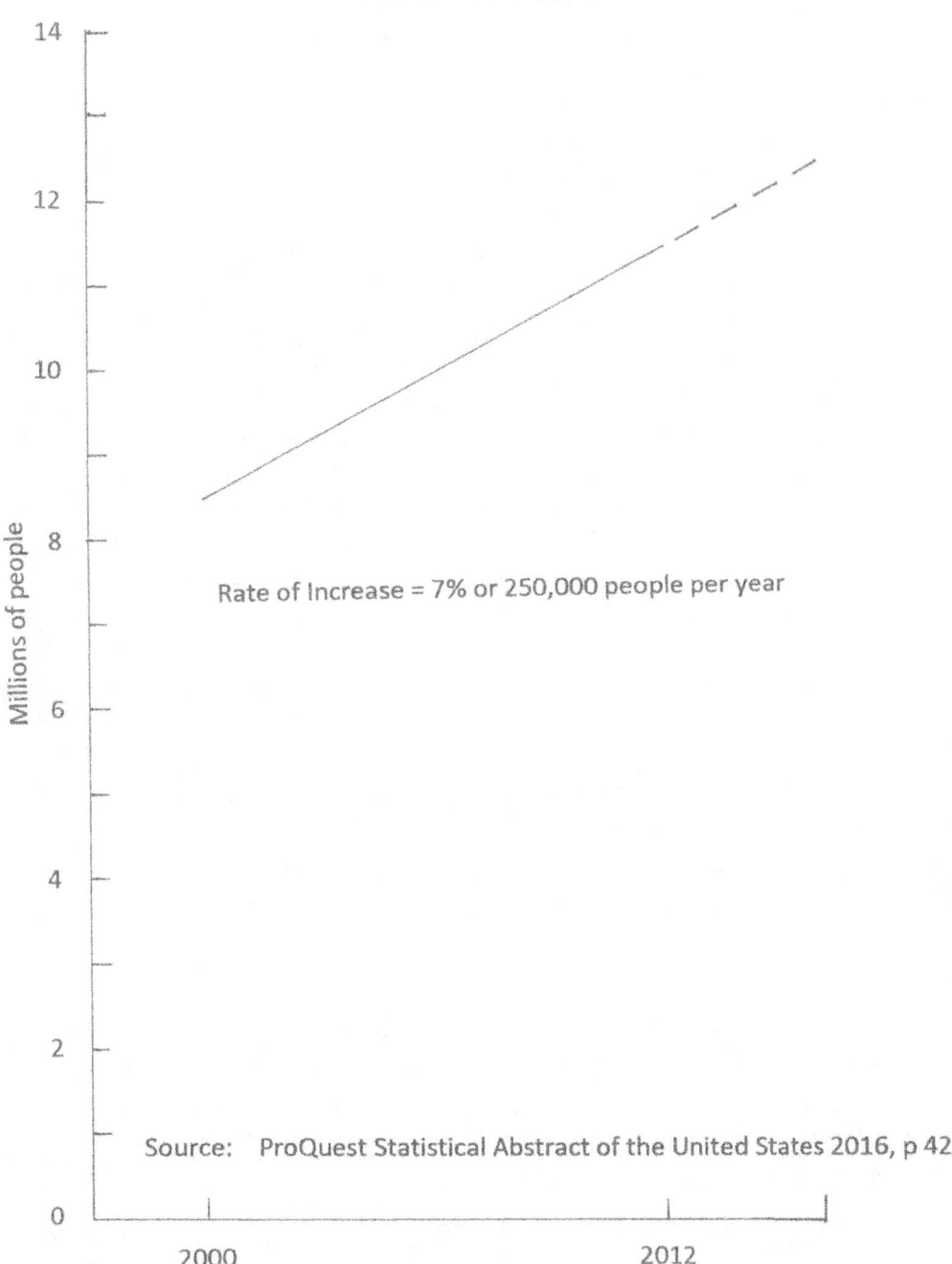

Rate of Increase = 7% or 250,000 people per year

Source: ProQuest Statistical Abstract of the United States 2016, p 42

"The United States have already felt the evils of incorporating a large number of foreigners into their national mass; by promoting in different classes different predilections in favor of particular foreign nations, and antipathies against others, it has served very much to divide the community and to distract our councils."

--- Alexander Hamilton
January 12, 1802

A SURGE OF CHINESE MIGRANTS VIA MEXICO

Los Angeles Times   Jun 8, 2016   p B2

The number of Chinese immigrants illegally crossing the Mexican border into California has skyrocketed in recent years, the result of a lucrative smuggling industry, mass migration from China and a diversifying pool of migrants settling in the United States.

From October to May, Border Patrol agents in the San Diego sector apprehended an estimated 663 Chinese nationals, compared with 48 in the entire previous year.

Wendi Lee, a spokeswoman for the Border Patrol, said criminal organizations involved in smuggling maximize their profits by transporting Chinese immigrants, often charging premiums..."We're talking anywhere from $50,000 to $70,000 per person."

The emigration rate of China's highly educated population is now five times as high as the country's overall rate..."China's wealthy elites and growing middle class are increasingly pursuing educational and work opportunities overseas for themselves and their families, facilitated by their rising incomes," according to a February report by the Migration Policy Institute...

"China is the world's largest country. In that sense, the recent increase in border crossings represents a drop in the bucket," said Muzaffar Chishti, director of the Migratrion Policy Institute's office at New York University's School of Law.   by Tatiana Sanchez

One of the biggest enforcement problems for immigration officials is the visa program, whereby visitors enter the country with a valid visa but overstay its time limit. Congress met with immigration officials, concerned because some of the 9/11 terrorists had overstayed their visas. The backlog is estimated at 5 million.

While visitors are fingerprinted when they enter the U.S., there is no tracking system to make sure they leave on schedule. Word gets out that the U.S. doesn't target visa holders who overstay, which encourages others to give it a try. According to the Pew Research Center, most who overstay are from Canada, followed by Mexico, Brazil, Germany and Italy.

Immigration officials report that the problem is too little manpower, not enough funding, and not enough information to track the visa holders. Officials are researching what works in other countries. Mexico has visitors fill out a card in duplicate, one turned in when they enter the country, and the other turned in when they leave. In Australia, information is put in the computer upon a visitor's arrival, then red-flagged if the departure date isn't met.

Compounding the problem is the vast size of the U.S. in population and area. A visa holder could be anywhere. In 2015, over 480,000 visa holders overstayed their departure date. The only penalty they face if caught is deportation.   --newsmax.com

REFUGEES TO THE UNITED STATES, 1971 - 1990

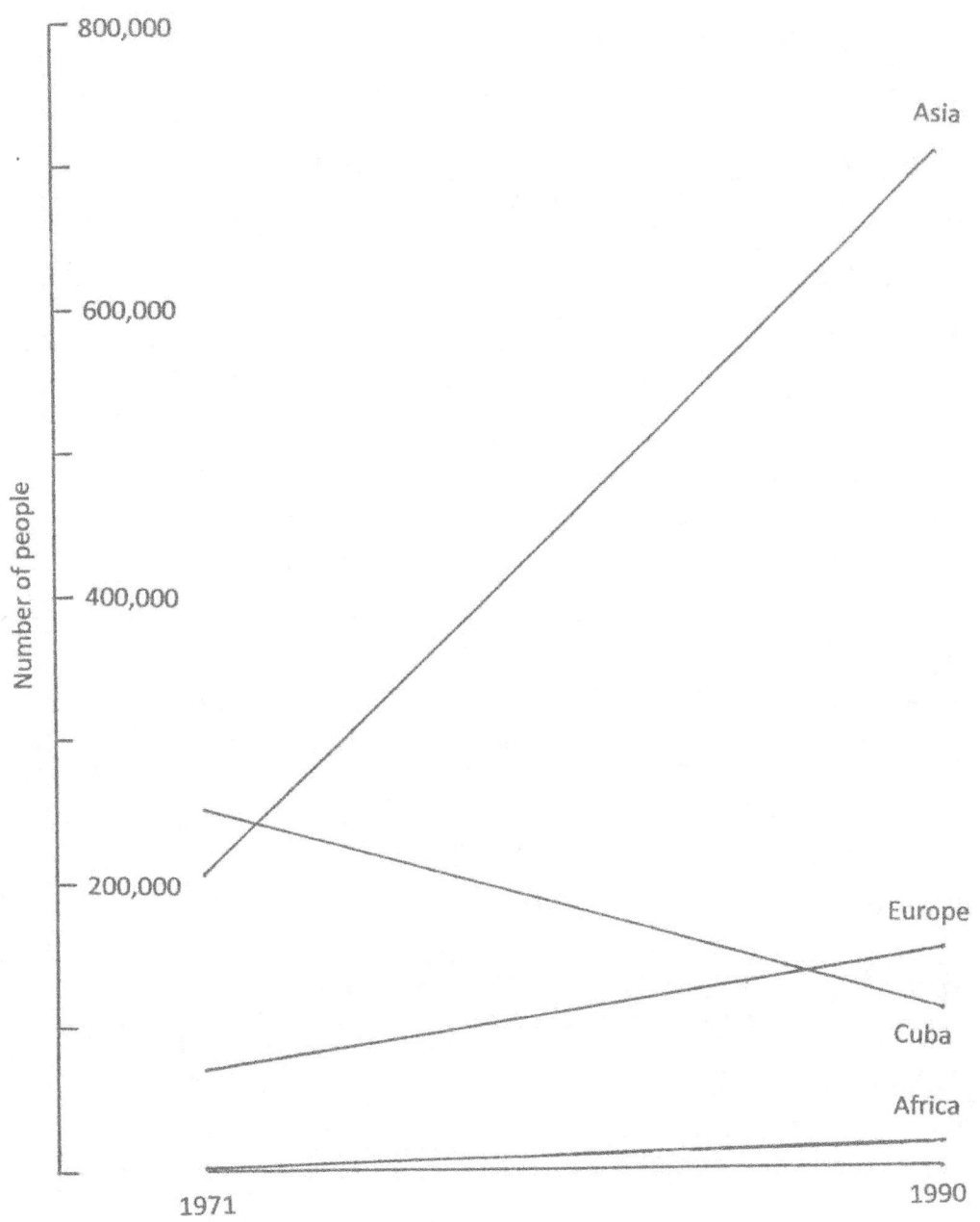

REFUGEE AND ASYLUM SEEKERS GRANTED ADMISSION
TO THE UNITED STATES, 2011 - 2013

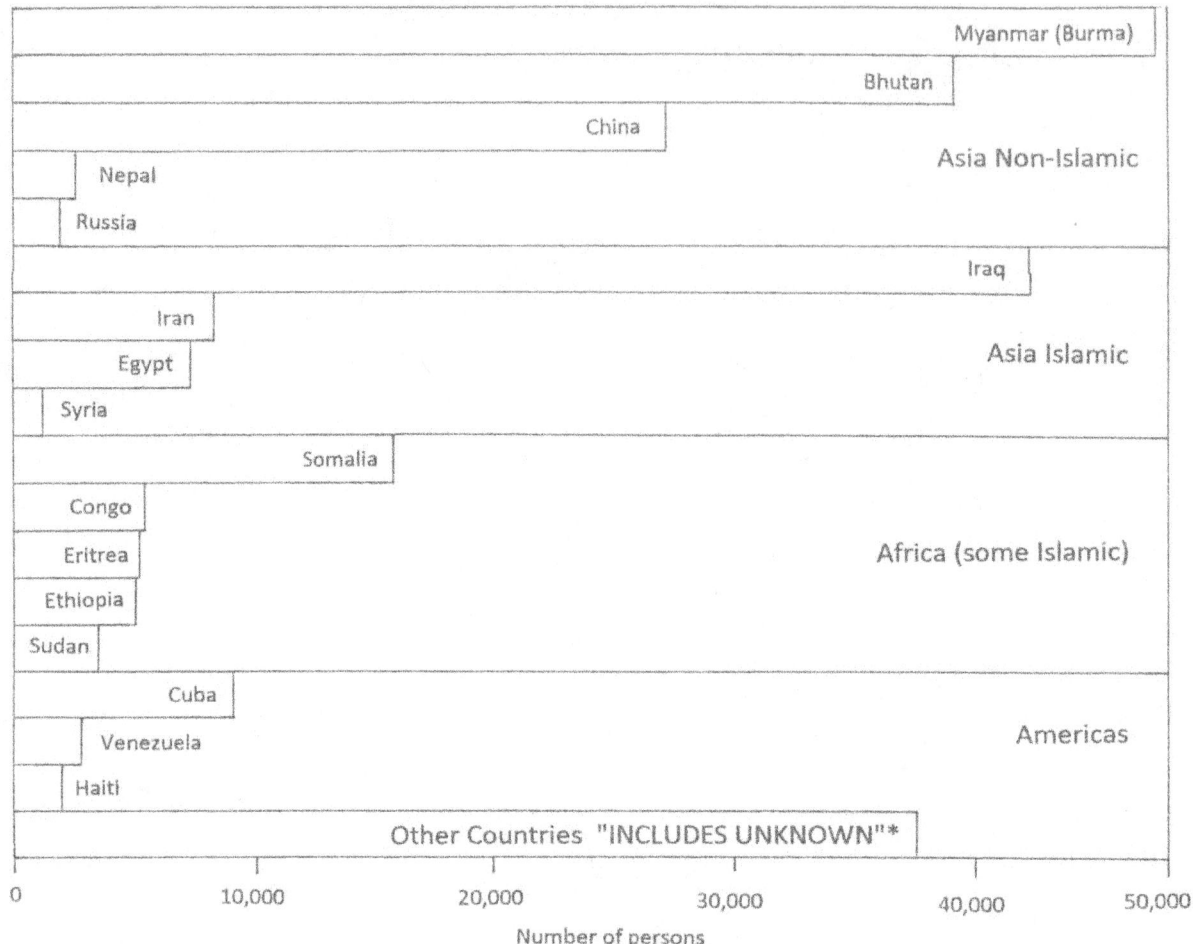

Myanmar (Burma)

Bhutan

China

Asia Non-Islamic

Nepal

Russia

Iraq

Iran

Asia Islamic

Egypt

Syria

Somalia

Congo

Africa (some Islamic)

Eritrea

Ethiopia

Sudan

Cuba

Venezuela

Americas

Haiti

Other Countries "INCLUDES UNKNOWN"*

Number of persons

0   10,000   20,000   30,000   40,000   50,000

TOTAL: 263,942 persons

Source: U.S. Department of Homeland Security
                 ProQuest Statistical Abstract of the United States 2016, p 42

*They throw away their papers on airplanes bound for the United States. At U.S. Customs,
they declare they are Asylum Seekers. They evidently don't reveal their home countries
or their identities, or they make something up. They have the resources for an expensive
airplane ticket. Homeland "Security" often grants them legal status, encouraging more Asylum
Seekers.

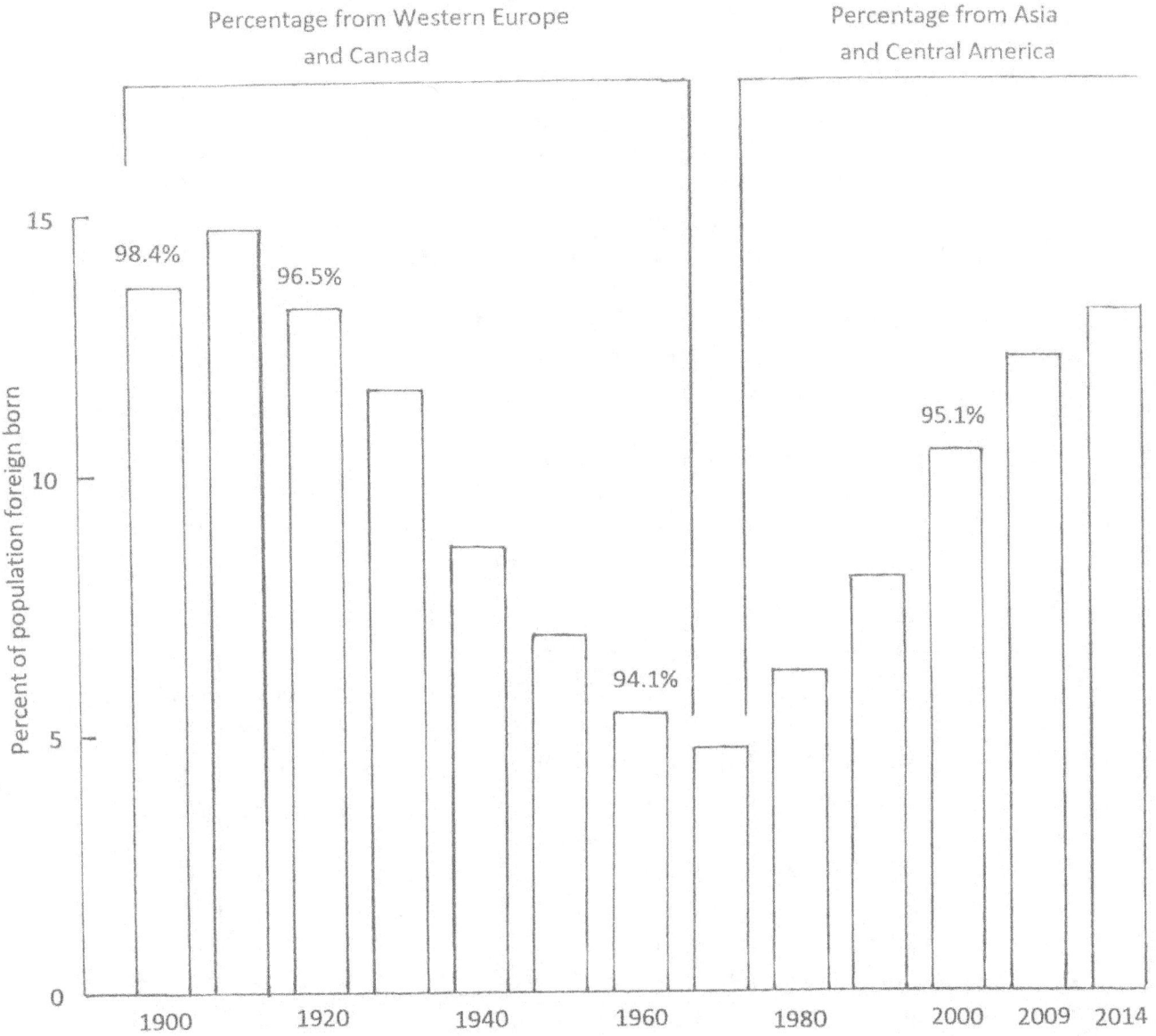

UNITED STATES FOREIGN BORN POPULATION BY COUNTRY OF ORIGIN
1900 - 2014

Percentage from Western Europe and Canada

Percentage from Asia and Central America

Percent of population foreign born

98.4%

96.5%

94.1%

95.1%

15

10

5

0

1900   1920   1940   1960   1980   2000 2009 2014

Note: The 1965 Immigration and Nationality Act removed restrictions on U.S. immigrants
          based on country of origin.

Source: The World Almanac and Book of Facts 2012, p 615; 2016, p 620

"There is no precedent for a sovereign country undergoing such a rapid and radical
transformation of its ethnic character in the entire history of the world."

--Peter Brimelow
"Alien Nation - Common Sense about America's Immigration Disaster,"
1995, p 57, Penguin Random House, New York, New York;
The Wylie Agency, LLC, New York, New York   Reprinted by permission

AFFIRMATIVE ACTION UPHELD

Los Angeles Times   Jun 24, 2016 p A1

WASHINGTON - The 30-year conservative campaign to strike down race-based affirmative action came to an apparent end Thursday when a University of Texas admissions policy was upheld by Justice Anthony M. Kennedy...often the deciding vote on divisive issues.

Kennedy said a university and its leaders deserve "considerable deference" as they seek "student body diversity" that is "central to its identity and educational mission."

The justices rejected a discrimination claim brought by a white student who had good but not excellent credentials when she was turned down for admission by the Austin campus in 2008. Abigail Fisher became the plaintiff in a suit that asked the court to rule that considering a student's race or ethnicity violated the Constitution's guarantee of equal protection of the laws.

The court's decision is a major victory for affirmative action...The ruling should give comfort to college officials across the nation who consider a student's race or ethnicity in admissions.   by David G. Savage

As of November 16, 2015, the number of international students at U.S. colleges and universities had the highest rate of growth in 35 years, increasing by 10% to a record high of 974,926 students. This strong growth confirms that the United States remains the destination of choice in higher education. The U.S. hosts more of the world's 4.5 million globally mobile college and university students than any other country in the world, almost double the number hosted by the United Kingdom, the second leading host country.

The private University of Southern California near downtown Los Angeles leads the nation in international student enrollment. Students from India were the largest group, with 1,571 students, followed by students from China, with 1,015. "USC is the top American university for international students by design, not by accident. Over the years, we have been strategically expanding our international presence in major cities around the world," said USC provost, Max Nikias. New York University and Columbia University are second and third, based on a study by Open Doors.   ---usc.edu

Most of the growth in foreign student populations are from China, India and Brazil. China and India comprise 45% of the total number, with 304,040 students from China and 132,888 from India on campuses throughout the country.

There were large increases in the number of students from Brazil, Kuwait and Saudi Arabia, all countries whose governments are investing heavily in international scholarships for their students, sending tens of thousands of them abroad to develop a globally competent workforce. International students' spending in all 50 states contributed more than $30 billion to the U.S. economy in 2014, according to the U.S. Department of Commerce. --opendoors.org

RACE, COUNTRY OF ORIGIN, REGION OF ORIGIN, COUNTRY OF NATIONALITY, COUNTRY OF BIRTH, ANCESTRY GROUP, HISPANIC ORIGIN, LATINO POPULATION, LATIN AMERICA, HISPANIC POPULATION, HISPANIC ORIGIN GROUPS, HISPANICS* (*may be of any race)

The U.S. Department of Commerce, when preparing the numbers for the ProQuest Statistical Abstract of 2016, uses all of the above categories. It also includes, in Table 9 on Resident Population: "White alone, not Hispanic," "White alone," "Black or African American alone," "American Indian, Alaska Native alone," "Asian alone," "two or more races," and "Hispanic Origin," an awkward list at best.

The abstract has a footnote for Hispanic origin, explaining that "Hispanic origin is considered an ethnicity, not a race. Hispanics may be of any race." Several tables have a footnote that says, "includes other races not shown separately," yet they include White, Black, Asian and "Hispanic origin."

Physical anthropologists report that there are three races: Caucasian, Negro and Mongolian. All three have distinct geographic origins.

Ethnicities usually self-classify by region of origin. Hispanics identify as Mexican, Columbian, Puerto Rican, or Spanish/Hispanic, among others. If Hispanics "can be of any race," why not also the Eskimo, the American Indian, Hawaiian, and, for that matter, Middle Easterners, Indians and Pakistanis, among others.

The problem lies with "Hispanics can be of any race." For one thing, it singles out Hispanics as a catch-all category, a mongrel category, which is demeaning. For another, it is untrue. Hispanics have a very distinctive ethnic or geographic origin: Central and South America. To allow persons from origins other than Central and South America to label themselves "Hispanic" or "Latino" is a distortion of data. It could also be fraudulent, in that persons who wish not to be identified by their regions of origin have a legal loophole allowing them to hide their true ethnicity or race.

The category "two or more races" is equally vague. "Ethnic origin" or "geographic origin" would be more accurate. It matters, as United States ethnic policy is geared toward more and more diversity.

> The federal Office of Management and Budget "defines the concept of race as outlined for the U.S. Census as not 'scientific or anthropological'... "The practice of separating 'race' and 'ethnicity' as different categories has been criticized by the American Anthropological Association..."   --Wikipedia, the free encyclopedia

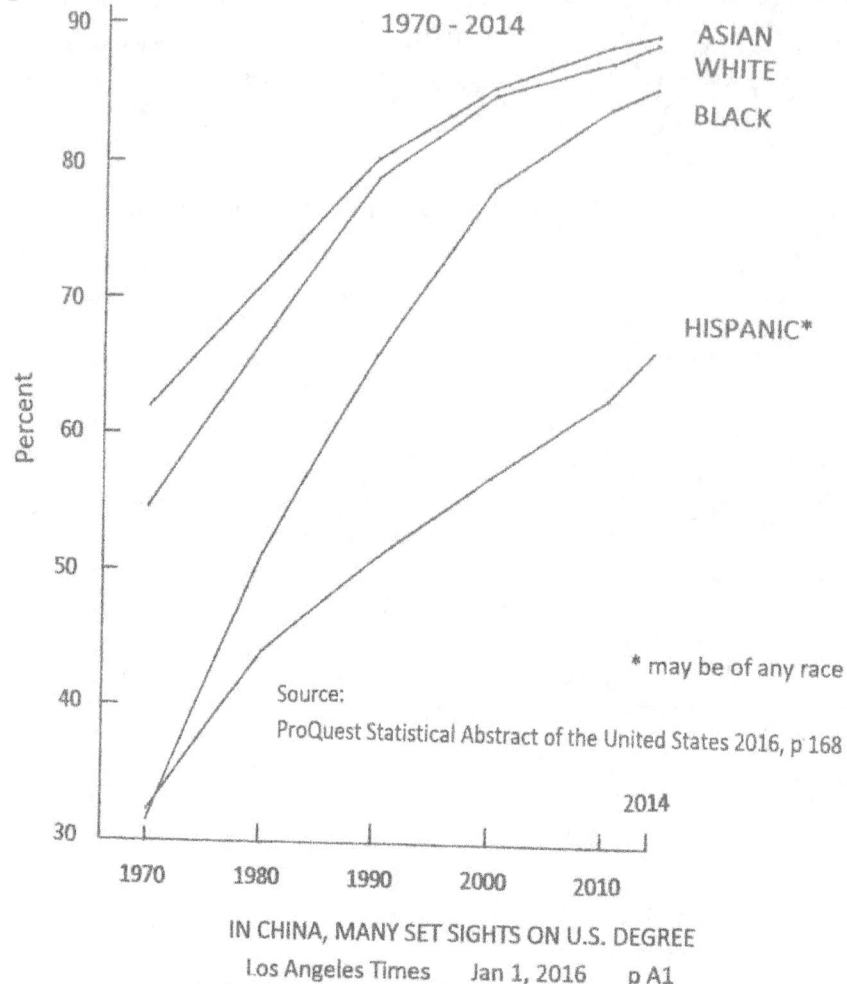

HIGH SCHOOL GRADUATES IN THE U.S. BY RACE AND HISPANIC ORIGIN
1970 - 2014

ASIAN
WHITE
BLACK

HISPANIC*

* may be of any race

Source:
ProQuest Statistical Abstract of the United States 2016, p 168

IN CHINA, MANY SET SIGHTS ON U.S. DEGREE
Los Angeles Times   Jan 1, 2016   p A1

Three months before the gaokao, China's all-or-nothing college entrance exam that can determine whether students become cashiers or CEOs...his family moved to the United States. After studying English for a year, he began to attend classes at Pasadena City College and hopes to transfer to UCLA.

More than 124,000 Chinese undergraduates are studying in the United States, according to the Institute of International Education. Many are affluent, announcing their presence with Lamborghinis, flashy clothes and the profligate spending that is the hallmark of the fuer dai - the derogatory term for sons and daughters of China's new wealthy class.

But a growing number are children from lower-middle class families who are looking for an alternative to an overcrowded and unforgiving Chinese educational system.

In China, a huge industry of intermediary agencies guarantees acceptance letters for a few thousand dollars, and they've successfully marketed American community colleges as a stop on the way to a degree at a four-year university.

The rising numbers of foreign students in publicly funded universities have irked some parents and legislators. "It used to be that Chinese kids wanted to go to Harvard, but now there are Chinese students at every level and type of U.S. institution," said Peggy Blumenthal, senior advisor to the President of the Institute of International Education.   by Frank Shyong

U.S. COLLEGE EDUCATION BY SEX AND RACE
1990 and 2010

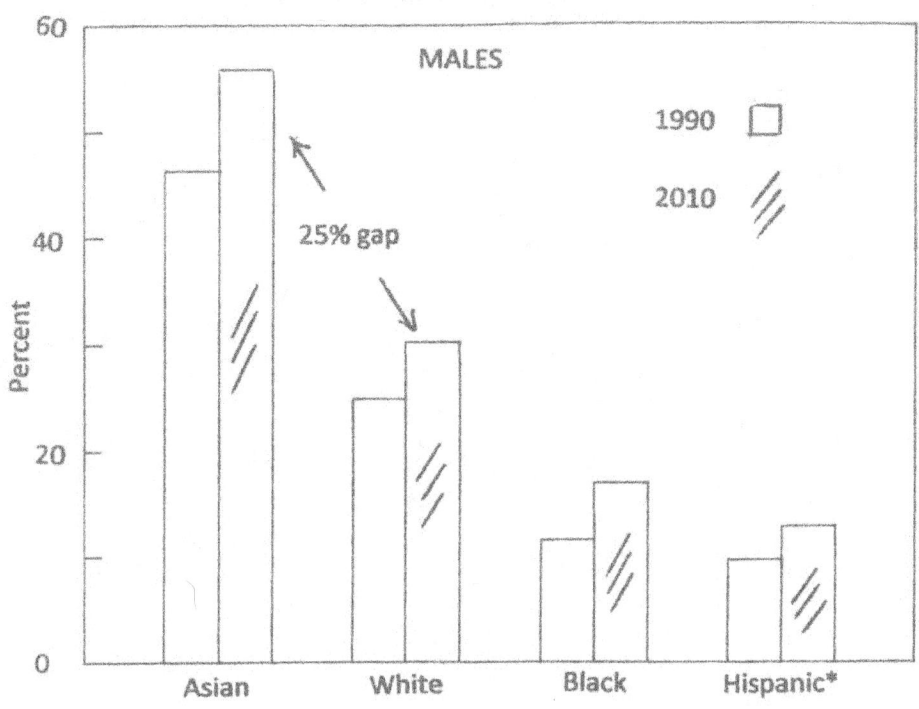

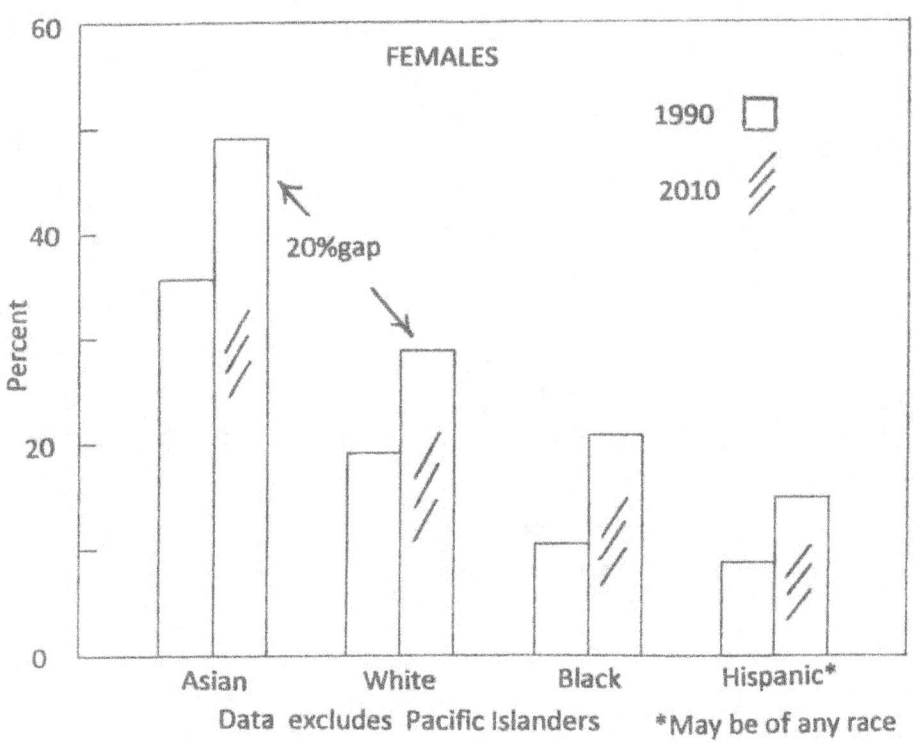

Data excludes Pacific Islanders   *May be of any race

Source: Statistical Abstract of the United States 1995, p 157; 2012, p 151

COLLEGE GRADUATES IN THE UNITED STATES BY RACE AND HISPANIC ORIGIN
1970 - 2014

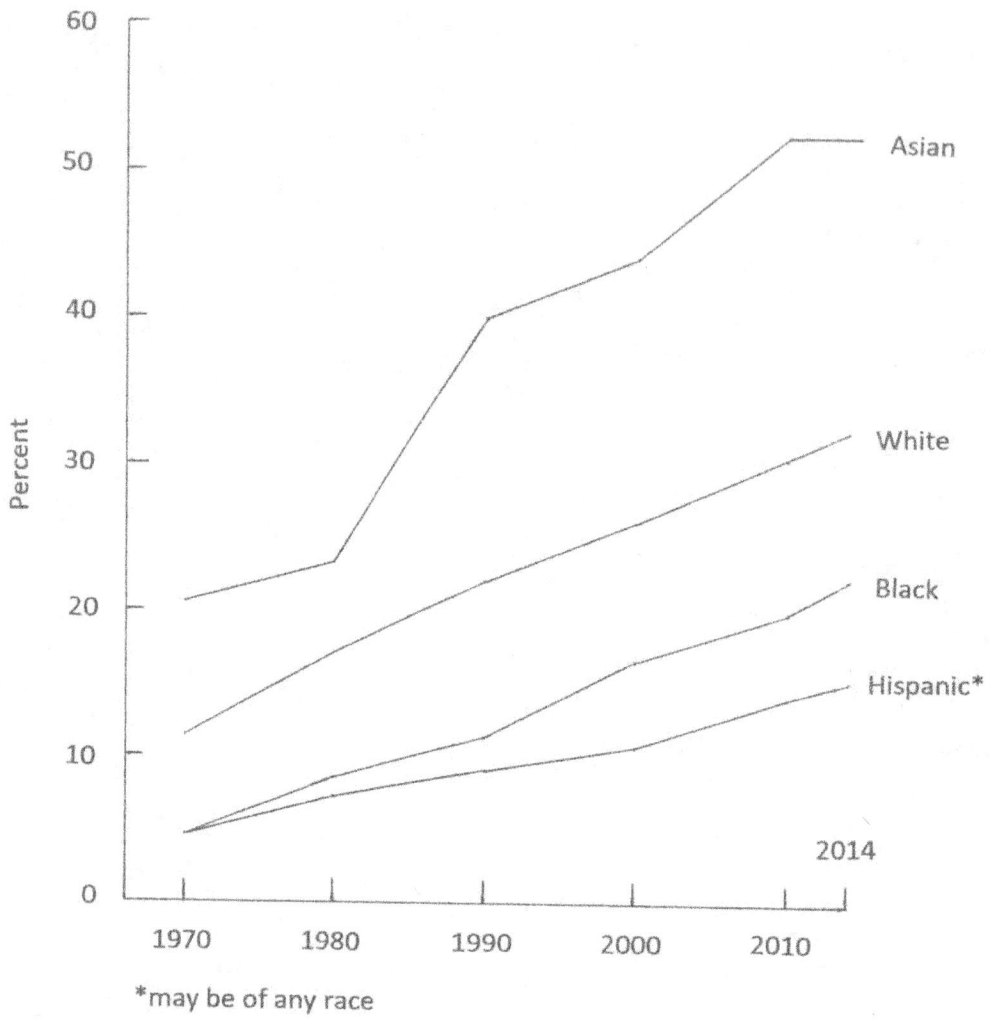

*may be of any race

Source: ProQuest Statistical Abstract of the United States 2016, p 168

For every foreign student enrolled in a U.S. college or university,
there is a U.S. student who is not.

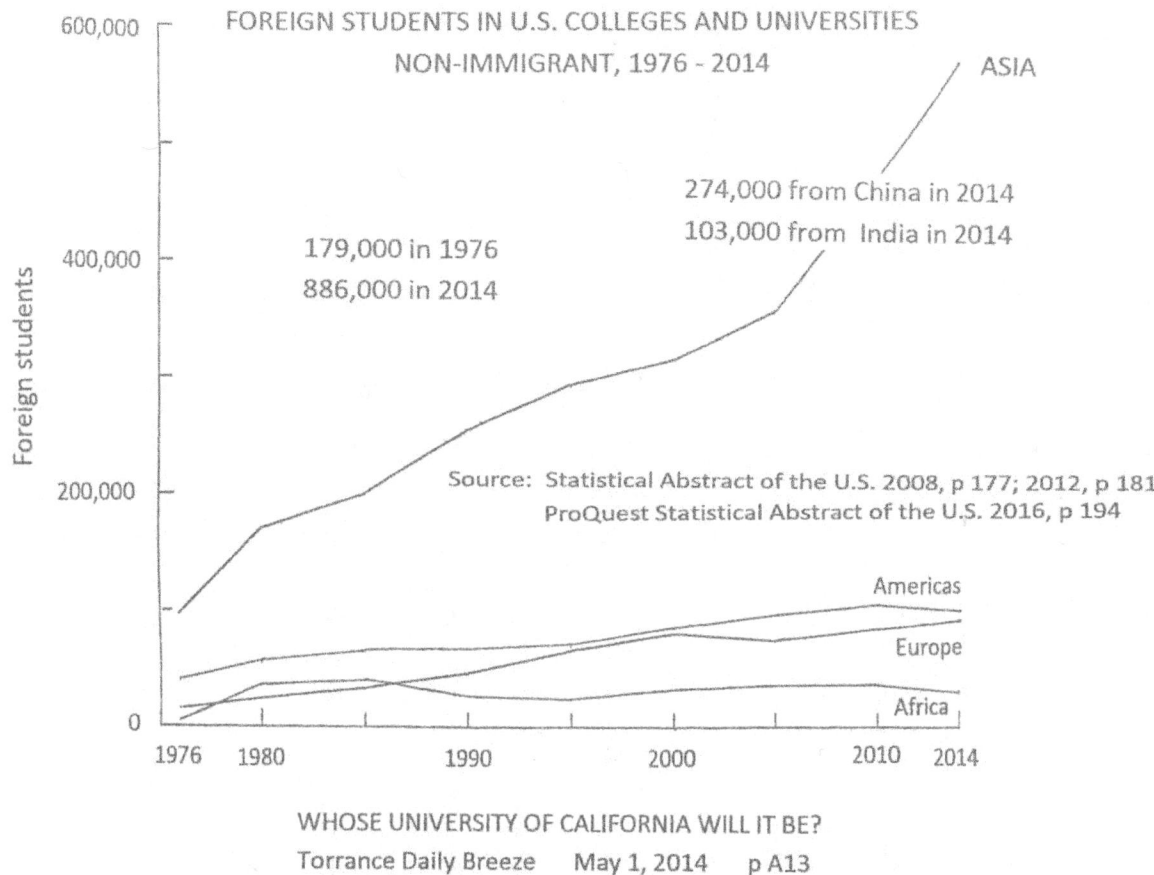

FOREIGN STUDENTS IN U.S. COLLEGES AND UNIVERSITIES
NON-IMMIGRANT, 1976 - 2014

ASIA

274,000 from China in 2014
103,000 from India in 2014

179,000 in 1976
886,000 in 2014

Source: Statistical Abstract of the U.S. 2008, p 177; 2012, p 181
ProQuest Statistical Abstract of the U.S. 2016, p 194

Americas

Europe

Africa

Foreign students

600,000

400,000

200,000

0

1976 1980   1990   2000   2010 2014

WHOSE UNIVERSITY OF CALIFORNIA WILL IT BE?
Torrance Daily Breeze   May 1, 2014   p A13

The squeeze on this state's most promising high school graduates became tighter than ever before. Will the nine undergraduate campuses of the University of California continue to be the fundamental goal and reward for the state's high schoolers...or will it become another playground for wealthy out-of-state and foreign students who can afford the almost $23,000 extra per year in tuition paid by non-California residents?

So far, that extra money - the difference between $13,200 in-state tuition this year and $36,078 for all others - has proved no hindrance to foreigners in particular. One reason: Governments of China and some Arab countries pay all tuition and expenses for many of their citizens who study at American universities.

UC officials maintain the out-of-staters displace no Californians in either the top 9 percent of their high school class or the top 9 percent statewide. Of course, UC used to accept the top 12% statewide. Plus the out-of-state proportion is higher at the most desired UC campuses - Berkeley and UCLA.

Which suggests that in academia, money talks, especially the more than $120 million in extra yearly tuition to be paid by new out-of-state students. Add in returning students and those in graduate and professional schools, and UC new gets nearly $1 billion more each year from out-of-staters than if the same slots went to Californians.

For the first time this year, UC took more Latino students than Anglos, 29% to 27%, and in-state Asian-Americans, 36%.   by Thomas D. Elias

U.S. MEDIAN ANNUAL EARNINGS BY RACE
1994 - 2009

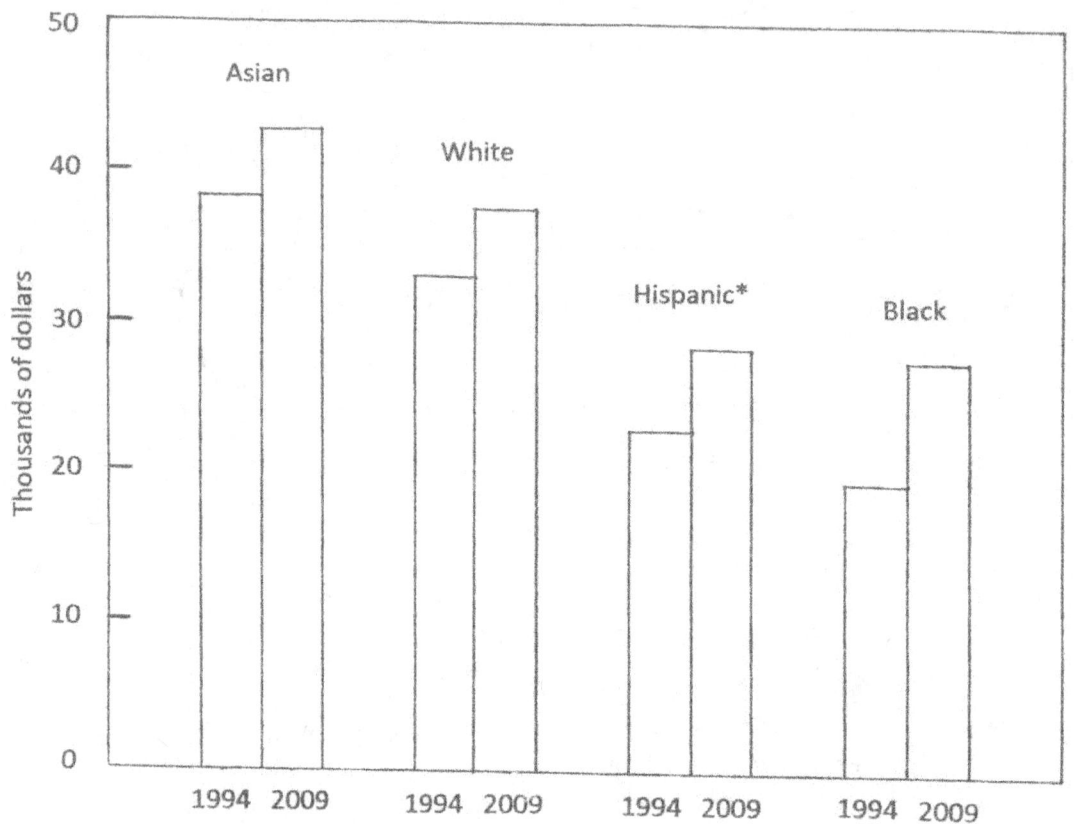

*Hispanic may be of any race

Source: World Almanac and Book of Facts 2012, p 114
           Statistical Abstract of the United States 1995, p 433

MEDIAN FAMILY INCOME IN THE UNITED STATES
BY RACE AND HISPANIC ORIGIN, 2013

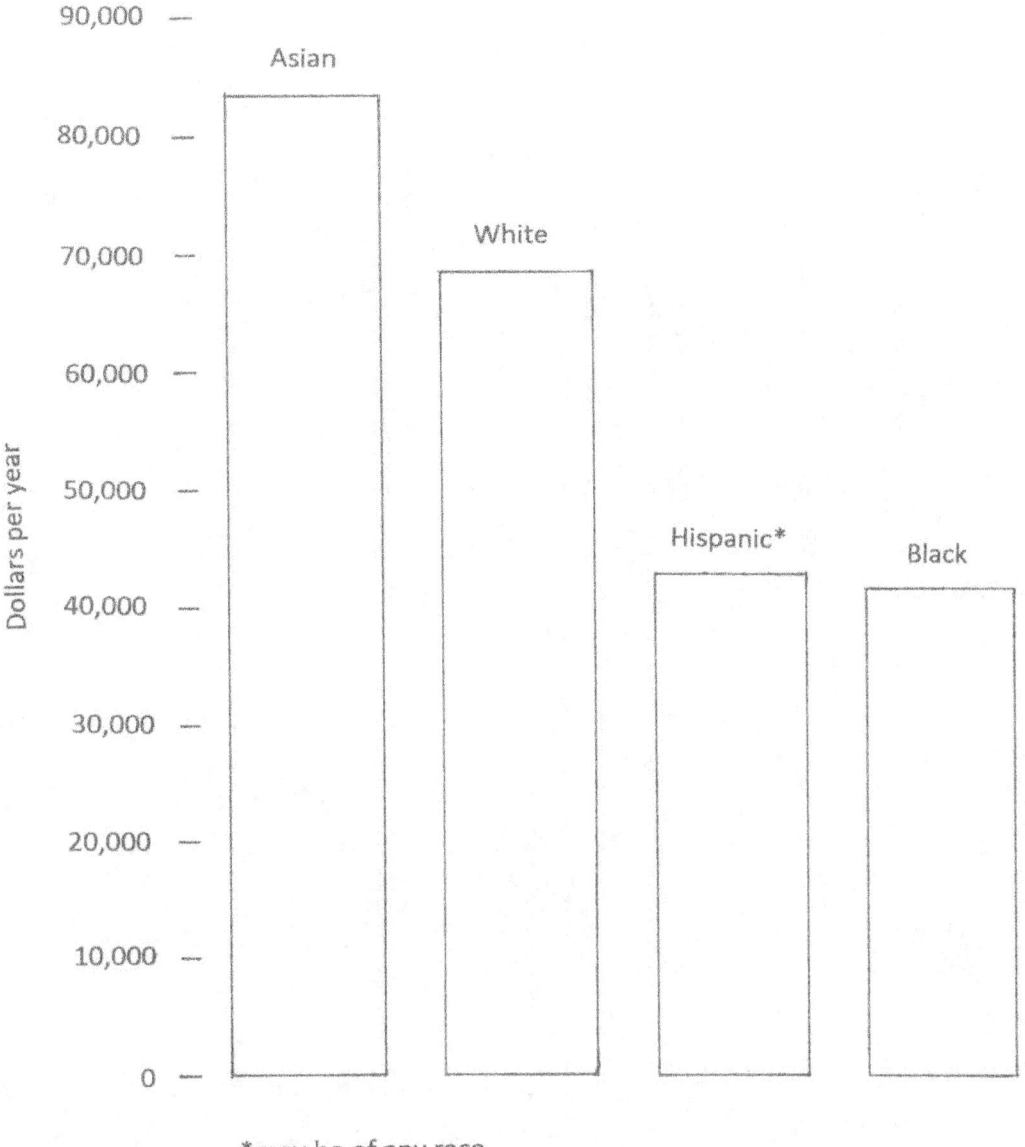

*may be of any race

Source: ProQuest Statistical Abstract of the United States 2016, p 36

POVERTY PERSONS IN THE UNITED STATES
2013

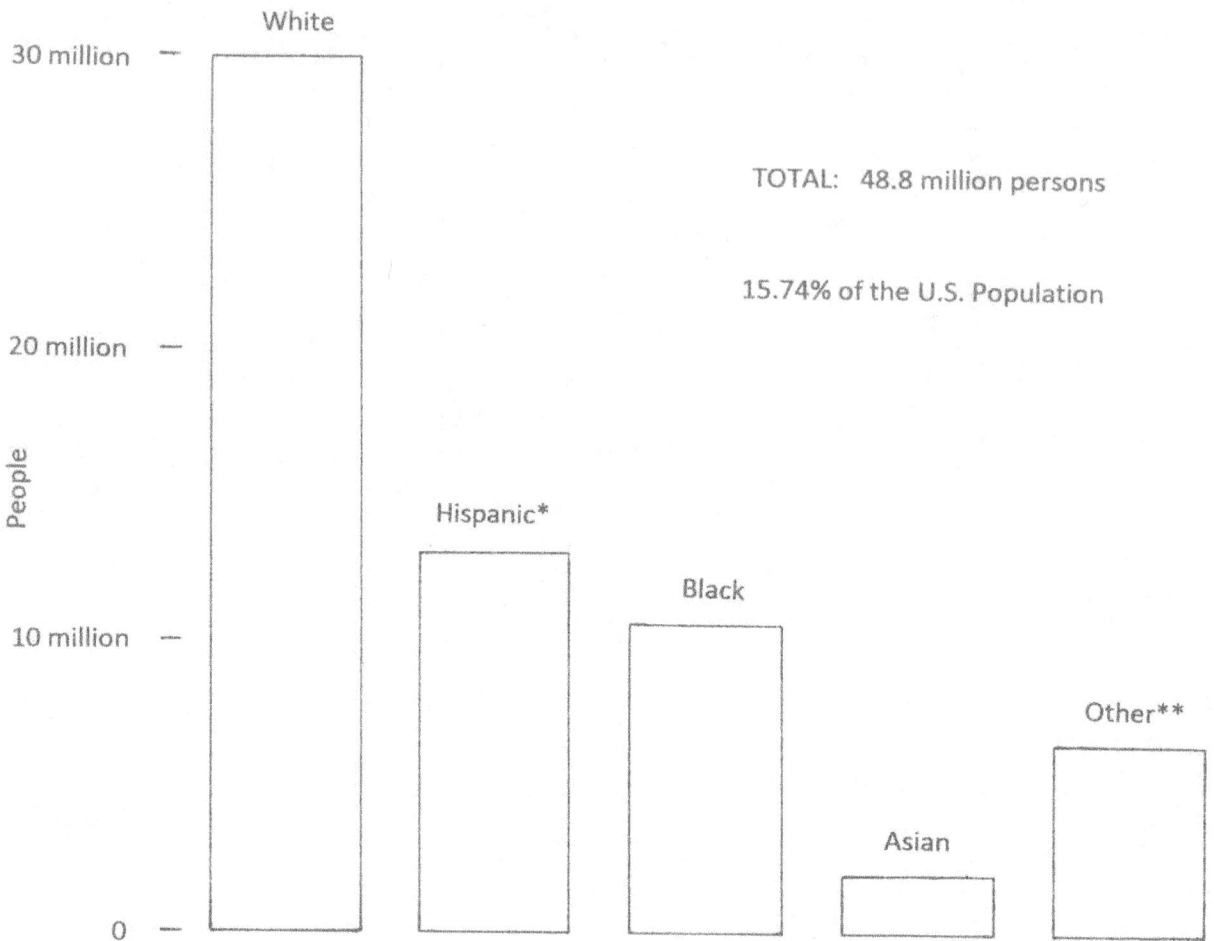

TOTAL: 48.8 million persons

15.74% of the U.S. Population

* may be of any race

** "Some other race alone, Two or more races, American Indian, Alaskan Native,
   Native Hawaiian or other Pacific Islander"

Source: Proquest Statistical Abstract of the United States 2016, p 36

"In June 2016 the International Monetary Fund warned the U.S. that its high poverty rate
needs to be tackled urgently by raising the minimum wage and offering paid maternity leave
to women to encourage them to enter the labor force."   --wikipedia.org

The academic contributors to the Routledge "Handbook of Poverty in the United States"
postulate that "new and extreme forms of poverty have emerged in the U.S. as a result of
neoliberal structural adjustment policies and globalization, which have rendered economically
marginalized communities as destitute 'surplus populations.'"   --wikipedia.org

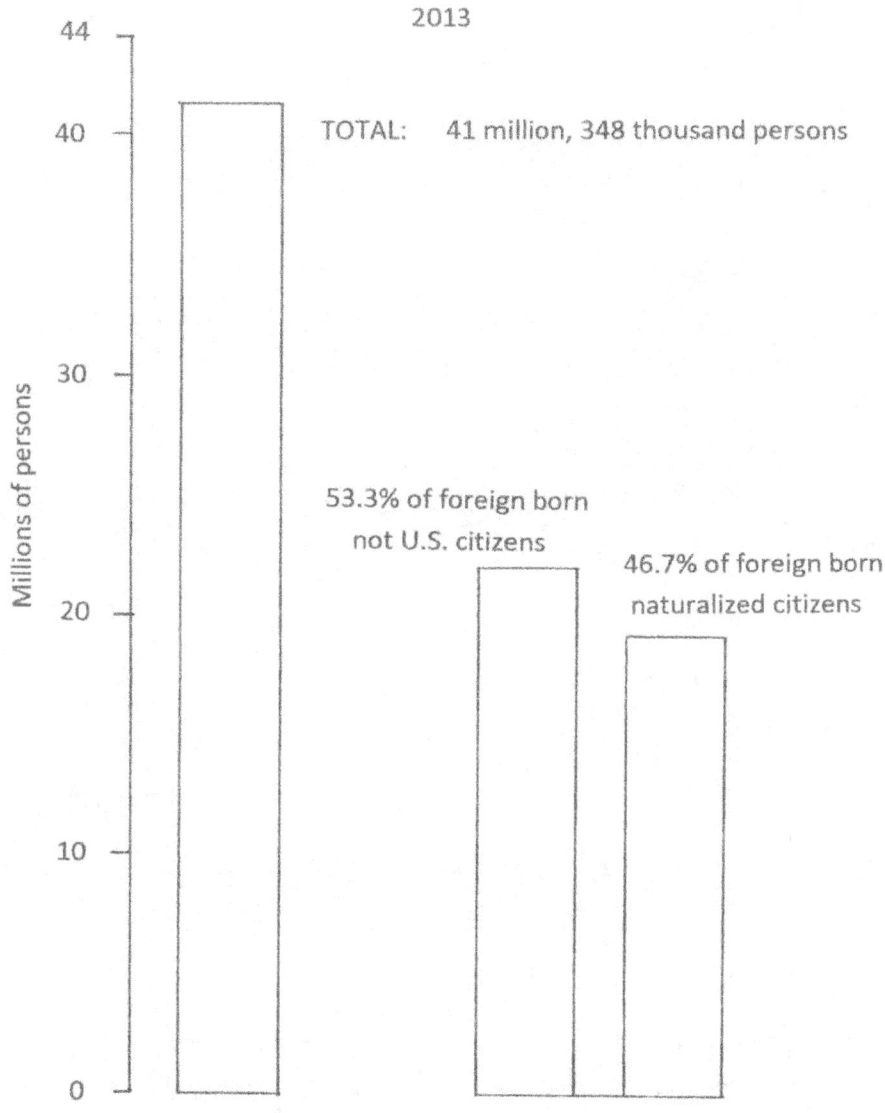

UNITED STATES FOREIGN BORN POPULATION
BY CITIZENSHIP STATUS
2013

TOTAL: 41 million, 348 thousand persons

53.3% of foreign born
not U.S. citizens

46.7% of foreign born
naturalized citizens

Millions of persons

Source: ProQuest Statistical Abstract of the United States 2016, p 40

In 2013, 22 million, 53 thousand persons were in the United States who were
not citizens, a much larger number than illegal immigration estimates.
Visa numbers are not available.

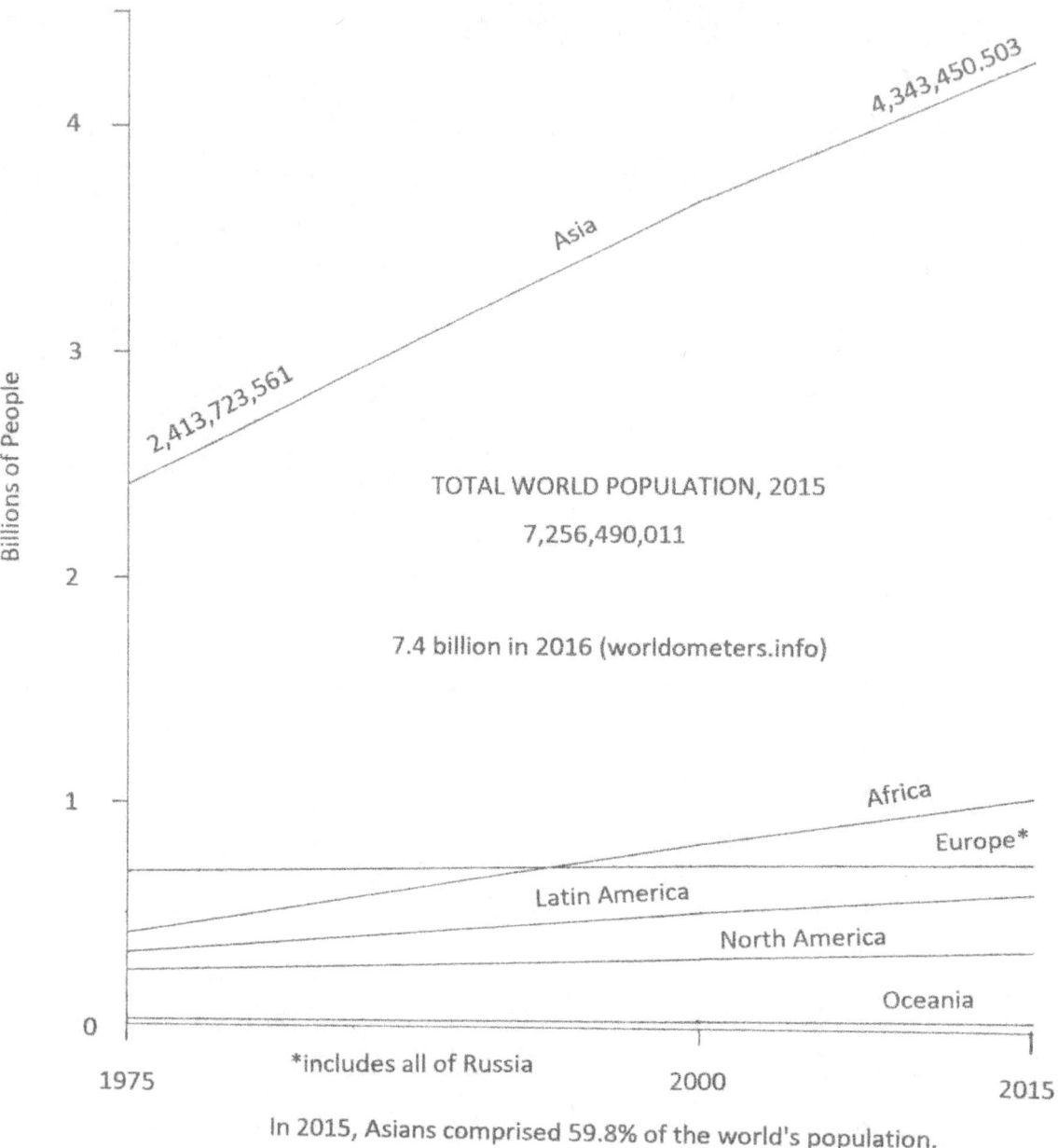

INCREASE IN GLOBAL POPULATION BY CONTINENT
1975 - 2015

Billions of People

4

3

2,413,723,561

Asia

4,343,450.503

TOTAL WORLD POPULATION, 2015

7,256,490,011

7.4 billion in 2016 (worldometers.info)

2

1

Africa

Europe*

Latin America

North America

Oceania

0

1975

*includes all of Russia

2000

2015

In 2015, Asians comprised 59.8% of the world's population.
In 1975, Asians comprised 59.0% of the world's population.
In 1950, Asians comprised 56.2% of the world's population.

Source: The World Almanac and Book of Facts 2016, p 730

Asians comprise whole cities, such as Gardena in California. One-third of
San Francisco is Asian. The state of Hawaii is Asian.

George Soros' nonprofit "Open Society Foundation" used $7.7 million from groups
wanting immigration reform to push "Comprehensive Immigration Reform" in 2013. The U.S.
Senate voted 68 to 32 in favor. When the bill reached the House of Representatives, it was
quashed by republicans at the urging of the still-active Tea Party. --Chuck Ross, "Daily Caller"

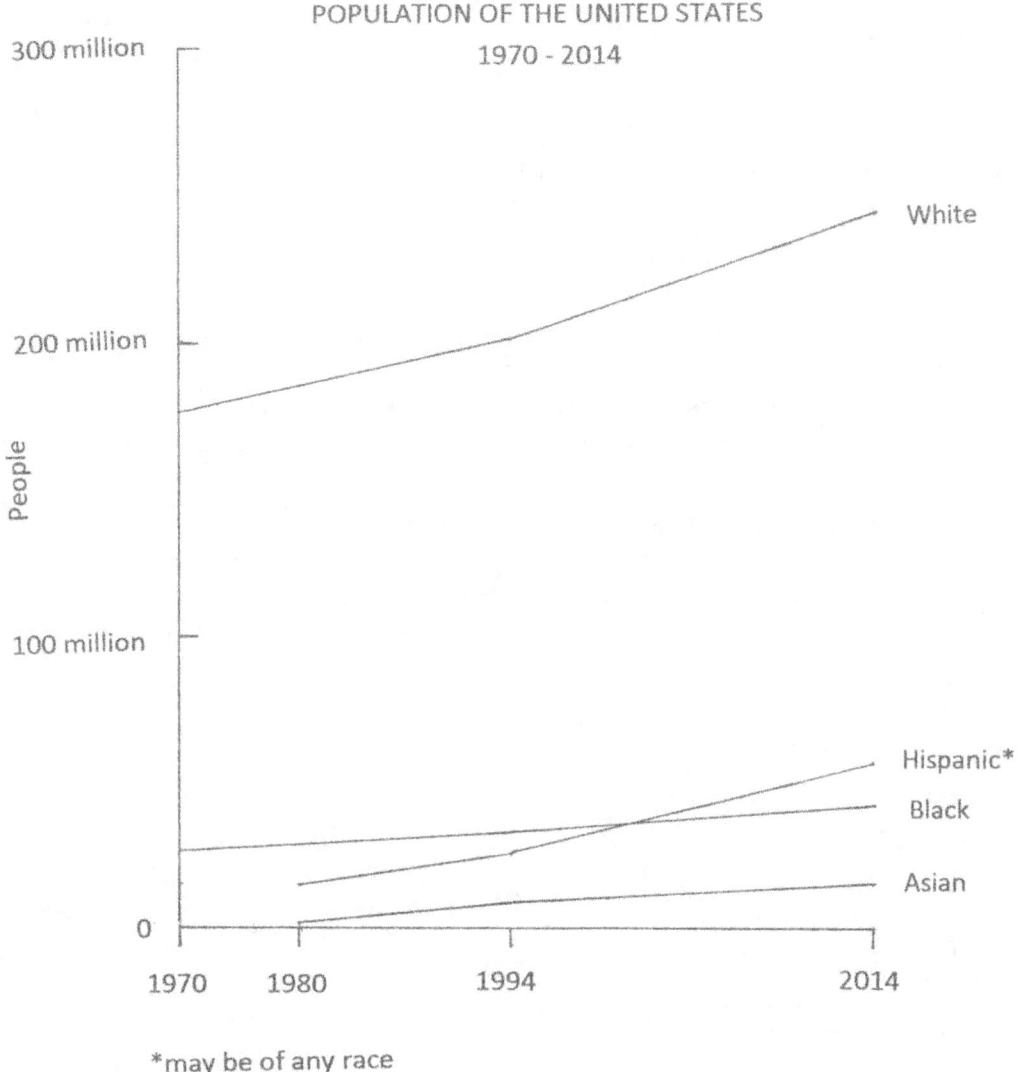

POPULATION OF THE UNITED STATES
1970 - 2014

300 million

200 million

People

100 million

0

White

Hispanic*

Black

Asian

1970   1980   1994   2014

*may be of any race

White population	1970 = 87.6%	White population	2014 = 68.22%
Black population	1970 = 11.1%	Black population	2014 = 11.66%
"Other" population	1970 = 1.3%	Hispanic population	2014 = 15.33%
		Asian population	2014 = 4.79%

Source: Statistical Abstract of the United States 1995, p 14

ProQuest Statistical Abstract of the United States 2016, p 12

WILL 'BREXIT' MARK THE END OF THE AGE OF GLOBALIZATION?

Los Angeles Times   June 25, 2016   p A1

WASHINGTON - For decades, financial and political leaders have preached the inevitability of globalization...But Britain's surprise vote to leave the European Union signals a new era for the post-World War II globalization drive, exposing deep populist anger and leaving open the question of how best to rein in an increasingly connected and interdependent world economy.

The backlash stems from a growing realization that the biggest winners of globalization have been international corporations, wealthy families, skilled and educated workers and those with easy access to capital.

Older working class families in many Western nations have instead struggled with stagnant wages, job losses and staggering debt. Income inequality has grown worse in many of the same countries that have embraced globalization.

At the core of the "Leave" campaign in Britain was the desire to curtail immigration and reclaim full sovereignty in Parliament.   by Don Lee

Websters Dictionary definitions:

DIVERSITY   noun   1, essential difference.   2, variety

DIVERSIFY   verb   to give variety to

UNITY   noun   the state of being unified or uniform
                         the quantity and integer
                         harmony among elements

UNITARY   adj   1, pertaining to a unit.   2, uniform.   3, unified

UNIFORM   adj   1, unchanging; even; regular.   2, the same as others
                 noun   a distinctive dress worn by all the members of a military force, a society, etc.

DIVERSITY IS THE POLAR OPPOSITE OF UNITY OR UNIFORM

"THE JUDICIAL POWER OF THE UNITED STATES SHALL BE VESTED IN ONE SUPREME COURT
AND SUCH INFERIOR COURTS AS THE CONGRESS MAY FROM TIME TO TIME
ORDAIN AND ESTABLISH"
Article III, Section 1
Constitution of the United States

"THE CONGRESS SHALL HAVE POWER TO CONSTITUTE TRIBUNALS
INFERIOR TO THE SUPREME COURT"
Article I, Section 8
Constitution of the United States

"When the people fear the government, there is tyranny. When the
government fears the people, there is liberty."   --Thomas Jefferson

THE UNITED STATES SUPREME COURT

The U.S. Constitution establishes a Supreme Court in Article III, Section 1:

Section 1.

The judicial Power of the United States shall be vested in one Supreme Court, and in such inferior Courts as the Congress may from time to time ordain and establish...

Section 2.

The judicial Power shall extend

to all Cases:

> in Law and Equity, arising under this Constitution, the Laws of the United States, and Treaties made, or which shall be made, under their authority
> affecting Ambassadors, other public Ministers and Consels;
> of admiralty and maritime Jurisdiction;

to Controversies
> to which the United States shall be a Party;
> between two or more States;
> between a State and Citizens of another State
> between Citizens of different States
> between Citizens of the same State claiming Lands under Grants of
> > different States, and
> between a State, or the Citizens thereof, and foreign States, Citizens or Subjects.

The Constitution goes on to say that the Supreme Court shall have original jurisdiction in all cases affecting Ambassadors, other public ministers or consuls, and those in which a state shall be a party (but) in "all the other CASES before mentioned, the supreme Court shall have appellate jurisdiction, both as to Law and Fact, with such Exceptions, and under such Regulations as the Congress shall make."

The Constitution says nothing more about CONTROVERSIES. One can conclude that controversies are not cases, and that therefore the U.S. Supreme Court can go beyond case law and inject itself in controversies, most specifically, "Controversies to which the United States shall be a Party."

Such an interpretation of the U.S. Constitution would give the Supreme Court oversight powers regarding Congressional and presidential activities and laws relative to the U.S. Constitution, which is the Supreme Court's abiding interest. But the Supreme Court as the third branch of the federal government does not exercise this power.

The U.S. has strayed far from Article I, Section 8 mandating Congress pay the debts, to regulate commerce, to impose duties and imposts on imports, and to establish or reinstate a true uniform rule of immigration. Nothing has been done toward establishing a militia, or toward limiting a standing army to two years' funding.

Limiting a standing army to two years' funding would curtail the perpetual state of warfare we have suffered since 2001, and the suffering we have caused on the other side of the world. If we didn't have a standing army, the art of negotiation, economic sanctions, special forces, drones, naval activities and air power would replace boots on foreign soil, with far less devastation of lives and property.

France has gendarmes, their version of militia. Gendarme presence in French communities helps to keep crime down. Such a system in the U.S. could wrest control from U.S. and foreign gang cartels in cities and neighborhoods across the country, and could have avoided their rise in the first place. It was militia, rag tag rebels under George Washington who fought and died to bring the United States freedom from England. Without the U.S. militia, the United States could not have become a sovereign nation.

The U.S. Constitution, a mere nine pages, is remarkably clear and brief. No doubt the founders wanted the average citizen to be able to understand it. There are legions of Constitutional scholars, but in the end, it comes down to common sense: all of the tenets of the Constitution are designed to protect the country and its citizens. Without adherence to the Constitution, we are not protected. Protectionism is a survival instinct we would be wise to reinstate.

One last but not least survival path the Constitution offers in Article I, Section 8 is that the Congress "shall have Power to constitute Tribunals inferior to the Supreme Court." A Tribunal is "a court of justice," and a tribune is "a person who defends or upholds popular rights," according to Websters. The founders of this country foresaw a time when things would be so bad we would be on the brink of revolution. It happened once already. With globalism we are close to another. Since the Supreme Court won't intervene to set the course back on track Constitutionally, maybe a Tribunal of the people, by the people and FOR the people, would.

Freedom of Expression

China has been controlled by one party, the Chinese Communist Party, since the People's Republic of China was formed in 1949. Human Rights Watch reports on-line that Chinese authorities "have unleashed an extraordinary assault on basic human rights and their defenders with a ferocity unseen in recent years - an alarming sign, given that the current leadership will likely remain in power through 2023."

China has psychiatric hospitals where troublemakers who haven't committed any crime are taken by the police without being charged and therefore have no trial dates. Sometimes authorities admit them under false names so their families cannot find them. Inside, they cannot protest against whatever treatment authorities want to use, including heavy sedation or electroshock "therapy" as a "re-education" technique.

There is "re-education through labor" in work camps, too, with sentences as long as four years without trial. Established in the 1950s under Mao Zedong, 350 work camps are scattered around the country. It is a catch-all system, not only for dissidents but also drug addicts, prostitutes, Christians and spiritual groups not allowed in China. The country's leadership takes the profit from the work performed by detainees' labor. China in 2012 announced they were going to reform the labor camp system, but, as with everything else in China, there is no way outsiders can measure results.

A pro-democracy activist laborer spent 22 years in prison because he sympathized with students protesting in Tiananmen Square in 1989. China dealt with workers much more harshly than students, and the complete fallout, including the number of deaths, from the government crackdown will likely never be known. What is known is that the laborer, 62 years old, was found dead by hanging from a bed sheet on the security bars of his window. His family doubts he committed suicide. He had been strong-willed and energetic throughout his prison sentence. In China, a ban on discussions of Tiananmen Square in public continues.

Chinese who file petitions to settle grievances might end up in labor camps if they're seen by authorities as stirring unrest. The grievance can be legitimate, for example, when a local official sells land that belongs to a farmer or peasant to developers for a large profit. There is also the case of a woman who filed a petition for tougher penalties against the men who raped her daughter. Authorities sentenced the woman to be re-educated for over a year for her negative view of society.

CHINA JAILS EQUAL RIGHTS ACTIVISTS

Los Angeles Times   Apr 12, 2015   p A3

BEIJING - Five young women were detained on initial suspicion, their lawyers, said, of "picking quarrels and provoking trouble" - a charge that can carry a prison term as long as five years. They were planning to mark International Women's Day with a public outreach campaign against sexual harassment on public transportation.

The detentions came even as the government has been pushing a high profile campaign to end some of the most egregious abuses in its legal system and implement what it calls "rule of law" - though the Communist Party hardly envisions a judiciary independent of its control...

University professors, think tanks, lawyers, judges, entertainers and others have been warned that ideals such as constitutionalism; freedom of the press, speech and assembly; judicial independence; and separation of powers are ill-suited to the Chinese situation.

Chinese authorities say the matter (of the detainees) is an internal affair.   by Julie Makinen

Anyone critical of Communist rule can be denied a passport with no explanation. Conversely, even with a valid passport, citizens returning to China can be turned away at the airport. Officers escort them to the next outbound flight. One citizen who helped organize the student protests in 1989 has had his passport applications repeatedly denied. Since he lives in Taiwan, he can't get home to see his aging parents, and they cannot get passports to leave China to see their son. Passport restrictions are particularly harsh on Tibetans.

Government crackdowns on dissidents in recent years have come under the banner of anti-terrorism, and can end with a death sentence.

World Report 2015: China | Human Rights Watch

Pervasive ethnic discrimination, severe religious repression, and increasing cultural suppression justified by the government in the name of the "fight against separatism, religious extremism, and terrorism" continue to fuel rising tensions in the Xinjiang Uighur Autonomous Region (XUAR).

In March, at least 30 people were killed when Uighur assailants attacked people with knives at the train station in Kunming, Yunnan Province. In May, 31 people died when a busy market in Urumqi was bombed. In August, official press reports stated than approximately 100 people died in Yarkand (or Shache) County in XUAR when assailants attacked police stations, government offices, and vehicles on a road. The Chinese government has blamed "terrorist" groups for these attacks.

Following the Urumqi attack, the Chinese government announced a year-long anti-terrorism crackdown in Xinjiang. Within the first month, police arrested 380 suspects and tried more than 300 for terror-related offenses. Authorities also convened thousands of people for the public sentencing of dozens of those tried. In August, authorities executed three Uighurs who were convicted of orchestrating an attack in Beijing's Tiananmen Square in October 2013. Fair trial rights remain a grave concern given the lack of independent information about the cases, the government's insistence on expedited procedures, the fact that terror suspects can be held without legal counsel for months under Chinese law, and China's record of police torture.

https://www.hrw.org/world-report/2015/country-chapters/china-and-tibet

Chinese officials are particularly sensitive when criticism is directed toward the massive wealth of Communist Party officials and their relatives. Foreign journalists who speculate on the subject are told to leave the country with the excuse that there are problems with their visas. The Party also denies visas to incoming journalists from the same publications. In recent years, the Party has issued "directives" as to correct reportage, pushing for pro-government rhetoric, and has cracked down on internet freedom.

Wealth

China has undergone the largest, fastest industrial development in human history, fueled mostly by twenty-five years of gargantuan exports. In the process, massive wealth has been created at the top. There are 370 members of the Central Committee, 24 members of the Politburo and about nine members of the Standing Committee at the top, where the big money goes. No one knows how rich the top party leaders are, but western estimates put their individual net worth at well over $1 billion. There are about 500,000 millionaires.

The Chinese are on the lookout for business ventures and real estate deals in the United States, Europe and elsewhere. Huge projects are purchased by holding companies, such as the State Administration of Foreign Exchange, called "SAFE," which has about $3 trillion available for investment. More recently, purchases are made directly through the better-known "China Investment Corporation" and "China Investment." SAFE has been moving cautiously since it lost $2.5 billion when Washington Mutual, the largest savings and loan entity in the United States, was closed by the U.S. government in the 2008 global recession.

Canada has been wooing Asian investors, and the Chinese came calling, with an oil company offer to purchase land in Alberta for $15 billion. The oil company was state-owned, so the offer was rejected, with the prime minister's remark, "When we say that Canada is open for business, we do not mean that Canada is for sale to foreign governments." Moreover, even though China is spending billions of dollars on purchases abroad, foreigners cannot make similar purchases in China.

The Workers

At the other end of the scale, 75% of the Chinese people receive about 15% of the country's disposable income. The inequality is leading to massive social unrest, especially for the tens of millions of workers who moved to the cities to be part of the manufacturing boom. The workers strike and get higher wages and better working conditions, but they know if they complain too much, they can be dragged off to jail, a work camp, or a mental institution. The labor force also correctly fears cheaper wage competition from nearby countries, such as Vietnam and Bangladesh. There is also the problem of residency. The Chinese must register in their birth villages, and if the city they've moved to denies them resident status, they are forced to live on the periphery where schools and health services are not available to them. If they obtain residency, they live in massive block buildings within bleak surroundings. Still, it seems they prefer it to the relentless poverty of the rural areas they left behind. A good wage is $284 per month.

In one way, China protects its workers by fining employers who hire foreign workers. The people are encouraged to turn in anyone they suspect is working in the country illegally. Any foreigner who wants to work in China must apply for documentation, including an employment certificate. They must also obtain a visa. It is not known what sort of penalty awaits an illegal worker who is caught.

Even though China raked in $56.9 billion from tourism in 2014, the country is increasingly hostile to other types of foreign visitors, notably non-governmental philanthropic groups, who face increased supervision and restrictions, one of which is that they must hire Chinese workers while in the country. The new rules would affect visiting orchestras and performers as well as environmental organizations such as Greenpeace and the voluntary aid group, Doctors without Borders.

Gay Rights

China decriminalized homosexuality in 1997. They treated it as a mental illness until 2001, when that designation officially ended, but clinics still "cure" homosexuality. One patient filed a lawsuit regarding his electroshock "therapy" in such a clinic in 2014. There are no laws to protect the gay community against discrimination, and no recognition of same-sex partnerships.

Religion

While the Chinese Communist Party espouses freedom of religion, the country is officially atheist. Buddhism is practiced by 18%, Christianity 5%, folk religion 22% and unaffiliated 52%. In practice, the party leadership bans religions with impunity and raids, audits, and spies on the religions it allows. Of late the government has come down hard on Christianity, expelling missionaries and refusing to acknowledge Pope Francis' invitation to establish a bond.

International Pressure

China is a member of the United Nations Human Rights Council, but it votes against measures to enhance human rights around the world. China voted against the Council's draft resolutions against human rights abuses in North Korea, Iran, Sri Lanka, Belarus, Ukraine and Syria, reported Human Rights Watch on-line.

Tibet

China ruled Tibet from the 1700s, but from 1911 to 1951 Tibet enjoyed independence. China then reasserted control, installing a Communist government in 1953. All land remained collectivized. The Tibetans rebelled from 1956 to 1959, in the area between the two countries. The Chinese army prevailed, and China outlawed Buddhism, causing the Dalai Lama and 100,000 of his followers to flee to India.

World Report 2015: China / Human Rights Watch

China's mass rehousing and relocation policy has radically changed Tibetans' way of life and livelihoods, in some cases impoverishing them or making them dependent on state subsidies. Since 2006, over 2 million Tibetans, both farmers and herders, have been involuntarily "rehoused"—through government-ordered renovation or construction of new houses—in the TAR; hundreds of thousands of nomadic herders in the eastern part of the Tibetan plateau have been relocated or settled in "New Socialist Villages."

--hrw.org

In 2008, Tibetan monks protested peacefully against Chinese rule, resulting in an immediate Chinese assault to halt the demonstrations. The protests escalated to anti-Chinese riots in the Tibetan capital, Lhasa. The Chinese sent troops to crush the rebellion, bringing international attention to the plight of the Tibetans, especially when monks calmly sat down on pavements, poured gasoline, and set themselves on fire.

Chinese suppression of Tibetan hopes for independence continues to this day. The Chinese Communist Party also discourages countries from offering the aging Dalai Lama a visa for travel. The country of South Africa has refused offering him a visa so as not to provoke the Communist regime. The Dalai Lama and his followers are beginning to think they will never see their homeland again, nor have Tibetan sovereignty.

CRUSADE IN CRISIS

Los Angeles Times   Jul 5, 2015   p A1

To hear the Dalai Lama laugh, it is easy to forget the cascade of disasters endured by the Tibetan Buddhist movement over the course of his life.

Yet the list is long, and growing longer, as an ascendant China consolidates control over Tibet. China's rising economic clout is slowly strangling the movement for Tibetan independence and, in the process, nudging the charismatic Tibetan spiritual leader off the world stage.

Under Chinese pressure, South Africa refused to grant him a visa last year to attend a gathering of Nobel laureates. Even Pope Francis, presumably worried about the fate of Chinese Catholics, declined to grant him an audience in December.

The 94,000-strong Tibetan community in India, which for years has operated as a government in exile, is shrinking as a result of tighter Chinese controls on borders and passports that keep the 6 million Tibetans living in China from leaving.

Tibetans are quietly requesting Chinese documents to go home, implicitly acknowledging that China's rule over Tibet is here to stay.

by Barbara Demick

Taiwan

China is relentless in insisting that Taiwan is a rebel province of mainland China. A democracy with multiple political parties, the island nation does not want to be enveloped into the Communist country. Taiwan's twenty three million people enjoy a prosperous, capitalist system with good trading partners, including the United States, which, since 1978, has not officially recognized Taiwan as an independent nation. Taiwan was controlled by Japan from 1895 to 1945. Since then, Taiwan has grown and prospered as a self-governing nation, with a literacy rate of 96%.

Taiwan has a new president, Tsai Ing-wen. Her political party is the Democratic Progressive Party. Most of its members want independence from China, and Tsai was voted in by a landslide victory. She is willing to talk to Beijing regarding trade and other matters, but not the subject of relinquishing sovereignty.

Disputed islands off the coast of Asia

China is aggressively asserting sovereignty over disputed islands in the region. The islands have rich mineral deposits and are also in strategic locations, allowing their owners sovereignty over a wide swath of territory. Five neighboring nations are feuding with China over the Paracel and Spratly Islands in the South China Sea.

China is also feuding with Japan over ownership of islands in the East China Sea. Japan calls the islands Senkaku Islands, and China calls them Diaoyu Islands. Japan has videos on-line of Chinese ships patrolling the waters around the islands.

The United States is silent on the matters of Tibet, Taiwan, and disputed islands in Asia. Meanwhile, Japan is arming and currently protesting U.S. military presence on Okinawa. There is general unease about the continuing economic rise of a militaristic, heavily armed China that appears to be growing more aggressive with her neighbors. China has a standing army of 2,333,000 troops, yet 10.6% of her people are undernourished, according to the World Almanac and Book of Facts 2016, p 762.

Pollution

The Chinese people suffer outdoor air pollution that is among the worst in the world. Part of the problem is the habit of smoking, which alone causes 25% of cancer deaths. Lung cancer has been the leading cause of death since 2010 and averages 7,500 deaths per day. Coal used in heating and cooking contributes to the airborne carcinogens. China is the world's largest producer and consumer of coal. The greatest source of pollution comes from the rapid industrialization of China since the 1980s, when the push for economic expansion abroad began, without much concern for environmental consequences. Factories are producing goods made of plastics, a derivative of oil, with widespread use of glue, solvents, dyes, paints and other carcinogenic materials in the manufacturing process as well as in finished goods.

Many thousands of Chinese are relocating to other countries due to environmental concerns. Smog has become a permanent shroud over most of mainland China. One youth said that he wishes there wasn't such a feverish concern over growth. "What about quality of life? I would rather have less concrete, less high rise buildings, less factories, less pollution and a smaller domestic product."

He may get what he wishes for. The Chinese government has been pushing factory owners to steadily increase wages, health coverage and other benefits for factory workers who are increasingly dissatisfied with, among other things, unhealthful working environments. In 2015, an explosion at a warehouse in Tianjin that was storing hazardous chemicals killed 173 workers and injured hundreds of others, causing widespread destruction and environmental damage.

Recently constructed cities in China stand empty because workers cannot afford to live in them. Companies leave factories empty in some districts for cheaper labor elsewhere. China reached its peak production around 2010, enjoying double digit growth in gross domestic product most years since the 1980s. By 2014, China's GDP had slowed to 8%, still a hefty number.

VLADIMIR PUTIN'S RUSSIA

After the collapse of the USSR in 1989, Russia and satellite countries were bordering on chaos and economic collapse. Vladimir Putin came to power in 2000 and has almost single-handedly rebuilt Russia economically and politically into the powerhouse that she is today.

One fact stands out above all others: Putin is indisputably Pro-Russian, a dedication as powerful as the Greats, Catherine and Peter. Since 1989, Putin has wanted to reconstruct his impoverished country. In 2003 he declared the Republic of Chechnya as part of Russia but with autonomy. Chechnya is now stable, with a regional government and parliamentary elections, despite occasional attacks by rebels in the Northern Caucasus.

Putin in 2005 implemented projects to improve health care, education, housing and agriculture. Between 2001 and 2007 the Russian economy grew by 7% annually, fueled by record-high oil prices and growth in manufacturing, construction, real incomes, credit, and a growing middle class, making Russia the seventh largest world economy. On May 7, 2012, Putin's inauguration day for his third term, he issued fourteen more goals for the Russian economy, including education, housing, better relations with the European Union and improved inter-ethnic relations. Literacy in Russia is now 99.7%.

In 2005 Russia undertook criminal prosecution of the country's richest man, Mikhail Khodorkovsky, President of YUKOS Company, for fraud and tax evasion. Khodorkovsky donated to both liberal and communist opponents of the Kremlin. After Khodorkovsky was arrested, YUKOS was declared bankrupt, and the company's assets were auctioned below market value; the greatest number of shares were acquired by a state-owned company, Rosneft. Critics saw the move as a broad shift toward "state capitalism."

In July 2014, YUKOS shareholders were awarded $50 billion in compensation by the Permanent Arbitration Court in The Hague, Netherlands.   --wikipedia.org

---

Putin's personal worth is estimated at $2 billion, shuttled through offshore companies, according to a source, the "Panama Papers," termed "reliable" by Putin. He has rebuilt his "dacha" near St. Petersburg, his home town, after a fire in 1996, and seven of his friends have built nearby, in what is now a gated community. Construction of his "palace" in the Black Sea village of Praskoveevka began in 2012 after Putin won his third term as President. Built on government land, guarded by government security, as befitting a head of state, it has three helipads. Its cost is reputed to be $1 billion as Putin adds finishing touches to it.

Between 2000 and 2010, Putin increased Russia's share of Europe's energy market by submerging gas pipelines that bypassed Ukraine. Russia also purchased rival Nabucco's Turkmen Gas and redirected it to Russian pipelines and constructed another gas pipeline in Russia's far east. Russia built the Trans-Siberian Oil Pipeline for markets in China, Japan and Korea, resulting in a "Treaty of Friendship" with China. Now there are joint Chinese-Russian military exercises on Russian soil.

Putin oversaw production of two new dams for hydroelectric power. By 2015 Russia had spent $42.7 billion to restore nuclear power, and a state-owned corporation, Rosatom, built nuclear power stations and units in Russia and abroad, including the construction in 2012 of "floating nuclear power plants" for Arctic coastal cities. Russia also spearheaded ice-resistant oil platform technology. A Russian-operated oil company, Rosneft, partnered with Exxon Mobil to produce arctic oil. Putin is increasing territorial claims in the arctic and has a military presence there.

On May 21, 2014, a $77 billion pipeline will provide natural gas from Russia's majority state-owned Gazprom to China's state-owned China National Petroleum Corporation for 30 years, at a profit for Russia of $400 billion. The same year, Putin signed $25 billion in energy, trade and finance agreements with China.

Putin is a "valued friend" of India. Russia helped Iran build a nuclear power plant. He traveled to Australia to meet with Prime Minister John Howard in 2007 to set up a deal for Australia to sell uranium to Russia. He put troops in Syria to help Assad remain in power. On September 11, 2013, Putin wrote an article that appeared in the New York Times regarding the U.S., Russia and Syria. Then, Putin helped Syria disarm itself of chemical weapons, but between 2000 and 2010 Russia sold $1.5 billion in arms to Syria, acknowledging that "Damascus is Moscow's seventh largest Client." Russia and Japan are not friendly. Both countries are currently claiming ownership of the Kuril Islands located in the Northern Territories, named Shikotan, Kunashiri and Etorofu.

In June 2013 the state Duma passed a law prohibiting display of the rainbow flag, a homosexual symbol, as well as publication of any homosexual content. Putin asserts that there is "no social or professional discrimination against homosexuality in Russia."

In 2014 during a Ukrainian Revolution, Putin sent troops to seize Ukraine's Crimea peninsula. The United Nations General Assembly passed a resolution supporting a Ukrainian Referendum that said 93% of Crimeans voted to secede from Ukraine and join Russia. "Of course, our troops stood behind Crimea's defense forces...to prevent bloodshed," Putin said, adding on December 4, 2014 that annexation of Crimea was a "historic event" that will not be reversed because Crimea is "Russia's spiritual ground."

Unrest in Eastern Ukraine began. The world united in sanctions against Russia, causing a significant setback in Russia's economy and plunging oil prices. Russia retaliated by curbing imports, but on August 26, 2014, Putin met with Ukraine President Poroshenko, who asked that Russia stop arming Russian separatist fighters. Poroshenko asked for a political compromise, where Russian-speaking people in Eastern Ukraine would be respected but remain Ukrainians. Putin backed off.

PUTIN CRITIC SLAIN IN MOSCOW

Los Angeles Times   Feb 28, 2015   p A3

Moscow - Boris Y. Nemtsov, one of Russian President, Vladimir Putin's fiercest critics, was shot dead in the shadow of St. Basil's Cathedral near Red Square early Saturday on the eve of a massive opposition march to show defiance of Kremlin aggression against Ukraine.

Nemtsov, 55, was shot seven times from a passing car.

Nemtsov had become somewhat critical about the fate of his country under Putin, who engineered constitutional changes before his 2012 reelection that should allow him to remain at the Kremlin's helm until 2024.

by Sergei L. Loiko and Carol J. Williams

Putin says of the murder of Gaddafi in Libya by rebels backed by NATO and the U.S. on October 2011, and the U.S. invasion of Iraq on March 19, 2003, and subsequent execution of Saddam Hussein on December 30, 2006: "What is happening in Libya? In Iraq? Where are they heading? Are they any safer?"

Putin supported the U.S. War on Terror in 2001, but he was against the U.S. invasion of Iraq. He says he favors a "democratic multi-polar world" and the strengthening of international law. In 1999 he said that "Communism is a blind alley, far away from the mainstream of civilization." In his famous "Munich Speech" of 2007, he criticized the United States of "almost uncontained hyper use of force in international relations," adding, "Of course, such a policy stimulates an arms race." When questioned, Putin says he has "no intention of attacking NATO." The United States is peeved because Russia has granted asylum to Edward Snowden, the National Security Agency employee who leaked to the world that U.S. intelligence can retrieve at will anybody's private phone conversations, e-mails and on-line discussions, including the cell phone conversations of Germany's Chancellor, Angela Merkel.

In 2007, Putin had an approval rating of 81%. In 2013 it was 62% but bounded back in 2014 to 85.9%, and in June 2015 to 89%, an all-time high, far above any U.S. politicians' approval rate. Hillary Clinton says Putin is a "bully" and "arrogant." Henry Kissinger says that "the west has demonized Putin." Donald Trump has said that he "could work with Putin." The bottom line is that Russian President Vladimir Putin is decidedly Pro-Russian, and no one can criticize him for that. He is making globalism work for Russia.

Thank you, Wikipedia, for 90% of this content.

Nuclear Arsenals by Country

Russia	7,300
United States	6,970
France	300
China	260
United Kingdom	215
Pakistan	130
India	120
Israel	80
North Korea	15

Only the nine countries listed hold nuclear weapons. The number of nuclear weapons around the world peaked in the mid-1980s. The arsenals have shrunk by two-thirds. Countries have given up nuclear weapons.

--ploughshares.org

"A WELL REGULATED MILITIA, BEING NECESSARY TO THE SECURITY OF A FREE STATE, THE RIGHT OF THE PEOPLE TO KEEP AND BEAR ARMS, SHALL NOT BE INFRINGED."

Amendment II
Constitution of the United States

"THE CONGRESS SHALL HAVE POWER ... TO RAISE AND SUPPORT ARMIES, BUT NO APPROPRIATION OF MONEY TO THAT USE SHALL BE FOR A LONGER TERM THAN TWO YEARS"

Article I, Section 8
Constitution of the United States

"America will never be destroyed from the outside. If we falter and lose our freedoms, it will be because we destroyed ourselves."   --Abraham Lincoln

U.S. FIREARM VIOLENCE, FATAL AND NONFATAL
1993 - 2011

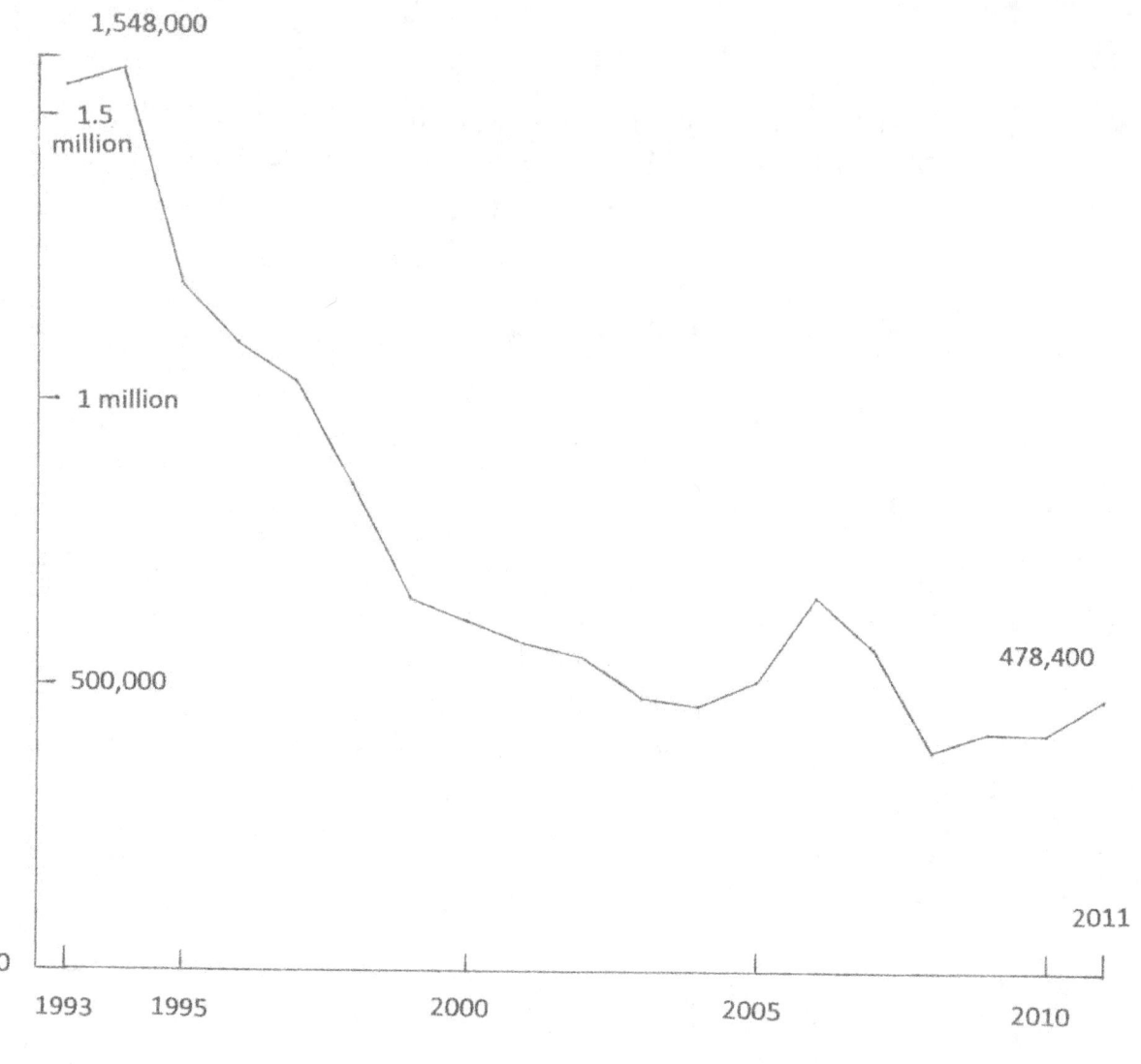

Source: Law Enforcement, Courts and Prisons
            ProQuest Statistical Abstract of the United States 2016, p 227

Firearm violence has declined dramatically from 1993 to 2011, likely due to tougher laws such as "Three Strikes, You're Out," as well as advancements in forensic science.

Due to mass shootings in the United States and around the world, there is political pressure to increase gun control. Los Angeles County passed a law immediately after the June 12, 2016 Orlando massacre prohibiting the carrying of a concealed weapon in public. It is foreseeable that perpetrators will ignore this law, and potential victims will be left defenseless.

District of Columbia v. Heller - June 26, 2008

U.S. Supreme Court struck down Firearm Control Regulation Act of 1975, which restricted residents from owning handguns except those registered prior to 1975. The Highest Court held that "the Second Amendment to the U.S. Constitution applies to federal enclaves and protects an individual's right to possess a firearm for traditionally lawful purposes such as self-defense within the home." The decision did not address extension of the Second Amendment to states.   --wikipedia.org

McDonald v. Chicago - June 28, 2010

76-year old retiree saw his neighborhood taken over by gangs and drug dealers. A hunter, McDonald legally owned shotguns, but felt them unwieldy in a robbery and wanted a handgun for his personal home defense. Chicago had a city handgun ban since 1982 and would not issue new registrations to own handguns, so McDonald effectively could not legally own a handgun. He and three others filed suit in 2008.

The U.S. Supreme Court found for McDonald, citing Heller v. D.C., finding "The Second Amendment protects the right to keep and bear arms for the purpose of self-defense," that "individual self-defense is the 'central component' of the Second Amendment right."   --wikipedia.org

California Assembly Bills 809 and 144 - October 11, 2012

In California it was legal to openly carry an unloaded handgun in public until Governor Jerry Brown signed Assembly Bill 144 modifying the open-carry unloaded handguns in public to match the restrictions on open-carry loaded weapons in public, effectively making it illegal to carry in public a weapon either loaded or unloaded. He also signed Assembly Bill 809 requiring registration of newly purchased long guns.
                                                                             --nraila.org

Peruta v. San Diego - June 9, 2016

The 9th Circuit Court of Appeals upheld a lower court's decision allowing San Diego's restrictive policy regarding carrying a concealed weapon in public to stand. Restrictive policies allow local governments to issue weapon-carry permits if applicant can show "good cause," which "distinguishes applicant from the mainstream and places the applicant in harm's way." The decision upheld the lower court's ruling that "there is no Second Amendment right for members of the general public to carry concealed weapons in public."   --wikipedia.org

The gun laws of California are some of the most restrictive in the United States.   Unlike most other states, California has no provision in its state constitution that explicitly guarantees private citizens the right to purchase, possess, or carry firearms. However, U.S. Supreme Court decisions of Heller (2008) and McDonald (2010) established that the Second Amendment applies to all states within the Union, and many of California's gun laws are now being challenged in the federal courts... The California Highway Patrol strictly enforces state firearms law anywhere in California.   --wikipedia.org

COUNTRIES WITH LARGEST ARMED FORCES, 2015

China	2,333,000	Colombia	297,000
United States	1,322,000	Taiwan	290,000
India	1,346,000	Mexico	267,000
North Korea	1,190,000	Japan	247,000
Russia	771,000	Sudan	244,000
South Korea	655,000	Saudi Arabia	227,000
Pakistan	644,000	France	215,000
Iran	523,000	Eritrea	202,000
Turkey	511,000	Morocco	196,000
Vietnam	482,000	South Sudan	185,000
Egypt	439,000	Germany	182,000
Myanmar	406,000	Afghanistan	179,000
Indonesia	396,000	Iraq	178,000
Thailand	361,000	Syria	178,000
Brazil	318,000	Israel	177,000

Source The Military Balance 2015
The World Almanac and Book of Facts 2016, p 133

COUNTRIES PURCHASING U.S. DEFENSE ARTICLES AND SERVICES

Deliveries, 2008-2011

Saudi Arabia	$ 5.9 billion
Egypt	$ 3.9 billion
Israel	$ 3.8 billion
Australia	$ 2.9 billion
Taiwan	$ 2.9 billion
Iraq	$ 2.6 billion
Japan	$ 2.5 billion
South Korea	$ 2.5 billion
Greece	$ 2.1 billion
Turkey	$ 2.0 billion

Total Revenue $31.1 billion, 46% from Islamic nations

Source Congressional Research Service, Library of Congress
The World Almanac and Book of Facts 2016, p 133

WEAPON SALES BY COUNTRY
1987 - 1991

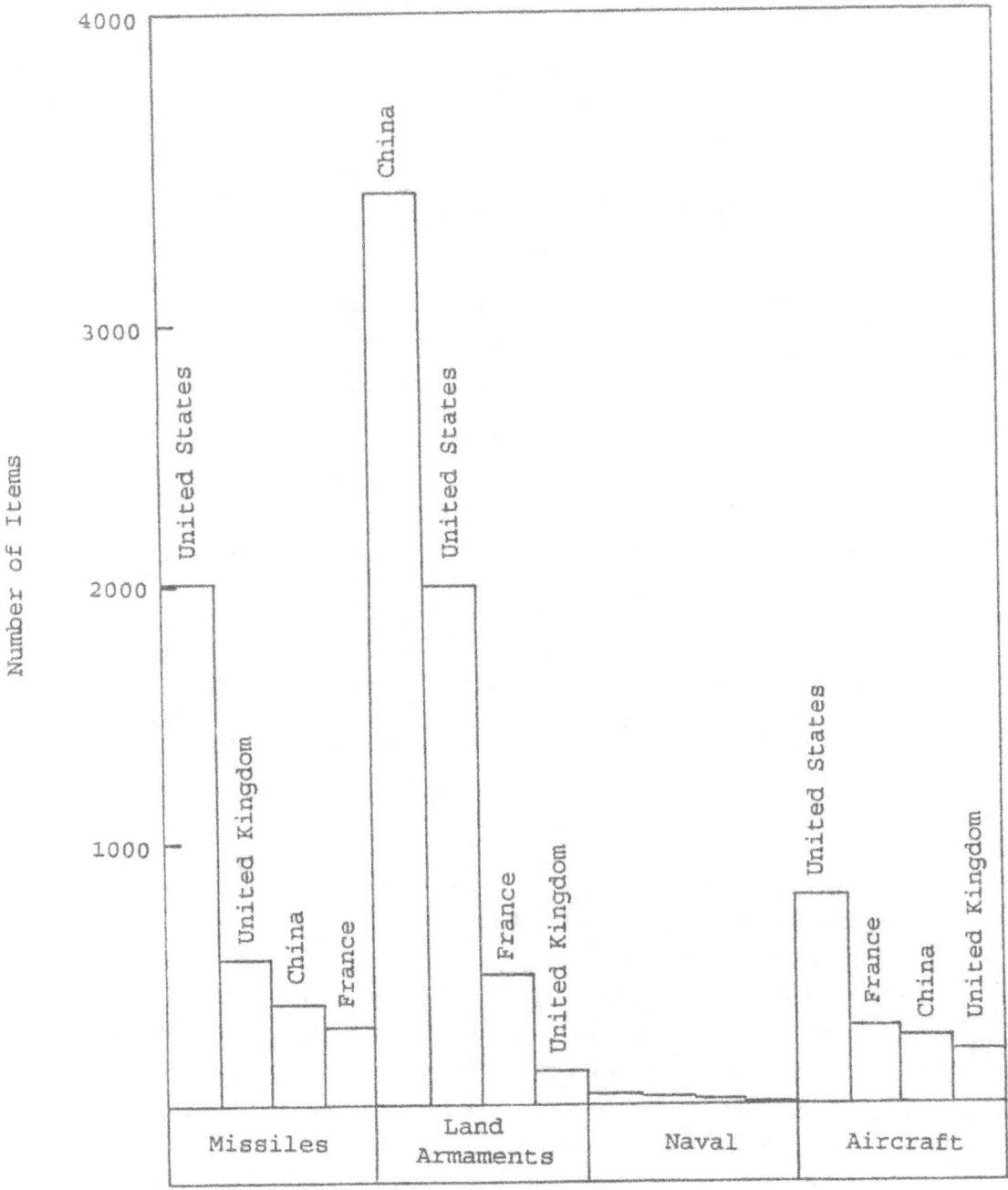

Source: Statistical Abstract of the United States 1995, p 357

Note: Recent data on types of weapons sold has not been located.

The Failed "War on Drugs"

Wikipedia reports that the Crips, primarily an African-American gang, were founded in Los Angeles in 1969. They formed loosely connected "sets," and, since they accepted all races, are one of the largest street gangs in the United States. They are also among the most violent, involved in murders, robberies and drug dealing.

CHICAGO MOTHER HAS LOST ALL 4 CHILDREN TO GUN VIOLENCE
Los Angeles Times   Feb 3, 2013   p A15

CHICAGO - By 2000, Shirley Chambers had lost three children to gun violence. She had one left, Ronnie Chambers, then 21. Because news of each death had arrived by telephone, she hated to hear a phone ring.

Around 13:30 a.m. this January 26, that dreaded sound awakened her, with news that she had feared for more than a decade. "I was told Ronnie had been shot," Chambers, 54, said in an interview. "I was so distraught. I jumped out of the bed and drove over to m sister's house on the west side...We stayed where we were until we got the news. I couldn't believe they were telling me m son was dead.

Police say a gunman or gunmen opened fire on a van that Ronnie Chamber was in. "It's so out of control," Chambers said. "These young men just have to stop it...All four of my children are gone now - all of them gunned down. It's too much to take."

by Dawn Turner Trice

The roots of the Crip gang go back to the l960s. With post World War II economic decline, jobs began to disappear, which in turn increased poverty. The Ford factory in South Gate moved elsewhere, as did many other industries that had provided solid manufacturing jobs. Whites moved to the suburbs, abandoning Los Angeles' alluvial plains, once a rich farming area due to rain and snow melt off from the nearby San Gabriel mountains. Black families moved in. Their sons formed "street clubs," producing PCP, marijuana and amphetamines to bring in cash; many were Korean and Vietnam War vets familiar with drugs. Some were crippled, which may be how they got their name.

By 1999 there were 600 Crip sets with 30,000 members transporting drugs throughout the United States. In midwest and southern prisons they formed alliances called "Folk Nation," to protect each other from rival gangs, one of which was their arch enemy, the Bloods.

In the 1960s, Black Panthers patrolled L.A. neighborhoods, offering protection from police harassment. When two Panthers were murdered in 1969, there was a void, so a 12-year old started a "blood" set, named after Piru Street in Compton. Members stuck together; unity was the key to their survival. Kids join at 13, to have help in school fights, freedom to go to movies, a sense of belonging and protection. The Bloods were outnumbered by the Crips two to one. They were the underdogs. The wars in the streets escalated, from Pasadena to Compton. No neighborhood was safe.

In 1993 in Pasadena on Halloween, a Blood was gunned down during the day. A witness said it was a Crip. The Bloods sent three armed members out hunting that night. They came across 11 teen-age boys trick-or-treating and opened fire, 30 shots in all, into the unsuspecting trick-or-treaters. It was called the "Halloween Massacre."

Law enforcement says the gangs will kill anyone, that they're "extremely dangerous." There was another massacre in the 1980s, the 54th Street Massacre, six to eight more victims. Street killing became the norm. In 1985, cocaine appeared on the streets of L.A. The Bloods turned it into crack, an extremely addictive form of cocaine and highly profitable. The streets became flooded with crack cocaine.

One of the bright spots in 2014 was and remains Compton, California, home of the iconic gangsta rap album, "Straight Outta Compton," produced 25 years ago by Dr. Dre. He inspires the local kids as a musician and successful businessman who just sold his headphone business, Beats Electronics, to Apple for $3 billion.

Compton has another inspiring leader in 32-year old Mayor Aja Brown, who was overwhelmingly elected to the post. Her modus operandi is to reach out to the older gang members, and Compton has dozens of gangs, to get them to come to city hall and sit down and talk, a groundbreaking approach. It's working. Homicides are down, even though it is three times the rate of Los Angeles, at 26 homicides per 100,000. During the gangsta rap era the rate was 100 murders. A recent shooting victim was a 16-year old boy as he was walking home from church.

She has gotten the murderous Crips and Bloods, both of whom call Compton home, to declare a truce. They have shown up at Mrs. Brown's outreach meetings, even though they are bitter enemies who haven't talked in decades. They respect her for her efforts to create jobs by attracting a business base to the city and spearheading an e-commerce development project, which will create 1,000 good jobs. And she's just getting started. Gang leaders now gather weekly. Mrs. Brown says, "Seeing people decide to choose love instead of hate is phenomenol."

By the 1990s it was about controlling the drug trade. 2,682 died in gang violence, many innocent bystanders. Drive-by shootings became common. The 1992 riots, caused by the acquittal of white policemen caught on video severely beating black Rodney King, were started by 2,000 gang members. They looted, set fire to cars and over six days caused 54 deaths and $1 billion in property damage, with no police in sight.   After that, the Crips and Bloods got together and decided to put down weapons. It lasted three months. By 1995 violence hit an all-time high with 807 murdered that year. "We have the history, the culture, and the language in L.A.," said a gang leader.

History.com reports that L.A. is the gang capital of the world. It is among the most culturally diverse cities in the world and also the most segregated. Los Angeles has a violent underworld. It is a vast war zone with 900 street gangs and 140,000 gang members mostly Black and Hispanic, but also Asian and white gangs.

FEDS TARGET GANG BORN IN L.A.
Los Angeles Times   Oct 12, 2012   p A1

Federal authorities Thursday named Mara Salvatrucha MS-13, the ruthless Latin American gang born three decades ago on the streets of Los Angeles, as a "transnational criminal organization," becoming the first street gang to join the list.

The designation gives the U.S. Treasury Department the power to freeze financial assets from the gang or its members and prohibits financial institutions from engaging in any transactions with members of the group.

Officials said the move is designed to reduce the flow of gang money within the United States and across the border. Authorities believe that money generated by MS-13 groups in the United States is funneled back to the group's leadership in El Salvador.

Among the other organizations to receive the designation are Japan's Yakuza organized crime syndicate and Mexico's Zetas, whose leader was killed by Mexican Marines on Sunday. An armed gang later stole his body from a funeral parlor.

MS-13 began among Salvadoran refugees - many of them young ex-soldiers - who came to Los Angeles to escape civil war in their home country in the 1980s. MS-13 has diversified into activities such as drugs, extortion, and human trafficking. The gang has been linked to at least five killings in the Washington D.C. suburbs, as well as shootings, machete attacks and stabbings. MS-13 has spread into Central America and across the United States, penetrating the Eastern Seaboard.

"They don't even dress like gang members anymore," said Los Angeles City Councilman Ed Reyes. The gang is now believed to have as many as 30,000 members.

by Hector Becerra, Danielle Ryan and Andrew Blankstein

The garment district in downtown Los Angeles is a ramshackle cluster of small businesses, but U.S. narcotics agents got wind of drug money laundering in the district when the Sinaloa drug cartel based in Mexico received $140,000 in ransom money from a family whose relative allegedly lost 100 kilos of the cartel's cocaine and was being tortured in Mexico.

The feds put the garment district under surveillance, gathering evidence, before making a sweeping raid in 2014 on over fifty businesses, finding $100 million in cash. The feds called the raid "Operation Fashion Police," and tightened money transfers from $10,000 to $3,000, as cash for garment purchases are shipped to Mexico. It's called the "black market peso exchange."

Knowing they were being watched, the money launderers changed their procedures. When a journalist asked how it was done now, the response was, "if I told you I would have to kill you."

The raid was reported by various news outlets. The feds were quick to say that the great majority of businesses in the district are lawful, generating $18 billion in annual revenue.

As long as Americans buy illegal drugs, the cartels will flourish, along with the violence that goes along with it throughout the Americas.

YOUTH DRUG SMUGGLING ARRESTS DROP AT BORDER
Los Angeles Times   Jun 21, 2016   p B4

It was as simple and as obvious as the poorly concealed bulge in the clothes of the teenager who approached the Customs and Border Protection officer assigned to Lane 59 at the San Ysidro Port of Entry.

Shuttled to a secondary inspection area, the youth...was asked what he was carrying. In response he stood up and lifted his shirt, revealing four sealed packages taped to his torso. The package contained 2.7 kilos of heroin, nearly six pounds. He told inspectors he had been paid $800...

Drugs flow across the border by land, sea and air, in underground tunnels, hidden in cars, packed inside toys and construction materials - and strapped to the bodies of willing youths tempted by the promise of ready cash and the reality that, if caught, their age would mean they would not be harshly sentenced.

Drug gangs target youths who can legally cross the border because they are U.S. citizens who may live in Tijuana and go to school in the United States, or have a border crossing card. They are paid no more than a few hundred dollars, which seems like big money to teenagers.   by Greg Moran

BACK HOME, THE PLACE THEY FEAR
Los Angeles Times   Aug 16, 2014 p A1

Relatives place the body of a 6-year old into a casket at the morgue in San Pedro Sula, Honduras, where the homicide rate is astronomical. The girl was caught in the crossfire of a gang dispute.

By the time Isaias Sosa turned 14, he'd already seen 15 bullet-riddled bodies laid out in his neighborhood of Cabanas, one of the most violent in this tropical metropolis. He rarely ventured out of his grandmother's home..."Everywhere here is dangerous. There is no security. They kill people all the time. It's a sin to be young in Honduras," he said...

Crossing the Rio Grande into Texas, Sosa was apprehended almost immediately by Border Patrol agents as he desperately searched for water. After a second unsuccessful attempt to enter the U.S. last fall, he now spends most of his days cooped up at home.

by Cindy Carcamo

In Los Angeles, neighborhood boundaries mean life and death. Dying is part of it. Black and Hispanic gangs control the streets, not law enforcement. They rule by fear and intimidation. When Hispanics arrived as agricultural workers in the 1950s, they were labeled "cholo." They had to be tough to survive. They began to organize in gangs.

Race rather than neighborhoods now plays the leading role in murders. Hispanics went after blacks for street control. Entire communities were taken as Hispanics began to outnumber blacks two to one, ever increasing their numbers. Many blacks left for Georgia or Louisiana for safety as Hispanics began to attack blacks who were not gang affiliated. For them, "if you're black, you're an enemy."

The 204th Street Hispanic gang at Harbor Gateway in south Los Angeles decided to kill "the first black" they encountered. Driving around, they saw a 14-year old black girl talking to neighbors. They fired at her four times. She died on the way to a hospital. She had no gang affiliation. She stayed in "safe" ground. Police say the 204th Street gang is a violent and racist gang that has no mercy.

Now, 75% of crimes are black versus brown. The violence is hate-based, with gang-related shootings every day. Los Angeles is fast becoming a Hispanic community. There are 25,000 black and 53,000 Hispanic gang members, and the Hispanics "want black turf," but they don't mind killing fellow Hispanics. The "Florencia 13" gang, Hispanic, shot into an innocent group, leaving two young Hispanic males wounded and bleeding, neither of whom were gang members.

CORONA RAID TARGETS MEXICAN MAFIA

Three hundred law enforcement officers swept into the once sleepy town of Corona, California, in Riverside County on June 9, 2016 after an investigation months in the making. They arrested 52 gang members, most from the Corona Varrio Locos, an offshoot of the Surenos of the Mexican Mafia, and some from the La Eme gang. The raid netted $1.6 million in illegal drugs plus 67 firearms, including assault rifles and semi-automatic weapons. 314 rounds of ammo and seven pounds of meth were also seized and $95,000 in cash. Those arrested were charged with felonies. "It will make our communities a little safer," commented one officer at the scene. "The Mexican Mafia controls the drug trade," he added as an afterthought.   --YouTube

All Hispanic gangs pay the Mexican Mafia to get protection in prison, where all races meet. It is a question of survival in prison. Hispanics dominate. They will attack other Hispanics in prison who associate with blacks, even for just playing dominoes, slicing their face with a razor, or worse. Murders based on hate increase among released prisoners, because the Mexican Mafia wants Latinos to expel blacks from their "growing" neighborhoods.

In Los Angeles, the quest for money and power is king. Gang life is a form of celebrity. Grafitti is a way of marking turf. The Crips don't recruit Hispanics anymore. There is deep distrust on both sides. "There are people who don't value life."

The Russian mafia is reputed to be in Glendale, California, as immigration increases from that source. Immigrants tend to cluster, until they have the numbers, and then they expand. It is a natural instinct, a safety factor, to be among people of similar background, culture and language.

Rodney King lamented, "Why can't we all just get along?" As violence rages in the Middle East and on the streets of America, and innocent people are victims of hate crimes the world over, his question remains.

There is a heroin epidemic in the U.S. The Mexican Drug Cartels are targeting the middle class, offering heroin cheaper and with a better high than prescription pain medications. Both are opiates. The danger is that heroin, often sold in pill form to look like a prescription medication, can be deadly if laced with other ingredients. The drug cartels send their peddlers into the suburbs, to the junior highs and high schools around the country, where buyers have discretionary income.

In Harford County, Connecticut, officials were seeing alarming rates of deaths from overdoses of prescription drugs. Law enforcement was told to crack down on prescription use by educating the public about the dangers of opiate prescriptions, and telling them to lock up their prescriptions at home. That made it harder for kids to get, so they turned to heroin, which was far easier to find. Both legal medications and heroin proved deadly in Harford County:

2010	prescription drug deaths	30	heroin deaths	12
2011	prescription drug deaths	15	heroin deaths	15
2012	prescription drug deaths	20	heroin deaths	14
2013	prescription drug deaths	14	heroin deaths	22

An addict told police when he was picked up, "It's as easy to get drugs as it is to get a pack of cigarettes at the gas station. That's anywhere around here." He went on to say that he started out on prescription drugs but, "It's cheaper to get heroin, you know, and it's more bang for your buck."

Another addict, a woman, said, "What people make in a forty hour week, I can make in three or four hours selling heroin." There are commuter dealers, where dealers buy heroin for $10 or $20 in Hartford, then go to the suburbs and sell it for $50 to $100. It is estimated that Hartford has 60,000 drug addicts.   --patch.com

> "Opiate drugs, including prescription painkillers and heroin, can produce withdrawal symptoms just hours after the last dose, and the symptoms can last for a week or more. Symptoms include nausea, muscle cramping, depression, agitation, anxiety and opiate cravings...unassisted withdrawal can lead to relapse."
> --americanaddictioncenters.org

Synthetic marijuana is coming from China to U.S. pot shops as "spices" or "bath salts." Registered as "controlled substances" they are cheap, ungraded and can cause sickness or death. Consumers don't know, it seems, or care, what's in them. When the government gets close to pulling certification, manufacturers change one component to stay legal.

GLOBAL TERRORISM

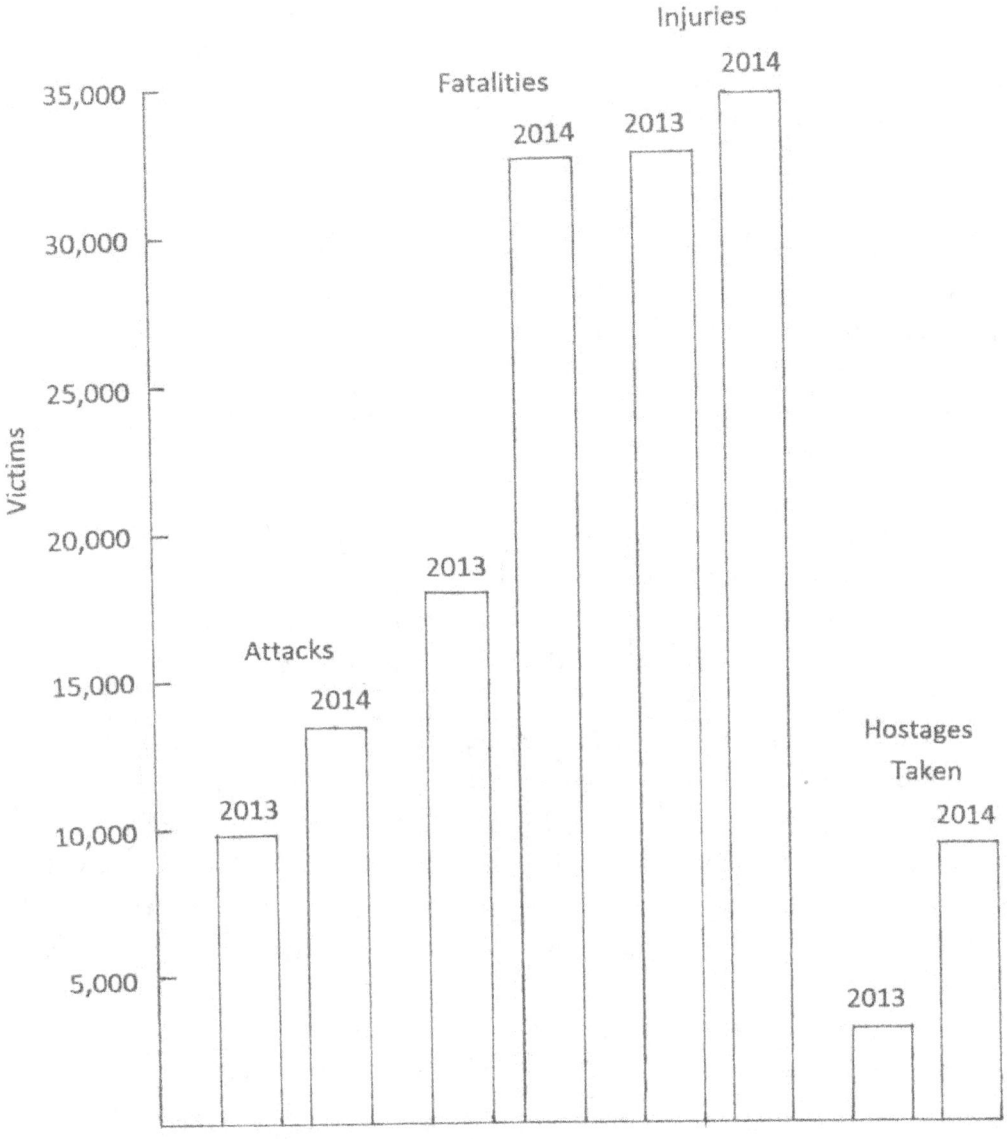

Top Countries: Iraq, Pakistan, Afghanistan, Nigeria, Syria

Perpetrators: Islamic State of Iraq and the Levant (ISIL)
                 Taliban
                 Al-Shabaab
                 Boko Haram
                 Maoists/Communist Party of India-Maoist

Source U.S. State Department, Bureau of Counterterrorism
        ProQuest Statistical Abstract of the United States 2016, p 899

Global Terrorism Index 2015

In 2014 the total number of deaths from terrorism increased by 80% when compared to the prior year. This is the largest increase in the last 15 years. Since the beginning of the 21st century, there has been over a nine-fold increase in the number of deaths from terrorism, rising from 3,329 in 2000 to 32,685 in 2014.

Terrorism remains highly concentrated with most of the activity occurring in just five countries - Iraq, Nigeria, Afghanistan, Pakistan and Syria. These countries accounted for 78% of the lives lost in 2014. Although highly concentrated, terrorism is spreading to more countries, with the number of countries experiencing more than 500 deaths increasing from 5 to 11, a 120% increase from the previous year. The six new countries with over 500 deaths are Somalia, Ukraine, Yemen, Central African Republic, South Sudan and Cameroon.

While the majority of countries in the world did not have a death from terrorism, the total number of countries which experienced at least one death increased to eight, raising the total to 67 countries in 2014. This includes Austria, Australia, Belgium, Canada and France which experienced high profile terrorist attacks last year.

Also notable over the past year is the major intensification of the terrorist threat in Nigeria. The country witnessed the largest increase in terrorist deaths ever recorded by any country, increasing by over 300% to 7,512 fatalities. Boko Haram, which operates mainly in Nigeria, has become the most deadly terrorist group in the world. Boko Haram pledged its allegiance to ISIL (also known as the Islamic State) as the Islamic State's West Africa Province (ISWAP) in March 2015. Deaths attributed to Boko Haram increased by 317% in 2014 to 6,644. ISIL was responsible for 6,073 terrorist deaths. 51% of terrorist deaths that are attributable to a terrorist group were by Boko Haram and ISIL.

There was also a shift in the distribution of targets during 2014, with an 11% decrease in the number of deaths of religious figures and worshipers. This was offset by a 172% increase in the deaths of private citizens. At least 437,000 people are victims of homicide globally each year, which is over 13 times more than the victims of terrorism.

The majority of deaths from terrorism do not occur in the West... The West is designated as the countries where ISIL has advocated for attacks. They include the United States, Canada, Australia, and European countries. The report highlights the striking prevalence of lone wolf attacks in the West. Lone wolf attacks account for 70% of all terrorist deaths in the West since 2006.

--static.visionofhumanity.org

Libya

U.S. airstrikes began August 1, 2016 to assist Libya's militia in the battle against Islamic State in the city of Surt, said to be the last stronghold of the terrorist group in Libya. By mid-August, the militia and its allies had retaken 70% of the city. U.S., British and Italian special forces are on the ground fighting with the militia and have met intense resistance in the attempt to clear out Islamic State neighborhoods block by block. 75% of Surt's residents have fled the city for outlying regions, telling horrific accounts of beheadings and beatings under Islamic State's year-long control.

President Obama authorized the three dozen air strikes to date in order to prevent Islamic State from becoming a stronghold in Libya. The U.S. has been shipping arms to the militants.

Surt is the city where Muammar Gaddafi was located and killed on August 20, 2011, resulting in a vacuum through which Islamic State rose to power. There is widespread speculation that when the fighting is over, the government will not be able to unify the numerous factions in the region, even though they are momentarily united in the fight against Islamic State.

Muammar Gaddafi was in Tripoli when fighting erupted in August 2011. He left in a truck convoy headed for Surt. A predator drone operated from a base near Las Vegas fired the first missiles at the convoy, hitting several trucks when the convoy was two miles west of Surt. French fighter jets as part of NATO forces continued the bombing. Gaddafi and several others left the convoy to hide in a drainage pipe near Surt. He was killed shortly thereafter. "Rebel fighters beat him before he was shot several times as he shouted for his life."

Omran Shaban, the Misrata fighter who discovered Gaddafi in the drain pipe and who had posed in photos with Gaddafi's golden gun, was captured by Green Resistance soldiers in Bani Walid. He was then paralyzed and severely tortured. The interim president of Libya secured his release, but he died some days later from his wounds in France.

Gaddafi was buried October 24, 2011 in an undisclosed location in the desert. His son was also in the convoy and killed. Prime Minister Jibril said, "Now that he's dead, Libya would need a meticulous plan for the transition to democracy. He declared Libya "liberated" at a ceremony in Benghazi October 23, 3 days after Gaddafi's death.

Hillary Clinton, Secretary of State at the time, "laughed and expressed delight" with Gaddafi's death, stating, "We Came. We Saw. He died."   --Wikipedia.org

Aiding and Abetting Terrorism

A 1987 video survives of Lt. Col. Oliver North testifying at the Iran-Contra hearings during the Reagan administration. He was being questioned by Senator Al Gore. "Did you not recently spend close to $60,000 for a home security system?"

Oliver North replied, "Yes Sir, I did."

Senator Gore continued, "Isn't that just a little excessive?"

"No sir," responded North.

"No? And why not?"

"Because the lives of my family and I were threatened, sir."

"Threatened? By whom?" Senator Gore questioned.

"By a Muslim terrorist, sir," North answered.

"Terrorist? What terrorist could possibly scare you that much?"

"His name is Osama bin Laden, sir," North replied.

At this point, Senator Gore tried to repeat the name, but couldn't pronounce it. Then he continued. "Why are you so afraid of this man?"

"Because, sir, he is the most evil person alive that I know of," North answered, "And the Muslims are trying to take over America and destroy it from the inside out and putting their people into our political offices."

"And what do you recommend we do about him?" asked Senator Gore.

"Well, sir, if it was up to me, I would recommend that an assassin team be formed to eliminate him and his men from the face of the earth,"

That was the end of the clip. The year before, in 1986, terrorist pilot Mohammad Atta blew up a bus in Israel. The Israelis captured, tried and imprisoned him, but as part of the Oslo agreement with the Palestinians in 1993, Israel had to agree to release "political prisoners." Israel refused, not wanting to release any "with blood on their hands." President Bill Clinton insisted that all prisoners be released. Thus, Mohammad Atta was freed. In 2001, he flew an airplane into Tower One of the World Trade Center. President Barack Obama is ending his second term quietly releasing suspected 9/11 terrorist prisoners at Guantanamo in Cuba.

TERRORISM REPLACES FIGHT FOR TERRITORY

Los Angeles Times   Jul 5, 2016   p A1

ISTANBUL, Turkey - As a U.S.-led coalition claws away territory from Islamic State in Syria and Iraq, the extremist group is shifting its emphasis away from building a caliphate to spreading terror around the world, according to terrorism experts.

While Al Qaeda prefers to use Arab fighters who are vetted and trained, Islamic State has deployed volunteers from non-Arab states and works with other local terrorist groups on the fly. Islamic State's reach is far greater than that of Al Qaeda. The carnage attributed to Islamic State is rising by the day. In Istanbul, at least 45 people were killed and more than 200 injured when three gunmen from Russia and Central Asia equipped with suicide belts attacked the main airport. Islamic State did not claim credit - and almost never does in Turkey.

The militants did claim credit in Baghdad, where a van packed with explosives was detonated early Sunday amid a crowd of families gathered at a shopping mall to break the Ramadan fast. At least 157 people were killed, many of them children.

In Saudi Arabia, assailants set off a bomb in Medina outside the Prophet's Mosque, one of the holiest sites in Islam. Though no one claimed responsibility for the attack, which killed four people, Islamic State has long been at odds with the Saudis.   by Roy Gutman

Cultural Diversity

Amnesty International reports that in Kashmir and Jammu, India, the "Armed Forces Special Powers Act," passed in 1990 "grants virtual immunity of the security forces from prosecution in civilian courts for alleged human rights violations." The interviewee in the report concludes that "space for civil society and dissent in India has been shrinking."

Human rights abuses appear to be increasing in many parts of the world, often by governments attempting to quell dissent, guards against prisoners, marauding gangs, and lone-wolf terrorists. Attacks motivated by ethnicity, territory or religion are giving way to random violence against random victims, especially since 9/11. The WTO and the Global Financial Crisis have further exacerbated unrest around the world.

Sometimes called "hate crimes" and "crimes against humanity," human rights abuses are not new. Human history is rife with examples. Stability and equality, the antidotes, are the responsibility of government.

Ethnic Violence in South Sudan

The Republic of South Sudan gained independence from Sudan on July 9, 2011, by 98.8% of the vote. South Sudan is Africa's newest country; its largest city, Juba, has a population of 300,000. Sudan was occupied by Egypt, then Anglo-Egypt until 1956, and the area south of Sudan adopted English as its official language in 2007. The majority religion is 60.5% Christian, mostly Anglicans from the Episcopal Church of the Sudan, 32.9% traditional African religion, and 6.2% Muslim, as of a 2012 report. The child marriage rate is 52%, and in this highly rural country cows are used to purchase young brides, sometimes multiple brides. The population of 12 million is 45% under age 15, with literacy rate of 27%. South Sudan belongs to the United Nations, the African Union, and East African Community.

Since independence, South Sudan has been declared the world's second "most fragile state," after Somalia, due almost intirely to internal conflict. There are campaigns of atrocities as government troops numbering 185,000 attempt to disarm sporadic rebellions. Among the Shilluk and Murle, government fighters burned scores of villages, raped hundreds of women and girls, and killed an untold number of civilians. Survivors report fingernails being torn out, burning plastic bags dripped on children to make parents hand over weapons, and villagers burned alive in their huts if rebels had spent the night there. In May 2011 government troops allegedly set fire to over 7,000 homes in Unity State.

In December 2013 President Salva Kiir Mayardit accused his Vice-President, Riek Machar, of an attempted coup d'etat, and fired him along with six others, starting another civil war. President Kiir is a Dinka, the country's largest ethnic group, and Machar is a Nuer, the country's second largest ethnic group, which lives mostly in the upper (White) Nile region. One million people were displaced, 400,000 fleeing to neighboring countries Kenya, Sudan and Uganda. The majority of atrocities were again carried out by the government side, including rape, hangings, castrations, houses lit on fire after dragging people inside, beatings of women who cried, house to house searches shooting civilians, and shooting at the swamps where people were hiding. A cease fire was declared October 2015.

An international aid agency calls South Sudan's "human rights abuses off the Richter scale." In April 2014 Navi Pillay, then U.N. High Commissioner for Human Rights, stated that more than 9,000 child soldiers had been fighting in South Sudan's civil war. Amnesty International reported that the army suffocated to death 60 people in a shipping container who were accused of supporting rebels.

During the civil war, President Kiir threatened to kill journalists who reported "against the country," resulting in seven journalists killed in 2015. Mr. Kiir established by decree 28 states instead of 10, formed "largely along ethnic lines." But in early August 2016, violence again is beginning to erupt in the north. Aid from the African Union is pending. It is estimated two million have died due to fighting and famine since independence.   --wikipedia.org

Police say a seventeen year old wife was drenched in kerosene and set alight after marrying against her family's wishes. "I need justice," pleads the husband, mourning his dead wife. The wife ran away and married, angering her Punjabi family who were furious that she had married an ethnic Pashtun without permission. She was "tricked" into returning home to her mother, who reportedly made no attempt to hide her crime, shouting to neighbors that she had killed her daughter for supposedly dishonouring her family.

The prime minister of Punjab pledged to close a loophole under Islamic law that allows many perpetrators of so-called "honour" killings to go free.

--theguardian.com/world/2016/Jun/08

More than 1,096 "honor" killings were reported in Pakistan last year, although the actual number of victims is likely to be far higher. A 28-year old died last month in northern Punjab. Her husband said he believed his wife, who was in Pakistan to visit relatives, was killed because her family disapproved of their marriage.

Authorities report that she was strangled. She had divorced her first husband, a cousin she had married in an arranged service, and married her current husband. They moved to Dubai in 2014. She converted from the Sunni to the Shia school of Islam when the pair married.   --theguardian.com/uk-news/2016/Aug/03

Yazidi women and girls as young as twelve are being advertised for sale as sex slaves slaves by ISIS fighters on the instant messenger apps Whatsapp and Telegram. Facebook owns Whatsapp. Both Whatsapp and Telegram use end-to-end encryption, so the companies themselves are not able to access messages of users.

Victims on ads are dressed in fine clothes and sometimes heavily made up.

An estimated 3,000 women and girls are currently held captive by ISIS. Most were taken prisoner in 2014 when ISIS fighters attacked their villages in northern Iraq. The Yazidis, a religious Kurdish community, have been attacked and killed by ISIS in both Iraq and Syria, in what constitutes an act of genocide, according to U.N. investigators.

Ahmed Burgus, director of Yazda in the UK, an organization formed to support the Yazidi community in the aftermath of the 2014 genocide, told "The Independent," "We condemn the inaction of social media websites such as Telegram, Facebook, Twitter and Whatsapp, for allowing the trade in women and children." Twitter announced on August 18, 2016, that they have closed 235,000 accounts suspected of terrorist postings.

The Yazda organizer is concerned that ISIS is using Yazidi children as recruiters, posing with index finger up, in apparent allegiance to ISIS. "A week ago, a Yazidi child called his family through Whatsapp and told his mother, 'You are a Kafir (a non-Muslim), and we are coming to kill you.'" Social media apps are the way ISIS is recruiting hundreds of Muslims every month. Whatsapp said they do what they can to fight extremist messaging, including disabling accounts , and they encourage people to report such sites.   --independent.co.uk/news/world

"Gangs and Sex Trafficking in San Diego," by Dr. Ami Carpenter, Faculty,
Joan B. Kroc School of Peace Studies, San Diego University, October 27, 2015

Today...we know that the actual (minimum) number of gangs involved in sex trafficking is...110 to be precise. We can also estimate for the first time, the minimum number of Commercially Sexually Exploited People (CSEP) in San Diego County per year. Currently that range is between 8830 and 11,773 per year, with an average age of entry between 14 to 15 years old.

Here are some of our major findings:

1. Sex trafficking is San Diego's 2nd largest underground economy after drug trafficking. The underground sex economy represents an estimated $810 million in annual revenue for facilitators of sex trafficking.

2. We estimate that 8,830 - 11,773 people are sex trafficking victims/survivors per year in San Diego County, but far fewer (1,766) come into contact with law enforcement.

3. 85% of pimps/sex trafficking facilitators interviewed were gang involved.

4. Pimps/sex trafficking facilitators are not primarily African American. Our sample of traffickers in prison contained roughly an equal number of white, black and Hispanic facilitators. In fact, the ratio of white to minority facilitators may be higher than is reported here given that our data does not account for the over-representation of blacks and Hispanics in California jails and prisons.

5. Nor does the relatively even split between black, Hispanic and white facilitators represent a complete picture - in the past 10 years, Somali gangs and Iraqi Chaldean groups have been indicted on sex trafficking charges, and Asian American and Native American gangs were under-represented in our data set. It is likely that our data underreports the nuances of facilitator ethnic/racial background.

6. 15 years old is the average age of entry into child-commercial sexual exploitation (CSEC).

7. Sex trafficking facilitators control 4.5 victim/survivors on average.

8. 42% of first-time prostitution arrests are in fact cases involving sex trafficking.

9. Domestic trafficking accounts for the majority of CSEP.

10. Transborder criminal networks are involved in trafficking minors and adults between Mexico and the United States. 20% of trafficking victims referred to service providers come from Mexico and 10 other countries.

11. Female recruiters and pimp/sex trafficking facilitators are perceived to be a significant and growing feature of the underground sex economy.

12. Significant CSEC recruitment is happening on high school and middle school campuses.

To learn more, go to Abolish Human Trafficking.org, a website dedicated to informing students and the general public about the realities of modern-day slavery.

—sandiego.edu/peace studies

Islamic treatment of homosexuality

Lesbian, gay, bisexual and transgender in Islam is influenced by the religious, legal and cultural history of the nations with a sizable Muslim population, along with specific passages in the Quran and statements attributed to the Islamic prophet Muhammad (hadith).

The traditional schools of Islamic law based on Quranic verses and hadith, and influenced by Islamic scholars such as Imam Malik and Imam Shafi, consider homosexual acts a punishable crime and a sin. The Quran cites the story of the "People of Lot" destroyed by the wrath of God because they engaged in lustful carnal acts between men.

Extreme prejudice remains, both socially and legally, in much of the Islamic world against people who engage in homosexual acts. In Afhganistan, Brunei, Iran, Mauritania, Nigeria, Saudi Arabia, Sudan, United Arab Emirates and Yemen, homosexual activity carries the death penalty. In others, such as Algeria, Maldives, Malaysia, Qatar, Somalia and Syria, it is illegal.

Most Muslim-majority countries and the Organisation of Islamic Cooperation (OIC) have opposed moves to advance LGBT rights in the United Nations.   --wikipedia.org

ISLAMIC STATE HUNTS FOR GAY MEN
Los Angeles Times   Jun 14, 2016   p A3

BEIRUT - The camera lingers on the jihadists suspending the man by his legs over the edge of the building. Blindfolded, his hands bound behind his back, he flails as he falls to his death, the video switching to slow motion as an Islamic chant, known as a nasheed, plays in the background.

The clip, from a 2015 video celebrating the anniversary of Islamic State's takeover of the Iraqi city of Mosul, is one of dozens of photo reports and videos depicting the fate of those accused by the militant group of "committing the act of (sodomy)": being thrown from a "tall height," usually a building. Those who survive have stones hurled at them by crowds waiting below...

The jihadists can rely on support for their cause from Muslim communities where intolerance of homosexuality is mainstream...Many countries across the Arab and Islamic world sentence people to death or subject them to lashings..."These atrocious acts exist on a continuum of violence. I think it's really important to underscore that there is violence by families, killing campaigns by militias...and there was indifference by governments even before the rise of ISIS, with not a single murderer being prosecuted."   by Nabih Bulos

Sharia Law

wikipedia, the free encyclopedia

Sharia law is the law of Islam. The Sharia (also spelled Shariah or Shari'a) law is cast from four sources:[1]

1. The Qur'an, which Muslims believe was verbally revealed by God to Muhammad through the angel Gabriel (*Jibril*).
2. The actions and words of Muhammad, which is called the *sunnah*
3. Consensus from the community by achieving recurrence
4. *qiyās* or legal reasoning

The Sharia law itself cannot be altered, but the interpretation of the Sharia law, called "fiqh," by imams is given some leeway.

As a legal system, the Sharia law covers a very wide range of topics. While other legal codes deal primarily with public behavior, Sharia law covers public behavior, private behavior and private beliefs.

According to the Sharia law and after due process and investigation:

- Habitual theft past a specific threshold, and after repeated warnings, is punishable by amputation of a hand.
- The punishment for adultery and fornication such that it becomes a public ordeal, according to the Holy Qur'an, is lashing. Before the revelation of these verses, Muhammad followed the Judaic law in implementing the punishment of death by stoning. This was only given if the person admitted to it repeatedly, was not intoxicated and knew the repercussions. Even then, if during the punishment he repented, he was to be released.
- A woman is allowed to be accompanied by another woman in giving testimony in court for financial affairs
- A female heir inherits half of what a male heir inherits. The concept being that Islam puts the responsibility of earning and spending on the family on the male. Any wealth the female earns is strictly for her own use. The female also inherits from both her immediate family and through agency of her husband, her in-laws as well.

Sharia law is divided into two main sections:

1. The acts of worship, or al-ibadat, called the 5 pillars of Islam:
    1. Affirmation (Shahadah): there is no god except Allah and Muhammad is his messenger. However, Allah is the same God of Isaac and Adam. Allah remains the same throughout time
    2. Prayers (Salah): five times a day
    3. Fasts (Sawm during Ramadan)
    4. Charities (Zakat)
    5. Pilgrimage to Mecca (Hajj)

--wikipedia.org

2. Human interaction, or al-mu'amalat, which includes:
    1. Financial transactions
    2. Endowments
    3. Laws of inheritance
    4. Marriage, divorce, and child custody
    5. Foods and drinks (including ritual slaughtering and hunting)
    6. Penal punishments
    7. Warfare and peace
    8. Judicial matters (including witnesses and forms of evidence)

Schools of sharia law

There are 5 schools of thoughts in Islam, four major schools of Sunni sharia law (Hanafi, Maliki, Shafi'i and Hanbali), and one major Shia sharia law (Jafari). The sharia (law) between these schools is same for topics covered in Quran, but in matters that is not covered explicitly in Quran, they sometimes differ from each other.

Laws and practices under Sharia

Marriage

- A Muslim woman can only marry a Muslim man and a Muslim man can only marry a Muslim or Ahl al-Kitāb . He/She cannot marry an atheist, agnostic or polytheist.[2]
- A Muslim minor girl's father or guardian needs her consent when arranging a marriage for her.
- A marriage is a contract that requires the man to pay, or promise to pay some of the wedding and provisions the wife needs. This is known as the dowry.
- A Muslim man may be married to up to four women at a time, although the Qur'an has emphasized that this is a permission, and not a rule. The Qur'an has stated that to marry one is best if you fear you cannot do justice between your wives and respective families. This means that he must be able to house each wife and her children in a different house, he should not give preferential treatment to one wife over another.

Crime and punishment

Sharia recognizes three categories of crime:[3]

1. Hudud: crimes against God with fixed punishment.
2. Qisas: crimes against Muslims where equal retaliation is allowed.
3. Tazir: crimes against Muslims or non-Muslims where a Muslim judge uses his discretion in sentencing.

Hudud crimes are five:[4] theft, highway robbery, zina (illicit sex), sexual slander (accusing someone of zina but failing to produce four witnesses), and drinking alcohol

Sharia requires that there be four adult male Muslim witnesses to a hudud crime or a confession repeated four times, before someone can be punished for a Hudud crime.[4]

--wikipedia.org

Murder, bodily injury and property damage - intentional or unintentional - is considered a civil dispute under sharia law.[5] The victim, victim's heir(s) or guardian is given the option to either forgive the murderer, demand Qisas (equal retaliation) or accept a compensation (Diyya) in lieu of the murder, bodily injury or property damage. Under sharia law, the Diyya compensation received by the victim or victim's family is in cash.[6][7]

The penalty for theft

Theft (stealing) is a hudud crime in sharia, with a fixed punishment. The punishment is cutting off the hand or feet of the thief.

The penalty for zina

Sharia law states that if either an unmarried man or an unmarried woman has pre-marital sex, the punishment should be 100 lashes.[8][9] There are some requirements that need to be met before this punishment can happen. For example, the punishment cannot happen unless the person confesses, or unless four eyewitnesses each saw, at the same time, the man and the woman in the action of illicit sex. Those who accuse someone of illicit sex but fail to produce four eyewitnesses are guilty of false accusation and their punishment is 80 lashes.[10] Maliki school of sharia considers pregnancy in an unmarried woman as sufficient evidence that she committed the hudud crime of zina.[11][12] The Hadiths consider homosexuality as zina.[13]

The penalty for apostasy

The punishment for apostasy is thought to be death by several schools of Muslim thought.

An example apostate was Hashem Aghajari, who was sentenced to death for apostasy in Iran (in 2002) after giving a controversial speech on reforming Islam. His sentence was reduced to 5 years in prison, but only after international and domestic outcry.

--wikipedia.org

Winston Churchill on Islam

Winston Churchill was a young soldier and journalist in 1899, when he penned his thoughts on Islam:

"How dreadful are the curses which Mohammadism lays on its votaries! Besides the fanatical frenzy... a degraded sensualism deprives this life of its grace and refinement...
Every woman must belong to some man as his absolute property, either as a child, a wife, or a concubine, delaying the final extinction of slavery until the faith of Islam has ceased to be a great power among men.
Individual Muslims may show splendid qualities, but the influence of the religion paralyzes the social development of those who follow it. No stronger retrograde force exists in the world."   --"The Russian War," 1st Edition, Vol. II, London, pp 248-250

First Muslim Woman Judge Carolyn Walker, hand-picked by President Obama, sworn in as judge of the 7th Municipal District, Brooklyn by holding the Holy Quran at Brooklyn Borough hall on December 10, 2015. **It was an Historic Day as Sharia law is now officially part of our Judicial System in America .**
Since the Quran forbids all law but Sharia Law, she will head the first Federally sanctioned Sharia Court in the nation .

wikipedia.org

In the United States, as of 2014, seven states have "banned Sharia law," or passed some kind of ballot measure that "prohibits the states' courts from considering foreign, international or religious law." Those states are Arizona, Kansas, Louisiana, South Dakota, Tennessee, North Carolina and Alabama. Sharia has become a political issue in several non-Muslim majority countries, with a petition to ban Sharia councils circulated in the United Kingdom.
--wikipedia.org

Hamtramck, Michigan: thenation.com

What's life like in America's first city with a Muslim-Majority City Council?

While there are few issues with non-Muslims locally, outsiders' assumptions forces local leaders like new City Council Member Saad Almasmari, a 28-year-old Yemeni, to stay busy repeating the obvious: He'll follow the constitution. He's there to serve all Hamtramck residents. No controversial Islamic laws. And so on.

That includes Sharia law, Almasmari's campaign manager and community organizer Ibrahim Aljahim assured me. "These people, they ran away from Sharia law in their countries and some fought against Sharia law. What makes you think they want to go to Sharia law here?" he asked, clearly exasperated.

The only legitimate sources of "tension" are the loud 6:30 AM calls to prayer, which many non-Muslims have complained about, and proposals to build mosques downtown.   --thenation.com

> "The practice, traditional in some cultures, of partially or totally removing the external genitalia of girls and young women for nonmedical reasons. It is illegal in many countries."
>
> —google.com

The United Nations Population Fund reports that three million girls undergo female genital mutilation (FGM) every year, largely in Africa and the Middle East. It has been a deep cultural tradition since the building of the pyramids.

Elderly women maintain high status in their tribes by performing the ritual on girls as young as ten who wait in line, listening to the screams of the girls before them, knowing they must undergo "the cut" in order to be marriageable. In most cases, the clitoris and inner and outer vaginal lips are removed. The remaining skin is stitched together, leaving an opening the size of a straw for urination and menstruation. The procedure explains the bloody sheet phenomenon upon marriage. Childbirth is extremely painful and life-threatening. Alice Walker was the first writer to bring this taboo subject to western awareness in her book, "The Color Purple." Gloria Steinem also wrote of it.

Because of large numbers of African and Middle East immigrants to Western Europe and the United States, the practice has spread to western culture. France has long had zero tolerance for FGM and has laws against it as a criminal act. It is difficult to enforce because it takes place behind closed doors.

The United States outlawed FGM in 1996, but visitors were being "cut" while on vacation, so the law was amended in 2012 to cover that exigency. Enforcement is spotty. An Ethiopian immigrant was convicted in 2006 in the U.S. for cutting off his daughter's clitoris with a pair of scissors.

"Often rationalized as a rite of passage into womanhood, in reality FGM is an extreme form of violence used to control girls' and women's sexuality. It involves a mixture of cultural, social and religious traditions associated with preparing for adulthood and marriage, and ideals of community, modesty and fidelity. Most instances occur in Africa, Asia and the Middle East, but Female Genital Mutilation is also practiced in Australia, Europe, New Zealand, Latin America and North America."   —equalitynow.org

ENVIRONMENTAL CONCERNS

ACTIVE CONTAINER SHIPS
IN PORTS OF LOS ANGELES
LONG BEACH ONE DAY
JUNE 19, 2016

Pollution from Container Ships

SHIP ARRIVALS, DEPARTURES
COMPILED BY MARINE EXCHANGE OF LOS ANGELES-LONG BEACH HARBOR INC.

ACTIVE VESSELS IN PORT AS OF SUNDAY, JUN 19 12:04

VESSEL	FLAG	BERTH FROM	OPERATOR	DESTINATION	TO SAIL
185-1 (T: SARAH C)	USA	C57 Santa Rosa, MEX	Curtin Maritime Corp.	TBA	
ALASKAN FRONTIER	USA	T121 Valdez, USA	Alaska Tanker	Cherry Point, USA	06/19
ANL BAREGA	CYP	A94 Papeete, PYF-Oakland	US Lines	Auckland, NZL	06/19
ANTON SCHULTE	MLT	212 Yantian, CHN	NYK Line (N.A.)	Oakland, USA	06/20
BELNOR	SGP	176 Praia Mole, BRA	Ultrabulk	Vancouver, CAN	06/19
CARNIVAL IMAGINATION	BHS	H4 Ensenada, MEX	Carnival Cruise	Avalon, USA	06/19
CASCADE SPIRIT	BHS	Anc-F13 Dumai, IDN-Sea (PAL)	Tesoro Maritime	Sea (PAL)	06/20
CHEMTRANS MOON	LBR	Anc-F8 Sea (PAL)	American Sun GMBH	TBA	06/23
CHETCO (T: PONO)	USA	LAMrngs Rainier, USA	Sause Bros. Towing	Columbia River, USA	06/25
CMA CGM LYRA	GBR	J266 Yantian, CHN	CMA-CGM	Oakland, USA	06/20
CP 38 (T: PONO)	USA	LAMrngs El Segundo, USA	Sause Bros. Towing	TBA	
CP 42 (T: PONO)	USA	LAMrngs El Segundo, USA	Sause Bros. Towing	TBA	
CP 43 (T: PONO)	USA	LAMrngs El Segundo, USA	Sause Bros. Towing	Ensenada, MEX	
CP 44 (T: LARGONA)	USA	D39 Ensenada, MEX	Connolly-Pacific	TBA	
CP 45 (T: DURANGO)	USA	D41 Ensenada, MEX	Connolly-Pacific	TBA	
CP 46 (T: AN TILLETT)	USA	D39 Ensenada, MEX	Connolly-Pacific	TBA	
DB LONG BEACH (T:	USA	D39 San Francisco, USA	Connolly-Pacific	San Francisco, USA	
DN MILLET	TUR	210 Ensenada, MEX	Turkish Cargo Line	Incheon, KOR	06/21
ELIZABETH I.A.	GRC	Anc-D6 Sea (PAL)	Elizabeth Special	La Paloma, URY	06/19
ESSIE C	MHL	Anc-F11 San Francisco, USA	Sterling Ocean Tankers	Rosarito, MEX	06/22
GUTHORM MAERSK	DNK	T140 Yokohama, JPN	Maersk Pacific	Oakland, USA	06/20
HALEIWA (T: PONO)	USA	LAMrngs Rainier, USA	Sause Bros. Towing	Columbia River, USA	06/25
HANJIN NETHERLANDS	PAN	T136 Pusan, KOR	Hanjin Shpg. Co.	Oakland, USA	06/19
K-MARINE IX	USA	271 Manzanillo, MEX	American Marine	TBA	
MANHATTAN (T: KAMAEHU)	USA	D41 Ensenada, MEX	Sause Bros. Towing	TBA	
MARJORIE C	USA	121 Hilo, USA-San Diego	Pasha Hawaii Holdings	Honolulu, USA	06/24
MARMAC 303 (T: RHEA)	USA	51 Morgan City, USA	Latham Maritime Inc.	TBA	
MAUNALEI	USA	C62 Shanghai, CHN	Matson Nav.	Honolulu, USA	06/22
MOMI ARROW	PAN	Anc-D2 Portland, USA	Gearbulk Shipping	Acajutla, SLV	06/27
NAVARINO	MLT	402 Pusan, KOR	PIL	Oakland, USA	06/20
NAVE CETUS	LBR	F209 Salina Cruz, MEX	Navios Corp.	Sea (PAL)	06/20
NS SPIRIT	LBR	Anc-F10 Vanino, RUS	SCF Management	TBA	
ODYSSEY	LBR	T16 Sea (Equator)	Barber Moss	TBA	
OREGON VOYAGER	USA	Anc-D1 San Francisco, USA	Chevron Shipping Co.	TBA	06/23
OVERSEAS NIKISKI	USA	Anc-B4 Anacortes, USA	Tesoro Maritime	Martinez, USA	
OVERSEAS RAPHAEL	MHL	Anc- Sea (PAL)	Aurora Shipping Co.	Sea (PAL)	06/19
PARAMOUNT HYDRA	IOM	B84A Rosarito, MEX-Sea	Oldson Ventures Ltd.	San Francisco, USA	06/20
SAGA ODYSSEY	HKG	Anc-B5x Vancouver, CAN	Saga Welco	Port Everglades	06/21
SAGA PIONEER	HKG	Anc-B3 Kaohsiung, TWN	Saga Welco	TBA	06/23
SEA LAUNCH COMMANDER	LBR	T16 Sea (Equator)	Barber Moss	TBA	
SEA RELIANCE (550-1)	USA	238 Martinez, USA	Intrepid Ship Mgmt	TBA	
SHARON SEA	LBR	Anc-F16 Sea (PAL)	Harren & Partner	TBA	
SIGNET ATLAS (T: BRITOIL	USA	Anc-B6 Balboa, PAN	Foss Maritime	Dutch Harbor, USA	06/21
TULA	MEX	189 Salina Cruz, MEX	TMM Division Maritima	TBA	
TWO HARBORS (T: A J)	USA	95 Manzanillo, MEX	Harley Marine	Seattle, USA	

VESSELS DUE TO ARRIVE SUNDAY, JUN 19 00:00

VESSEL	FLAG	BERTH FROM	OPERATOR	DESTINATION	TO SAIL
AZALEA ISLAND	PAN	Anc-D5 Nagoya, JPN	MOL	Oita, JPN	06/25
BROTONNE BRIDGE	HKG	128 Ningbo, CHN	K Line	Oakland, USA	06/22
CRESTY	CYP	Anc-I9 Pittsburg, USA	Norden A.S.	Santa Rosalia, MEX	06/25
DIJKSGRACHT	NLD	Anc-B10 Chimbote, PER	Spliethoff	Zhanjiagang, CHN	06/19
EVER URSULA	PAN	404 Yantian, CHN	Evergreen Shpg.	Oakland, USA	06/21
SEASPAN HAMBURG	HKG	Anc-B9 Oakland, USA	Hapag-Lloyd Cont. Line	Manzanillo, MEX	06/19

The International Maritime Organization estimates that carbon dioxide emissions from global shipping is 2.2% of human-made carbon dioxide emissions in 2012. There are 100,000 transport ships at sea globally, of which 6,000 are container vessels. Shipping cargo tonnage has been increasing at 4% annually since the 1990s.

Smokestack discharge from container ships accounts for 18-30% of nitrogen oxide and 9% of sulfur oxide released into the earth's air. The fuel used in oil tankers and container ships is high in sulfur. Sulfur in the atmosphere creates acid rain, which damages crops and buildings and causes respiratory problems in people, including risk of a heart attack.

Shipping container engines emit noise which travels long distances beyond the ship, a threat to marine life, especially whales, who rely on sonar for communication. Southern California has seen a number of beached, dying whales in recent years.

Ballast discharge from large vessels contains water contaminated with viruses, bacteria, and non-native exotics that can cause extensive ecologic and economic damage to aquatic life.

There are an unknown number of collisions with sea life, mostly whales, who breach regularly for air. At greatest risk is the North Atlantic Right Whale. With only 400 or less remaining, collisions are an extinction threat.   --wikipedia.org

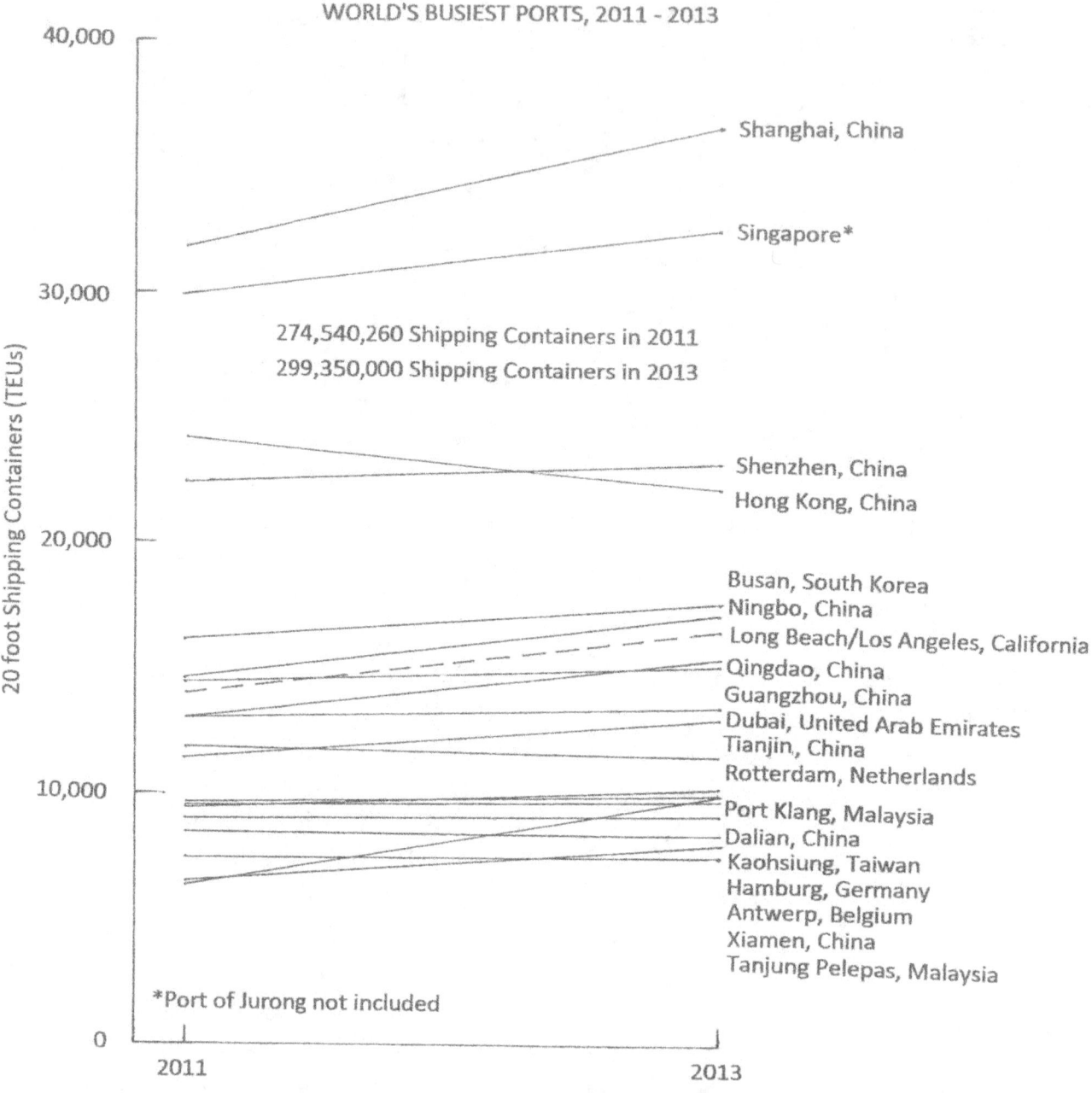

WORLD'S BUSIEST PORTS, 2011 - 2013

40,000

Shanghai, China

Singapore*

30,000

274,540,260 Shipping Containers in 2011
299,350,000 Shipping Containers in 2013

20 foot Shipping Containers (TEUs)

Shenzhen, China
Hong Kong, China

20,000

Busan, South Korea
Ningbo, China
Long Beach/Los Angeles, California
Qingdao, China
Guangzhou, China
Dubai, United Arab Emirates
Tianjin, China
Rotterdam, Netherlands

10,000

Port Klang, Malaysia
Dalian, China
Kaohsiung, Taiwan
Hamburg, Germany
Antwerp, Belgium
Xiamen, China
Tanjung Pelepas, Malaysia

*Port of Jurong not included

0

2011   2013

Other west coast ports heavily used for foreign goods include Oakland, CA;
Richmond, CA; Portland, OR; Longview, WA; Tacoma, WA; Seattle, WA.

The Ports of Houston and South Louisiana are also heavily used for foreign goods.

Source: United Nations Conference on Trade and Development
               The World Almanac and Book of Facts 2016, p. 76

The Ports of Long Beach and Los Angeles built a freeway exclusively for trucks
called the "Alameda Corridor" to expedite transit of foreign goods to the trains
of downtown Los Angeles for shipment across the country.

France gets 3/4ths of its electricity as nuclear power. She has 58 operating power plants
      and one under construction.

China has 38 operating nuclear power plants and 28 under construction.

Russia has 34 operating plants.

India has 21 operating plants and 6 under construction.

South Korea has 24 operating plants and 4 under construction, but about a hundred older
      reactors are being retired.

Japan has 48 nuclear power plants still operating.

Sweden has 10, Finland 4, Ukraine 16, and United Kingdom 16 operational nuclear plants.

Chancellor Angela Merkel announced May 30, 2011 that Germany's fourteen
nuclear power stations will be shut down by 2022.   In 2016 Italy is closing all its
nuclear stations. Belgium, Spain and Switzerland are phasing out nuclear power,
as are the Netherlands, Sweden and Taiwan. Austria built a nuclear power station
but never started it.

As of 2011, Australia, Austria, Denmark, Greece, Ireland, Italy, Latvia, Lichtenstein,
Luxembourg, Malaysia, Malta, New Zealand, Norway, Philippines and Portugal
have no nuclear facilities and remain opposed to them.

There are no nuclear power stations in Greece, Turkey, Croatia or Israel.

Belarus, Jordan, Turkey, United Arab Emirates and Vietnam are considering nuclear power.

— wikipedia.org

    The United States has 59 nuclear power plants with 100 commercial reactors
licensed to operate, since most plants have two units. There are three stations in the
western half of the United States. The other 56 are in the eastern half of the country.
The newest plants are located south of the Great Lakes. The greatest concentration
of plants are in the northeast.   --energyjustice.net

Decommissioning San Onofre's Nuclear Power Plant in California

The San Onofre Nuclear Power Plant decommissioning will cost $4.4 billion. One third of that money will come from trust funds set up by customer billings, and two thirds from investments. Unit 1 has already been shut down, shorter than the life span of 30 years for nuclear power plants, because of premature wear on over 30,000 tubes in replacement steam generators installed in 2010 and 2011. Senator Barbara Boxer said the unit was a "danger to the 10 million people living within 50 miles" near San Clemente, California.

--wikipedia.org   --songscommunity.com/decommissioning

More than 4,000 tons of radioactive waste are stored at San Onofre, buried across the 405 Freeway, 42 yards from the ocean. Edison International, which holds 78.2% ownership of the plant, wants to bury the nuclear waste from the decommissioning on the bluffs. There was a huge meeting on June 12, 2016, with residents protesting the California Coastal Commission's decision to approve Edison's plan. Discussion centered on the fifty canisters already at the "high level nuclear dump." "Each half-inch thick canister has more waste than was released at the Chernobyl accident, and now there's a hundred more to come."   --wikipedia.org

Decommissioning the Clinton and the Quad Cities in Illinois

Chicago's Exelon Corporation owns "the most nuclear plants in the United States." Exelon will be shutting down two in Illinois in two years, the Clinton built in 1987, and the Quad Cities nuclear plant consisting of 2 reactors built in 1973, both over 40 years old. The plants had cost overruns, extended shutdowns, chronic safety problems, and some of the highest electrical rates in the nation.   --la.indymedia.org

U.S. Nuclear Regulatory Commission

The NRC reports that on average, Americans receive a radiation dose of 620 millirem annually. Half comes from natural background radiation: radon in the air, smaller amounts from cosmic rays and the earth itself. The other half comes from man-made sources of radiation, including medical, commercial and industrial sources. In general, a yearly dose of 620 millirem from all radiation sources has not been shown to cause humans any harm. A full body CT scan results in a dose of 1,000 millirem; a pelvis x-ray is a dose of 70. Nuclear medicine is 400 millirem.

There is also radioactivity in organic matter, including food, the highest in brazil nuts, but also bananas, carrots, white potatoes and lima beans. Even water contains small amounts of uranium and thorium. The average person receives an average internal dose of 30 millirem of radioactivity per year from the food and water that we eat and drink.

According to the Congressional Research Service, there were 62,683 metric tons of commercial spent fuel accumulated in the United States as of the end of 2009. The total increases by 2,000 to 2,400 tons annually.   --nrc.gov

Fossil Fuel Emissions

Richard Heede of the Climate Accountability Institute in Snowmass, Colorado, spearheaded a study that showed that ninety "top emitters" worldwide produced 63% of cumulative global emissions of industrial CO2 and methane between 1751 and 2010, a total of 914 billion metric tons (gigatons) of CO2. Seven were cement manufacturers, and the rest were oil, gas and coal companies.

His study was published in the journal "Climate Change" November 21, 2013. Heede commented to "The Guardian," "There are thousands of oil, gas and coal producers in the world, but the decision makers, the CEOs, or the ministers of coal and oil: they could all fit on a Greyhound bus or two."

Michael Mann, a climate scientist says that the study increases the accountability of fossil fuel burners. "You can't burn fossil fuels without the rest of the world knowing about it." Bill Moyers added that fifty are investor-owned companies, 31 are state-owned, and there are 9 government industries on the list.　　　　　--thinkprogress.org

Fossil Fuels and Earthquakes

Hydraulic fracturing injects millions of gallons of water into oil and gas-containing geologic formations deep underground. "Earthquakes are caused by fluid injection during hydraulic fracturing in proximity to pre-existing faults. Secondarily, earthquakes are caused by the disposal of fracking wastewater via underground injection." Texas, Oklahoma and Ohio are examples. California is at risk.

The earthquakes are chronic but were thought to be minor. They can be "large and damaging," new research shows. Oklahoma places restrictions on wells in earthquake-prone areas. Texas also. Insurance companies have increased rates on their earthquake policies in some areas.

In 2011 there was a 5.7 magnitude earthquake in Oklahoma. A resident is suing the oil company responsible at the site in Oklahoma's highest court. A favorable finding would make wells a legal liability.

Many states ignore the issue. Arkansas suspended injection wells after an "earthquake swarm" in 2011.　　　　　--earthworksaction.org

"The earth does not belong to man. Man belongs to the earth.
This we know. All things are connected like the blood which unites
one family. All things are connected."　　　　　--Chief Seattle

Fossil Fuels and Benzene

In 1995 the Environmental Protection Agency exempted oil and gas development waste from being classified "hazardous." In 2015 there are 1.1 million active oil and gas wells in the United States. Most hydraulically fracture large quantities of liquid and solid waste. The Resource Conservation and Recovery Act (RCRA) declared the waste "nonhazard, subject to state discretion."   --earthworksaction.org

Benzene is a natural constituent of crude oil and is a human carcinogen. It is classified as an aromatic hydrocarbon, a colorless and highly inflammable liquid with a sweet smell. Benzene is used to make other chemicals. More than half of benzene production is used to make polymers and plastics like polystyrene. 20% of benzene is used to manufacture cumene, needed to produce phenol and acetone for resins and adhesives. 10% of benzene production is used to make cyclohexane for manufacture of nylon fibers used in textiles and engineering plastics. Smaller amounts of benzene are used to make rubbers, lubricants, dyes, detergents, drugs, explosives and pesticides.

In 2013 the biggest user of benzene was China, then the USA. Now its production is expanding to the Middle East and Africa. In 1907 benzene was used in a decaffeinated coffee called Sanka, later discontinued. In the early 20th century it was also used as an after-shave lotion because of its pleasant smell. Later it was used as a significant component in Liquid Wrench, which lasted until the late 1970s, as well as paint strippers, rubber cements and spot removers.

Before the 1950s, gasoline often contained benzene additive of several percent because benzene increases the octane rating and reduces knocking. Now, in the U.S., concern over its negative health effects and the possibility of benzene entering the groundwater have led to stringent regulation of gasoline's benzene content with limits typically around 1%. European regulations also put a 1% limit on benzene content. The U.S. EPA introduced new legislation in 2011 that lowered the benzene content in gasoline to 0.62%.

In 2005 the water supply to the city of Harbin, China, with 9 million people was cut off because of a major benzene exposure. Benzene leaked iknto the Songhua River, which supplies drinking water to the city, after an explosion at a Chinese National Petroleum Corporation factory in the city of Jilin on November 13, 2005.

Benzene enters the human body from automobile exhaust, auto service stations, industrial emissions and smoking. Benzene rapidly metabolizes in the body, is exhaled or excreted through the urine, but most persons in developed countries have some measurable baseline levels of benzene and other aromatic petroleum hydrocarbons in their blood.

Benzene exposure increases the risk of cancer, is a notorious cause of bone marrow failure, aplastic anemia and acute leukemia. Benzene is ubiquitous, as gasoline and hydrocarbon fuels are in use everywhere. Human exposure to benzene is a global health problem.
                                                                --wikipedia.org

Genetically Modified Foods

The European Union has a standing policy not to import genetically modified foods from the United States or elsewhere. Europe does not produce GM foods. it is estimated that 70% of the food that Americans eat is genetically modified or comes from a genetically modified source. In California, voters turned down a ballot measure that would have required identification of genetically modified foods, likely due to a barrage of advertisements from producers of GM foods saying that foods would be more expensive if GM labeling were required.

On October 18, 2012, "GMO Answers" gave the following information:
1. GMO seeds are not sterile. Monsanto has a patent on sterile seeds, called the Terminator Gene, but has promised not to use the patent.
2. GMO seeds can produce plants that withstand Roundup. Farmers must pay royalties for these seeds.
3. Organics prohibit the "use" of GMO, but if pollen blows, it isn't being "used." It is difficult to control wind effects, especially in canola and corn.
4. Due to the rise in commercial seed companies, farmers bought seeds yearly, long before GMO seeds were introduced, because replanting from hybrid seeds yields inferior quality.
5. Most seeds are not GMO modified. Those that are include corn, soybeans, cotton (for oil), canola (for oil), squash and papaya, plus GMO alfalfa for animals.

"GMO Answers" that GMO crops do not harm bees. Bee colony collapse disorder (CCD) became a national concern about ten years ago, when CCD destroyed 33% of hives in 2006. GMOs allow more crops on less land in drought with fewer insecticides. One out of every three mouthfuls we eat is thanks to bees. A bee parasite has a virus that infects bees. Other factors include bacterial diseases, low genetic diversity and bees having to travel long distances for nutrition.   --gmoanswers.com

Food and Water Watch responds: GMOs allowing stronger herbicides and pesticides affects not just what we eat but what's in the soil, air and water. More GMOs means more chemical use. Roundup is potentially carcinogenic. Planting GMOs means using the associated chemicals, which end up in the environment and threaten the health of farm workers and their families as well as the communities they live in.

The pests are catching up. They build up resistance to chemicals. The more chemicals we use, the faster they adapt. It is an "arms race of dangerous chemicals where people and the environment will be the losers." The biotech and food companies don't want labeling of GMO foods. Monsanto, Dow, Dupont and Syngenta sell GMO seeds and related products to farmers. The industry is dominated by a handful of companies. Monsanto owns the seed companies that once were competitors. GMOs are spreading around the world, along with the pesticide Roundup, also by Monsanto.   --foodandwaterwatch.org

Wikipedia reports that pesticides vary in their effect on bees. If a bee comes into contact in some manner with a pesticide but dies before returning to the hive, no harm is done. But a bee returning to the hive can cause colony death. Pesticides are now considered a main cause of colony collapse, and the toxic effects of neonicotinoids on bees are confirmed. Sub-lethal effects are disorientation, reduced foraging, impaired memory and learning, and a shift in communication behaviors. If there is an over-accumulation of acetylcholine, the result is paralysis and death. The U.S. Department of Agriculture says pesticides, pathogens and parasites all are present in high levels in affected hives.   --wikipedia.org

On August 24, 2016 the news reported that the Swiss company Syngenta was being bought by the state-owned China National Chemical Corporation for $43 billion. The deal was held up while the United States scrutinized its impact on the American food supply chain. Sygenta was formed in 2000 by the merger of Novartis and Zenica Agrochemicals. Syngenta is a global agribusiness that produces agrochemicals and seeds. As a biotech company, it conducts genomic research. As of 2014, Syngenta was the world's largest crop chemical producer. Sales in 2015 were approximately $13.4 billion, over half of which were to emerging markets.   --npr.org   --Syngenta.com

Organophosphates form the basis of many insecticides, herbicides and nerve agents. The EPA says organophosphates are "very highly acutely toxic to bees, wildlife and humans." Organophosphates are widely used in solvents, plasticizers, additives and insecticides such as malathion, parathion and diazinon. Prenatal exposure to organo-phosphate pesticides lowers IQ and may contribute to attention-deficit disorder.
                                                                                --wikipedia.org

The Bayer Company in Germany investigated organophosphates for use in insecticides. The German military said no to pesticide use, but came up with the warfare agent Serin, which was used in the mass poisonings in the Tokyo subway system in 1995. Serin was also delivered by rockets as a chemical warfare agent in Damascus, Syria, in 2013. It was used by Saddam Hussein as a nerve gas in Iraq in the 1980s. During World War II, in 1941, organophosphates were reintroduced worldwide for pesticide use.
                                                                                --emedicine.medscape.com

The U.S. has long known of the toxicity of pesticides, since Rachael Carson's 1962 groundbreaking book, "Silent Spring," detailing the absence of birds because of DDT. John Robbins, of the Baskin Robbins ice cream family, retreated to live in the woods with his family and write "Diet for a New America," published in 1985 during the height of Reagan's factory farming of agricultural animals. Robbins writes in painful-to-read detail of the use of pesticides, herbicides, fungicides and other agents sprayed on animals living in tight confinement throughout their lives, and of the alarming rise in cancer, heart disease and other ailments in humans from ingesting chemically laden foods.

Plastics

Public Radio International reports that plastics are destroying ocean ecosystems. five countries dump more plastic in the oceans than the rest of the world combined. Soda bottles, plastic bags, cigarette butts "bob atop the ocean for miles on end." And, according to Ocean Conservancy, a U.S. environmental non-profit, the other 95% is submerged beneath.

> China, Indonesia, the Philippines, Thailand and Vietnam account for 60% of the ocean's garbage.

In these five countries, only 40% of trash is properly collected. As Asia adopts a taste for "consumer junk," often wrapped in plastic, the refuse is piled high in communal dumps where wind picks it up. Even sanctioned garbage dumps are near rivers that flow into the sea. Asians recycle plastic bottles only. Those that collect the bottles receive fifty cents for ten hours' work. Mini-plastic pouches are sold to Asians, small affordable quantities, so there are a lot of small plastic containers that add up. Garbage trucks often dump loads by the roadside.

> Ninety percent of the garbage ends up in the ocean.

The Ocean Conservancy estimates that 1 million metric tons of plastic trash ends up in the seas every year. Plastic trash is toxic. It also chokes marine life by ensnaring them. Plastic trash "warps ecosystems, creating environmental havoc."   pri.org

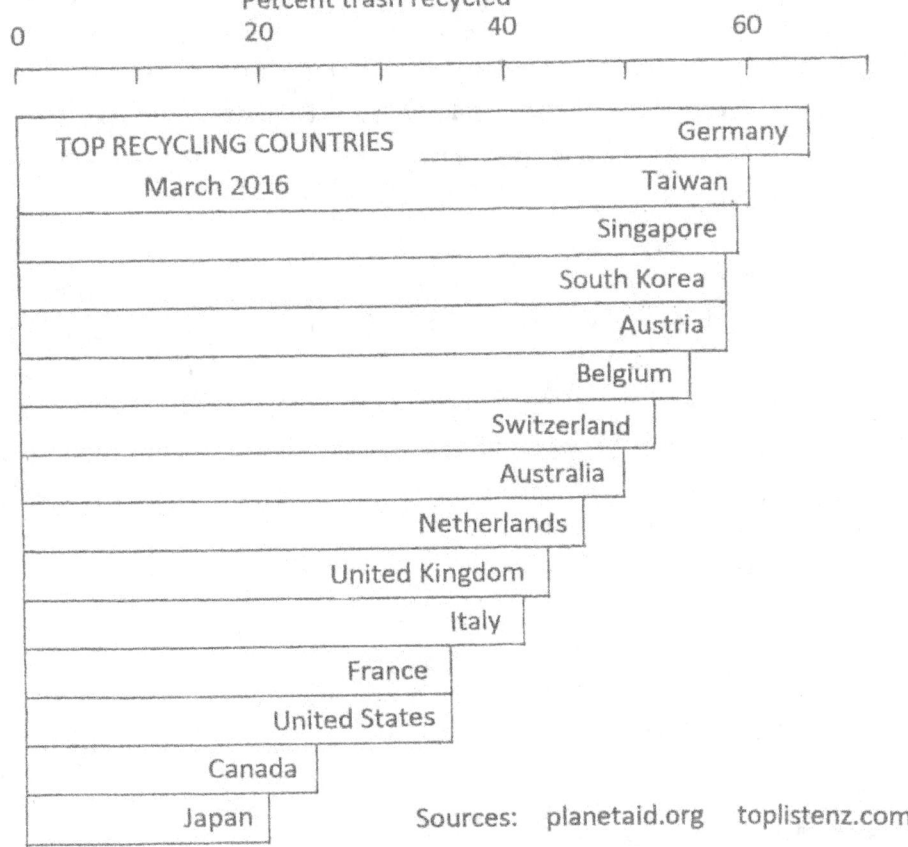

206

The Brazilian Rainforest

Beef production is wiping out the Amazon Rainforest. 65.7% of deforestation is due to cattle ranching. In the last three decades, about a fifth of the forest has been lost. Brazil is the largest exporter of beef. From 1996 to 2004, its beef exports increased from $1.6 million to $1.9 billion. The land presently supports between 180 to 190 million head of cattle. The U.S. imported $200 million a year in beef from Central America. The chief importers now are China and Russia.   --onegreenplanet.org

The Brazilian government plans to reduce forest clearing of 2100 square miles every year by 2018. In 2013 26 Brazilian beef producers faced fines of $300 million for buying cattle illegally raised on deforested Amazon rainforest. Still, illegality goes on.
--onegreenplanet.org

On August 1, 2016, the U.S. Department of Agriculture announced the reopening of U.S. beef exports to the Brazilian market. Brazil has removed all barriers in the agreement with the U.S. Brazil has 200 million consumers, a growing middle class. U.S. beef exports to Brazil and 15 other countries in 2015 reached $6.3 billion, due to the efforts of the U.S. Department of Agriculture to eliminate BSE-related, mad cow restrictions.   --usda.org

Amazon tapper Chico Mendes wanted to improve the lot of the rubber tappers and preserve the rainforest from which they extracted their living. The tappers encountered bitter conflict from cattle ranchers and other large landowners who wanted to continue cutting down the forest. Mendes, assassinated on December 22, 1988, lives on as an international symbol of environmental courage - and of hope for the forests of the Amazon.
--Kenneth Brower, "One Earth," Collins Publishers 1990, p 122

Chinese state oil company Andes Petroleum is proceeding with operations to drill for oil on indigenous lands. The government of Ecuador must halt these plans and respect the rights of indigenous peoples and the environment. Environmental activists are killed in increasing numbers globally. We activists have written: "To Ecuador's Minister of Hydrocarbons and the Director of China's Andes Petroleum: China must not finance drilling in Yasuni-ITT, one of the most biodiverse places on the planet and the home of Ecuador's last indigenous communities living in voluntary isolation. Ecuador must honor its constitution and respect the rights of the environment and indigenous peoples."
--amazonwatch.org

Deforestation globally is responsible for up to 20% of global greenhouse gas emissions.
wwf.org.uk

Climate Change and the Amazon Rainforest

Global climate change is happening now. The United Nations Framework Convention on Climate Change (UNFCCC) defines climate change as a change in climate attributable directly or indirectly to human activity, and that occurs in addition to natural processes of climate variability observed over comparable periods of time. When released into the atmosphere through the burning of fossil fuels, deforestation, and other human practices, carbon dioxide and other greenhouse gases like methane absorb infrared radiation from the sun, trapping heat in Earth's atmosphere and altering the global atmosphere. Major and immediate impacts of climate change include increased flooding, storms, drought, and food insecurity, according to a recent World Bank report.

In a February 2010 *report*, the World Bank estimated that the "tipping point" for the Amazon could be approximately 20% deforestation. If reached, this threshold could trigger a dramatic die-back of the Amazon rainforest. With 17% to 18% of the Amazon already deforested, another similar amount degraded, forest fires running rampant, and global temperatures already on the rise, the Amazon ecosystem could face ecological collapse sooner than previously expected.

As the source of one-fifth of all fresh water on the planet, the Amazon Basin's hydrological system plays a critical function in regulating the global and regional climate. Water condensation, evaporation, and transpiration over the Amazon are key drivers of the global atmospheric circulation, affecting precipitation across South America and much of the Northern Hemisphere. Among the regions directly linked to the Amazon by a complex weather system is the Rio de la Plata basin of southeastern South America, one of the most important agricultural zones on the planet. Recent climate models indicate that deforestation has also had the effect of reducing precipitation as far afield as the lower Midwest of the United States.

U.S. High Elevation Forests

Across the west, high elevation forests are dying at an alarming rate. Five-needle pines, critical for sustaining vast and essential ecosystems, are witnessing an unprecedented level of threats. We must work to prevent irreversible damage. The Whitebark Pine faces a combination of mountain pine beetles, white pine blister rust, fire suppression and climate change, jeopardizing the health of high elevation forests. To offset the damage to some extent, 50 million trees have been planted.   -- americanforests.org

Trees Suffering in Southern California

Thousands of trees are dying due to two invasive beetles:

The polyphagous shot hole borer beetle reproduces in trees such as maples, oaks, elders and cottonwoods in southern California. The beetle is also invading sycamores and willows. The beetle holes look like shotgun holes across the trunks. The beetles are epidemic in the city of Whittier. Beetles bring with them a fungus that feeds on the tree between the bark and the wood. The fungus kills the tree two or three years before the tree would otherwise die from multiple generations of the beetles. The beetles arrive in wood products from Southeast Asia. They could also be in the wood pellets that arrive. There could be hundreds of beetles in a pallet.

The goldspotted oak borer is rampant in Los Angeles, Riverside, San Diego and Orange Counties in southern California. These borers attack oaks already weakened by the southern California drought going into its fifth year.   July 15, 2016   --pe.com/articles/trees

Citrus Trees

The Asian citrus psyllid was first noticed in China in 1943, then South Africa in 1947. It has spread everywhere in Asia except Japan. The psyllid carries a bacteria in its gut that causes huanglongbing, or "Yellow Dragon Disease," when the psyllid eats citrus leaves, leaving fruit green and bitter. There is no cure for an infected tree. As of 2004, the psyllid was absent from the U.S. or Europe, but since then it has wiped out 90,000 acres of Florida citrus groves. A single tree was found to be infected in the town of Hacienda Heights in Southern California in 2012. The U.S. Department of Agriculture funded CalPoly Pomona to breed stingless wasps the size of a flea from Pakistan that forage on the Asian psyllid; hundreds of thousands of the wasps have been released, and the USDA wants a million released annually. The wasps are being harvested under tents in Riverside. 80% of citrus fruit sold in the U.S. is grown in California.
                    --hungrypests.com   --nationalgeographic.com

West Antarctica Glaciers

Jet Propulsion Laboratory, California Institute of Technology

> The six west Antarctica glaciers are past the point of no return.
> They are on an unstoppable path to complete meltdown.

It's just a matter of time until they disappear into the sea. We can slow the process down but we can't stop it. This is where we see the most dynamic change in the speed and thinning of these glaciers. We have been watching forty years of changes in velocity. There is a continuous increase in the discharge of ice. We are also watching also their retreat inland.

But most is what we can't see. There is a grounding line where glaciers detach from the bed and become afloat in the ocean. They melt more strongly then. We imaged this area in 1992, and in 2011 when we looked again we went, "Wow."

Josh Willis, a NASA scientist, wrote "Sea Level Rise from Space." There is about a kilometer a year retreat. They will disappear completely within a couple of centuries. Hundreds of millions of people living on coastlines around the world are at risk of sea levels rising. In Asia, sea levels are rising fast. They are rising as well on the United States east coast, the Gulf of Mexico, and all around Florida. Off the California coast, some sea level is falling.

--jpl.nasa.gov

Coral Reefs and Ocean Warming

Earth Justice

Coral reefs are the "rainforests of the ocean." They are biodiversity hotspots that take up less than 1% of the marine environment but home to 25% of the oceans' marine life. Clear, warm shallow waters provide sunlit nutrients and the algae that sustains coral. Stunningly beautiful, coral reefs protect coasts from hurricanes, and chemicals from coral provide medicine for cancer, AIDs and other diseases.

> Coral reefs are extremely vulnerable to warm water temperatures.

When temperatures are too high, the algae living in coral dies, creating large areas of dead bleached coral reefs. The catastrophic 1998 bleaching in the Great Barrier Reef of Australia will become more commonplace in the future. The increase of greenhouse gases in the atmosphere also leads to more acidification of ocean waters, which can harm coral and inhibit the production of coral reefs.

On May 13, 2014, Earth Justice won a lawsuit against the National Marine Fisheries Service, pushing for better protection for the parrotfish and coral. Now the agency must do more to protect and restore Caribbean reefs.   --earthjustice.org

Global Warming

Natural Resources Defense Council

Eight degrees Fahrenheit. It may not sound like much - perhaps the difference between wearing a sweater and not wearing one on an early spring day. But for the world in which we live, which climate experts project will be at least 8 degrees warmer by 2100, should global emissions continue on their current path, this small rise will have grave consequences, ones that are already becoming apparent, for every ecosystem and living thing - including us.

According to the National Climate Assessment, human influences are the number one cause of global warming, especially the carbon pollution we cause by burning fossil fuels and the pollution-capturing we prevent by destroying forests. The carbon dioxide, methane, soot and other pollutants we release into the atmosphere act like a blanket, trapping the sun's heat and causing the planet to warm. Evidence shows that 2000 to 2009 was hotter than any other decade in at least the past 1300 years. This warming is altering the earth's climate system, including its land, atmosphere, oceans, and ice, in far-reaching ways.

Higher temperatures are worsening many types of disasters, including storms, heat waves, floods, and droughts. A warmer climate creates an atmosphere that can collect, retain, and drop more water, changing weather patterns in such a way that wet areas become wetter and dry areas drier. "Extreme weather events are costing more and more," says the deputy director of NRDC's Clean Power Plan initiative. "The number of billion-dollar weather disasters is expected to rise."

According to the National Oceanic and Atmospheric Administration, in 2015 there were 10 weather and climate disaster events in the United States - including severe storms, floods, drought and wildfires. In the years between 2011 and 2015, you see an annual average cost of $10.8 billion.

The increasing number of droughts, intense storms and floods we're seeing as our warming atmosphere holds - and then dumps - more moisture poses risks to public health and safety, too. Prolonged dry spells mean more than just scorched lawns. Drought conditions jeopardize access to clean drinking water, fuel out-of-control wildfires, and result in dust storms, extreme heat events and flash flooding. Elsewhere around the world, lack of water is a leading cause of death and serious disease. At the opposite end of the spectrum, heavier rains cause streams, rivers and lakes to overflow, which damages life and property, contaminates drinking water, creates hazardous-material spills, and promotes mold infestation and unhealthy air. A warmer, wetter world is also a boon for food-borne and waterborne illnesses and disease-carrying insects such as mosquitoes, fleas and ticks.   --nrdc.org

> Today's scientists point to climate change as the biggest global health threat of the 21st century.   --nrdc.org

Paris Agreement to Reduce Greenhouse Emissions

Carbon Tracker reports that the United States, China and the European Union combined emit as much carbon annually as the rest of the world. At the Paris Summit in December, 2015, China committed to using 20% non-fossil fuels by the year 2030, when the country will have reached its peak carbon dioxide emissions, calculated at 10 billion metric tons per year.

At the Paris summit, 195 countries adopted the first ever legally binding global climate deal, with enforcement to begin in 2020. The governments agreed to:
- Commit to the long-term goal of keeping the increase in global average
     temperature well below 2 deg C above pre-industrial levels
- Aim to limit the increase to 1.5 deg C, which would significantly reduce risks and
     impact of climate change
- Have global emissions peak as soon as possible
- Have rapid reductions thereafter in accordance with best available science.

The governments will meet every five years to assess accomplishing the above goals and to provide transparency.

The United Nations Framework Convention on Climate Change reached a goal of limiting global warming to 2 degrees Celsius (3.6 deg Fahrenheit), but concluded that it would "take more effort from the United States and China to achieve that goal." China will have to "cap coal use, scale up renewables and efficiency, and reconfigure fossil resources and carbon pricing."

The China emissions trading scheme is already in place in seven cities and provinces and will go national in 2016. China is currently emitting double the emissions of the U.S., and if no change is forthcoming, China will be emitting triple the U.S. quantity in 20 years. India is rapidly industrializing, and in 2025 India will be equal to U.S. current emissions. Further, India won't allow the west to limit growth on energy resources. India will be under pressure, however, due to the U.S. and China agreement in Paris to reduce emissions. Coal is facing stiff competition in the U.S. from renewables and natural gas. U.S. coal is losing 3/4ths of its value because of less profitability compared to natural gas.

Carbon Tracker says that United States oil companies are "in denial" that there is any outcome other than burning an unlimited amount of fossil fuels.

President Obama and Xi Jinping met on March 31, 2016, at which time both agreed to accelerate the reduction of carbon dioxide before 2030. Xi Jinping said his goal was to reach 20% of non-fossil fuel use by 2020, rather than 2030.   --carbontracker.org

Worst Invasive Reptiles

slate.com

Nile crocodiles and green anacondas like hot, muggy spaces. Sometimes they are smuggled into the United States unintentionally in airplane cargo holds or in shipping containers but most often, they arrive legally.

> Dangerous reptiles are shipped to the U.S. legally for the exotic pet trade.

The environmental damage that non-native species cause in the United States every year is $120 billion. The Miami International Airport is a major hub for wild animal trade, legal and otherwise. Between 2000 and 2004, "the U.S. imported...588,000 individually counted animals, plus 3 tons of animals that were weighed but not individually counted." Many were not even identified. Some are for pets. Some go on a dinner plate. "The global trade in animals is so huge and complex that we shouldn't be surprised when creatures slip through the cracks and disappear into the nearby woods." If they form populations, we call them "established." If they harm natives or eat their food, we call them "invasive."

Some of the non-native species now here include:

Green Anaconda - from South America. The heaviest snake in the world. 4 in Florida found.

Yellow Anaconda - only 4 found in Florida. Possibly established. Potentially invasive.

Nile crocodile - largest reptile in the world, a verified man-eater from Africa. Diet is wildebeest. A few seen in the Everglades. The fear of them becoming invasive is so great that the Fish and Wildlife Service granted Florida officials permission to shoot any Nile crocodile on sight.

African python - large constrictor showing up in West Miami near Everglades. Youngsters. Established. Potentially invasive.

Black and white tegu - large lizard from South America. 4 to 5 feet long, spotty black and white. Increasingly common in south Florida. Loves eggs. Gopher tortoise eggs threatened. Established and likely invasive.

Reticulated python - from Southeast Asia. Largest snake in the world. No evidence of breeding.

Boa constrictor - Very popular in the pet trade. Invasive. On the 444 acres of Deering Estate in Miami for decades.

Nile monitor - looks like a Komodo dragon. 8 foot long lizard, a voracious eater of anything smaller than itself. In several different counties in Florida, West Palm Beach, Cape Coral, Homestead Air Reserve Base. Invasive in south Florida.

Burmese python - one of the largest snake species on earth, in Florida Everglades and spreading. Have established a "large breeding ground" since the end of the 20th century. Native to Southeast Asia. Deer, alligators, birds and rats have been found in their stomachs. Have spent $1.2 million so far trying to control. The snake is a constrictor, has been seen more that 15 feet long. 104 killed on a hunting day. Tens of thousands to hundreds of thousands in number. Beyond control.   --slate.com

Burmese Python (continued)

The Burmese python is spreading throughout southern Florida. Two thousand have been removed from the Everglades and surrounding areas since 2002. They were first documented to be established in 2000. They are the result of accidental or intended release by pet owners, and they are causing devastating consequences on the Everglades ecosystem. "The proliferation of the pythons and the introduction of new foreign species can further threaten many of the endangered plants and animals we are working diligently to protect."

--nps.gov

The Key Largo wood rat and wood stork, both federally protected, are disappearing.

--slate.com

salon.com

There has been a "devastatingly huge collapse" of the small animal population in the Florida Everglades. Between 2003 and 2011, sightings of raccoons and opossums declined 99%. Bobcats, too. "all of us were shocked by the results," said Bob Reed, co-author of a study and chief of the Invasive Branch of the U.S. Geological Society. For the study, transmitters were attached to rabbits. "Every adult marsh rabbit we were tracking ended up in a python. The radios were transmitting from inside the pythons." The study, published in the Proceedings of the Royal Society B: Biological Sciences, concludes,

> Only with the recovery of the mammal populations will it be possible to restore the health and functionality of this World Heritage Site.

--salon.com

Endangered Species

Elephant

worldwildlife.org

Once common throughout Africa and Asia, elephant numbers were severely depleted throughout the twentieth century, largely due to the massive ivory trade. Poaching, conflict, and habitat destruction continue to threaten the species. Rampant ivory poaching reduced elephants in Tanzania's oldest and largest protected areas by 90% in fewer than 40 years. Since 2009, Mozambique and Tanzania have lost more than half their elephants. Elephants help maintain forest and savannah ecosystems for other species and are integrally tied to rich biodiversity. In 1989, the International Trade in Endangered Species of Wild Fauna and Flora (CITES) banned the international trade in ivory. Thriving, unregulated domestic ivory markets in a number of countries continue, which fuel an illegal international trade. Poaching to meet growing demand from affluent Asian countries is driving up the rate of poaching. ETIS, the Elephant Trade Information System, helps identify routes and countries of particular importance in illegal trading.

CHINA OFFICIALS LINKED TO IVORY SMUGGLING
Los Angeles Times   Nov 7, 2015   p A3

JOHANNESBURG, South Africa - Visits to Africa by high-level Chinese delegations, including a presidential trip, have been used to smuggle ivory, contributing to an explosion in poaching that has cut Tanzania's elephant population in half over five years, according to a report released Thursday by an environmental group...

A Chinese national was caught trying to enter the port of Dar es Salaam, the Tanzanian capital, with 81 illegal tusks intended for two mid-ranking Chinese naval officers, said the group...The visit by Chinese President Xi Jinping in March 2013 coincided with another boom in sales that reportedly caused black market prices for ivory to double. Chinese officials rejected the report as groundless...

Two smugglers speaking to undercover investigators for the environmental group said that in the two weeks before Xi's visit, Chinese buyers flooded the market. As the customers snapped up thousands of pounds of ivory, the price doubled to $320 a pound, the smugglers said. Diplomatic bags were used to smuggle the ivory to China on the presidential plane, according to the report...

The report analyzed the eight biggest seizures of poached ivory in Tanzania since 2009, which totaled 26.5 tons, equivalent to the loss of nearly 4,000 elephants.

"When President Jakaya Kikwete assumed office in 2005, the country had about 142,000 elephants. By the time he steps down in late 2015, the population is likely to have plummeted to about 55,000."   by Robyn Dixon

Rhinoceros

Vietnam is the largest consumer of rhino horn, and Mozambique is the major source of rhinoceros. "Mozambique, Tanzania and Vietnam are still not doing enough," says a conservationist. Zanzibar, Tanzania, is a major trafficking hub in illegal smuggling.
--worldwildlife.org

Shark

wikipedia.org

Shark fins are imported in massive amounts by Vietnam. And the economic growth of China has put this expensive delicacy within reach of a growing middle class. In 2012 China passed a ban on shark fin imports, but in January 2013, restaurants were selling artificial shark fins, one-third of which had dangerous amounts of cadmium and methylmercury. Since 2011 shark fin soup consumption dropped 50% to 70%. There was a worldwide drop in shark fin prices, and a move away from shark fishing in parts of Africa. After cutting fins off, sharks are thrown back into the ocean alive, unable to swim or hunt. They die of suffocation from not being able to swim, starvation or predation.

Malaysia banned shark fin soup. Hawaii, California, Oregon, Washington, Illinois and Guam banned the sale and possession of shark fins, eliminating availability of the soup. Chinese-American groups seek to overturn the ban. Shark fin soup is a social dish in Chinese culture. It is also a status symbol, since it is so expensive.

Canada banned shark fin soup in 2011, but Calgary overturned the ban due to protests by the Chinese community. The International Union for Conservation of Nature (IUCN), the oldest global environmental organization, estimates that 100 million sharks are killed each year. In 2010, the convention of the International Trade in Endangered Species (CITES) rejected shark regulation on hammerhead, white tip and dogfish sharks, failing to get the required 2/3rds vote. China and Japan spearheaded the opposition. In 2013 CITES overcame the Chinese and Japanese opposition, so the three shark species will now join the protection afforded the great white, basking and whale shark. The whale shark, the world 's largest fish, is endangered. In 2014 Western Australia began to allow shooting of great white, bull and tiger sharks close to shore, a potential threat to swimmers. The shot bodies are discarded at sea.
-- wikipedia.org

"For if one link in nature's chain might be lost, another might be lost, until the whole of things will vanish by piecemeal."   --Thomas Jefferson

Blue Fin Tuna

The Atlantic blue fin tuna, also known as the northern blue fin tuna, swims in the west and east Atlantic as well as the Mediterranean. It is extinct in the Black Sea. Its great size, speed and power has the admiration of fishermen, writers and scientists. The Atlantic blue fin is heavily targeted for the Japanese raw fish market. The species has declined in the last 40 years, 72% in the east Atlantic and 82% in the west Atlantic. It has been an important game species for sports fishermen since the 1930s, particularly in the United States but also in Canada, Spain, France and Italy.

In the 1970s, Canada started farming blue fin tuna in St Mary's Bay. In captivity the fish can grow to hundreds of kilos. Taken young from the Mediterranean and South Australia, the fish are a $220 million market, but a threat to wild species since the young are removed from the sea before reproducing. The farms are not sustainable because they rely on ranching juveniles from the ocean, rather than captive breeding. The blue fin's slow growth and late maturity compound the problem. In 2010, 30 million tons of small fish were removed from the ocean, the majority to feed farmed fish. The Japanese appetite for sushi is the predominant threat to the Atlantic blue fin. The Japanese came up with the miles-long nets, which were globally banned in the 1970s. Overfishing continues despite warnings of current precipitous decline. There is a global quota of 15,000 tons per year, 10,000 tons to allow recovery, but 60,000 tons per year are actually being taken. Now, a reduction to 7,500 tons would be necessary to sustain the population. In 2010, the United Nations opposed a US-backed effort of a total ban on Atlantic blue fin tuna fishing and trading. The leading opponent was Japan, rallying others to defeat the ban 68 to 20. The population is fragile. In 2012 a quota compromise of 13,500 tons per year of Atlantic blue fin tuna was passed.

The Pacific blue fin tuna, the species "Thunnus Thynnus," called "Tunny" for short, by 2013 faced a "drastic population decline estimated at 96% due to overfishing." It was found widely in the north Pacific ocean previously. From 2000 to 2004, 16 to 29,000 tons of Pacific blue fin was caught each year. It has passed from threatened status to "vulnerable." In 1979 the Japanese farmed the Pacific blue fin at Kinki University, and in 2002 succeeded in breeding them. The Pacific blue may have high levels of mercury, harmful to humans. Ninety percent caught in the wild are juveniles, severely impacting the blue fin's ability to increase its numbers.

80% of both Atlantic and Pacific blue fin tuna are consumed in Japan as sashimi or sushi. On January 5, 2013, a 489 pound Pacific blue fin was sold at a new year auction, the most prestigious auction, for $1.76 million, or $3,603 per pound.

Greenpeace and Blue Ocean Institute both have placed ALL blue fin tunas on their "Red List," which means "threatened or endangered."   -- wikipedia.org

Totoaba and Vaquita

nationalpublicradio.org

The totoaba is a sea bass, and the vaquita is the world's smallest porpoise with a permanent smile on its face. Both exist only in the Gulf of California, in the Sea of Cortes, consisting of 5,000 square miles. Both species are endangered. The Chinese crave the swim bladder of the totoaba, saying it makes one more beautiful as an anti-aging product. The dried bladder turns up on the "Dried Seafood Street" in Hong Kong and can cost $100,000. It is usually served as a soup. Totoaba is called "fish cocaine" due to its price. It is a multi-billion black market industry.

Fishing for totoaba has been banned in Mexico. Illegal fishing boats troll at night, casting nets that have holes for fish smaller than the totoaba to escape, but the unfortunate vaquita porpoise is the same size as the totoaba and cannot escape. The porpoise has declined 92% since 1997, and with only 60 left is on the edge of extinction.

The World Wildlife Fund is helping the Mexican government which is aggressively targeting the fishing boats and their nets night and day. The government flies over the Gulf of California looking for poachers in the protected habitat, and the Sea Shepherd, an environmental activist ship, assists by chasing off the fishing boats, or finding their nets and releasing the catch. Often they find dead totoabas, their bellies cut open for the swim bladder, the only part of the fish poachers want. Intervention kept 30 kilos of swim bladders off the Hong Kong market at a value of $750,000. A previous bust prevented 600 bladders from crossing Mexico and U.S. borders destined for China. The Mexican government is paying their fishermen $2,000 a month not to fish in the protected waters, but bagging totoaba would net them more. "If the oceans die, we die," said Dan Villa of the Sea Shepherd.   --npr.org

Significance of Loss of Species

webofcreation.org

Within the next 30 years, as many as half of the species on the earth could die in one of the fastest mass extinctions in the planet's 4.5 billion year history. Such a dramatic and overwhelming mass extinction threatens the entire, complex fabric of life, including Homo sapiens (the species responsible for the crisis).

The National Wildlife Federation says "Every day, an estimated 100 plant and animal species are lost to deforestation, 36,000 a year." Scientists have identified the key causes of the crisis. In particular, the loss of species is caused by the growing size of human populations, and the rate at which humans consume resources and cause changing climate. Dredging, draining, bulldozing, and paving land for housing developments, malls, business parks, and new roads all destroy natural habitat, as does clearing and burning forests, over-harvesting plants and animals, use of pesticides, draining and filling wetlands, destructive fishing practices, air, water and soil pollution.   --webofcreation.org

BANGKOK, 3 February 2014

Experts sometimes describe Southeast Asia as a "hotspot" for emerging infectious diseases (EIDs) because several major outbreaks have started in this region. Now, with unprecedented levels of connection between animals and people through urbanization, and of people with other people through increased air travel, scientists say the threat level for new diseases is high.

"[Economic growth] has created in the region a greater concentration and interconnection of animals, people, and products than is found almost anywhere else in the world," said Chris Gregory, an epidemiologist with the Thailand International Emerging Infections Programme.

With visa-free travel on the horizon for the 10 countries in the Association of South East Asian Nations (ASEAN), and the proliferation of low-budget airlines, experts predict that a more rapid spread of diseases may soon follow.

More people on the move to more places can take more than their luggage to their destinations. "Cross-national migration, mostly for economic

irinnews.org

reasons from lower-income to higher-income countries, is also significant and likely to further increase after the opening of ASEAN borders in 2015," said Gregory, the epidemiologist.

"Lower airline fares and more flights mean it's an opportunity for people with these diseases to travel more frequently and more quickly."

"We have to remember that greater connectivity means information is more linked-up, too. Someone in Laos or Cambodia can look up a doctor in Bangkok or Singapore and get on a flight the next day to seek care for an illness that he or she thinks can't be, or won't be, adequately treated at home."

kk/pt/he

irinnews.org

"Elmhurst Hospital Center in Elmhurst, the most diverse neighborhood in New York City and maybe in the world, serves 1.7 million patients a year, and offers translation services in a hundred and fifty-three languages. The Colombians, Bangladeshis, Koreans, Belarussians, Burmese, Chinese, Vietnamese, Croatians, Mexicans, and other immigrants who live nearby use Elmhurst for their care, and their communities back home often know about the hospital as well. It is not unusual for the exotically sick to fly to LaGuardia or J.F.K. from overseas to check into Elmhurst. Diseases rare enough to merit special-case-study attention in The New England Journal of Medicine are, at Elmhurst, relatively common."

--Rivka Galchen
"Annals of Medicine, Every Disease on Earth: Elmhurst Hospital's Medical Melting Pot," The New Yorker/Conde Nast, May 13, 2013, p 51
Reprinted by permission

> Ellis Island was the gateway for over 12 million immigrants to the United States as an inspection station from 1892 to 1954. Those with visible health problems or diseases were sent home to their countries of origin. About 2% were denied admission. Ellis Island was sometimes known as "The Island of Tears."　　　　　　　--wikipedia.org

Poliomyelitis

Dr. Jonas Salk invented the polio vaccine in 1955. There is the inactivated or dead polio vaccine, which is injected, and the oral polio-weakened virus which is taken orally, which was invented by Albert Sabin and put into commercial use in 1961. Polio vaccinations are on the World Health Organization's list of essential medicines. There is a global polio eradication initiative doctors are fighting for. Polio is still endemic in Afghanistan, Pakistan and Nigeria. Neighboring countries are vulnerable due to weak public health and immunity services.

　　　　　　　--wikipedia.org

Tuberculosis

TB kills 1.5 million people every year. Half a million more develop dry-resistant TB. It is just as contagious but harder to treat. A drug, Situro, discovered by Johnson & Johnson in 2004 and approved by the FDA in 2012, is saving lives. Situro was added to WHO's list of essential medicines in 2015. Tuberculosis is highly contagious and can be transmitted by air. In the 1950s, people with the disease were quarantined in sanitariums so as to control the spread of the disease. One of the nation's four sanitariums specializing in TB is located near Los Angeles. The dry climate weakens the bacterial disease over time. Tuberculosis can remain dormant for decades. Most new cases are Asian immigrants. --wikipedia.org

With tuberculosis contagion strictly controlled, and the introduction of the Salk vaccine to prevent polio, the United States in the 1950s was remarkably disease-free. Vaccinations against mumps, measles, rubella, chicken pox and small pox were routinely and freely given and universally taken in every elementary school, and venereal disease was rare. AIDS had not appeared. Viral infections from common colds, poison oak and poison ivy infections, and the occasional ringworm persisted, but none were life-threatening and usually lasted less than a week.

Globalism changed all that.

> About a third of the world's population carries dormant tuberculosis.

Zika

No vaccine exists. Mosquito control is the only remedy. Zika is mild to carriers, but can cause microcephaly and other serious brain defects if passed from a pregnant woman to her unborn child. As of August 19, 2016, there were 2,260 cases of Zika in the United States and Washington, D.C. Zika is widespread in Puerto Rico with 7,855 cases. In the U.S. Virgin Islands there are 101 cases. New York has 579 cases, Florida has 405, California 137, Texas 108, New Jersey 66 and Virginia 62. Mostly the cases are travelers returning home from infectious areas. There is active transmission in Mexico and throughout South America and in the Caribbean. Hillary Clinton in Miami pledged $1.8 billion in emergency funds to fight Zika. Meanwhile, China has put the U.S. on its Zika watchlist; all goods to China must be certified mosquito-free, as of August 5, 2016, a major headache for container ports in the U.S.   --cdc.gov

Ebola

Risk from the Ebola virus in the U.S. is low. It is mainly in Liberia, Sierra Leone and Guinea. In 2014 Ebola was an epidemic in West Africa, the largest in history in multiple countries. Bats are the likely host. Ebola is transmitted through blood, sweat, vomit and saliva through broken skin or mucous membranes. Ebola victims who have malaria have a better chance of surviving Ebola. Symptoms are headache, vomiting, fever, stomach pain and diarrhea. The first case in the U.S. was in Dallas, September 30, 2014.   --ochealthinfo.com

Chikungunya

This virus is mosquito-borne. There is no cure. A case was reported on the island of St. Martin in 2013. Chikungunya is widespread throughout the world, in Central and South Africa, Alaska, Central and South America, France and northeast Italy, India, China, Indonesia and Croatia as of April 22, 2016.   It has been in the Americas less than one year, mostly in the Dominican Republic. Similar to Dengue fever, the word comes from contortions of the body from a stooped appearance and joint pain. It usually goes away in months or years, but it can contribute to the death of older people. There were 37,480 confirmed cases in the Americas in 2015. Mosquitos breed in coconut husks, tires, and saucers under potted plants. It is in 60 countries.   --cdc.gov

Dengue Fever

Dengue fever consists of four viruses. It is related to the West Nile virus and yellow fever. It is mosquito-borne and thrives in tropical and sub-tropical regions. In 2009 there was an outbreak of Dengue in Key West, Florida. Person to person contact is not possible. It is spread through mosquito bites and is widespread. Symptoms include severe joint and muscle pain, pain behind the eyes, nausea, vomiting, skin rash. Symptoms can progress to death.   --webmed.com

The West Nile Virus

The West Nile Virus is transmitted to humans by mosquitos , with birds as the primary host. 80% of people carrying the virus have no symptoms. There is no vaccine. Mosquito abatement is the only prevention. There are two West Nile viruses, one is West Nile encephalitis, or inflammation of the brain. The other is West Nile poliomyelitis, which causes spinal cord inflammation, a syndrome similar to polio. The West Nile virus thrives in the warm, tropical regions of the world. It first appeared in the West Nile region of Uganda in 1937. Then there was an outbreak in Romania in 1996. The West Nile has now spread globally. The first case in the U.S. was in 1999 in New York City. Now it has spread across the United States, Canada, the Caribbean and Latin America.

A new strain of the West Nile Virus was identified in Italy in 2012. In the U.S., 286 people died from the disease in 2012, mostly in Texas. It was reported in Orange County, California in 2016, due to the evidence of infected dead birds. 97 people in Orange County had the disease in 2015, resulting in 8 deaths. In 2016 in Central and Southern California, 1007 dead birds infected with the virus were counted, as well as 161 Sentinel chickens that tested positive. There were 24 new human cases in California in August, 2016.   --westnile.ca.gov

Middle East Respiratory Syndrome

First seen in Saudi Arabia in 2012, MERS had spread to 25 other countries by 2015. The Saudi Ministry of Health reported 1,250 cases since the outbreak began, with 536 deaths.
--World Almanac and Book of Facts 2016, p 830

Severe Acute Respiratory Syndrome

SARS, transmitted through the air, has spread from Hong Kong to Vietnam, Singapore, Canada and Germany. Caused by the Corona virus, it is one of scores of viruses transmitted through live animal trading, a widespread practice throughout Asia.   -healthsummit.org

Nipah Virus

In Bangladesh, the Nipah virus spreads from date palm bats to humans. In Malaysia, the virus spreads from bat to pig to humans.   --healthsummit.org

Hendra Virus

The Hendra virus is transmitted from bats to horses to humans, often spread, such as in Australia, by horses housed outside in a paddock with fruit trees during the flying fox birthing season. There is a new vaccine for horses with Hendra, the HeV vaccine, which allows the horses to remain clinically healthy, but post-exposure therapeutics are needed for humans. Bats are the source of a range of diverse groups of viruses. Even with viruses that are closely related, an all-for-one treatment approach is not possible.   --healthsummit.org

Solar Powered Airplane

On July 25, 2016, the first solar airplane to fly around the world landed in Abu Dhabi, United Arab Emirates. European Bertrand Piccard is the visionary behind the Solar Impulse 2, a small plane with the wing span of a 747 and batteries to hold the sun's energy, allowing flight at night. The speed is 47 miles per hour. The giant European consortium, Airbus, is following Solar Impulse 2's lead into clean energy for commercial aircraft. --theguardian.com

Carb Fix

The United States and Europe are testing a program whereby carbon dioxide and water are mixed about 1000 feet underground, then sent 600 feet deeper, where the mixture leaches with mineral deposits in basalt bedrock, forming a limestone-type rock within two years, permanently transforming the carbon dioxide. This innovative technology, allowing power plants to get rid their carbon dioxide byproduct in an environmentally friendly way, has been successful in Reykjavik, Iceland.   --theguardian.com

Net Zero Housing

Germany, Scandinavia and Switzerland are leading the world in buildings designed to be carbon neutral. Along with rooftop solar panels, special windows, thick walls and insulation help regulate inside temperatures while a filtration system provides fresh air throughout the structure. Germany is mandating this "passive" approach to all new construction and encouraging renovation of existing structures. Upfront cost is less than 5% higher, but the long-term savings are much higher.   --en.wikipedia.org

California Green

Governor Jerry Brown used to be called "Governor Moonbeam," but now his vision has resulted in California being 20% clean with more to follow. "We must lead by example," he says. He wants the state's 1700 public buildings to be green, all state vehicles to be zero emissions, solar panels installed on prisons and hospitals, and all purchase order products to be carbon neutral. California has 230,000 residential rooftop solar grids and a growing number of residents purchasing electric cars. California has the three largest photovoltaic facilities in the world as of July 2015, with proposals for several larger ones pending. The world's largest solar thermal project, the Ivanpah, is located 40 miles southwest of Las Vegas. Using a $1.375 billion loan from the U.S. Department of Energy, it deploys 347,000 heliostat mirrors focusing solar energy on boilers located on centralized solar power towers. Another solar thermal plant, Genesis, is located in Riverside County. California has three primary wind farms, near San Francisco, Bakersfield and Palm Springs.   --en.wikipedia.org

Individual Lives Matter.

In the effort to help our overtaxed planet, localism is better than globalism. It is better for individuals to seek improvement in their surroundings rather than be handed edicts from on high. People have it within their power to make a difference in life. Consider, for example, the historic flooding in mid-August, 2016, in Baton Rouge, Louisiana. In some parishes, 90% of citizens lost their homes and everything they owned. They didn't sit down in despair or wait for some government agency to offer help. They individually, house by house, began putting their wrecked furniture, clothing, photo albums, appliances, household items and spoiled food out by the curb when the water had receded sufficiently. They did it quietly and efficiently, their lifelong possessions ruined, the work before them immense. Pets and people trapped by high water were saved by strangers who came with their boats from miles around, even from different states, to help out. There was hardly any loss of life.

The same individual spirit was at work in the tiny hilltop town of Amatrice, Italy, in late-August, 2016. The entire village suddenly crumbled under a powerful earthquake. Lives, possessions and masonry disappeared under tons of rubble. No one waited for government assistance. Men helped each other lift rocks as big as they could manage, flinging them down the nearest hillside in their angst to find and save survivors. Aftershocks made their work especially dangerous. A golden retriever was found alive after nine days under the rubble. There was a state funeral for 37 victims, but the final count is still not and may never be known.

Individuals interact in communities, but not far beyond, for most. Barring geophysical and human upheavals, individuals have the power to make their lives better. It's the little things. Like planting a tree. There is connection with the elements when outdoors, for one thing, and handling a tree, digging soil for it, spreading roots that have been compressed in a pot, are life-enhancing, and not just for the tree. The bigger picture is that planting the tree adds a sustaining source of oxygen for the lungs all around it, but also the tree rids the air of the carbon dioxide we emit from our bodies, our cooking, and our cars. One tree. Maybe a few plants. A couple more trees. Thinking becomes expansive. The falling leaves become nutrient-rich mulch. Toss the fertilizer. One individual can create an ecosystem.

> For the first time in my life I saw the horizon as a curved line. It was accentuated by a thin seam of dark blue light - our atmosphere. Obviously, this was not the ocean of air I had been told it was so many times in my life. I was terrified by its fragile appearance.
>
> --Ulf Merbold, German Astronaut

Airbus solar research — 224
Amatrice, Italy — 225
Apple, Inc. — 75, 76, 84
Arizona v United States — 124
Automobiles
  Foreign Trade Zones in U.S. — 97
  Imports — 101
  Manufacture for U.S. Market — 104
  U.S. Market Share — 106
  Defects — 106, 107
Banks
  Failures in U.S. 1930-2015 — 55
  Failures v Fed Prime Rate — 56
Baton Rouge, Louisiana — 225
Benefits for non-citizens — 4
Bilderberg Group — 70
Bloods Gang — 178
Brazilian Rain Forest — 207-209
Brewer, Jan, Gov of Arizona — 124
Brimelow, Peter — 130, 144
Brower, Kenneth — 207
Brown, Jerry, Gov of Calif. — 224
Britain
  Thatcher, Margaret — 103
  London Diversity — 132
  Brexit from European Union — 157
Bush, H.W. — 50, 98, 135
  Amnesty for Illegal Aliens — 124
  Savings and Loan Scandal — 51
Bush, George — 22
Bush, Jeb — 50, 62
Campaign Funding
  Presidential — 70
  Court Decisions — 61
  Dem Nat Committee, Chinese — 101
Canada — 103, 163, 216
Carson, Ben — 62
Carson, Rachel — 205
Carter, Jimmy — 49, 50
China — 161- 167
  Portion of U.S. fed debt — 3
  Rare earth metals — 40, 108
  Most Favored Nation Status — 98
  Import Goods to U.S. — 98
  Purchase Influence U.S., Canada — 103
  WTO founder — 105
  Trade in Kano, Nigeria — 105
  Second largest economy — 107
  Pokeno, New Zealand — 108
  Europe trade disputes — 108

China
  Communist Party — 161- 163
  Pollution — 167
  Shark fin soup — 216
  Totoaba, porpoise endangered — 218
Chagoury Group — 64
Churchill, Winston — 195
Citi Group — 55, 57
Citizens United v Fed Elec Comm — 61
Climate change
  Glaciers melting — 210
  Affect on coral reefs — 210
  Global warming, NRDC — 211
  Paris Agreement — 212
Clinton Whitewater — 52, 53
Clinton Foundation — 66
  Foreign donations — 63, 66
  Status — 64
  Assets — 67
Clinton Global Initiative — 65
Clinton, Chelsea — 70
Clinton, Bill
  Interview — 64
  Speech in 1994 — 99
  Chinese visitors to White House — 101
  On immigration — 124
  On terrorist prisoners — 187
Clinton, Hillary — 62
  E-mail controversy — 68
  Friends of Hillary and Bill — 68-71
  Recipient of Public Unions — 81
  On Putin — 170
Constitution, U.S. — 160
  1, 10, 35, 58, 72, 92, 114, 117
  158, 172
Controversies, U.S. Supreme Ct — 159
Consumer Price Index, 1960-2014 — 21
Corporations
  Tax Rate by Countries — 29
  CEO pay v paying taxes — 30
  Earnings deferred 2000-2012 — 31
  Tax havens — 31
  Real taxable income rate 2015 — 32
  Income tax share of GDP — 32
  Effective corporate tax rate — 32
  Debt 1916 - 1970 — 39
  Net profits by industry 2015 — 46
  Net profits 1947-2015 — 74
  U.S. largest, 2015 — 75, 76
  World's largest 2015, — 77, 78

Corporations
    Mergers and acquisitions 84
    Outsourcing, in-off-shoring jobs 83
    Downsizing jobs 85
    Profits v legal immigration 91
    World's most powerful, 1992 100
Cosco, Chinese Overseas Ship Co 103
Council on Foreign Relations 70
Crimea 169
Crips Gang 177, 178
Cuba 123, 187
Defense
    Countries purchase from US 175
    Countries large armed forces 175
    Weapons sold by countries 176
Debt
    Individual, corporate & fed 39
    State and local, 2015 10
Deregulation 55
    Carter 49
    Reagan 49, 50, 80
    Clinton and H.W. Bush 57
Disability insurance 4, 24
Disease 219
    Pests killing U.S. trees 209
    Human 221-223
Diversity, definition 157
Dodd Frank Reform Act 56,57
Dodd, Senator Christopher 63
Dollar, purchasing power 43
Dow Jones, 1900-2015 73
Dre, Dr. 178
Education, Federal outlays 7
    Affirmation action upheld 145
    Foreign students 145, 147, 150
    High School grads by race 147
    College grads by sex and race 148
    College grads by race 149
Eisenhower, Dwight 24, 39, 124
Ellis Island 221
Endangered species 218
    Elephant 215
    Rhinocerous 216
    Shark 216
    Blue fin tuna 217
Estate tax, U.S. 34
Ethnic-race federal classify 146
European Exchange Rate Mech 71
Evans-Pritchard, Ambrose 53
Exelon Corp, Chicago, Ill. 201

Factory Farming in U.S. 5, 205
Federal Deficit 2
    Investors in 3
    By presidential term 23
    Debt history, 1916-1970 39
Federal
    Depts spend less than $100 b 6
    Depts spend more than $100 b. 8
    Govt assistance programs 11
    Involvement in foreign affairs 22
    Receipts, 1980-2015 28
Federal Reserve 38, 43, 45
    Owns portion of federal debt 3
    Profit, 2015 46
    System 47
    Prime interest rate 48
    Prime interest rate 1978-81 49
    Prime interest rate 2001-09 54
    Prime interest v bank failures 56
Feinstein, Dianne, Senator 103
Firearms
    Victims in U.S. 173
    Gun laws in U.S. 174
    Chicago family 177
Female genital mutilation 197
Foreign business in US 104,111, 112
Ford, Gerald 38
Fossil fuels 202, 203
Foster, Vince 53
France 160, 197
Gaddafi, Muammar 170, 186
Genetically modified foods 204
Germany 29, 200, 206, 224, 225
Global recession 56, 73, 74, 93, 163
Glass-Steagall Act 55-57
Gold
    World's leading producers 36
    Standard abandoned 1933 37
    Completely abandoned 1971 39
    Rethinking 40
    Eagle certificate 41
    Owned by U.S. 42
    Holdings of other countries 42
Gompers, Samuel 80
Gore, Al, Senator 187
Great Depression 39, 47
Greenspan, Allen 54
Griffin, G. Edward 45
Hamilton, Alexander 46, 140
Hawaii 129, 155

Health
  Health, services outlays, 2014   9
  Health care outlays, 2016   17
  Corporation profits, 2012   17
  Waste   18
  Fraud   19
  Expenses by country   20
Heroin   183
Hoffa, Jimmy   80
Hogan Lovells law firm   69, 70
Honduras   181
Hong Kong reverts to China   103
Hostage crisis 1979-1981   50
House of Saud   50, 69
  Saudi Arabia   188
Human Rights
  China   163
  Abuses in world   188
Iceland, carbon containment   224
Indonesia universal health care   20
Institute of Medicine   18
Immigration
  Costs, no budget provided   12
  Entitlements, fed deficit   13
  Nativity v jurisdiction   116
  Birth tourism   116
  Language required   117-120, 122
  Loyalty oath   121, 122
  Uniform rule   121
  Imm. and Nationality Act '65   123
  ICE agents sue fed gov't   125
  Classes of admission   126, 127
  Asians top foreign born   128, 130
  Quotas from W. Europe   128
  Geographic source   129
  Diversity laws   131 -133
    Compliance   134
  EB-5 citizenship sale   135
  Naturalization   136
  Amnesty 1980-93   137
  Amnesty 2000-13   138
  Country of birth '13   139
  Visa visitors overstay   141
  Chinese via Mexico   141
  Refugees 1971-90   142
  Refugees 2011-13   143
  Foreign 1900-2014   144
Iran   50, 187

Islam
  Legal system   121
  Honor killings   190
  Homosexuality   192
  Sharia Law   193-195
  Judge, City Council   196
Israel   187
Japan
  Own U.S. fed debt   3
  Jetro   97
  Wage disparity US   98
  Japan v US trade '95   99
  Founder of WTO   105
  Okinawa   167
  Blue fin tuna   217
  2nd largest economy   107
Jefferson, Thomas   158, 216
Kahn, Khizr Muazzam   69
Kaiser Permanente   15
Kennedy, John   81
Kennedy, Ted   123
King, Rodney   179, 182
Kelly, Kitty   50
Korean War   39, 123
Labor unions, US   79
  Private sector   80
  Public sector   81
Lamm, Richard   139
Lewis, Michael   57, 82
Libya   186
Lincoln, Abraham   172
Lobbying   59, 60, 63, 70, 81
  Lobby Disclosure Act   63
Lone-wolf terrorism   185
Los Angeles, Calif.   179-181
Lynch, Loretta   69
Manuf v serv.   102, 106, 113
Marijuana, synthetic   183
Mattera, Phillip   100
Medical profits, 2012   17, 19
Medicare, US, balance   4
Mexican Mafia   182, 183
Merkel, Angela   179, 200
Mezvinsky, Edward   70
Middle class decline US   113
Militia   160, 172
MS-13 El Salvador gang   179
Mukasey, Michael   68

NAFTA	98, 103
Nasdaq, 1970-2015	73
NRDC	211
NCBI Employ by race	86
Nemtsov, Boris	170
New York's Elmhurst	220
Nixon, Richard	38, 70, 80
North, Oliver	187
Nuclear	
Arsenals by country	171
Power by country	200
Decom San Onofre	201
Obama	
Budget 2016	1
Clinton Foundation	66
Guantanamo	187
Cost of wars	22
Obamacare	
Premiums	14, 16
Rise in premiums	15
Office personnel, fed	136
Oil companies	
Subsidies	30
Environmental	202, 203
Largest US	75, 76
Largest non-US	78
Operation Wetback	124
Opiate drugs	183
Osama bin Laden	187
Oxfam International	74
Panama Canal	107
Pfaelzer, Mariana	124
Piccard, Bertrand	224
Political Action Committees	59-62
Pollution	
In ports	198-199
Plastics	206
Population global	
Increase 1990-2016	115
% increase Asian	155
Population US	
By race, 1970-2014	156
High school grads	147
College by sex, race	148
College by race	149
Median income by race	151
Median income by race, 2013	152
Poverty, U.S. by race	153
Foreign v US citizen	154
Port of Long Beach	103

Prescriptions for Hepatitis C	19
Proposition 187, Calif	124
Putin, Vladimir	168-170
Rail Mexico to US	107
Rand, Ayn	84
Reagan, Ronald	49, 50, 51
	80, 82, 84, 205
Foreign trade zones	97
Trip to Japan	98
Amnesty for illegals	124
Realtor.com	84
Recycling countries	206
Refugees, US	123, 142, 143
Reptiles, invasive	213, 214
Resolution Trust Crp	51, 53
Robbins, John	205
Roosevelt, Franklin	37, 80
Roosevelt, Theodore	122
Rothschild, Lynn F.	70
Russia	168-170
Sanders, Bernie	62
Savings & Loan Crisis	49
Bush family	51
Bill and Hillary	53
Seattle	97
Chief	202
Sex Trafficking by ISIS	190
by gangs in San Diego	191
Soros, George	70, 71, 155
South Sudan	189
Speechnow. v Fed Elec.	61
Standing army, U.S.	160
State, local govt expn	10, 39
Steinem, Gloria	197
Switzerland	
Davos, mtgs for govt, business	74
Geneva, WTO home	105
Sygenta Corp	204, 205
Taiwan	166, 167
Takata air bags	107
Tax	
Personal income US	33, 34
Personal by country	34
Estate, US	34
Fed taxes US 1980-15	28
Tea Party	155
Tibet	165-167
Trade, intl 1940-2014	93
by country, 2013	94
US deficit/country '14	95

Trade,

    US deficit/country '10 — 96

    deficit with Japan — 97

    Intl trade goods 2010 — 109

    Intl trade goods 2014 — 110

    US mfg job loss — 112, 113

    US custom, duty tax — 28

Tribunals — 160

Trident Imports — 97

Truman, Harry — 39, 80

Trump, Donald — 62, 69, 170

Unity definition — 157

    Uniform — 157

    Uniform Rule — 121

Ukraine — 170

Vietnam War — 23, 39, 123

Villa, Dan — 218

Voter ID laws — 125

Wages

    Real weekly 1947-92 — 44

    Earnings by race — 87

    Women v men/occup — 88

    Women v men/edu — 89, 90

    Foreign v US wage — 98

Walker, Alice — 197

Wanda Group — 85

Walmart — 83

War on drugs

    Failure — 177

    Money laundering — 180

    Across borders — 180

    Racial violence — 181

War on terror — 22

    Costs — 23

    Three 911 field ops — 26

    Foreign financing — 25

    Arms transfers — 26

    Defense contractors — 27

    Putin position on — 170

    Victims — 184

    Increase — 185

Weyerhauser Corp — 97

Whitewater — 52, 53

World's largest econ — 107

World Trade Org — 105, 112

    Loss mfg jobs US — 106

    Europe grievances — 108

World Recession '08 — 54, 56

Yukos — 168

ABOUT THE AUTHOR

Lynn Stewart holds a Bachelors of Arts Degree in Sociology from the University of California at Berkeley. She has lived in Seattle and Southern California and has seven grandchildren.

www.ingramcontent.com/pod-product-compliance
Lightning Source LLC
Chambersburg PA
CBHW081822280526
45789CB00007B/2301